GENERAL PRINCIPLES AS A SOURCE OF INTERNATIONAL LAW

This book provides a comprehensive analysis of an often neglected, misunderstood and maligned source of international law. Article 38(1)(c) of the Statute of the International Court of Justice sets out that the Court will apply the 'general principles of law recognized by civilized nations'. This source is variously lauded and criticised: held up as a panacea to all international law woes or denied even normative validity. The contrasting views and treatments of General Principles stem from a lack of a model of the source itself. This book provides that model, offering a new and rigorous understanding of Article 38(1)(c) that will be of immense value to scholars and practitioners of international law alike.

At the heart of the book is a new tetrahedral framework of analysis – looking to function, type, methodology and jurisprudential legitimacy. Adopting an historical approach, the book traces the development of the source from 1875 to 2019, encompassing jurisprudence of the Permanent Court of International Justice and the International Court of Justice as well as cases from international criminal tribunals, the International Criminal Court and the World Trade Organization. The book argues for precision in identifying cases that actually apply General Principles, and builds upon these 'proper use' cases to advance a comprehensive model of General Principles, advocating for a global approach to the methodology of the source.

Volume 81 in the series Studies in International Law

Studies in International Law

Recent titles in this series

The Impact of Investment Treaty Law on Host States: Enabling Good Governance
Mavluda Sattorova

Allocating International Responsibility Between Member States and International Organisations
Nikolaos Voulgaris

Predictability and Flexibility in the Law of Maritime Delimitation, 2nd edition
Yoshifumi Tanaka

Feminist Engagement with International Criminal Law: Norm Transfer, Complementarity, Rape and Consent
Eithne Dowds

Asylum Control and Access to Protection: Admission, Readmission and Human Rights
Mariagiulia Giuffré

Intertemporal Linguistics in International Law: Beyond Contemporaneous and Evolutionary Treaty Interpretation
Julian Wyatt

The Responsibility to Protect and the Failures of the United Nations Security Council
P M Butchard

The Role of Multilateral Environmental Agreements: A Reconciliatory Approach to Environmental Protection in Armed Conflict
Britta Sjostedt

Prosecutorial Discretion at the International Criminal Court
Anni Pues

Judicial Deference in International Adjudication: A Comparative Analysis
Johannes Hendrik Fahner

Human Rights Commitments of Islamic States: Sharia, Treaties and Consensus
Paul McDonough

Intervention in Civil Wars: Effectiveness, Legitimacy, and Human Rights
Chiara Redaelli

For a complete list of titles in this series, see www.bloomsburyprofessional.com/uk/series/studies-in-international-law

General Principles as a Source of International Law

Art 38(1)(c) of the Statute of the International Court of Justice

Imogen Saunders

•HART•

OXFORD • LONDON • NEW YORK • NEW DELHI • SYDNEY

HART PUBLISHING
Bloomsbury Publishing Plc
Kemp House, Chawley Park, Cumnor Hill, Oxford, OX2 9PH, UK
1385 Broadway, New York, NY 10018, USA
29 Earlsfort Terrace, Dublin 2, Ireland

First published in Great Britain 2021

A catalogue record for this book is available from the British Library.

Library of Congress Cataloging-in-Publication data

Names: Saunders, Imogen, author.

Title: General principles as a source of international law : Art 38(1)(c) of the Statute of the International Court of Justice / Imogen Saunders.

Description: Oxford, UK ; New York, NY : Hart Publishing, an imprint of Bloomsbury Publishing, 2021. | Series: Studies in international law ; volume 81 | Includes bibliographical references and index.

Identifiers: LCCN 2020049937 (print) | LCCN 2020049938 (ebook) | ISBN 9781509936069 (hardback) | ISBN 9781509946624 (paperback) | ISBN 9781509936083 (pdf) | ISBN 9781509936076 (Epub)

Subjects: LCSH: International Court of Justice—History. | Permanent Court of Arbitration. | International law.

Classification: LCC KZ6275 .S28 2020 (print) | LCC KZ6275 (ebook) | DDC 341.5/52—dc23

LC record available at https://lccn.loc.gov/2020049937

LC ebook record available at https://lccn.loc.gov/2020049938

ISBN: HB: 978-1-50993-606-9
ePDF: 978-1-50993-608-3
ePub: 978-1-50993-607-6

Typeset by Compuscript Ltd, Shannon

Acknowledgements

I HAVE BEEN thinking about this book, on and off, for almost 18 years. The genesis of this project was when I was a member of the University of Western Australia Jessup Moot team, for which I needed to plead reliance on a General Principle. I quickly grew frustrated with what I saw as lack of clarity and precision surrounding Article 38(1)(c) in the literature and the jurisprudence. 'But what *are* they? And how do you find one?' was a common refrain, and my thanks to Bronwyn Grieve, Sarah Knuckey, Andrew Lodder, Benjamin Spagnolo and Julie Taylor both for being there when it all started, and for putting up with my many rants on the subject.

The project took shape with the guidance of two mentors who were instrumental in supporting and challenging me to encourage the development of my ideas, analysis and theories. At the first stage, my attempts to answer my own questions grew into the subject matter for my honours dissertation for my LLB degree. Justice James Edelman was an ever-patient and encouraging supervisor, whose only hesitation was that perhaps this topic was too big to be fully addressed in 10,000 words. He was, as is so often the case with Justice Edelman, right.

I took up the project again when I started my PhD at the Australian National University under the supervision of Professor Don Rothwell. Professor Rothwell was stalwart in his calm wisdom, guidance and reassurance. I thank both Justice Edelman and Professor Rothwell for being wonderful and generous supervisors: this book would not exist without them. Thank you also to Professors Andrew Mitchell, Dinah Shelton and the late Ivan Shearer for their help during my doctoral process. The kind, wise and constructive feedback offered by my PhD examiners, Professors Phillip Alston and Fleur Johns, has been invaluable as I have written this book, the latest expression of my quest to settle the General Principles question – thank you to both.

I have made my academic home at the Australian National University College of Law since 2007, and the collegiality I have enjoyed has been outstanding. It is a warm and supportive environment and I am lucky to work here. Thank you to the three Deans under whom I have been an ANU College of Law member – the late Professor Michael Coper, Professor Stephen Bottomley and Professor Sally Wheeler. Warmest thanks also to my colleagues both at ANU and elsewhere for their kind words of encouragement, corridor chats, coffee runs, discussions in beer gardens, sage advice and always being willing to answer my questions or assuage my concerns, no matter how trivial.

I owe a big debt of thanks to Bede Thompson, who has been my research assistant for the final stages of this book and instrumental in getting my unruly referencing in order. Being able to trust in his professionalism and impeccable work has been a lifesaver. Thank you too to the team at Hart Publishing, and in particular Sinead Moloney and Sasha Jawed, who have been so generous to me during delays brought on by the bushfires in Australia in January 2020 and the COVID-19 pandemic. This has been an interesting time to write a book!

Finally, my deepest gratitude to all of my family, but in particular to Tony, who was there at the very beginning of this project, and to Toby and Millie, who arrived along the way – you have been unflinchingly and fiercely supportive of me and my goals, and I am forever grateful.

Contents

Introduction

> I have never been convinced of the supposed importance of 'general principles of law' as a source of general international law ...[1]
>
> *Sir Robert Jennings*

THIS BOOK EXAMINES Article 38(1)(c) of the Statute of the International Court of Justice (ICJ Statute). Article 38 of the Statute sets out the sources of law that the International Court of Justice (ICJ) may have recourse to:

> 1. The Court, whose function is to decide in accordance with international law such disputes as are submitted to it, shall apply:
>   a. international conventions, whether general or particular, establishing rules expressly recognized by the contesting states;
>   b. international custom, as evidence of a general practice accepted as law;
>   c. the general principles of law recognized by civilized nations;
>   d. subject to the provisions of Article 59, judicial decisions and the teachings of the most highly qualified publicists of the various nations, as subsidiary means for the determination of rules of law.[2]

The relevance of Article 38 has extended beyond the parameters of the ICJ, and is viewed as the basis for the study of sources of international law.[3] Accordingly, each provision is essential to the understanding of international law. Both conventional and customary international law are relatively uncontroversial in nature, scope and content. The general principles of law recognised by civilised nations (referred to throughout this book as 'General Principles'), however, still raise debate; simultaneously derided as a 'historical remnant of the 1920s'[4] and as a subsidiary source of law;[5] yet also lauded as 'the ultimate seedbed and gap filler of international law',[6] which 'play a prominent role in the creation of

[1] R Jennings, 'The Identification of International Law' in B Cheng (ed), *International Law: Teaching and Practice* (Stevens, 1982) 3, 4.

[2] Statute of the International Court of Justice, Art 38.

[3] M Koskenniemi, 'Introduction' in M Koskenniemi (ed), *Sources of International Law* (Routledge, 2000) xi.

[4] R Jennings, 'What is International Law and How Do We Tell It When We See It?' (1981) 37 *Schweitzerisches Jahrbuch für Internationales Recht* 59, 71.

[5] G Schwarzenberger and ED Brown, *A Manual of International Law*, 6th edn (Professional Books, 1976) 27.

[6] DJ Bederman, *The Spirit of International Law* (University of Georgia Press, 2002), 30.

the law'.[7] Contrast the quotation from Sir Robert Jennings at the head of this Introduction with the view of M Cherif Bassiouni in 1990 – 'it is quite likely that "General Principles" will become the most important and influential source of international law in this decade'.[8] Even Jenning's view above, from 1982, differs from his description of the source in 1967 as 'a salutary addition to Article 38', valuable for the 'progressive development of the law'.[9] How do we reconcile such opposing views of General Principles?

This fracture in the assessment of the importance of General Principles is linked to a common perception of an under-utilisation of General Principles by the Permanent Court of International Justice (PCIJ) and the ICJ.[10] This under-utilisation is often overstated – while references to source in the PCIJ were often vague, post-PCIJ practice has seen more direct discussion of General Principles. The reality is the source has been used or discussed in over 80 PCIJ and ICJ judgments, Separate Opinions, Dissenting Opinions and Declarations,[11] as well as in cases before the International Criminal Tribunal for the Former Yugoslavia, the International Criminal Court, the Inter-American Court of Human Rights, the European Court of Human Rights and decisions of the World Trade Organisation Appellate Body and Panels.[12] Moreover, as one former judge of the ICJ, Jimenez de Arechaga, wrote, 'general principles of law, though rarely mentioned in the Court's judgments, should not be underestimated as to their influence on the minds and the intellectual processes of judges'.[13]

In recent years, General Principles have received more academic attention,[14] including being put on the programme of works for the International Law Commission.[15] This has, however, not led to greater clarity about the use or

[7] R Kolb, 'Principles as Sources of International Law (with special reference to Good Faith)' (2006) 53(1) *Netherlands International Law Review* 1, 9.

[8] MC Bassiouni, 'A Functional Approach to "General Principles of International Law"' (1990) 11 *Michigan Journal of International Law* 768, 769.

[9] R Jennings, 'The Sources of Law' (1967) 121 *Recueil des cours* 329, 340.

[10] WW Bishop, 'Sources of Law' (1965) 115 *Recueil des cours* 214, 237; M Koskenniemi, 'The Pull of the Mainstream' (1990) 88(6) *Michigan Law Review* 1946, 1947–48; A Pellet and D Müller, 'Article 38 ' in A Zimmerman, CJ Tams, K Oellers-Frahm and C Tomuschat (eds), *The Statute of the International Court of Justice: A Commentary*, 3rd edn (Oxford University Press, 2019) 819, 924. M Dixon, *Textbook on International Law*, 6th edn (Oxford University Press, 2007) 43; P Sands and J Peel, *Principles of International Environmental Law*, 3rd edn (Cambridge University Press, 2012) 117.

[11] See chs 4 and 5. It is far more common for such discussion to occur in the individual Opinions/ Declarations of Judges rather than in the Judgment of the Court.

[12] See ch 6.

[13] J de Arechaga, 'Discussion' in A Cassese and JHH Weiler (eds), *Change and Stability in International Law-Making* (Walter de Gruyter, 1988), 50.

[14] See in particular N Jain, 'Judicial Lawmaking and General Principles of Law in International Criminal Law' (2016) 57(1) *Harvard International Law Journal* 111; CT Kotuby Jr and LA Sobota, *General Principles of Law and International Due Process: Principles and Norms Applicable in Transnational Disputes* (Oxford University Press, 2017); M Andenas, M Fitzmaurice, A Tanzi and J Wouters (eds), *General Principles and the Coherence of International Law* (Brill Nijhoff, 2019); M Đorđeska, *General Principles of Law Recognised by Civilised Nations (1922–2018)* (Brill Nijhoff, 2020).

[15] ILC, *First Report on General Principles of Law* (29 April–7 June and 8 July–9 August 2019) UN Doc A/CN.4/732.

purpose of the source. Rather, under-utilisation has been replaced in some cases by over-utilisation, with cases referring to 'principles' *without* clear links to Article 38(1)(c) being held out as uses of General Principles. Paradoxically, both the under-utilisation and over-utilisation of General Principles stem from the same foundation: the lack of a clear and accepted model of General Principles. As long as academic definitions and understandings of General Principles are at odds with the jurisprudence of international courts and tribunals, it is unlikely General Principles will be relied on to found any decisions: by the same token, it is more likely academics and commentators will overreach in categorising cases as examples of General Principles to fit their own understanding of the source.

As such, this book has one key aim: to create a model of General Principles that is consistent and justified on the basis of the historical development of the source, the treatment of the source by key international institutions and international legal theory. To do so, I first develop a tetrahedral framework of analysis in chapter 1 that looks to *function, methodology, type* and *jurisprudential legitimacy.* These touching (and at times overlapping) four faces are used throughout this book to interrogate fundamental questions about General Principles. I attempt to unpack assumptions about the source, arguing that too often, unwritten beliefs about one or more of the sides of the tetrahedron colour conclusions about the whole source. It is only by breaking down the source into these four aspects that it can be rebuilt in a way that is consistent with its historic development and use, and normatively justifiable in light of international legal theory.

To achieve these aims, I apply the framework developed in chapter 1 to the historical development of General Principles prior to their inclusion in the Statute of the PCIJ (chapter 2); to relevant judgments of the PCIJ (chapter 3) and the ICJ (chapters 4 and 5), and selected key international courts and tribunals (chapter 6). It is only after the analyses of the primary sources that I explore the writings of commentators on the source in greater depth (chapter 7). In this way, I seek to avoid Anthony Clark Arend's salient criticism that

> debate frequently centers on the scholars' paradigms and not the behaviour of the international actors that they are supposed to be evaluating. In theory, legal scholars do not create rules of international law; rather they muster empirical evidence that supports the existence of a particular rule. But to do this, they need to examine real-world behaviour. Increasingly, legal scholarship seems to have been removed from this basic, but often very time consuming and complicated exploration of the behaviour of international actors.[16]

While 'scholar's paradigms' are important for this work, such paradigms are assessed against the background of the behaviour of the primary actors. As Martti Koskenniemi states, 'However international legal ideas cannot simply

[16] AC Arend, *Legal Rules and International Society* (Oxford University Press, 1999) 7.

live as abstractions. They must also have concreteness: they must reflect what actually takes place in the political and economic world.'[17]

By placing the analysis of General Principles in the context of their historical development, the model this book proposes is not simply abstract but will reflect the actual development and use of the source. As has been pointed out, history is no more objective than law;[18] and the history explored in this book, anchored in a traditional source of international law, is somewhat unavoidably 'rooted in nineteenth and early twentieth century European history'.[19] In an attempt to expand this, and avoid the 'inadequacies and inconsistencies' of this mainstream narrative noted by Matilda Arvidsson and Miriam Bak McKenna,[20] chapter 8 explores the idea of 'global' General Principles.

The focus for analysis is not on the *specific* content of General Principles – that is, I do not attempt to make a list of known or accepted General Principles. Rather, the focus is on understanding the source itself – where it fits within the creation of international law, with the other sources of international law, and how it is used to find norms. Although some specific General Principles will be mentioned to illustrate a point, or explored where they demonstrate something about the source itself, there will generally be no exhaustive discussion on what international courts, tribunals or publicists consider the content of existing General Principles to be.

Although there is inherent value in having a complete understanding of Article 38(1)(c) in itself, the importance of the analysis developed here is not limited to merely satisfying theoretical curiosity. A confluence of global events – continuing globalisation of the world, and the increased recognition of different legal systems; the increasing scope of international law, both in terms of the *content* of international law and utilisation of the ICJ and other international courts and tribunals; and the unprecedented access to information that has been delivered by technological developments – means that General Principles are poised to become an important source of international law. They are potentially able to respond to new challenges in international regulation faster and more flexibly than either treaty or custom. General Principles can only take this role, however, if there is a consistent and cohesive understanding of the fundamental aspects of the source: this book seeks to provide that.

[17] M Koskenniemi, 'International law in the World of Ideas' in J Crawford and M Koskenniemi (eds), *The Cambridge Companion to International Law* (Cambridge University Press, 2012) 47, 60.

[18] A Kemmerer, 'We do not always need to look to Westphalia … A Conversation with Martti Koskenniemi and Anne Orford' (2015) 17 *Journal of the History of International Law* 1, 3.

[19] M Arvidsson and MB McKenna, 'The turn to history in international law and the sources doctrine: Critical approaches and methodological imaginaries' (2020) 33(1) *Leiden Journal of International Law* 37, 40.

[20] ibid.

1

A Framework for Analysing General Principles

I. INTRODUCTION: A TETRAHEDRAL FRAMEWORK

TO BUILD A model of General Principles, we initially need to know three things: first, the role that General Principles play (their *function*); second, the type of content that can form a General Principle (their *type*); and, third, how they are found (their *methodology*).

The fourth aspect that must be considered is the jurisprudential underpinning of the source's legitimacy. If we think of the first three questions as the three vertical sides of a tetrahedron, the fourth aspect is the horizontal floor: touching and informing all other aspects.

Figure 1.1 General Principles: A Tetrahedral Framework

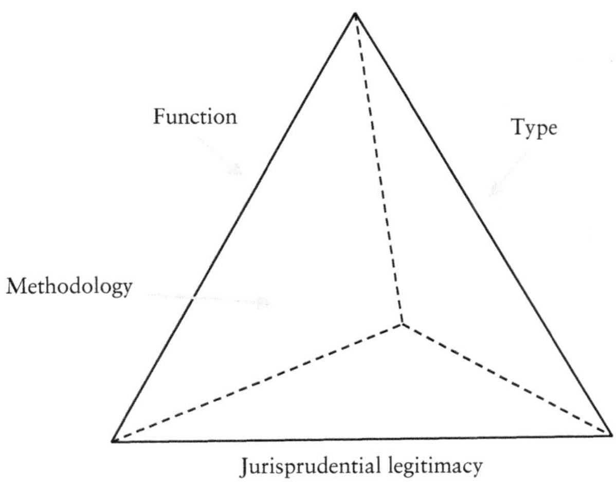

As will be seen in this book, these four aspects are interrelated. A certain characterisation of the judicial legitimacy of the source often leads to assumptions about the other three aspects as well. Too often these interrelated aspects are not separated out and the underlying assumptions interrogated. Accordingly, the analysis in this book attempts to partition the four elements of the source. This ensures that the final model of General Principles is not coloured by unwritten assumptions about any of the four aspects. Doing so also offers up some explanation, as discussed later in chapter 7, why different national schools of international law[1] offer contrasting views of General Principles.

This chapter sets out a brief introduction to each of the four sides of the tetrahedron. It will engage with the work of commentators only to the extent necessary to illustrate the different possibilities under each aspect of the source. It purposefully does not dive too deeply into these theoretical discussion to avoid prejudging the analysis that follows. The aim of *this* chapter is provide a structure of analysis only: the following chapters will apply this structure to the jurisprudence of the PCIJ, ICJ, other international courts and tribunals, and then turn to scholarly commentary of the source.

II. JURISPRUDENTIAL LEGITIMACY: A BRIEF CONSIDERATION OF POSITIVISM AND NATURAL LAW

Martti Koskenniemi describes the 'material' aspect of a source of international law as

> the explanation of sources as the history, cause or basis from which law 'emerges'. This ('material') aspect of sources seeks to provide for the law's legitimacy, pointing to its origin in a legislative process, natural reason, a principle of justice or policy that resonates with our political sensibility and that we usually take as good reason for applying the standard based on it.[2]

It is this same material aspect that is termed jurisdictional legitimacy in this book. Within Koskenniemi's explanation, the tensions between a positivist and natural law approach to sources are immediately obvious. While 'legislative process' indicates a positivist approach, 'natural reason' or 'justice and policy' suggest a natural law basis.

The key distinction between positivism and natural law for the purpose of this book is necessarily a reductionist one. In short, natural law posits that there are 'true and valid standards of right conduct',[3] and that that law is binding because of its inherent morality and justice.[4] A natural law conception of General Principles sees jurisprudential legitimacy tied up in the content of the

[1] For a general discussion of national conceptions of international law, see A Roberts, *Is International Law International?* (Oxford University Press, 2017).

[2] M Koskenniemi, 'Introduction' in M Koskenniemi (ed), *Sources of International Law* (Ashgate, 2000) xiii.

[3] J Finnis, 'Natural Law: The Classical Tradition' in J Coleman and S Shapiro (eds), *The Oxford Handbook of Jurisprudence and Philosophy of Law* (Oxford University Press, 2002) 1, 3.

[4] J Finnis, *Natural Law and Natural Rights* (Oxford University Press, 1987) 34.

norm itself. This immediately prioritises type over methodology, and impacts the function of the source as certain norms may be more binding (more moral) than others.

In contrast, employment of a positivist Hartian rule of recognition[5] accords jurisprudential legitimacy based on the process by which the General Principle is found. Under strict legal positivism, law is a social reality and is created (or 'posited'), not discovered.[6] Positivist laws are no more or less valid than each other: a law is either valid or it is not.[7] Methodology is now foregrounded, as it is the methodology that confers validity, and consideration of type is restricted to simply what type of norm can satisfy the prescribed legitimacy granting methodology – beyond this, the content of the General Principle is irrelevant. Function is also affected, as each norm is equally valid and none can override another.

Of course, modern conceptions of international law are not confined to contrasts between pure natural law and strict positivism. As Fuller argued, positivism reaches a limit when determining what gives the law-making process – the rule of recognition – itself legitimacy. Unless the process gains legitimacy by itself being created by a valid law-making process (thereby creating an infinite regress), its fundamental nature must instead be gained from the validity of its content.[8] Kelsen's 'basic norm', or *grundnorm*,[9] provides this root source that imbues the law-making process with its power. Kelsen states that 'the basic norm is not valid because it has been created in a certain way, but its validity is assumed by virtue of its content'.[10]

What makes up the *grundnorm* of international law will influence how we understand General Principles: the implication of a *grundnorm* based in consent is discussed in the next section on function. Thus positivist law itself has a natural law basis: an ultimate foundation in content rather than procedure. This book does not seek to maintain a bright-line distinction between positivism and natural law, and recognises that the two necessarily co-mingle. Yet one can still characterise a position as (more or less) positivist or (more or less) one of natural law. In the context of General Principles, the characterisation of the jurisprudential legitimacy can also follow the same lines. This in turn impacts on the rest of the tetrahedral framework.

[5] HLA Hart, 'Positivism and the Separation of Law and Morals' (1958) 71(4) *Harvard Law Review* 593.

[6] MP Golding, 'Kelsen and the Concept of "Legal System"' in RS Summers (ed), *More Essays in Legal Philosophy* (University of California Press, 1971) 69, 70.

[7] U Fastenrath, 'Relative Normality in International Law' (1993) 4 *European Journal of International Law* 305, 307.

[8] L Fuller, 'Positivism and Fidelity to Law – A Reply to Professor Hart' (1958) 71 *Harvard Law Review* 630, 640–41.

[9] H Kelsen, *General Theory of Law and State*, tr A Wedberg (Harvard University Press, 1945) 401.

[10] ibid.

III. FUNCTION: A BINDING SOURCE OF INTERNATIONAL LAW?

Sources of international law can be either formal[11] or subsidiary[12] sources. A formal source gives rise to binding norms of international law.[13] Of the sources contained in Article 38 of the ICJ Statute, both convention[14] and custom[15] are formal sources of law.[16] If the requirements either for a treaty to be made (the express consent of those countries entering into it)[17] or for custom to be formed (the state practice and *opinio juris* of a vast majority of affected states)[18] are met then a new norm of law is created. In the case of conventions, that norm is binding only on those countries who entered into the treaty.[19] For customary law, the norm is binding on all states in the international community,[20] with the exception of 'persistent objectors' states.[21] In contrast, a subsidiary source of law does not create international norms but is a way of determining the content of norms. The opinions of publicists and decisions of national courts[22] are subsidiary sources.[23] An opinion of a publicist, no matter how qualified, does not in itself give rise to a binding norm of international law. Such opinion, however, may be instrumental in determining the precise content of a norm of international law, or in providing documentary evidence of such a norm.[24]

Unlike the other three sources under Article 38(1), some contention remains as to the *function* of Article 38(1)(c). Some commentators consider the source as norm-creating only in the context of the ICJ and not part of international

[11] Sometimes referred to as primary or normative sources.

[12] Sometimes referred to as secondary or material sources. As the phrase 'material source' has another meaning under source theory, this terminology will be avoided. See Koskenniemi, 'Introduction' (n 2) xiii.

[13] GG Fitzmaurice, 'Some Problems Regarding the Formal Sources of International Law' in JHW Verzijl (ed), *Symbolae Verzijl: présentées au Professeur JHW Verzijl, à l'occasion de son Lxx-ième anniversaire* (Martinus Nijhoff, 1958) 153.

[14] Statute of the International Court of Justice [1945] ATS 1, Art 38(1)(a) ('ICJ Statute').

[15] ibid Art 38(1)(b).

[16] G Danilenko, *Law-Making in the International Community* (Martinus Nijhoff, 1993) 48, 77.

[17] ibid 45; M Bos, *A Methodology of International Law* (Elsevier Science Publishers, 1984) 57.

[18] *North Sea Continental Shelf (Federal Republic of Germany v Denmark; Federal Republic of Germany v Netherlands)* (Merits) [1969] ICJ Rep 3, 44 ('*North Sea Continental Shelf*'); *Military and Paramilitary Activities in and against Nicaragua (Nicaragua v United States of America)* (Merits) [1986] ICJ Rep 14, 98 ('*Nicaragua*'); American Law Institute, *United States of America Restatement (Third) of Foreign Relations Law* (1987) §102(2).

[19] Vienna Convention on the Law of Treaties (adopted 23 May 1969, entered into force 27 January 1980) 1155 UNTS 33 ('VCLT'), Art 34; Danilenko, *Law-Making* (n 16) 58.

[20] *North Sea Continental Shelf* (n 18) 44.

[21] *Fisheries Case (United Kingdom v Norway)* (Merits) [1951] ICJ Rep 116, 131 ('*Fisheries Case*').

[22] ICJ Statute (n 14) Art 38(1)(d).

[23] G Schwarzenberger, *International Law as Applied by International Courts and Tribunals*, vol 1, 3rd edn, (London, Stevens and Sons 1957) 26–27; A Pellet and D Müller, 'Article 38' in A Zimmerman, CJ Tams, K Oellers-Frahm and C Tomuschat (eds), *The Statute of the International Court of Justice: A Commentary*, 3rd edn (Oxford University Press, 2019) 819, 945.

[24] Pellet and Müller, 'Article 38' (n 23) 945.

law per se,[25] or merely subsidiary, serving to help interpret norms established by convention or custom.[26] The more widely held view is that General Principles are a formal source of law. This is often tempered by the restriction that they will only be applied if treaty or custom is absent[27] (although this restriction is not universally adopted).[28] This view often sees the primary role of General Principles as filling gaps in international law.[29] While many commentators choose one view, others see General Principles as a hybrid source – simultaneously formal and subsidiary in effect.[30]

The link between jurisprudential legitimacy and function can be seen in the analysis of sources of law as hard and soft rhetoric; both of which rest on a *grundnorm* of consent underpinning the legitimacy of international law.

A. 'Hard' and 'Soft' Rhetoric: Consent and Voluntarism

The positivist and natural law divide as it applies to Article 38 sources has been conceptualised as a contrast between 'hard' and 'soft' justifications of law:

> Sources rhetoric provides two rhetorical or persuasive styles which we might call 'hard' and 'soft'. A 'hard' argument will seek to ground compliance in the 'consent'

[25] H Kelsen, *The Law of the United Nations: A Critical Analysis of its Fundamental Problems* (Stevens and Sons, 1950) 533; H Kelsen, *Principles of International Law*, first pub 1952, 2nd rev edn (Holt, Rinehart and Winston, 1966) 539–40.

[26] See H Bokor-Szegö 'General Principles of Law' in M Bedjaoui (ed), *International Law: Achievements and Prospects* (UNESCO and Martinus Nijhoff, 1991) 213, 217.

[27] See, eg, B Cheng in HC Gutteridge, 'The Meaning and Scope of Article 38(1)(c) of the Statute of the International Court of Justice' (1952) 38 *Transactions of the Grotius Society* 125, 132; H Lauterpacht, *Private Law Sources and Analogies of International Law*, first pub 1927 (Archon Books, 1970) viii; G Schwarzenberger and ED Brown, *A Manual of International Law*, 6th edn (Professional Books, 1976) 27; M Bogdan 'General Principles of Law and the Problem of Lacunae in the Law of Nations' (1977) 46(1) *Nordisk Tidsskrift for International Ret* 37, 44; American Law Institute, *United States of America Restatement (Third) of Foreign Relations Law* (1987) §102(4); JI Charney, 'Universal International Law' (1993) 87 *American Journal of International Law* 529, 534; Fastenrath, 'Relative Normality' (n 7) 328; S Hall, 'The Persistent Spectre: Natural Law, International Order and the Limits of Legal Positivism' (2001) 12(2) *European Journal of International Law* 269, 298; D Mitchell, 'The Prohibition of Rape in International Humanitarian Law as a Norm of Jus Cogens: Clarifying the Doctrine' (2005) 15 *Duke Journal of International and Comparative Law* 219, 233; DP Harris, 'Carrying a Good Joke Too Far: Trips and Treaties of Adhesion' (2006) 27 *University of Pennsylvania Journal of International Economic Law* 681, 695; BB Jia, 'The Relations between Treaties and Custom' (2010) 9 *Chinese Journal of International Law* 81, 91.

[28] Schwarzenberger, *International Law* (n 23) 55–56; JG Lammers, 'General Principles of Law Recognized by Civilised Nations' in F Kalshoven, PJ Kuyper, and JG Lammers (eds), *Essays on the Development of the International Legal Order in Memory of Haro F Van Panhuys* (Sijthoff and Noordhoff, 1980) 53, 65.

[29] H Lauterpacht, *The Function of Law in the International Community* (Clarendon Press, 1933) 115.

[30] MC Bassiouni, 'A Functional Approach to "General Principles of International Law"' (1990) 11 *Michigan Journal of International Law* 768, 775–76.

> of the state to be bound. A 'soft' argument relies on some extra consensual notion of the good and the just.[31]

'Hard' and 'soft' here are not 'international hard law' (generally viewed as the traditional sources of international law)[32] and 'international soft law' (generally viewed as those non-binding instruments of international law)[33] but rather *reasons* for compliance with international law. In such a divide, the 'hard' sources derive their validity from the consent of states, not their content, reflecting a positivist viewpoint. States must volunteer to be bound by norms.[34] On the other hand the 'soft' sources require validation from their content – something 'good' or 'just' – to be binding, and thus reflect a natural law approach. The first approach can also be explained as validity through an objective rule of recognition that provides a law-making process. The process is objectively ascertainable, and is completely divorced from the subject matter of the law. When a rule is formed through this process, it is valid, regardless of its content. How then does this apply to the Article 38 sources of international law?

i. Treaties

Treaties fall under the 'hard' justification, or positivist approach.[35] They are 'quintessentially hard: the ultimate expression of sovereign consent'.[36] The valid rule of recognition is the express consent of states to be bound – and treaties derive their validity from such consent, not from their subject matter.[37] It should be noted, however, that even this divide is fluid: the approach of viewing some treaties, such as United Nations Charter, as higher, more valid or more fundamental *because* of their content infuses this positivist source with a natural law flavour.[38]

ii. Customary International Law

Customary international law is usually viewed as a positivist source of law, based on *implied* consent. However, some publicists justify adherence to custom

[31] D Kennedy, 'The Sources of International Law' (1987) 2(1) *American University Journal of International Law and Policy* 1, 20.

[32] JE Alvarez, 'The New Dispute Settlers: (Half) Truths and Consequences' (2003) 38 *Texas International Law Journal* 405, 421.

[33] C Chinkin, 'Normative Development in the International Legal System' in D Shelton (ed), *Commitment and Compliance: The Role of Non-Binding Norms in the International Legal System* (Oxford University Press, 2000) 21, 30.

[34] V Degan, 'Some Objective Features in Positive International Law' in J Makarczyk, *Theory of International Law at the Threshold of the 21st Century: Essays in Honour of Krzysztof Skubiszewski* (Kluwer Law International, 1996) 123.

[35] Hall, 'The Persistent Spectre' (n 27) 284.

[36] Kennedy, 'The Sources of International Law' (n 31) 24.

[37] Although note that treaties that violate *jus cogens* norms are void: VCLT (n 19) Art 53.

[38] Kennedy, 'The Sources of International Law' (n 31) 27; A McNair, *The Law of Treaties* (Clarendon Press, 1961) 215–16.

with a 'soft' approach – 'binding because it is just to do things as they have been done'.[39] Although this view of custom does not link validity inherently to content, the source does not fulfil strict positivist criteria either. The valid rule of recognition for custom consists of the dual requirements of state practice and *opinio juris*,[40] although even here there is contention. Some scholars argue that the process of recognition relating to custom is not objectively ascertainable, as the requirements are subject to debate and change over time:

> Within the coordinates of legal positivism, the preconditions laid down in various doctrinal writings are nothing but speculative arguments. Thus in legal positivism, the validity, and with this the normativity of the legal propositions, is not certain but remains dependent upon the relative authority of such arguments.[41]

Thus unlike treaties, where validity is derived from the express consent of states, custom's validity is measured by external requirements as to methodology that are subject to judicial and doctrinal interpretation. Under this view, the validity of customary norms directly corresponds to the authority of the doctrinal interpretation of the theories. This strict positivist jurisdictional legitimacy of custom directly impacts on the function of the source, rendering custom invalid (non-binding) if the doctrinal interpretation of methodology is deemed to lack the relevant authority. It should be noted that this is an extreme view of legal positivism, and is not shared by most international law jurists:[42] nonetheless, it illustrates the fundamentally inter-connected nature of the aspects of the tetrahedral model.

Further, just as the 'hard' justification for adherence to treaties has been softened, the 'soft' justification for of custom has been made harder by emphasis on the consent of states by doctrines such as the persistent objector,[43] as well as an increased emphasis on *opinio juris* – where 'the repeated practice of states was coupled with a psychological intent to be bound'.[44] Modern consideration of customary international law generally considers it to be a positivist source of law with a binding function.[45]

iii. General Principles

The analysis above rests on a Kelsenian *grundnorm* of consent: that the validity of international law rests on its voluntary nature. Both custom and convention

[39] Kennedy, 'The Sources of International Law' (n 31) 24.
[40] *North Sea Continental Shelf* (n 17) 44; *Nicaragua* (n 17) 98.
[41] Fastenrath,'Relative Normality' (n 7) 322.
[42] Hall, 'The Persistent Spectre' (n 27) 274.
[43] *Asylum Case (Columbia v Peru)* (Judgment) [1950] ICJ Rep 266, 277–78; M Akehurst, 'Custom as a Source of International Law' (1974–75) 47 *British Yearbook of International Law* 1, 24.
[44] Kennedy, 'The Sources of International Law' (n 31) 26.
[45] Hall,'The Persistent Spectre' (n 27) 284.

express the wills of states,[46] and because it is considered 'right' that states only be bound by what they agree to, and 'that law should reflect what States generally will',[47] the sources of custom and convention give rise to binding norms. While custom and convention create laws divorced from their content, legitimate only because of the valid law-making process, the law-making process itself is valid only because it is right that it should be.

This construction of the primacy of consent in international law impacts the *function* of General Principles as well. Degan argues that adherence to voluntarism leads to the denial of the binding character of Article 38(1)(c):

> On this voluntaristic ground most authors deny the obligatory character for States of such general principles of law which are not embedded in treaties or customary law. And *vice versa*, if for a legal norm can be proved its conventional or customary character, even if the matter is of an obvious fiction, such a norm, according to this teaching, ceases to be a 'general principle of law, recognized by civilized nations'.[48]

Thus the *jurisprudence* of international law impacts on the function of General Principles. It suggests that General Principles are not binding and are capable of being subsumed by the other two sources; in this view, they are a truly secondary source of law.

In contrast, Schwarzenberger argued that as General Principles are expressly accepted by treaty – by virtue of their inclusion in the ICJ Statute – an argument that the source is fundamentally incompatible with sovereignty and thus inoperable 'runs counter to the established rule of treaty interpretation that treaty clauses must be interpreted in such a manner as not to make any of them inoperative or useless'.[49] Here, the function of General Principles leads to conclusions about their jurisprudence – General Principles are binding because of their inclusion in the ICJ Statute, thus their validity derives from the positivist law-making process of treaty creation.

IV. TYPE

The second face of the tetrahedron, type, asks what kind of content can become a General Principle. As with function, this aspect is also underpinned and affected by the jurisprudential legitimacy of the source. There are two preliminary questions to consider: first, the significance of the distinction drawn between rules and principles; and, second, whether General Principles are limited to certain types of content.

[46] Koskenniemi, 'Introduction' (n 2) xiii.
[47] ibid.
[48] Degan, 'Some Objective Features' (n 34) 127.
[49] Schwarzenberger, *International Law* (n 23) 56.

A. Principles and Rules

The concept of a 'principle' is often conceived of as different from a 'rule'. Sir Gerald Fitzmaurice argued that principles underlie rules and give reasons for their existence: while rules answer 'What?', principles answer 'Why?'[50] We must consider whether General Principles are actually *principles* as properly understood, or whether the judges decline to differentiate between principles and rules. It is suggested by Maurice Mendelson that, for the most part, the distinction is not observed: 'although there is quite a debate among legal theorists as to the difference and hierarchical relation between rules and principles, none of this finds any reflection in the utterances of the ICJ, which tends to treat the two terms as synonymous'.[51] Nonetheless, there is an inherent assumption in the work of some publicists that General Principles can *only* be true principles: non-specific, over-arching, fundamental and foundational,[52] being 'general propositions underlying the various rules of law which express the essential qualities of juridical truth itself'.[53] Such a view impacts on both the jurisprudential legitimacy and the methodology of the source: as true principles derive at least some legitimacy from their content, rather than an objective rule of recognition. The view of General Principles as true, natural law principles is further argued by Finnis:

> [T]he terms 'recognized' and 'civilized' ... point towards the assumption – fully justified – that there are true principles – traditionally called natural law – underlying this and every other legal order ...[54]

B. Content of General Principles

Some commentators suggest that General Principles are inherently procedural norms of international law.[55] This view is inherent in Degan's critique of voluntarism.[56] Degan refers to General Principles that apply to agreements

[50] G Fitzmaurice, 'The General Principles of International Law Considered from the Standpoint of the Rule of Law' (1957) 92 *Recueil de Cours* 1, 7.

[51] M Mendelson, 'The International Court of Justice' in V Lowe and M Fitzmaurice (eds), *Fifty Years of the International Court of Justice: Essays in Honour of Sir Robert Jennings* (Cambridge University Press, 1996) 80.

[52] See, eg, JHW Verzijl, *International Law in Historical Perspective*, vol 1 (AW Sijthoff, 1968) 59; R Kolb, 'Principles as Sources of International Law (with special reference to Good Faith)' (2006) 53(1) *Netherlands International Law Review* 1, 29; Bogdan, 'General Principles of Law' (n 27) 48.

[53] B Cheng, *General Principles of Law as Applied by International Courts and Tribunals* (Stevens and Sons, 1953) 24.

[54] Finnis, *Natural Law and Natural Rights* (n 4) 54.

[55] See GJH van Hoof, *Rethinking the Sources of International Law* (Kluwer Law and Taxation Publishers, 1983) 13.

[56] Degan, 'Some Objective Features' (n 34) 127.

and legal situations such as good faith, prescription and circumstances precluding wrongfulness,[57] as well as principles of arbitral and judicial procdure.[58] Degan argues that the validity of these principles 'depends on the fact of the very existence of the legal order'.[59] This is because without the first category of principles, 'any legal relations of States ... are impossible ... [t]hey are a necessary prerequisite for any kind of legal relations'.[60] The principles in the second category are necessary to make judicial settlement possible.[61] By limiting General Principles to those fundamental procedural norms that allow legal relationships and judicial settlement to function, Degan is able to justify their validity by their inherent operation within the international legal order.

Must all General Principles be of this type? Or are there other types of General Principles, perhaps substantive in nature? This question is necessarily related to the rules/principles question – while the principles Degan refers to fit within the true meaning of 'principle', what of General Principles, which may, in fact, be rules? Some commentators argue that substantive rules are indeed capable of being General Principles.[62] Simma and Alston extend the argument further, and suggest that in the context of human rights, *jus cogens* norms are better understood as examples of General Principles rather than customary norms.[63] This argument necessarily links back to jurisprudential legitimacy: as *jus cogens* norms are imbued with their higher normative status by reason of their content.

V. METHODOLOGY

The final facet of the tetrahedron is methodology: how are General Principles ascertained? Like the others, discussion of this facet is underpinned by the jurisprudential legitimacy of the source. There is also a clear overlap between type and methodology, as already explained.

There are four areas to explore: first, which forum the 'laws recognised by civilized nations' are drawn from; second, how General Principles are found (ie by a comparative approach, or otherwise); third, whether the methodology of General Principles authorises judicial discretion; and, finally, what the role of 'appropriateness' is in the methodology of General Principles.

[57] ibid.
[58] ibid 129.
[59] ibid.
[60] ibid 128.
[61] ibid 129.
[62] See JHH Weiler, 'Discussion: The Classical Sources of Law Revisited' in A Cassese and JHH Weiler (eds), *Change and Stability in International Law-Making* (Walter de Gruyter, 1988) 47.
[63] B Simma and P Alston, 'The Sources of Human Rights Law: Custom, Jus Cogens and General Principles' (1988–89) 12 *Australian Yearbook of International Law* 82, 104.

A. Domestic/International Forum

Some publicists take the view that the inclusion of the words 'as recognized by civilized nations' means that this recognition must be *in foro domestico* – that is, within the municipal systems of states.[64] Others argue that the principle can be drawn from principles of international law.[65] A question then arises, when is a 'civilized nation'[66] taken to have recognised something internationally? Can a conception of General Principles that includes deductions from existing international law (or the structure of international law itself) fulfil the requirement of 'recognition'? Some analysts suggest such recognition is fulfilled by drawing from expressions of state consent/practice such as resolutions and declarations of the United Nations General Assembly.[67]

B. Comparativism/Categoricism

There are two main approaches for finding General Principles. The first employs a comparative law approach, comparing the laws from different systems. While this is often in the context of *domestic* legal systems, this is not necessarily the case. Within this category, it is unclear which systems should be considered,[68] and how many systems a law must be in to be sufficient.[69] Nonetheless, despite these unanswered issues, the basic methodology of comparativism is fairly well understood.[70]

The second, less conceptually clear approach has been termed 'categoricism'[71] and identifies principles that 'form the basis of all law'.[72]

[64] Pellet and Müller, 'Article 38' (n 23) 924.

[65] ILC, *First Report on General Principles of Law* (29 April–7 June and 8 July–9 August 2019) UN Doc A/CN.4/732, para 174.

[66] See ch 7 for further discussion of the term 'civilized': see also ch 8 for discussion of Global General Principles.

[67] B Simma, 'The Contribution of Alfred Verdross to the Theory of International Law' (1995) 6 *European Journal of International Law* 1, 18; K Zemanek, 'The United Nations and the Law of Outer Space' (1965) 19 *Book of World Affairs* 199.

[68] R Schlesinger, 'Research on the General Principles of Law Recognised by Civilised Nations' (1957) 51 *The American Journal of International Law* 734, 751.

[69] Bos, *A Methodology of International Law* (n 17) 70; W Friedmann, 'The Uses of "General Principles" in the Development of International Law' (1963) 57 *The American Journal of International Law* 279, 284; Schwarzenberger, *International Law* (n 23) 45.

[70] Although see N Jain, 'Judicial Lawmaking and General Principles of Law in International Criminal Law' (2016) 57 *Harvard International Law* Journal 111; N Jain, 'Comparative International Law at the ICTY: The General Principles Experiment' (2015) 109(3) *American Journal of International Law* 486. See further discussion in ch 6.

[71] C Ford, 'Judicial Discretion in International Jurisprudence, Article 38(1)(c) and General Principles of Law' (1994) 5 *Duke Journal of Comparative and International Law* 35, 74.

[72] F Jalet, 'The Quest for General Principles of Law Recognized by Civilized Nations' (1963) 10 *University of California Law Review* 1041, 1086.

This method follows Lord Asquith's reasoning in the *Abu Dhabi* arbitration. He applied certain principles of English statutory interpretation because they were 'so firmly grounded in reason as to form part of … [a] "modern form of nature"'.[73] The exact methodology of categoricism is unclear. Some principles are derived with reference to one municipal legal system and others without reference to any municipal systems.[74] It can be argued that categoricism tends to a natural law methodology, as the validity of principles found in this manner often relates to their content. It is important, however, to maintain the distinction between jurisprudential legitimacy and methodology: it must not be assumed that a natural law conception of General Principles will always be accompanied by a categoricist methodology.

Both comparativism and categoricism go to the requirement of generality. Comparativism requires a horizontal generality, assessed laterally across legal systems (usually domestic, but not always). This could include both principles and rules. Catagoricism, on the other hand, can be considered as a more vertical generality, looking to abstractions of principles rather than lateral commonality.

C. Judicial Discretion

Some scholars argue that General Principles explicitly authorise the use of judicial discretion by the ICJ.[75] Using a Dworkinian model, there are two types of judicial discretion – strong (or pure or absolute) discretion and weak (or guided) discretion.[76] Pure or absolute discretion allows judges to decide 'upon a course of action unguided by rule or principle and solely as a matter of subjective determination'.[77] Pure discretion cannot exist under positivist law, as there is no valid law making imbuing the norm with validity.

Guided discretion exists where there are a number of possible alternatives, and the judge must choose between these. Guided discretion in the context of interpretations of legal texts (such as legislation) was espoused by Kelsen, who saw each differing alternative interpretation as equally valid and lawmakers free to choose among them.[78] This view was shared by Hart, who considered 'problems of the penumbra' – problems 'which arise outside the hard core of standard

[73] *In the Matter of an Arbitration between Petroleum Development and the Sheikh of Abu Dhabi* (1952) 1 *International and Comparative Law Quarterly* 247, 251.

[74] Ford, 'Judicial Discretion' (n 71) 74.

[75] ibid 64.

[76] R Dworkin, *Taking Rights Seriously* (Harvard University Press, 1977) 31–33.

[77] J Edelman, 'Judicial Discretion in Australia' (2000) 19 *Australian Bar Review* 285, 285.

[78] H Kelsen, *Pure Theory of Law*, 2nd edn, tr Max Knight (University of California Press, 1945) 351; Fastenrath, 'Relative Normality' (n 7) 307.

instances or settled meaning'[79] where a judge must decide between a number of possible alternatives. Hart stressed that the need for discretion does not equate to need for morality in the law.[80] In contrast to this positivist view, Dworkin argued that within the confines of such guided discretion (which he called interpretative adjudication), a correct interpretation existed, more valid than the others, based on what would 'show the ... law in the best possible light'.[81] Accordingly, guided discretion is not possible under this natural law view, as there are not a number of possible alternatives but only one, which is right by virtue of its content. In this manner, the judicial decisions in Dworkin's 'hard cases' are guided by principle,[82] where 'principle' reflects some moral right.[83]

Finally, there is the possibility that no judicial discretion is authorised: this scenario was covered by Raz:

> I suppose there might be a legal system which contains a rule that whenever the courts are faced with a case for which the law does not provide a uniquely correct solution they ought to refuse to render judgment. In such a system there would be no judicial discretion.[84]

i. Discretion and Gaps in International Law

It should be noted, however, that Kelsen did not view guided discretion as a means for filling gaps in law: in his theory of law, gaps cannot exist.[85] Kelsen characterises all legal disputes as being whether the 'valid norm to be applied in the concrete case ... establishes or does not establish the alleged legal obligation'.[86] Kelsen argues that in the absence of legal obligation, individuals are guaranteed freedom from obligation, and any attempt to impose a new obligation is unacceptable judicial discretion.[87] Thus Kelsen sees Raz's supposition as the reality of law. Although Kelsen's discussion focused on domestic law, this conception of law seems consistent with the view of the PCIJ in the *Lotus* case: that in the absence of international law, restrictions on states cannot be presumed.[88]

Lauterpacht, in contrast, espoused a view of 'legal constructivism',[89] which sees the role of General Principles as specifically acting to fill gaps, or *lacunae*,

[79] Hart, 'Positivism and the Separation of Law and Morals' (n 5) 607.
[80] ibid 615.
[81] R Dworkin 'Law's Ambitions for Itself' (1985) 71 *Virginia Law Review* 173, 175.
[82] R Dworkin, 'Hard Cases' (1975) 88(6) *Harvard Law Review* 1057, 1060.
[83] ibid 1059.
[84] J Raz, 'Legal Principles and the Limits of Law' (1972) 81 *Yale Law Journal* 823, 845.
[85] H Kelsen, 'On the Theory of Interpretation' (1990) 10 *Legal Studies* 127, 132.
[86] ibid 132.
[87] ibid 133.
[88] *SS 'Lotus' (France and Turkey)* (Merits) [1927] PCIJ Series A No 10, 18.
[89] Koskenniemi, 'Introduction' (n 2) xiii.

in international law.[90] Lauterpacht approves of Brierly's conception of such gaps:

> Surely when we speak of 'gaps' in the law, international or municipal, we are using a tendencious metaphor appropriate to critics, but not one of the jurist's terms of art. We are thinking of contingencies in which we know that the only answer a court can give to the complainant state or individual is that his grievance constitutes, as the law stands, no cause of action. We do not mean that the law has *no* rule for these contingencies, but merely that we do not like the rule that the law directs the court to apply.[91]

Using General Principles in this way not only impacts on the function of the source (that is, to fill the gaps left by treaty and custom), but also allows judicial discretion. This is discretion that seems to be linked to content: replacing a non-desired outcome with a rule that the court 'likes' more. This view fits Kelsen's crictisms of the notions of gaps: a gap is 'nothing more but the difference between the positive law and a system held to be better, more just, more nearly right'.[92] Under Kelsen's view, regardless of the high morality of the other system, the positive law must be applied: 'even the statute that is bad in the view of the official applying it is to be applied'.[93] In contrast, Brierly and Lauterpacht would allow discretion to fill the 'gap' or alter the norm. Lauterpacht sees such 'discretion' as a reference to General Principles.[94] This supposes fundamental concepts about the jurisprudential legitimacy and methodology of General Principles – notably, in giving rise to such discretion, they are not based on an objective process and rule of recognition. They are favoured by the judge because of their content – they are 'better' than the existing rule – and thus are not a positivist source of international law.

The analysis of the history of the source will reveal, first, whether it was *meant* to authorise discretion, while analysis of the treatment of the source by the PCIJ, ICJ and other international courts and tribunals will reveal whether it *has* been used to justify discretion. If judicial discretion is employed under the auspices of General Principles then analysis of what type of discretion has been used may give information about the jurisprudential construction of the source: is it Hartian positivist discretion, devoid of content; or is a Dworkinian 'principle' guided discretion, protecting moral rights? If General Principles are being used to fill a lacunae in the law, does this mean they cannot be a positivist source in line with Kelsen's pure theory of law?

[90] H Lauterpacht, 'Some Observations on the Prohibition of "Non Liquet" and the Completeness of Law' in Verzijl (ed), *Symbolae Verzijl* (n 13) 196, 205.

[91] JL Brierly, 'The General Act of Geneva' (1930) 11 *British Yearbook of International Law* 119, 128; Lauterpacht, 'Some Observations' (n 90) 206.

[92] Kelsen, 'On the Theory of Interpretation' (n 85) 133.

[93] ibid.

[94] Lauterpacht, 'Some Observations' (n 90) 205.

D. Appropriateness

The final issue to consider is whether there is some other step in the process in finding a General Principle such that it is appropriate for the norm to be a norm of *international* law. This is particularly relevant if the appropriate forum for finding General Principles is found to be the domestic forum – do such principles need to possess some inherent quality such that they are capable of being drawn from the domestic level and applied at the international level? Such a concern was raised by Judge McNair in the *International Status of South-West Africa*.[95] If such quality is needed, how is it assessed? Is it because of the inherent validity of the norm (going to both type and jurisprudential legitimacy)? Is it because of the manner of recognition – say, on the international plane (going to methodology)? Appropriateness could also impact function: if judicial discretion is required to assess appropriateness, as suggested by Schwarzenberger,[96] this could on some views render Article 38(1)(c) 'devoid of any formal character'.[97]

VI. CONCLUSION

This chapter sets out a framework of analysis, looking to jurisprudential legitimacy, function, type and methodology: the framework itself gives rise to questions that touch on multiple faces of the tetrahedron. These include, but are not limited to:

- Are General Principles binding?
- How do they interact with other sources of law?
- Do General Principles have an objective rule of recognition?
- If so, what is it?
- Does Article 38(1)(c) authorise judicial discretion? And if so, what kind?
- What does 'recognized by civilized nations' mean?
- Is this domestic or international recognition?
- What are 'civilized nations'?
- Are General Principles rules, or principles? Or both?
- Is horizontal generality sufficient, or is vertical generality required?
- Are General Principles limited to any particular type of content?

The list could go on.

[95] *International Status of South-West Africa* (Advisory Opinion) [1950] ICJ Rep 128, 148 (Separate Opinion of Judge McNair).

[96] Schwarzenberger, *International Law* (n 23) 46.

[97] J d'Aspremont, *Formalism and the Sources of International Law: A Theory of the Ascertainment of Legal Rules* (Oxford University Press, 2011) 171.

In attempting to answer these questions, this book will, where possible, break down use and analysis of the source into the four aspects of the framework. This is admittedly an artificial exercise at times. Nevertheless, interrogating the distinctions between the sides of the tetrahedron will allow a more rigorous final model of General Principles, based on the historical development of the source, its use in international courts and tribunals, and scholarly commentary.

2

History of Article 38(1)(c)

> [When] the draftsmen of the Statute of the Permanent Court of International Justice listed 'the general principles of law recognized by civilized nations' among the norms to be applied by the Court, they were giving official international recognition to a species of rabbit in the judicial hat. While all lawyers know that the rabbit is there and will be produced at need, they have rarely shown much interest in its pedigree.
>
> *Percy E Corbett*[1]

I. INTRODUCTION

ARTICLE 38 OF the Statute of the International Court of Justice (ICJ Statute) was drawn in its entirety from the same numbered Article of the Statute of the Permanent Court of International Justice (PCIJ Statute).[2] This chapter examines the introduction of Article 38 into the PCIJ Statute, tracing the formation of the article through the late nineteenth and early twentieth centuries, up to its inclusion in the finalised PCIJ Statute. The tetrahedral model developed in chapter 1 will be used to analyse this historical development.

In the formation of the PCIJ, an Advisory Committee of Jurists was formed to draft the PCIJ Statute ('Advisory Committee'). The introduction of Article 38 in its modern form is commonly traced back to the proposal of the President of the Committee, Baron Edouard Descamps,[3] made at the 13th Meeting.[4]

[1] PE Corbett, 'The Search for General Principles of Law' (1961) 47(5) *Virginia Law Review* 811, 814.

[2] Statute of the Permanent Court of International Justice contained in Protocol of Signature of the Statute of the Permanent Court of International Justice (opened for signature 16 December 1920, entered into force 1 September 1921) 200 LNTS 494 (PCIJ Statute).

[3] A Belgian Minister of State, Former Secretary-General of the Interparliamentary Union, Former President of the *Institut de Droit International*, and nominated 27 times for a Nobel Peace Prize from 1901–15. See A Eyffinger, *The 1899 Hague Peace Conference: 'The Parliament of Men, the Federation of the World'* (Kluwer Law International, 1999) 135–36; 'The Nomination Database for the Nobel Peace Prize, 1901–1956' (*Nobel Prize*, 2020) available at https://old.nobelprize.org/nomination/archive/show_people.php?id=2387.

[4] A Pellet and D Müller, 'Article 38' in A Zimmerman, CJ Tams, K Oellers-Frahm and C Tomuschat (eds), *The Statute of the International Court of Justice: A Commentary*, 3rd edn (Oxford University Press, 2019) 819, 827; J d'Aspremont, *Formalism and the Sources of International Law: A Theory of the Ascertainment of Legal Rules* (Oxford University Press, 2011) 97; M Đorđeska, *General Principles of Law Recognized by Civilized Nations (1922–2018)* (Brill Nijhoff, 2020) 26.

This proposal was discussed by the Advisory Committee, before a new formulation of the third source was suggested by the American and British participants at the Committee, Elihu Root[5] and Lord Walter Phillimore,[6] being 'the general principles of law recognized by civilized nations'.[7] Although Article 38 is clearly founded on Descamp's proposal, and the current wording of Article 38(1)(c) on the Root-Phillimore amendment, the recognition of a source of law in other than convention or custom had, in fact, been discussed for at least 21 years previous to the Advisory Committee's work. There are clear parallels with the various conceptions of this third source and the debate that surrounds General Principles today. By setting out this context, a more holistic understanding of the Advisory Committee's discussions can be gained. This chapter focuses on the recognition of the source within international agreements, and in particular in those agreements setting up international adjudicative bodies, as these are both the most analogous to the Statute of the PCIJ and most indicative of state practice. However, it should be noted that a third source of law was also used in some arbitral decisions during the same period.[8]

II. DEVELOPMENT PRE-WORLD WAR I

Although arbitration itself has its roots as far back as Ancient Greece,[9] and was widely used in the Middle Ages,[10] modern international arbitration is traced back to the Jay Treaty between the United States of America and the United Kingdom in 1794.[11] The Jay Treaty set up three arbitral commissions[12] to deal

[5] The former US Secretary of State and former US Secretary of War, first President of the Carnegie Endowment for International Peace, a member of the Permanent Court of Arbitration, and the winner of the 1912 Nobel Peace Prize. See CR Rossi, *Equity and International Law: A Legal Realist Approach to Decision Making* (Transnational Publishers, 1993) 100; M White, 'Equity – A General Principle of Law Recognised by Civilised Nations?' (2004) 4(1) *Queensland University of Technology Law and Justice Journal* 103, 107–08.

[6] An expert in international, ecclesiastical and admiralty law, the former Lord Justice of the Court of Appeal of the Privy Council (UK), and President of the International Law Association in 1905. See J Sankey and H Mooney, 'Phillimore, Walter George Frank, first Baron Phillimore (1845–1929)' in *Oxford Dictionary of National Biography*, online edn (2008) available at www.oxforddnb.com/view/article/35511.

[7] Permanent Court of International Justice: Advisory Committee of Jurists, *Procès-verbaux of the Proceedings of the Committee* (Van Langenhuysen Brothers, 1920) 15th Meeting.

[8] For example, 'the general principles of the law of nations on the denial of justice', which considered 'the rules common to most legislations or taught by doctrines' in *Antone Fabiani Case* (1905) 10 UNRIAA 83, 117. See P Dumberry, *A Guide to General Principles of Law in International Investment Arbitration* (Oxford University Press, 2020) 14; CT Kotuby Jr and LA Sobota, *General Principles of Law and International Due Process* (Oxford University Press, 2017) 8–9.

[9] A Nussbaum, *A Concise History of the Law of Nations*, rev edn (Macmillan, 1954) 7; WL Penfield, 'International Arbitration' (1907) 1(2) *American Journal of International Law* 330, 335.

[10] JH Ralston, *International Arbitration from Athens to Locarno* (Stanford University Press, 1929) 174; Penfield, 'International Arbitration' (n 9) 337.

[11] JW Salacuse, *The Law of Investment Treaties* (Oxford University Press, 2009) 362.

[12] Ralston, *International Arbitration* (n 10) 191; MO Hudson, *International Tribunals: Past and Future* (Carnegie Endowment for International Peace and Brookings Institution, 1944) 3.

with issues stemming from the American Revolutionary War.[13] The commissions proved popular, with one delivering 536 awards over five years.[14] Following the success of the arbitration clauses in the Jay Treaty, many other states began incorporating such clauses into other treaties.[15] As a result, by the end of the nineteenth century, over 100 treaties referred to international dispute settlement resolution via arbitration,[16] and arbitrations had been held between many European, African, South American and North American countries.[17] Following this increase in popularity in international arbitration, a need for consistency in arbitration was identified: 'the time seemed to be ripe for the creation of a permanent agency for arbitration'.[18] A number of international instruments and reports were created between 1873 and 1920, which provided for a variety of international arbitration schemes. It is these documents that provide us with the first expressions of General Principles as a source of international law.

A. Arbitral Procedure Regulations 1875

The late nineteenth century brought about many developments in international law, not least the establishment of the *Institut de Droit International* ('Institute of International Law') in 1873.[19] The Institute asked Levin Goldschmidt, a German scholar, to prepare a draft of procedural regulations for international courts of arbitration in 1873.[20] This draft was discussed at the 1874 Geneva meeting of the Institute,[21] and unanimously adopted, with some amendments, by the Institute in plenary session at the Hague in 1875 ('Arbitral Procedure Regulations').[22]

[13] Nussbaum, *A Concise History* (n 9) 129.

[14] While Salacuse puts the number at 536, Hudson reports 565 awards were made: Salacuse, *The Law of Investment Treaties* (n 11) 362; Hudson, *International Tribunals: Past and Future* (n 12) 3.

[15] LB Sohn, 'International Arbitration in Historical Perspective: Past and Present' in AHA Soons (ed), *International Arbitration: Past and Prospects* (Martinus Nijhoff, 1990) 9, 12.

[16] E Descamps, 'General Survey of the Clauses of Mediation and Arbitration Affecting the Powers Represented at the Conference' in JB Scott (ed), *The Proceedings of the Hague Peace Conferences* (Oxford University Press, 1920) 191.

[17] Hudson, *International Tribunals: Past and Future* (n 12) 4–5.

[18] MO Hudson, *The Permanent Court of International Justice 1920–1942* (Macmillan, 1943) 4.

[19] JB Scott (ed), *Resolutions of the Institute of International Law Dealing with the Law of Nations* (Oxford University Press, 1916) viii.

[20] L Goldschmidt, 'International Arbitral Procedure' (1874) 6 *Revue de droit international et de Législation Comparée* 421, tr in Scott (ed), *Resolutions* (n 19) 205; H Lauterpacht, *The Function of Law in the International Community* (Clarendon Press, 1933) 9; WM Reisman, 'Revision of the South West Africa Cases' (1966) 7(1) *Virginia Journal of International Law* 1, 8.

[21] Scott (ed), *Resolutions of the Institute of International Law* (n 19) 1.

[22] Institute de Droit International, *Projet de règlement pour la procédure arbitrale internationale* [1875] Res 1; tr in Scott (ed), *Resolutions of the Institute of International* (n 19) 1.

Both the initial draft and the adopted version of the Arbitral Procedure Regulations contain a section addressing the sources of law to be considered by tribunals. Section 22 of Goldschmidt's draft reads:

> Unless the arbitral tribunal is permitted, either by the *compromis* or by a subsequent convention of the contracting parties, to decide simply according to its equitable judgment, or unless, on the contrary, it is prescribed that it decide according to definite rules agreed upon, the legal judgment of the facts of the case will be rendered in conformity with the principles of law which are applicable by virtue of the rules of international law.[23]

The draft adopted by the Institute of International Law amended the provision in its Article 18: '[t]he arbitral tribunal gives judgment according to the principles of international law, unless the *compromis* imposes upon it different rules or leaves the decision to the free discretion of the arbitrators'.[24]

Both versions refer to the 'principles of law' or 'principles of international law' without defining these principles further. Goldschmidt's draft regulations, however, were presented interspersed with his statement of reasons. There are several points contained in these reasons that link the development of 'general principles of law', as understood in Article 38(1)(c), with this early expression of the third source of international law.

The first discussion comes in the introductory remarks to the draft regulations. Goldschmidt stated that where states agree by treaty to submit to an arbitral decision, the procedural rules the arbitral tribunal must consider are first and foremost those included in the treaty itself.[25] Where the treaty does not provide, the tribunal will consider subsidiary rules:

> These rules are drawn in the first place from the practice – very limited in truth – of international law. In the second place, they are the result of *independent* deductions, in which we have taken into account legal principles accepted in the matter of arbitrations in various civilized countries.[26]

Accordingly, when considering the procedural rules to be adopted by the arbitral tribunal, Goldschmidt saw the sources as, first, the treaty by which the parties have agreed to arbitrate, second, the 'practice of international law' and, third, the independent deductions based on legal principles accepted in civilised countries. A clear parallel can be seen between these three sources and Articles 38(1)(a), (b) and (c) of the concluded PCIJ Statute. From the passages above, two points about the methodology of this third source are immediately clear. First, it draws from domestic forums: those principles accepted in domestic arbitrations. Second, the '*independent* deductions' of the tribunal

[23] Goldschmidt, 'International Arbitral Procedure' (n 20) 228.
[24] Institute de Droit International, *Projet de règlement* (n 22) 5.
[25] Goldschmidt, 'International Arbitral Procedure' (n 20) 212.
[26] ibid.

echo the idea of judicial discretion associated with General Principles.[27] This link is further supported by Goldschmidt's next deliberation, concerning the difficulties in considering legal principles from different countries:

> These principles can not be utilized *directly*, first, because there are considerable differences in the practices of different countries in this matter also; then, because an international *compromis* can not be subjected to all the principles of civil arbitration, but requires special rules ...[28]

Both these points have variously been raised in the discussion of Article 38(1)(c) – first, the difference between legal systems saw some commentators questioning whether any 'general principles of law' could in fact exist.[29] Second, the idea of appropriateness for General Principles is well established,[30] and Goldschmidt's concern echoes Judge McNair's warning 77 years later that the transposability of municipal laws to the international stage must be 'as an indication of policy and principles rather than as directly importing these [private law] rules and institutions'.[31] Combining the notion of non-direct application with independent legal deductions, we approach the view of Schwarzenberger: that *limited* judicial discretion is necessary to ensure the appropriateness of a General Principle.[32]

Two further observations can be drawn from the commentary accompanying Section 22 of the draft, the first relating to jurisprudential legitimacy and the second to function. Goldschmidt noted that there had been 'considerable agitation' whether the arbitrator should consider law or equity,[33] and concluded that the arbitrator should decide

> according to the principles of existing international law. He will apply to the *international* points in the dispute the *international* law existing between the parties by virtue of treaties or custom; in the second place, general international law ...[34]

Here we have the first explicit listing of the three sources of international law – conventional law, customary international law and 'general international law'. Goldschmidt did not expand on what was meant by 'general international law', but again we can see the structural similarity to Article 38(1)(a), (b) and (c). It should be noted that the use of the term 'general international law' muddies the water – this term is often used as synonymous with non-conventional

[27] See ch 1.

[28] Goldschmidt, 'International Arbitral Procedure' (n 20) 212.

[29] See especially H Kelsen, *The Law of the United Nations: A Critical Analysis of its Fundamental Problems* (London Institute of World Affairs, 1950) 533.

[30] See discussion in ch 1.

[31] *International Status of South West Africa* (Advisory Opinion) [1950] ICJ Rep 128, 148 (Separate Opinion of Judge McNair).

[32] G Schwarzenberger, *International Law as Applied by International Courts and Tribunals*, vol 1, 3rd edn (Stevens and Sons, 1957) 46.

[33] Goldschmidt, 'International Arbitral Procedure' (n 20) 212.

[34] ibid 229.

international law, encompassing both custom and General Principles.[35] Here, however, it is clearly separated from customary law. It is also clear that the third source of law that Goldschmidt considered was *not* unfettered equitable principles.[36] Rather it is 'positive law' that the arbitrator must apply, suggesting a jurisprudential legitimacy based in positivism.[37] Second, the order of the sources suggests that this third source, while norm-creating, will only be applied where treaties or custom do not: its function is gap-filling, only acting where treaty and custom are silent.

B. Permanent Court of Arbitration: 1899 and 1907

The draft Arbitral Procedure Regulations, as adopted by the Institute of International Law, were utilised as a basis for discussion at the 1899 Hague Peace Conference ('First Peace Conference'), discussing the possibility of a Permanent Court of Arbitration (PCA).[38] A convention was formed at the First Peace Conference ('First Hague Convention') to establish the PCA.[39] The idea was subsequently revisited at the 1907 Hague Peace Conference ('Second Peace Conference') and another convention was drafted ('Second Hague Convention').[40] Article 48 of the First Hague Convention establishing the PCA states:

> The Tribunal is authorized to declare its competence in interpreting the *compromis* as well as the other Treaties which may be invoked in the case, and in applying the principles of international law.[41]

This article is also repeated at Article 73 of the Second Hague Convention.[42] This provision is a development from the articles contained in the Arbitral Procedural Regulations, in that it expressly envisions a two-step process of the sources of international law: first, the *compromis* and other conventional law; and, second, the 'principles of international law'. However, no further definition of 'principles of international law' was given. Baron Descamps, later President of the Advisory Committee of Jurists, was a member of the Third Commission on Pacific Settlement of International Disputes involved with the drafting of

[35] See, eg, R Jennings, 'The Identification of International Law' in B Cheng (ed), *International Law: Teaching and Practice* (Stevens and Sons, 1982) 3, 4; *Military and Paramilitary Activities in and against Nicaragua (Nicaragua v United States of America)* (Merits) [1986] ICJ Rep 14, 153 (Separate Opinion of President Singh).

[36] Goldschmidt, 'International Arbitral Procedure' (n 20) 228–29.

[37] ibid 229.

[38] Scott, *Resolutions of the Institute of International Law* (n 19) ix.

[39] Convention (I) on Pacific Settlement of International Disputes (adopted 29 July 1899, entered into force 4 September 1900) 187 CTS 410 ('Convention (I)').

[40] Convention (II) on Pacific Settlement of International Disputes (adopted 18 October 1907, entered into force 26 January 1910) 205 CTS 233 ('Convention (II)').

[41] Convention (I) (n 39) Art 48.

[42] Convention (II) (n 40) Art 73.

the PCA Conventions. In this role, he 'asked that Article 48 be completed by a provision setting forth the rules according to which the arbitrators should give judgment'.[43] Unfortunately, his request was not met – Descamps reported that 'the point was considered, properly speaking, as not coming within the field of arbitral procedure'.[44] Given the reluctance of the drafters to expand on these principles, the process provided is not as sophisticated an approach as that advanced by Goldschmidt in 1873.

Although the Hague Conventions established the PCA, which is still in operation today, they are nonetheless relevant to the formulation of Article 38(1)(c) in that, first, they form part of the general background against which that article was drafted and, second, they are the direct predecessors to two other conventions that arose from the Second Hague Peace Conference in 1907: the Court of Arbitral Justice Convention[45] and the Prize Court Convention.[46] It should also be noted that although neither Hague Convention expressly set out that PCA tribunals *could* refer to General Principles, in practice they have done so.[47]

C. Court of Arbitral Justice: 1907

The PCA, was, it is argued, misnamed: 'The Permanent Court of Arbitration is not really a Court. Nor is it in any accurate sense a tribunal, though it is often referred to as "the Hague Tribunal"; instead it is a device for facilitating the creation of *ad hoc* tribunals.'[48] Criticism of the PCA on this basis was raised at the Second Peace Conference. James Brown Scott, the United States delegate to the Second Peace Conference, writes:

> [I]t is evident, as was said at the Second Peace Conference that 'the Permanent Court is not permanent, because it is not composed of permanent judges; it is not accessible, because it has to be constituted for each case; it is not a court, because it is not composed of judges'.[49]

[43] E Descamps, 'Report to the Conference from the Third Commission on Pacific Settlement of International Disputes' in JB Scott (ed), *The Reports to the Hague Conferences of 1899 and 1907* (Clarendon Press, 1917) 42, 83.

[44] ibid.

[45] *Draft Convention Relative to the Creation of a Court of Arbitral Justice*, extracted in full in JB Scott, *An International Court of Justice: Letter and Memorandum of January 12, 1914, to the Netherland Minister of Foreign Affairs, in behalf of the Establishment of an International Court of Justice* (Oxford University Press, 1916) 100.

[46] Convention Relative to the Creation of an International Prize Court (signed 18 October 1907) 205 CTS 381.

[47] See, eg, *Netherlands v Portugal (Island of Timor)* (1915) 9(1) *American Journal of International Law* 240, 244; *United States v Netherlands (Island of Palmas (or Miangas))* (1928) 2 RIAA 829, 866; *Larsen v Hawaiian Kingdom* (2001) 119 ILR 566 para 13; *Guyana v Suriname* (Award of 17 September 2007) ICGJ 370 (PCA 2007) paras 418–420.

[48] Hudson, *The Permanent Court of International Justice* (n 18) 11.

[49] Scott, *An International Court of Justice: Letter and Memorandum* (n 45) 7.

Accordingly, the United States' delegates to the Second Peace Conference were instructed to propose the creation of a permanent court composed of judges, to overcome the shortcomings of the PCA,[50] referred to subsequently as a Court of Arbitral Justice (CAJ). The proposed Court was not intended to displace the PCA but rather to operate alongside it.[51] The Court never came into existence,[52] but a Convention was drafted – the Draft Convention Relative to the Creation of a Court of Arbitral Justice ('CAJ Draft Convention').[53] The CAJ Draft Convention was mostly focused on issues surrounding the appointing of judges to the Court.[54] It did not specify the sources of law to be considered by the Court, but rather stated that the CAJ would follow the rules of procedure as laid down in the Convention for the Pacific Settlement of International Disputes.[55] Accordingly, those provisions set out in the Hague Conventions, including the two-tiered Article 73 allowing for the consideration of 'principles of international law', separate from conventional law, would apply.

The report made to the Second Peace Conference from the First Commission Recommending the Creation of a Court of Arbitral Justice[56] did provide more detail on the types of law that the proposed court would consider, and is useful in the consideration of the history of General Principles. In particular, in the commentary to Article 1 of the CAJ Convention, discussing the phrase 'the continuity of arbitral justice', a link was drawn between the need to have judges representing different nationalities and the inclusion of municipal law principles in the international law judgments of the Court:

> If the Court is to develop an international, not a national system of law, it seems to need no argument that the various systems of law should find representation within the Court and upon the bench. In a national court this proposition is so axiomatic that it would neither be questioned or discussed, but the problem is here complicated by the fact that many systems of law exist and that these various systems must find adequate representation. Different systems of law exist in different States, but an international court must embrace the various systems of the world.[57]

From this, an idea emerges that the contention around and attention paid to the national origins of judges on the CAJ,[58] rather than being an issue separate

[50] ibid 8.

[51] ibid.

[52] O Spiermann, *International Legal Argument in the Permanent Court of International Justice: The Rise of the International Judiciary* (Cambridge University Press, 2005) 5.

[53] *Draft Convention Relative to the Creation of a Court of Arbitral Justice*, extracted in Scott (ed), *The Reports* (n 43) 100.

[54] See, eg, *Draft Convention Relative to the Creation of a Court of Arbitral Justice*, Arts 1–10, 20, extracted in full in Scott, *An International Court of Justice: Letter and Memorandum* (n 45).

[55] ibid 100: see Art 20.

[56] JB Scott, 'Report to the Conference from the First Commission Recommending the Creation of a Court of Arbitral Justice' in Scott (ed), *The Reports* (n 43) 232.

[57] ibid 242.

[58] This was also a concern in the development of the Statute of the PCIJ.

from General Principles, may in fact be rooted in that same concern: that rules or principles common to all, or most, municipal systems find expression as a source of law in the international courts. This link foreshadows, perhaps, ideas expressed by publicists such as Virally, that the requirement of generality in Article 38(1)(c) is satisfied by virtue of the diverse nationality of judges on the ICJ.[59] The commentary to Article 1 continues:

> If the Court is to judge according to equity and international law, it must not be the equity of any one system, but the equity which is the resultant of the various systems of law. Just as the individual rarely frees himself from this environment, so the jurist is influenced by his system of law and the training in it. Supposing, therefore, that each is influenced by his training, it is necessary to have judges trained in the various systems of law in order that the equity administered by the Court may be truly the spirit of the laws. For the purpose of the Court municipal law must be nationalized. In this case, and in this case only, can the judgement be equitable in any international sense, for the judgement so formed will be based on international equity as well as international law.[60]

Two issues arise from this commentary. First, although not expressed in the CAJ Convention, the source of international law being discussed is very similar to modern conceptions of Article 38(1)(c): 'municipal law must be nationalized' could be an early expression of the requirement of appropriateness – the necessity of transposability of principles from municipal systems into international law.[61] Second, the 'spirit of the laws' and the 'equity which is the resultant of the various systems of law' echo in later conceptions of Article 38(1)(c) as being overarching norms of 'juridical truths'.[62] However, without any explicit consideration of the sources of law in the CAJ Convention, the most comprehensive treatment of the third source of law up to this point remains Goldschmidt's draft of the Arbitral Procedure Regulations.

D. International Prize Court: 1907

i. General Principles of Justice and Equity

As well as the formation of the CAJ, delegates to the Second Hague Peace Conference discussed the formation of an International Prize Court. Proposals for such a court had been made throughout the eighteenth and nineteenth

[59] M Virally 'The Sources of International Law' in M Sørenson (ed), *Manual of Public International Law* (Macmillan, 1968) 116, 146; See also PE Corbett, 'The Search for General Principles of Law' (1961) 47(5) *Virginia Law Review* 811, 824; GJH van Hoof, *Rethinking the Sources of International Law* (Kluwer Law and Taxation Publishers, 1983) 142–43.

[60] Scott, 'Report to the Conference' (n 56) 242.

[61] Pellet and Müller, 'Article 38' (n 4) 930–31.

[62] B Cheng, *General Principles of Law as applied by International Courts and Tribunals* (Stevens & Sons, 1953) 24.

centuries, including a study begun in 1875 by the Institute of International Law.[63] Although the subject was not on the agenda of the Conference, both the British and German delegates made proposals for the creation of a Prize Court.[64] As a result, the Second Peace Conference created the Convention Relative to the Creation of an International Prize Court ('Prize Court Convention').[65] Unlike the CAJ Draft Convention, the Prize Court Convention did consider what law should be applied by the Court. Article 7 provided that if a question of law to be decided were covered by a treaty in force between the parties to the dispute, then the Court was to be governed by the treaty provisions. Otherwise:

> In the absences of such provisions, the Court shall apply the rules of international law. If no generally recognized rule exists, the Court shall give judgement in accordance with general principles of justice and equity.[66]

The commentary to Article 7, prepared by the First Commission on the Draft Convention relative to the Creation of an International Prize Court, explains further what is meant by 'general principles of justice and equity'. The commentary first states the normal position – 'even in the absence of a formal treaty, there may be a recognized customary rule which passes as a tacit expression of the will of the States'[67] – and then goes on to ask, 'But what will happen if positive law, written or customary, is silent?'[68]

In the context of a Prize Court, when determining whether seizure of prizes (ships, cargo and the like) has been done legitimately, the silence could be construed as permissive, allowing the national law of the captor to prevail,[69] a situation that tends to favour the captor.[70] The First Commission did not take that view, instead providing for the 'general principles of justice and equity'. There are two important points to take from the introductory question above. First, the drafters of the Prize Court Convention clearly had in mind the situation where neither convention nor custom could apply to a question of law – the same situation later referred to as a lacuna by the drafters of the PCIJ Statute,[71] and one of the strongest justifications for the inclusion of Article 38(1)(c) in the PCIJ Statute.[72] Second, the general principles in Article 7 are referred to when

[63] Hudson, *The Permanent Court of International Justice* (n 18) 71.

[64] ibid.

[65] Convention Relative to the Creation of an International Prize Court (n 46).

[66] ibid Art 7.

[67] L Renault, 'Report to the Conference from the First Commission on the Draft Convention relative to the Creation of an International Prize Court' in Scott (ed), *The Reports* (n 43) 758, 769.

[68] ibid.

[69] Renault, Report to the Conference' (n 67) 769.

[70] HB Brown, 'The Proposed International Prize Court' (1908) 2(3) *American Journal of International Law* 476, 477.

[71] See, eg, Permanent Court of International Justice: Advisory Committee of Jurists, *Procès-verbaux* (n 7) 13th Meeting, 296.

[72] W Phillimore, 'Scheme for the Permanent Court of International Justice' (1920) 6 *Transactions of the Grotius Society* 89, 94.

'positive law' is silent, perhaps giving an indication that such principles are not, in fact, positivist in origin.

The commentary goes on to explain the meaning of General Principles:

> [W]e believe that we ought to propose to you a solution, bold to be sure, but calculated considerably to improve the practice of international law. 'If no generally recognized rule exists, the Court shall give judgment *in accordance with the general principles of justice and equity*.' It is thus called upon to *create the law* and to take into account other principles than those to which the national prize court whose judgment is appealed from was required to conform.[73]

This propounds an activist role for judges, allowing them to *create* law where no custom or convention applies, in line with Brierly's and Lauterpacht's conception of discretion and lacuna.[74] From the discussion in chapter 1 we can see such discretion would be incompatible with Kelsenian positivism.[75] Thus, the jurisprudential legitimacy of this third source points away from positivism and more towards natural law.

Further, although the paragraph refers to 'other principles' to which the judges can refer in this creation, it does not set out what those principles are, nor how they are found. It could be argued that the judicial discretion given to judges under Article 7 was not intended to be unfettered but instead limited by law drawn from 'other principles'. Without a clear understanding of what exactly these 'other principles' are, however, such an argument seems spurious.

As well as contributing to the context in which the PCIJ Statute was developed, there is another link between the First Commission drafting the Prize Court Convention and the PCIJ Statute. Both Léon Bourgeois[76] and Francis Hagerup[77] were members of the First Commission drafting the Prize Court Convention.[78] Thirteen years later, Hagerup was a member of the Advisory Committee of Jurists charged with the drafting of the PCIJ Statute,[79] while Bourgeois presented the final report of the Advisory Committee to the League of Nations.[80]

[73] Renault, 'Report to the Conference' (n 67) 769.

[74] JL Brierly, 'The General Act of Geneva' (1930) 11 *British Yearbook of International Law* 119, 128; H Lauterpacht, 'Some Observations on the Prohibition of "Non Liquet" and the Completeness of Law' in JHW Verzijl (ed), *Symbolae Verzijl: Présentées au Professeur JHW Verzijl, à l'occasion de son Lxx-ieme anniversaire* (Martinus Nijhoff, 1958) 196, 205–06.

[75] H Kelsen, 'On the Theory of Interpretation' (1990) 10 *Legal Studies* 127, 132.

[76] The so-called 'spiritual father of the League of Nations', a French politician, later President of the Council of the League of Nations and recipient of the 1920 Nobel Peace Prize: see I Abrams, *The Nobel Peace Prize and the Laureates* (Science History Publications, 2001) 94.

[77] A Norwegian politician and diplomat, later chairman of the *l'Institut de Droit International*, and founder of the Norwegian journal *Tidsskrift for Rettsvitenskap*: see GG Wilson, 'George Francis Hagerup' (1921) 15(3) *American Journal of International Law* 418, 418–19.

[78] Renault, 'Report to the Conference' (n 67) 758.

[79] See n 115.

[80] League of Nations, 'Procès-verbal of the Eight Meeting of the Council, San Sebastian, 30th July–5th August 1920' [September 1920] (6) *League of Nations Official Journal* 1, 304, 318.

ii. The Prize Court's Failure: A Bold Solution Goes Too Far

It is clear that the drafters of the Prize Court Convention were aware of the evolving and developing role of international law, and the subsequent difficulty of codifying such a system: 'If we were to wait until the system of international law is complete, before having judges to apply it, the event would be a prospective one which even the youngest of us could hardly expect to see.'[81] Accordingly, the drafters were prepared to allow the judges of the Prize Court to play a dynamic role in the development of international law through their inclusion of the 'general principles of justice and equity'.

This 'bold solution' was, however, too bold for states to be comfortable with. Britain's representative to the 1907 Conference, Sir Edward Grey, wrote a letter to the other naval powers of the time,[82] proposing a conference 'with the object of arriving at an agreement as to what are the generally recognized principles of international law'.[83] The reason behind the meeting was the feeling that

> the establishment of the International Prize Court would not meet with general acceptance so long as vagueness and uncertainty exists as to the principles which the court, in dealing with appeals brought before it, would apply to questions of far-reaching importance affecting naval policy and practice.[84]

The 10 naval states met in London for the London Naval Conference of 1908–09, at which they drew up the Declaration of London,[85] which attempted the codification of the particular principles of maritime law that would be applied by the Court. The discretion awarded to the judges to create the law through use of 'general principles of justice and equity' by the drafters of the Prize Court Convention was removed, being replaced with a positivist codification of the principles that could be applied. The Declaration was signed by all the states but never entered into force.[86] Various modifications were then proposed to the Convention, including an additional protocol, which was signed but never ratified.[87] Although there was early optimism that the Prize Court would succeed,[88] by 1912 'it was clear that the Declaration of London would not be ratified by certain States of great naval strength, so that even before the outbreak of war in 1914, the effort to create an international prize court had come to grief'.[89] Thus, when the third source of law was cast as a natural law source,

[81] Renault, 'Report to the Conference' (n 67) 769.

[82] Austria-Hungary, France, Germany, Italy, Japan, Russia, Spain, the United States of America and the Netherlands.

[83] Letter from Edward Grey to the principal maritime powers dated 27 February 1908, extracted in JB Scott (ed), *The Declaration of London February 26, 1909* (Oxford University Press, 1919) 13–15.

[84] ibid 13.

[85] Declaration of London (adopted 26 February 1909) 208 CTS 338.

[86] Hudson, *The Permanent Court of International Justice* (n 18) 77.

[87] ibid 78.

[88] JB Scott, 'An International Court of Prize' (1911) 5(2) *American Journal of International Law* 302, 315.

[89] Hudson, *The Permanent Court of International Justice* (n 18) 78.

based on unrestrained judicial activism, it failed. As will be seen, this context is vital for understanding the work of the Advisory Committee of Jurists.

E. Development 1910–14

Although the Prize Court itself had stalled, momentum towards an international court continued. The United States delegates sought to take advantage of the meeting of states at the London Naval Conference, and proposed that the Prize Court be extended in its scope so as to be invested with the jurisdiction of the CAJ.[90] The Conference decided to pursue this idea through diplomatic channels rather than conclude anything at London – accordingly, a note was circulated to all the powers participating in the Conference.[91] In response, delegates from Germany, the United States, France and Great Britain met in Paris in March 1910 and drafted a Convention to put into effect the CAJ Draft Convention.[92] This Convention dealt mainly with the issue of judges in the CAJ and did not address the question of what sources of law the proposed court would consider. This Convention was predicated on the Prize Court Convention's being ratified, and so did not progress beyond the draft stage. Regardless of these setbacks, certain people, including James Brown Scott, continued their efforts to establish the CAJ. Scott wrote to the Netherlands Minister of Foreign Affairs, Jonkheer Loudon, on 12 January 1914, urging the Netherlands's participation in the proposed establishment of the CAJ in the Peace Palace in The Hague. Again, the central issue was the appointment of judges, and Scott's letter and accompanying memorandum devote much consideration to this issue. The documents stress the difference between arbitration as a 'continuation of diplomatic procedure'[93] and adjudication in the CAJ as the 'impartial application of principles of law and justice'.[94] It should be noted that at one point in the memorandum Scott lists the sources of international law as 'custom, as evidenced by the practice of nations, and treaties and conventions',[95] apparently excluding the third source. Scott's diplomatic efforts were cut short by the outbreak of war in July–August 1914. No more work was done on the proposed Court until after peace had been declared.

Thus, before World War I, a third source of international law additional to treaties and custom was emerging. The nature of this source was not settled,

[90] Scott, *An International Court of Justice: Letter and Memorandum* (n 45) 12.

[91] ibid.

[92] *Draft Convention concluded at Paris in March 1910, by Representatives of Germany, the United States, France and Great Britain to put into effect the Draft Convention recommended by the Second Peace Conference Relating to the Establishment of a Court of Arbitral Justice*, extracted in JB Scott, *An International Court of Justice: Letter and Memorandum* (n 45) 91.

[93] Scott, *An International Court of Justice: Letter and Memorandum* (n 45) 19.

[94] ibid.

[95] ibid 60.

with a clear schism between, on the one hand, a positivist conception drawing from municipal laws with limited judicial discretion to determine appropriateness and, on the other, a natural law source drawing from 'justice and equity' and requiring judicial discretion to the point of activism. This schism between two alternative models continued in the post-War discussions.

III. DEVELOPMENT POST-WORLD WAR I

Following the end of World War I, the League of Nations was formed and attention was redirected towards the establishment of an international court of justice. At the second session of the Council of the League of Nations, the Council decided to appoint an Advisory Committee to prepare plans for the establishment of the PCIJ, and to present a report of these plans to the Council.[96]

Before commencing work, the Advisory Committee was issued a number of documents concerning the draft Statute of the PCIJ, including various drafts of the Statute prepared by different countries.[97] Under the nomenclature in use at the time, these were referred to as 'draft schemes' and contained different formulations of the sources of law to be considered by the PCIJ.

A. The Draft Schemes

i. Draft Scheme of Denmark, Norway and Sweden: 1918

One of the first documents to be prepared was the Draft Scheme drawn up by delegates from Denmark, Norway and Sweden in 1918.[98] Article 27 of that scheme states:

> If the legal point at issue is provided for in an agreement actually in force between the parties, such agreement shall form the basis of the decision.
>
> If no such provision exists, the Court shall decide the case according to the established rules of International Law. In default of generally recognised rules, the Court shall base its decision on the general principles of Law.[99]

[96] Permanent Court of International Justice: Advisory Committee of Jurists, *Procès-verbaux* (n 7) chs I, III.

[97] Permanent Court of International Justice: Advisory Committee of Jurists, *Documents Presented to the Committee Relating to Existing Plans for the Establishment of a Permanent Court of International Justice* (Washington DC, 1920).

[98] *Draft Scheme of a Convention Concerning an International Judicial Organisation. Drawn up by the Three Committees Nominated Respectively by the Governments of Denmark, Norway and Sweden*, extracted in Permanent Court of International Justice: Advisory Committee of Jurists, *Documents* (n 97) 169.

[99] ibid Art 27.

The structure of this article is very similar to Article 7 of the Prize Court Convention (see section II.D.i), with 'general principles of justice and equity' being replaced with 'general principles of Law'.

The Draft Scheme also provided an alternative wording for the second paragraph of Article 27. The explanatory statement to the Draft Scheme, prepared by the Swedish delegation, explains such alternatives as instances where the Swedish delegation felt 'it should record not only the solution which appeared most advisable, but any other which also seemed acceptable'.[100] Accordingly, while the above formulation was the most advisable, the acceptable alternative states:

> If no such provision exist, the Court shall decide the case according to the established rules of International Law, or, if rules of this kind do not exist, the Court will decide according to what, in its opinion, should be the rules of International Law.[101]

Here, 'general principles of Law' have been replaced by judicial discretion. Two issues can be drawn from this alternative formulation. First, as it is presented in the alternative, it seems to suggest that 'general principles of Law' were not intended to be purely discretionary in nature. Second, the alternative formula could lead to natural law connotations, as the judges decide not what is but what *should* be the law. Does this indicate that 'general principles of Law' in the first connotation were intended to be free of such natural law qualities? This differentiation is in line with the development of the source prior to the War.

The Draft Scheme alternative wording was adopted by three later independent drafts from each of the countries involved in the original Draft Scheme – the 1919 Swedish Draft Convention,[102] the Danish Draft Scheme[103] and the Norwegian Draft Scheme.[104]

[100] *Explanatory Statement: Extract of the Report Addressed by the Swedish Commission to the Minister for Foreign Affairs*, extracted in Permanent Court of International Justice: Advisory Committee of Jurists, *Documents* (n 97) 153.

[101] *Draft Scheme* (n 98) alternative Art 27.

[102] *Draft of a Convention Respecting a Permanent International Court of Justice drawn up by a Swedish Governmental Commission 1919*, Art 17, extracted in Permanent Court of International Justice: Advisory Committee of Jurists, *Documents* (n 97) 241.

[103] *Draft Scheme Concerning the Organisation of a PCIJ prepared by the Committee Appointed by the Danish Government*, Art 15, extracted in Permanent Court of International Justice: Advisory Committee of Jurists, *Documents* (n 97) 205.

[104] *Report on the Organisation of a Permanent International Tribunal Submitted by the Norwegian Committee Appointed to Enquire into Certain Questions Concerning the League of Nations*, Art 15, extracted in Permanent Court of International Justice: Advisory Committee of Jurists, *Documents* (n 97) 233.

ii. Swiss Avant-projet*: 1918–19*

The Federal Council of Switzerland appointed a Commission Consultative in late 1918 to draw up a draft scheme for the PCIJ.[105] Article 42 of the scheme sets the sources out in the order in which they are to be utilised: first, any treaties existing between the parties; second, the 'principles of law'; and, third, where no generally recognised rule of law exists or is recognised by the parties, the judge decides 'in accordance with justice and equity'.[106]

Here, again, is a scheme much like the one in the alternative (and ultimately adopted) wording of the Swedish, Danish and Norwegian scheme. In this case, the 'principles of law' refer to customary international law, and hence the structure is convention, then custom, then 'justice and equity'. The scheme does not set out what is meant by 'justice and equity', but the wording seems to hand wide discretion to the judge, unfettered by limits. This is similar to the alternative conception in the four Scandinavian schemes, as well as the formulation in the Prize Court Convention.

iii. Five Powers Plan

Following their various individual plans, the Governments of Norway, Denmark, the Netherlands,[107] Sweden and Switzerland sent delegates to a Conference at The Hague to draft a combined plan, often referred to as the 'Five Powers Plan'. This plan reverted back to the alternative wording of the original Draft Scheme of Denmark, Norway and Sweden, focusing on judicial discretion, and Article 2(2) of the Five Powers Plan stated:

> In the absence of such treaty provisions, the Court shall apply the recognised rules of international law or, should no rules applicable to the case exist, shall enter judgment according to its own opinion of what the rules of international law on the subject should be.[108]

Here again, the 'recognised rules of international law' clearly refer to customary law. The structure is then conventional law, customary law and then judicial discretion. Again, the reference to what the law *should* be suggests a natural law basis for this third source.

[105] Secretariat of the League of Nations, 'Memorandum on the Different Questions Arising in Connection with the Establishment of the Permanent Court of International Justice' in Permanent Court of International Justice: Advisory Committee of Jurists, *Documents* (n 97) 3, 59.

[106] Federal Council of Switzerland, *Statut Constitutional de la Ligue de Nations* (1919), Art 42, extracted in Permanent Court of International Justice: Advisory Committee of Jurists, *Documents* (n 97) 267.

[107] The original Dutch scheme does not contain any reference to the sources of law to be considered by the Court, and hence has not been discussed in this chapter.

[108] *Draft for the Establishment of the Permanent Court of International Justice Provided for in Article 14 of the Covenant of the League of Nations (Plan of the Five Neutral Powers)*, Art 2(2), extracted in Permanent Court of International Justice: Advisory Committee of Jurists, *Documents* (n 97) 301.

iv. Proposals of the German Government: 1919

The German Government also communicated its proposals for the Statute of the PCIJ to the League of Nations. Article 35 states that the decision of the tribunal is passed 'according to international agreements, international customary law and according to the general principles of law and equity'.[109] Here we have a departure from the inclusion of judicial discretion. Rather, the German scheme is reflective of Article 7 of the Prize Court Convention.[110] It was also the first scheme to explicitly (rather than relying on accompanying commentary or the like) list the sources of law in a form very similar to the eventual Article 38(1)(a), (b) and (c). Unlike previous schemes, Article 35 does not contain instructions as to the order in which the sources may be considered, save any implicit hierarchy based on the order of mention.

v. Draft Prepared by Clovis Bevilaqua

The documents presented to the Advisory Committee also contained a draft prepared by Clovis Bevilaqua, the Brazilian representative on the Advisory Committee. This provided that, in the absence of treaties or recognised principles of international law, the Court 'shall deliver judgment in conformity with the general principles of law and equity'.[111] As with the German scheme, this reflects back to the wording of the Prize Court Convention; however, instead of 'justice and equity' the reference is to 'law and equity'. Law is a concept different from justice, and this difference may suggest less emphasis on morality (and thus natural law) in these later conceptions.

vi. Memorandum, Permanent Secretariat

These draft proposals were accompanied by a memorandum prepared by the Legal Section of the Permanent Secretariat of the League of Nations. The memorandum stated the sources of law for the PCIJ to be '[b]y reference, in the order named, to treaties, customary international law, general principles of law and equity',[112] citing the Central American Court Convention, the Swiss project, the original Scandinavian Draft Scheme and the German project as

[109] *Proposals of the German Government for the Establishment of a League of Nations*, Art 35, extracted in Permanent Court of International Justice: Advisory Committee of Jurists, *Documents* (n 97) 129.

[110] Convention Relative to the Creation of an International Prize Court (n 46), Art 7.

[111] *Draft for the Organisation of the Permanent Court of International Justice by Mr Clovis Bevilaqua*, Art 24, extracted in full in Permanent Court of International Justice: Advisory Committee of Jurists, *Documents* (n 97) 353.

[112] Secretariat of the League of Nations, *Memorandum on the Different Questions Arising in Connection with the Establishment of the Permanent Court of International Justice*, contained in Permanent Court of International Justice: Advisory Committee of Jurists, *Documents* (n 97) 103.

support for this formulation.[113] The Convention establishing the Central American Court of Justice provided that the Court would be governed by 'its free judgement, with respect to points of law, by the principles of International Law'.[114]

B. Discretion and General Principles

From the documents presented to the Court, two distinct proposals emerge. Every scheme lists the primary source of law as conventional law as applicable between the two parties. Most schemes then have recourse to customary international law (although most do not mention the term 'customary'). In determining the third source – what Court should refer to in the absence of these conventions or custom – the proposals split. One approach is that of judicial discretion, giving power to the judges to determine what the law should be. The other does not allow for such wide discretion, tethering judges to 'general principles of law and equity'. Thus, in the lead-up to the formation of the PCIJ, the third source of international law was unclear. What was certain, however, is that when the phrase 'general principles' was used, it was as an *alternative* to unfettered judicial discretion, not a manifestation of it.

IV. ARTICLE 38(1)(C) AND THE PCIJ

A. Advisory Committee of Jurists

It was against the background of these two approaches that the Advisory Committee discussed the sources of law the PCIJ would apply. The Advisory Committee was formed of 10 members, representing 10 different interested nations.[115] The members were high-ranking lawyers, politicians and diplomats. All had great experience, and some were elder statesmen – Albert de Lapradelle was the youngest at 49,[116] while Elihu Root, Lord Walter Phillimore and Baron

[113] ibid.

[114] *Convention for the Establishment of a Central American Court of Justice*, extracted in full in 'Supplement: Official Documents' (1908) 2 *American Journal of International Law* 231.

[115] Mineichiro Adatci (Japan), Rafael Altamira (Spain), Clovis Bevilaqua (Brazil), Edouard Descamps (Belgium), Francis Hagerup (Norway), Albert de Lapradelle (France), Bernard Loder (the Netherlands), Walter Phillimore (England), Arturo Ricci-Busatti (Italy) and Elihu Root (the United States of America).

[116] de Lapradelle was born in 1871: see M Koskenniemi, 'Nationalism, Universalism, Empire: International Law in 1871 and 1919' (draft prepared for the 'Whose International Community? Universalism and the Legacies of Empire' Conference, Columbia University Department of History, 19–20 April 2005) 30.

Eduoard Descamps were all in their seventies.[117] It is interesting, but perhaps not surprising, that the three oldest also had the three strongest, and most opposed, views in the debate over General Principles. In addition to these 10 members there were three other people present at the meetings – Raoul Fernandes, first standing in a consultative capacity for Clovis Bevilaqua but later replacing him, James Brown Scott as advisor to Root, and Åke Hammerskjöld as an observer.[118] The Advisory Committee met from 16 June 1920 to 24 July 1920, for a total of 35 meetings, with Descamps presiding as chair.

The proceedings of the Advisory Committee are set out in the *procès-verbaux* published by the PCIJ.[119] It is these *procès-verbaux* on which this section will primarily rely. It should be noted that they might not be a wholly accurate report of the discussions that took place – they were often post-edited by the members of the Advisory Committee,[120] sometimes so much so that 'the revised minutes appear to convey a different impression from that to be gained in the session or from a perusal of the original minutes'.[121] Nonetheless, these *procès-verbaux*, along reports of the proceedings written contemporaneously,[122] provide the background for the introduction of General Principles into the Statute of the PCIJ.

As was the case with the CAJ Conventions before it, much of the work of the Committee was concerned with discussing the method of appointment of judges[123] and the compulsory jurisdiction of the Court.[124] The sources of law were discussed in the 13th, 14th and 15th Meetings. Much of the discussion was between Descamps and Root. While Descamps supported a model of General Principles with natural law aspects, Root was highly resistant to what he viewed as a subjective source of law. Tension between the two delegates had been ongoing throughout the meeting process, but when the discussion turned to sources of law, Hammerskjöld observed, 'Root threw off the veil and entered into open war with Descamps'.[125]

[117] Descamps was born in 1847: see Eyffinger, *The 1899 Hague Peace Conference* (n 3) 135. Phillimore was born in 1845: see P Towle, *Democracy and Peace Making: Negotiations and Debates, 1815-1973* (Routledge, 2000) 39. Root was born in 1845: see ES Mihalkanin, *American Statesmen: Secretaries of State from John Jay to Colin Powell* (Greenwood, 2004) 430.

[118] See generally O Spiermann, '"Who Attempts Too Much Does Nothing Well": The 1920 Advisory Committee of Jurists and the Statute of the Permanent Court of International Justice' (2002) 73 *British Yearbook of International Law* 187, for publication of private reports written by Åke Hammerskjöld.

[119] Permanent Court of International Justice: Advisory Committee of Jurists, *Procès-verbaux* (n 7).

[120] Spiermann, 'Who Attempts Too Much' (n 118) 191–92.

[121] JB Scott, *The Project of a Permanent Court of International Justice and Resolutions of the Advisory Committee of Jurists* (Carnegie Endowment for International Peace, 1920) 10.

[122] ibid; Phillimore, 'Scheme for the Permanent Court of International Justice' (n 72); see also Spiermann, 'Who Attempts Too Much' (n 118).

[123] Spiermann, 'Who Attempts Too Much' (n 118) 201.

[124] ibid 202.

[125] ibid 213.

i. 13th Meeting of the Committee

Discussion at the 13th Meeting initially concerned compulsory jurisdiction, and it is in this context that the sources of law the Court should consider were introduced. Root argued that nations would only be satisfied with a Court exercising compulsory jurisdiction if the limits of that jurisdiction were clearly laid down: '[t]he States would not accept a Court which had the right to settle disputes in accordance with rules established by the Court itself, and by the interpretation of more or less vague principles'.[126] Root argued that the failure of the Prize Court Convention lay in the vagueness of Article 7 of that Convention: 'Nations will submit to positive law, but will not submit to such principles as have not been developed into positive rules supported by an accord between all States.'[127]

Root thus supported a positivist leaning, state-consent-based approach to the sources of law to be considered by the PCIJ. The issue was not discussed further at that point, as the other members felt the issue of sources of law was 'quite distinct from that of the competence of the Court'.[128] The Advisory Committee returned to the question of sources of law when it had settled the subject-matter jurisdiction of the Court, later in the meeting. In his role of President of the Committee, Descamps circulated his draft of the four sources:

> The following rules are to be applied by the judge in the solution of international disputes; they will be considered by him in the undermentioned order:
>
> 1. Conventional international law, whether general or special, being rules expressly adopted by the States;
> 2. International custom, being practice between nations accepted by them as law;
> 3. The rules of international law as recognised by the legal conscience of civilised nations;
> 4. International jurisprudence as a means of the application and development of law.[129]

Descamps' draft does not embrace the pure judicial discretion suggested by some of the earlier conventions and draft schemes. It does not, however, follow the alternative conception of 'general principles of law and equity'[130] drawn from the laws of nations.[131] Indeed, in introducing the concept of the 'legal conscience of civilised nations', Descamp's formulation is not necessarily linked to municipal law at all.

[126] Permanent Court of International Justice: Advisory Committee of Jurists, *Procès-verbaux* (n 7), 13th Meeting, 286.
[127] ibid 287.
[128] ibid.
[129] ibid 306.
[130] *Proposals of the German Government for the Establishment of a League of Nations* (n 109), Art 35; *Draft for the Organisation of the Permanent Court of International Justice by Mr Clovis Bevilaqua* (n 111), Art 24.
[131] Goldschmidt, 'International Arbitral Procedure' (n 20) 212.

There was little contention among the Advisory Committee as to the first two sources. There was, however, much discussion as to the third and fourth sources.[132] The discussion started with Root's expressing his disapproval of clauses 3 and 4 of Descamps' draft:

> Did it refer to something which had been recognized but nevertheless had not the character of a definite rule of law? It was the same with clause 4. These two clauses constituted an enlargement of the jurisdiction of the Court which threatened to destroy it. If these clauses were accepted, it would amount to saying to the States: 'You surrender your rights to say what justice should be.' Was it possible to compel nations to submit their disputes to a Court which would administer not merely law, but also what it deems to be the conscience of civilised people.[133]

In contrast, the Dutch delegate and future President of the PCIJ, Bernard Loder,[134] saw the duty of the PCIJ to develop international law, and viewed clauses 3 and 4 of Descamps' proposal as serving this aim:

> Rules recognized and respected by the whole world had been mentioned, rules which were, however not yet of the nature of positive law, but it was precisely the Court's duty to develop law 'ripen' customs and principles universally recognised and to crystallize them into positive rules; in a word, to establish an international jurisprudence.[135]

Other committee members disapproved of giving the Court the power to expand international law beyond the restraints of convention and custom,[136] or to act as a legislator.[137] Phillimore saw the role of customary international law as so important that clauses 3 and 4 must either come within the limits of custom (and thus, it would seem, be redundant), or be an unacceptable expansion of international law – 'it was not possible to go beyond the bounds of [international custom]'.[138]

Francis Hagerup drew the Advisory Committee's attention to the underlying reason for clause 3 as expressed in the various drafts:

> [T]here might be cases in which no rule of conventional or general law was applicable. A rule must be established to meet this eventuality to avoid the possibility of the Court declaring itself incompetent (*non liquet*) through lack of applicable rules.[139]

[132] Permanent Court of International Justice: Advisory Committee of Jurists, *Procès-verbaux* (n 7), 13th Meeting, 306.
[133] ibid 293–94.
[134] 'History, International Court of Justice', available at www.icj-cij.org/en/history.
[135] Permanent Court of International Justice: Advisory Committee of Jurists, *Procès-verbaux* (n 7), 13th Meeting, 294.
[136] ibid 295.
[137] ibid 296.
[138] ibid 295.
[139] ibid 296.

Hagerup thus identified the issue of the lacuna in international law, and explicitly connected it with the third source under discussion. The 13th Meeting ended at this point, and the discussion of sources of law was reignited at the 14th Meeting of the Advisory Committee.

ii. 14th Meeting

At the 14th Meeting, Descamps made a speech supporting his draft of sources. He spoke of the need for a third source, to be utilised where convention and custom did not apply, an 'objective justice'.[140] Descamps saw this objective justice as encompassing two different sources, the 'concurrent teaching of the authors whose opinions have authority' and the 'legal conscience of civilised nations'.[141]

In this formulation, Descamps saw the work of publicists as a material source of law, stating that 'when the greater part of juriconsults agree upon a certain rule the presumption in favour of that rule becomes so strong that only a person who makes a mock of justice would gainsay it'.[142] In regard to the second proposition, the 'legal conscience of civilised nations', Descamps referred to the Maartens clause from the 1899 Hague Convention on the Laws and Customs of War on Land – 'the rule of the principles of the law of the nations, as they result from the usages established among civilised peoples, from the laws of humanity and the dictates of the public conscience'.[143]

In light of this, it is clear that the 'conscience' that Descamps referred to in clause 3 of his proposal was indeed divorced from municipal law and instead tied to some higher 'public conscience' – a natural law conception. This is confirmed by Descamps' reference to an 'objective justice'.

Following Descamps' speech, the Advisory Committee returned to the issue of a possible lacuna in international law, as previously identified by Hagerup. Root was asked by several members of the Committee as to his views on a *non liquet*, given his opposition to Descamps' draft. It is clear that Root's opposition was grounded in his fear that states would not accept a Court with compulsory jurisdiction if that jurisdiction extended to pronouncing judgments on rules other than 'the universally recognised rules of International Law', which Root saw as being convention and custom.[144] In line with this, Root felt that if neither convention nor custom could be applied to a case, the Court should either declare itself incompetent to deal with the issue, or limit itself to making a recommendation, rather than a binding judgment.[145]

[140] ibid 14th Meeting, 322.
[141] ibid 323.
[142] ibid.
[143] ibid 323–24; Convention with Respect to the Laws and Customs of War on Land (adopted 29 July 1899, entered into force 4 September 1900) 32 Stat 1803, preamble.
[144] ibid 308.
[145] ibid 309–10.

In response, Descamps argued that the conception of the law of nations as composed 'not only by rules recognised by the civilised nations, but also by the demands of public conscience' was not a new phenomenon, nor an expansion of international law.[146] Root had also expressed concern that the interpretation of 'general principles of law' would differ from country to country, rendering such a source 'subjective conceptions of the principles of justice'.[147] In contrast, Descamps advanced a conception of such general principles that seems firmly rooted in natural law ideas:

> Concerning Mr Root's statement that the principles of justice varied from country to country, that might be partly true as to certain rules of secondary importance. But it is no longer true when it concerns the fundamental law of justice and injustice deeply engraved on the heart of every human being and which is given its highest and most authoritative expression in the legal conscience of civilised nations. That was the law which could not be disregarded by a judge, a law which in practice whether it is wished to or not, a judge would never disregard.[148]

Descamps thus saw such a rule as limiting, rather than encouraging, judicial discretion, as judges would have to consider whether their opinions were in 'agreement with the conception of justice of civilised nations'.[149] This passage also seems to suggest that these fundamental laws would be non-derogable – even if judges *wished* to overrule them, they could not. The obvious comparison here is the development of the doctrine of *jus cogens* – which would fit into this conception of General Principles.

Another conception of the source was advanced by Arturo Ricci-Busatti, the Italian delegate. He returned to the language of 'general principles of law'. He saw these general principles as 'general rules of equity and justice which come into play in each case',[150] using the example of 'that which is not forbidden is allowed'.[151] This was 'not a question of creating rules which do not exist, but of applying the general rules which permit the solution of any question'.[152] Ricci-Busatti's interpretation did not provide any guidance as to how these general rules were to be found, nor any objective way of measuring generality. In this manner, this proposition could again be seen as a natural law conception, speaking of empirical truths or fundamental rules that the judges must discern with no reference to particular evidence or use of that rule. It should be noted that the general rules to which Ricci-Busatti referred were procedural in nature.[153]

[146] ibid 310.
[147] ibid 309.
[148] ibid 310–11.
[149] ibid 311.
[150] ibid 315.
[151] ibid 314.
[152] ibid 315.
[153] ibid.

iii. 15th Meeting

The question of sources was revisited at the 15th Meeting, where a draft prepared by Root and Phillimore was circulated.[154] The text stated:

> The following rules are to be applied by the Court within the limits of its competence, as described above, for the settlement of international disputes; they will be considered in the undermentioned order:
>
> 1. conventional international law, whether normal or special, being rules expressly adopted by the States which are parties to a dispute;
> 2. international custom being recognised practice between nations accepted by them as law;
> 3. the general principles of law recognised by civilised nations;
> 4. the authority of judicial decisions and the opinions of writers as a means for the application and development of law.[155]

Here we can see the first inclusion of General Principles in its modern form. Root had been persuaded to accept a further source of law in addition to treaty and custom – although it seems that some of this success was because the wording of the source was 'based on a ruling of the Supreme Court of the United States'.[156] Phillimore later explained the need for a compromise between his position and the 'Continental' delegates. A schism had opened in relation to the concept of *non liquet*:

> Here we had to fight some dangerous suggestions, that if there was no definite rule of law, the Court should decide on what it thought ought to be the law; and we had further to deal with a curious Continental way of looking at cases which arises from their being bound by Codes. We found that Continental jurists were so afraid of injustice being done by following the strict letters of their Codes, that they ended up giving their judges a kind of power to do abstract justice, almost throwing their Codes to the wind. We therefore had to express ourselves with considerable care.[157]

Root and Phillimore, with their common law backgrounds, thus sought to restrain the possibility of unfettered judicial discretion in light of a possible lacuna in international law. General Principles was inserted to 'meet the fears of our foreign friends'[158] – to provide a method of finding applicable law where treaty and custom did not exist. The inclusion of Article 38(1)(c) in the draft Statute must be read in this light – rather than *authorise* judicial discretion, it was intended to curtail it.

[154] Spiermann, 'Who Attempts Too Much' (n 118) 217.
[155] Permanent Court of International Justice: Advisory Committee of Jurists, *Procès-verbaux* (n 7), 15th Meeting, annex 1.
[156] Spiermann, 'Who Attempts Too Much' (n 118) 217.
[157] Phillimore, 'Scheme for the Permanent Court of International Justice' (n 72) 94.
[158] ibid.

Also circulated to the Advisory Committee at the 15th Meeting was a statement made by Raoul Fernandes, attempting to conciliate the views of Descamps and Root. The statement referred to general principles at the national level as 'latent rules', which a judge does not create but brings to light – 'such a rule is quite legitimate because it is logically contained in a principle already recognised by the Nation concerned'.[159] The statement goes on:

> What is true and legitimate in national affairs, for reasons founded in logic and not in the arbitrary exercise of sovereignty, cannot be false and illegal in international affairs, where moreover, legislation is lacking and customary law is being formed very slowly, so that the practical necessity of recognising the application of such principles is much greater.[160]

First, it should be noted the high import that is given to such principles – necessary because of the slow and sometimes cumbersome nature of conventional and customary law. As will be discussed in chapter 8, these concerns are no less pertinent today. Second, a notion emerges from Fernandes' statement of the *inherent* morality of these principles by reason of their inclusion in the laws of many states. This argument is the precursor to that developed by Judge Ammoun in *North Sea Continental Shelf*,[161] and will be discussed further in chapters 4 and 7.

As it happens, such reconciliation between the views of Descamps and Root was unnecessary. Root and Phillimore had been able to persuade Descamps that their formulation was 'not so unlike his own as to make defeat too bad',[162] and Descamps agreed with the Root-Phillimore draft as circulated.[163] However Fernandes' work was welcomed as coinciding with the general ideas of the Committee and Root's plan.[164]

Root's plan was generally accepted, although Ricci-Busatti argued the sources should be read simultaneously.[165] Ricci-Busatti also favoured inserting 'the general principles of equity' as a source, but this did not find support.[166] Descamps replied to Root's views on the order of the sources, stating that although the sources could be read simultaneously in certain cases, a 'classified graduation' was desirable.[167] Ricci-Busatti reiterated his view, stating that the proposed words 'in the undermentioned order'

[159] Permanent Court of International Justice: Advisory Committee of Jurists, *Procès-verbaux* (n 7), 15th Meeting, 346.

[160] ibid.

[161] *North Sea Continental Shelf (Federal Republic of Germany v Denmark; Federal Republic of Germany v Netherlands)* (Merits) [1969] ICJ Rep 3, 136 (Separate Opinion of Judge Ammoun).

[162] Spiermann, 'Who Attempts Too Much' (n 118) 217.

[163] Permanent Court of International Justice: Advisory Committee of Jurists, *Procès-verbaux* (n 7), 15th Meeting, 331.

[164] ibid.

[165] ibid 332.

[166] ibid 333–34.

[167] ibid 336.

> might also suggest that a judge was not authorised to draw upon a certain source, for instance point 3, before having applied conventions and customs mentioned in points 1 and 2. This would be a misinterpretation of the Committee's intentions.[168]

Although General Principles were introduced against the background of the discussion of a lacuna, Ricci-Busatti's argument suggests that this is not the only role for them. He argued that a judge *would* be authorised to draw upon General Principles without first having applied convention and custom and finding them lacking. Descamps still supported the inclusion of the order of the sources, arguing it reflected a 'natural classification' of the sources,[169] but he conceded the point, and the words 'in the undermentioned order' were omitted from the final draft of Article 38. This is important for the discussion of the function of the source.

The Advisory Committee also considered the methodology of General Principles. The two main views were that General Principles are a subset of customary law, and must be derived from that;[170] and alternatively, that General Principles are rooted in national law. In support of the second point, Phillimore stated that General Principles are 'these which were accepted by all nations *in foro domestic*, such as certain principles of procedure, the principle of good faith, and the principle of *res judicata*'.[171] Phillimore referred to such principles as 'maxims of law'.[172] Albert de Lapradelle agreed that 'principles which formed the bases of national law were also sources of international law,' and said for these principles to be sufficiently recognised they must have obtained 'unanimous or quasi-unanimous support'.[173] Lapradelle also saw merit in keeping the provision open-ended: 'it [is] preferable to keep to a simple phrase: such, for example, as "the general principles of law" without indicating exactly the sources from which these principles should be derived'.[174]

The Advisory Committee then turned its attention to the procedure that the Court would follow, and did not revisit the discussion on the sources of law.

B. Passage through the League of Nations

Once the Advisory Committee had completed its draft scheme for the PCIJ, this was presented to the Council of the League of Nations. The Council considered the draft scheme at its 8th and 10th sessions, and made amendments to a number of articles.[175] No amendments were made to Article 38.

[168] ibid 337.
[169] ibid 337.
[170] ibid 335.
[171] ibid.
[172] ibid.
[173] ibid.
[174] ibid 336.
[175] Hudson, *The Permanent Court of International Justice* (n 18) 118.

The amended draft scheme was then submitted to the members of the League of Nations pursuant to Article 14 of the Covenant of the League of Nations, and was then referred by the League of Nations to the Third Committee.[176] The Third Committee held 10 meetings on the amended draft scheme, and a sub-committee of the Third Committee held a further 11 meetings.[177] The Statute was finally adopted by the PCIJ on 13 December 1920.[178] Throughout the Statute's progress through the various committees of the League of Nations, no amendment had been made to Article 38 as endorsed by the Advisory Committee.

V. CONCLUSION: APPLYING THE TETRAHEDRAL FRAMEWORK

A. Jurisprudential Legitimacy

The source as first introduced by Descamps to the Advisory Committee rested on natural law principles of 'the fundamental law of justice and injustice deeply engraved on the heart of every human being',[179] laws that, because of their nature, could not be disregarded by judges even if they wanted to. The main opponent to the inclusion of Article 38(1)(c), Root, opposed it precisely because it was not a source consistent with consent-based (ie positivist) international law.

The usage of the terms such as 'general principles of … equity',[180] 'international equity'[181] and 'general principles of justice and equity'[182] in the third source of law in the earlier conventions and draft schemes, also support the conception of a source where the content of the norms is important in determining the validity of the norms – that is, a natural law conception. The term 'equity', however, was specifically omitted from the final draft of the sources, over the protestations of one member of the Advisory Committee.

Although Descamp was persuaded to accept the Root-Phillimore proposition, there remains an inherent tension between his natural law conception of the 'conscience of mankind' and Root's refusal to entertain a non-positivist source of law. The compromise between the two views is certainly a restriction on Descamp's initial conception, but it also seems to be a weakening of a strict consent-based approach. Fernandes' explanatory statement, accepted by the rest

[176] ibid 119.

[177] ibid.

[178] ibid 122.

[179] Permanent Court of International Justice: Advisory Committee of Jurists, *Procès-verbaux* (n 7), 15th Meeting, 310.

[180] *Draft for the Organisation of the Permanent Court of International Justice by Mr Clovis Bevilaqua* (n 111), Art 24; *Proposals of the German Government for the Establishment of a League of Nations* (n 109), Art 35.

[181] Scott, 'Report to the Conference' (n 56) 242.

[182] Convention Relative to the Creation of an International Prize Court (n 46).

of the Advisory Committee, of such principles as 'true and legitimate'[183] also suggests a deviation from strict positivism. Thus although the third source of international law evolved from a positioning of a positivist conception against a natural law one, the ultimate inclusion of General Principles is an uneasy compromise between the two.

B. Function

Although there was discussion by the Advisory Committee of the order of the sources of law, it is clear that Article 38(1)(c) was intended to operate as a formal source of international law, alongside convention and custom. This intention is evident in the work of the Advisory Committee, which, despite early reluctance on the part of some members to accept a source other than convention or custom, endorsed the source as fulfilling a necessary role to provide rules of law where otherwise there would be a lacuna. It is also reflected in the inclusion, from the beginning of the Advisory Committee's deliberations on the sources of law, of the words 'as a means for the application and development of law' as relating to the fourth source (judicial decisions and publicists) but not the third. In addition, although the source was introduced as a solution to any lacuna, any expression as to the order in which the sources of law must be applied was explicitly rejected by the Advisory Committee. Indeed, one member expressly stated that a judge would be authorised to use General Principles without first having exhausted conventional and customary international law.

The status of General Principles as a formal source of law is also reflected in the developments leading up to the Advisory Committee's works. None of the Conventions or draft schemes discussed in this chapter that included 'general principles' as a source of law made any indication that this source was not a formal source equivalent in law-making capability to convention and custom, although most schemes did specify that the source would only be used in the absence of the first two sources.

C. Methodology

Two main issues relating to methodology arose from the development of the source: the role of judicial discretion, and the forum from which General Principles should be drawn.

[183] Permanent Court of International Justice: Advisory Committee of Jurists, *Procès-verbaux* (n 7), 15th Meeting, 346.

i. The Role of Judicial Discretion

Although the source can be said to have developed from natural law considerations, it is clear that such considerations are tempered by the practical requirements of the recognition of principles by nations. The Advisory Committee warned against judicial legislation: Article 38(1)(c) was never intended to give judges unfettered power to make laws. The Root-Phillimore formulation was aimed at limiting potential judicial discretion in the face of a lacuna. Accordingly, there is no role for *pure* judicial discretion.

This view is supported by the various conventions and draft schemes that led up to the PCIJ: as was discussed, two distinct variations of the third source emerged. One was based on judicial discretion, the Court deciding 'according to what, in its opinion, should be the rules of International Law',[184] while the other was the 'general principles of law', in various formulations. The source of General Principles is distinct from a source that allows pure judicial discretion: there must be some objective methodology that guides judges in their discovery of norms under this source. This view is particularly understandable in the light of the failure of the Prize Court, due to – it was argued – too great a role for judicial discretion.

Although it is clear that General Principles were intended to be a source separate from discretion, it cannot be denied that the source was introduced with the aim of letting the Court develop international law, particularly in situations where the alternative would be the Court's declaring itself *non liquet*.

ii. The Forum from which General Principles are Drawn: The Role of Municipal Law

Descamps' initial draft did not necessarily tie the principles to municipal laws: rather they rested on the 'legal conscience' of nations.[185] Later discussion by the Committee made it clear that the appropriate forum from which to draw General Principles was municipal law. This conception is also supported by the various conceptions of the source in the Conventions and documents preceding the PCIJ.[186]

[184] *Draft Scheme of a Convention Concerning an International Judicial Organisation* (n 98), alternative Art 27.

[185] Permanent Court of International Justice: Advisory Committee of Jurists, *Procès-verbaux* (n 7), 13th Meeting, 287.

[186] See, eg, Goldschmidt, 'International Arbitral Procedure' (n 20) 212; Scott, 'Report to the Conference' (n 56) 242.

D. Type of General Principles

i. Principles and Rules

Throughout the development of Article 38(1)(c) the terms 'principles' and 'rules' were used interchangeably. There was no discussion about the philosophical difference between the two terms. In the discussions of the Advisory Committee, Descamps talked of 'principles' and 'laws', while Loder and Fernandes used the term 'rules'. Descamps' initial formulation of Article 38(1)(c) used 'rules', while the Root-Phillimore draft used 'principles'. The significance (if any) of this alteration was not discussed by the Advisory Committee. This is entirely consistent with the development of the source prior to the work of the Advisory Committee. Within the Arbitral Procedural Regulations, 'principles of international law' and 'rules of international law' are used interchangeably to refer to international law generally. Although General Principles are discussed as 'legal principles', they are also 'subsidiary rules'. The reference to 'principles of international law' in the Hague Conventions seems to encompass custom; while custom is termed 'the rules of international law' in the Prize Court Convention.

Inasmuch as we can draw *any* information about the distinction between rules and principles from this history, we can say that the development of the third source of law, as indeed the development of international law more generally, was not concerned with any theoretical distinction between rules and principles – the instruments used the terms as synonymous.

ii. Procedural General Principles

It should also be noted that although many of the principles explicitly recognised by members of the Advisory Committee as 'general principles' were procedural in nature, there was no indication by any members that the source was limited to only founding norms with a procedural content. Indeed, Descamps talked of General Principles as 'fundamental laws of justice',[187] which seems to go beyond norms of a purely procedural nature.

iii. Jus Cogens

Finally, Descamps' description of the General Principles as non-derogable gives a link between the source in its infancy and the concept of *jus cogens* norms. As will be seen in chapter 7, some scholars argue that *jus cogens* norms are not, in fact, customary but are better understood as General Principles.[188]

[187] Permanent Court of International Justice: Advisory Committee of Jurists, *Procès-verbaux* (n 7), 14th Meeting, 310.

[188] See, eg, H Mosler, *The International Society as a Legal Community* (Springer, 1980) 135; A Cassese 'Discussion' in A Cassese and JHH Weiler (eds), *Change and Stability in International*

In summary, the development of General Principles as a source of law from 1875 to their inclusion in the PCIJ Statute in 1920 reveals five clear features of the source. First, the jurisprudential legitimacy of the source fits into neither bright-line positivism nor strict natural law: a compromise reached as a way forward by the Advisory Committee of Jurists. Second, it was always intended to be a binding source of law, alternative to treaty and custom. Third, it does not authorise unfettered judicial discretion. Fourth, there is no significance in the choice of the term 'principle', at least in so far as it does not indicate that *rules* are excluded by the source. Fifth, General Principles are drawn from the domestic forum.

Of note, even in this early work on the source, issues were identified that continued to be discussed throughout the development of General Principles through the twentieth century and, indeed, today – the possibility of a link to *jus cogens* norms, the link between General Principles and judicial diversity, the disparity of laws between countries, and the need for some kind of appropriateness for domestic laws to be transformed into international norms.

Having considered how General Principles were developed up until their inclusion in the PCIJ Statute, the next stage is to assess how the source was *actually* treated by the Court, which is the work of chapter 3.

Law Making (Walter de Gruyter, 1988) 55; MC Bassiouni, 'A Functional Approach to "General Principles of International Law"' (1990) 11 *Michigan Journal of International Law* 768, 779–80; B Simma, 'International Human Rights and General International Law: A Comparative Analysis' (1993) 4(2) *Collected Courses of the Academy of European Law* 153, 226; D Shelton, 'Normative Hierarchy in International Law' (2006) 100 *American Journal of International Law* 291, 299.

3

Consideration of Article 38(1)(c) by the PCIJ

I. INTRODUCTION: SEPARATING THE WHEAT FROM THE CHAFF

HAVING CONSIDERED THE development of Article 38(1)(c) until its inclusion in the Statute of the Permanent Court of International Justice (PCIJ), this chapter will now consider the use of the General Principles by the Court. Although the judgments of the PCIJ make reference to 'principle[s] of international law',[1] 'general rules',[2] 'general conception[s] of law',[3] 'principle[s] universally accepted',[4] 'principles … generally accepted'[5] and the 'general principles of law',[6] it is often hard to ascertain whether these are actually a reference to General Principles. Indeed, in many of these cases it would be 'daring to consider the Court has alluded to general principles of Article 38(1)(c)'.[7] The Court's terminologies are 'vague and cryptic formulas which may equally apply both to principles of customary international law and to general principles in the sense of para 1(c)',[8] and are often the result of a judge's having 'simply expressed a hunch, a hunch probably based upon the legal systems with which he happened to be familiar'.[9] Antonio Cassese argues that many of the principles commonly identified as General Principles are

[1] *Factory at Chorzów (Claim for Indemnity) (Germany v Poland)* (Merits) [1928] PCIJ Series A No 17, 29 (*Chorzów Factory* (Merits)).

[2] *Interpretation of the Greco-Turkish Agreement* (Advisory Opinion) [1928] PCIJ Series B No 16, 20.

[3] *Chorzów Factory* (Merits) (n 1) 29; A Pellet and D Müller, 'Article 38' in A Zimmerman, CJ Tams, K Oellers-Frahm, and C Tomuschat (eds), *The Statute of the International Court of Justice: A Commentary*, 3rd edn (Oxford University Press, 2019) 819, 926.

[4] *Electricity Company of Sofia and Bulgaria (Belgium v Bulgaria)* (Interim Protection Order) [1939] PCIJ Series A/B No 79, 199; Pellet and Müller, 'Article 38' (n 3) 926.

[5] *Mavrommatis Jerusalem Concessions (Greece v Britain)* (Merits) [1925] PCIJ Series A No 5, 30 (*Mavrommatis Jerusalem Concessions*).

[6] *Certain German interests in Polish Upper Silesia (Germany v Poland)* (Merits) [1926] PCIJ Series A No 7, 19.

[7] Pellet and Müller, 'Article 38' (n 3) 929.

[8] ibid.

[9] R Schlesinger, 'Research on the General Principles of Law Recognized by Civilised Nations' (1957) 51 *American Journal of International Law* 734, 734.

actually general tenets of international law, not found pursuant to an application of Article 38(1)(c):

> The principles themselves were not identified through a detailed investigation of the legal systems of the various members of the international community. This, itself, corroborates the view that they were actually not applied *qua* general principles obtaining in foro domestico, but as general tenets capable of being induced from the rules of international law or deduced from legal logic.[10]

Cassese's statement, while illustrating the difficulty of pinpointing *when* the PCIJ is in fact referring to General Principles, also illustrates the problem with undertaking analysis of the jurisprudence with unquestioned assumptions regarding General Principles. Cassese limits 'true' General Principles to those with a comparative *methodology*, drawing from domestic systems. He rejects 'general tenants' found by induction – but these are also considered as applications of Article 38(1)(c) by some scholars,[11] and offer an alternative conception of the source.[12]

Nonetheless, the point remains that it is hard to ascertain at times whether the PCIJ was actually referring to General Principles in its judgments, or in the Separate and Dissenting Opinions of judges. This difficulty has led to methodological approaches to General Principles that actually muddy the water of analysing the source rather than providing illumination.

The first is the assumption that use of the term 'principle' by the PCIJ necessarily indicates a General Principle. This assumption, while understandable, is not justified or sustainable. As seen in chapter 2, 'principles of international law' was used to reference customary international law in the development of the sources of international law.[13] In addition to this, the term 'principles of international law' was often used by the PCIJ in reference to international law as a whole.[14]

The second unhelpful approach is the tendency for some works, often those focusing on the *content* of general principles, to accept *all* judgments that contain norms of a certain type (for example good faith) as being expressions of norms found pursuant to Article 38(1)(c). The temptation to do so is

[10] A Cassese, *International Law*, 2nd edn (Oxford University Press, 2004) 192.

[11] H Mosler, *The International Society as a Legal Community* (Sijthoff and Noordhoff, 1980) 134–35; GJH van Hoof, *Rethinking the Sources of International Law* (Kluwer Law and Taxation Publishers, 1983) 144.

[12] Albeit one not often utilised in judgments, as seen here and in chs 4 and 5.

[13] See, eg, Convention (I) on Pacific Settlement of International Disputes (adopted 29 July 1899, entered into force 4 September 1900) 187 CTS 410, Art 48; Convention (II) on Pacific Settlement of International Disputes (adopted 18 October 1907, entered into force 26 January 1910) 205 CTS 233, Art 73; Federal Council of Switzerland, *Statut Constitutional de la Ligue de Nations* (1919), Art 42, extracted from Permanent Court of International Justice: Advisory Committee of Jurists, *Documents Presented to the Committee Relating to Existing Plans for the establishment of a Permanent Court of International Justice* (1920), ch 10.

[14] See, eg, *SS 'Lotus' (France v Turkey)* [1927] PCIJ Series A No 10, 16 (*SS Lotus*).

easy to understand, especially when faced with a plethora of judgments from many different international courts and tribunals, all of which express a norm of substantially similar content. The reality is, though, that only some of the judgments do so using language that even on a generous reading can be taken as referring to Article 38(1)(c): a far smaller number expressly refer to the source itself.

These two approaches become problematic not for establishing that the particular norm in *question* applies at international law, but rather when attempting to use these cases to ascertain features of Article 38(1)(c) as a source of law *itself*. This chapter will focus on separating out the 'wheat' (the proper use of General Principles) from the 'chaff' (the misuse of General Principles).

Within the wheat exists a spectrum of cases ranging from where a reference to Article 38(1)(c) is at least persuasively arguable to those that refer to it expressly and unequivocally. It is only the latter cases that can be reliably used to build a model of Article 38(1)(c), as it is only these cases that we can say with confidence actually are using the source of law. These cases will be analysed with reference to the tetrahedral framework – what do they tell us about the *function*, *type*, *methodology* and *jurisprudential legitimacy* of the source?

The purpose of this chapter is not to list the content of the General Principles found by the Court, nor to examine the application of such content. While consideration of the four tetrahedral factors necessitates some discussion of content, this will not go beyond what is necessary for analysis of these factors. The enumeration of the instances where General Principles have been found, and the identification of the content of such General Principles, is a necessary by-product of this process but not the primary goal.

Explicit references to Article 38(1)(c) by the PCIJ are few, and are located exclusively in Separate or Dissenting Opinions by individual judges: Judge Anzilotti in the *Interpretation of Judgments Nos 7 and 8*[15] and *River Meuse*;[16] Judge Hudson in *River Meuse*;[17] Judge Séfériadès in *Lighthouses in Crete and Samoa*;[18] and Judge Van Eysinga in *Panevezys-Saldutiskis Railway*.[19] However, in addition to these opinions, there are instances where, on construction, a judgment or an opinion can properly be taken to be referring to Article 38(1)(c).

This chapter will also set out some of the chaff – those cases that are cited by commentators as containing an Article 38(1)(c) General Principle but which,

[15] *Interpretation of Judgments Nos 7 and 8 (The Chorzów Factory) (Germany v Poland)* (Interpretation) [1927] PCIJ Series A No 13, 27 (Dissenting Opinion of Judge Anzilotti) (*Interpretation of Judgments Nos 7 and 8*).

[16] *Diversion of Water from the Meuse (Netherlands v Belgium)* (Merits) [1925] PCIJ Series A/B No 70, 50 (Dissenting Opinion of Judge Anzilotti) (*River Meuse*).

[17] ibid 76 (Separate Opinion of Judge Hudson).

[18] *Lighthouses in Crete and Samoa (France v Greece)* (Merits) [1937] PCIJ Series A/B No 71, 138 (Separate Opinion of Judge Séfériadès) (*Lighthouses in Crete and Samoa*).

[19] *Panevezys-Saldutiskis Railway (Estonia v Lithuania)* (Merits) [1939] PCIJ Series A/B No 76, 40 (Dissenting Opinion of Judge Van Eysinga) (*Panevezys-Saldutiskis Railway*).

on textual analysis, either do not refer to a source of law at all, or use language so ambiguous that the source cannot be made out. It cannot list *all* instances of misuse of General Principles.[20] Analysis here is instead limited to the most egregious misuse: either mischaracterisations that have been repeated across various articles and books, gaining credence as they are reiterated; or mischaracterisations that have been relied upon by commentators to distill meaning about the source itself.

The jurisprudence of the PCIJ is heavily self-referential, and often cases can only be properly understood in light of previous judgments. Any attempt to structurally isolate analysis of wheat from chaff is unhelpful, as the historic context of the cases is often key to a proper construction of the text. Further, many cases contain multiple instances of General Principles – or are claimed to do so. In some instances, wheat and chaff reside alongside each other within the same case. As such, analysis in the next section proceeds in chronological order.

II. CASES IN CHRONOLOGICAL ORDER

A. *SS Wimbledon*

In March 1921, German authorities refused permission for the steamship *Wimbledon* to pass through the Kiel Canal, on the basis it was carrying munitions and artillery stores destined for the Polish Naval Base at Danzig. As a result of this refusal, Britain, France, Italy and Japan brought the first contentious case before the PCIJ, alleging a breach of the Treaty of Versailles.[21] Germany argued that its then position as a neutral in respect of the war between Poland and Russia meant it was able to withhold permission for any weaponry headed to either party, notwithstanding the general rights of free passage provided in the Treaty of Versailles. The question for the Court became the interaction between the treaty provisions and Germany's 'rights consequent on neutrality in an armed conflict'.[22]

The case has been cited by Bin Cheng as support for the existence of the general principle *salus populi supreme lex esto*: the overriding interest of the self-preservation of the state,[23] as well as for informing content of the general

[20] One recent work alone purports to find reliance on General Principles in 64.4% of the PCIJ's judgments and 81.4% of the ICJ's judgments, in stark contrast to other works on the source. See M Đorđeska, *General Principles of Law Recognised by Civilised Nations (1922–2018)* (Brill Nijhoff, 2020) 218.

[21] *SS Wimbledon (Britain, France, Italy & Japan (with Poland as Intervener) v Germany)* (Merits) [1923] PCIJ Series A No 1 (*SS Wimbledon*).

[22] ibid 9.

[23] B Cheng, *General Principles of Law as applied by International Courts and Tribunals* (Stevens, 1953) 30.

principle of good faith in international law, specifically that parties contracting to a treaty cannot be intended to presume anything leading to impossible consequences.[24]

i. Salus populi supreme lex

Bin Cheng argued:

> The well-known maxim *salus populi supreme lex* may thus properly be regarded as one of the general principles of law recognised by civilised nations, within the contemplation of Article 38(1)(c) of the Statute of the World Court.[25]

Bin Cheng rested this proposition in part on the Dissenting Opinion of Judges Anzilotti and Huber in *SS Wimbledon*, and in particular on two paragraphs taken from that judgment:

> The right of a State to adopt the course which it considers best suited to the exigencies of its security and to the maintenance of its integrity, is so essential a right that, in case of doubt, treaty stipulations cannot be interpreted as limiting it, even though those stipulations do not conflict with such an interpretation.[26]
>
> This right possessed by all nations, which is based on generally accepted usage, cannot lose its *raison d'être* simply because it may in some cases have been abused ...[27]

No reference is made to the source of this right, including no mention of Article 38(1)(c), or 'general principles' – the right is not described as a General Principle but as a right 'possessed by all nations' and 'based on generally accepted usage'. 'Possessed by all nations' is of little help as it applies to custom and General Principles alike.[28] Equally, 'generally accepted usage' could refer to general acceptance of this principle in municipal legal systems (and thus, perhaps, suggest it is a general principle of law); but the word 'usage' could reference the actual usage of the right by states – that is, state practice – supporting the right as a norm of customary international law. Indeed, the phrase 'general usage of States' was commonly used in the pre-PCIJ development of international law to refer to custom rather than General Principles.[29]

ii. Good Faith – Impossible Consequences

Bin Cheng also refers to the Dissenting Opinion as informing the content of the General Principle of good faith in treaty relations, specifically that 'contracting

[24] ibid 106.
[25] ibid 31.
[26] *SS Wimbledon* (n 21) 37 (Dissenting Opinion of Judges Anzilotti and Huber).
[27] ibid 36.
[28] Assuming that the *function* of General Principles is a binding source of law – see discussion in ch 1.
[29] A D'Amato, *The Concept of Custom in International Law* (Cornell University Press, 1971) 49 (quoting F Gény writing in 1899).

parties [cannot] be presumed to have intended anything which ... leads to impossible circumstances'.[30]

The Dissenting Opinion states that 'it must not be presumed that the intention was to express an idea which leads to contradictory or impossible consequences or which, in the circumstances, must be regarded as going beyond the intention of the parties'.[31] There is nothing to suggest this general proposition is a General Principle – no indication is given as to the source of the statement. Indeed, Ole Spiermann has attributed this passage to Judge Huber's 'sociological' approach to international law',[32] rather than to an application of General Principles. Accordingly, no inferences can be drawn about Article 38(1)(c) from this statement alone.

Thus this case has been *misused* in respect of General Principles – it is highly doubtful the dissenting judges were referring to the source at all. This conclusion finds support in the work of Lauterpacht, who accepts that Anzilotti and Huber's judgment is *not* an example of restrictive interpretation of treaties as a General Principle.[33]

B. *Mavrommatis Palestine Concessions*

This case[34] concerned a Greek national, Mavrommatis, who was contracted to construct an electric tramway in, and supply electricity and drinking water to, Jerusalem; and to supply electricity and drinking water to Jaffa. The contracts were originally made with the Ottoman authorities of Palestine. Post-World War I, Great Britain was granted a mandate to administer Palestine. The British authority refused to recognise Mavrommatis' contracts as binding upon it. Greece brought the action on behalf of her nationals, arguing ultimately that Britain was obliged to give compensation for the loss suffered by Mavrommatis due to the non-performance of the contracts. The case lead to two judgments – the first, *Mavrommatis Palestine Concessions*, deals with Great Britain's preliminary objections to jurisdiction. The second, *Mavrommatis Jerusalem Concessions*,[35] dealt with the substantive claim of Greece regarding the contracts relating to construction in Jerusalem.

Mavrommatis Palestine Concessions has been cited as relevant to General Principles in three ways: Pellet and Müller cite the case as an instance of the

[30] Cheng, *General Principles of Law* (n 23) 106.

[31] *SS Wimbledon* (n 21) 36 (Dissenting Opinion of Judges Anzilotti and Huber).

[32] O Spiermann, *International Legal Argument in the Permanent Court of International Justice: The Rise of the International Judiciary* (Cambridge University Press, 2005) 178.

[33] H Lauterpacht, 'Restrictive Interpretation and the Principle of Effectiveness in the Interpretation of Treaties' (1949) 26 *British Yearbook of International Law* 48, 57–58.

[34] *Mavrommatis Palestine Concessions (Greece v Britain)* (Jurisdiction) [1924] PCIJ Series A No 2 (*Mavrommatis Palestine Concessions*).

[35] *Mavrommatis Jerusalem Concessions* (n 5).

Court's rejecting the comparative methodology for finding General Principles.[36] Bin Cheng cites this case as an example of the General Principle *allegans non contraria est audiens*.[37] Schlesinger and Bassiouni cite the Dissenting Opinion of Judge Moore as applying the General Principle that a court must have jurisdiction before it can act.[38]

i. Rejection of the Comparative Methodology

In considering Britain's objection to the PCIJ's jurisdiction, the Court stated, '[t]he Court has not to ascertain what are, in the various codes of procedure and in the various legal terminologies, the specific characteristics of such an objection'.[39] This is actually an instance of *misuse* of General Principles by commentators: Alain Pellet and Daniel Müller have used this judgment to suggest that the Court 'thus showed a clear disinclination towards the use of the comparative method'[40] in regard to Article 38(1)(c).

In fact, the statement of the PCIJ in *Mavrommatis Palestine Concessions* is not linked to Article 38(1)(c) at all. Rather, it is a general statement by the PCIJ of how it determines its own competence:[41] a task the PCIJ was expressly empowered to do under Article 36(4) of its Statute.[42] Thus although the PCIJ 'forcefully denied' the relevance of domestic law analogies[43] to determine its own competence, in doing so it was *not* rejecting domestic law analogies for the methodology of General Principles.

ii. Allegans Contraria Non Est Audiendus

Bin Cheng uses this case as an example of the application of the rule:

> Nor indeed may a State, while denying that a certain treaty is applicable to the case, contend at the same time that the other party in regard to the matter in dispute has not complied with certain provisions of that treaty.[44]

[36] Pellet and Müller, 'Article 38' (n 3) 929.

[37] Cheng, *General Principles of Law* (n 23) 143.

[38] Schlesinger, 'Research on the General Principles of Law' (n 9) 736; MC Bassiouni, 'A Functional Approach to General Principles' (1990) 11 *Michigan Journal of International Law* 768, 793.

[39] *Mavrommatis Palestine Concessions* (n 34) 10.

[40] Pellet and Müller, 'Article 38' (n 3) 929.

[41] S Rosenne, *The Law and Practice of the International Court, 1920–2005*, vol II, 4th edn (Brill, 2006) 818–20.

[42] Somewhat confusingly, Rosenne refers to the principle of *compétence de la compétence* as a 'general principle' (eg ibid 815). The cases, however, refer to it as a 'rule of general international law' or as 'consistently accepted by general international law', language more in line with customary international law. See ibid 816–17.

[43] ibid 819. However, behind the face of the judgments it is clear domestic law was on the judges' minds: see Spiermann, *International Legal Argument* (n 32) 194–95.

[44] Cheng, *General Principles of Law* (n 23) 143.

Bin Cheng argues that in applying the rule, the PCIJ was using a General Principle.[45] The relevant section of the case dealt with the application of certain Articles of the Protocol governing Britain and Greece. Britain sought to rely on a right contained in Article 4, while denying that Article 4 applied to the present case. The Court stated, '[t]he British Government cannot insist on the exercise of this right so long as it denies that the concession fall[s] under the terms of that article'.[46]

Although an example of the *allegans contraria non est audiendus* principle, there is no mention of Article 38(1)(c) or the term 'general principle' by the Court. Rather, the rule is stated without context or hint as to where it originated. Accordingly, it cannot be concluded that the Court intended this statement to be taken as an application of Article 38(1)(c).

iii. Jurisdiction

Finally, it is suggested that the Dissenting Opinion of Judge Moore applies the General Principle that a court must have jurisdiction before it can act.[47] The two relevant paragraphs from the Dissenting Opinion are:

> There are certain elementary conceptions common to all systems of jurisprudence, and one of these is the principle that a court of justice is never justified in hearing and adjudging the merits of a cause of which it has not jurisdiction.[48]
>
> The requirement of jurisdiction, which is universally recognised in the national sphere, is not less fundamental and peremptory in the international.[49]

Although Judge Moore does not explicitly refer to 'general principles' or Article 38(1)(c), it does seem that 'conceptions common to all systems of jurisprudence' fall within their ambit, and that this is a situation where it can be reasonably concluded that the principle referred to was, in fact, a General Principle: one drawn from the domestic forum and applicable on the international level. Unlike in *SS Wimbledon*, there is no language to suggest this is principle of custom rather than a General Principle.

In order to demonstrate the content and acceptance of the principle, Judge Moore turned to the decisions of national courts, stating:

> [T]he decisions of the Courts of the United States as to the fundamental character of the question of jurisdiction are practically identical in terms with those of the highest Court in France and, no doubt, of the highest Courts in at least some other countries.[50]

[45] ibid.

[46] *Mavrommatis Palestine Concessions* (n 34) 33.

[47] Schlesinger, 'Research on the General Principles of Law' (n 9) 736; Bassiouni, 'A Functional Approach' (n 38) 793.

[48] *Mavrommatis Palestine Concessions* (n 34) 57–58 (Dissenting Opinion of Judge Moore).

[49] ibid 59.

[50] ibid.

This (admittedly non-comprehensive) comparison between different national jurisdictions, coupled with the words 'common to every legal system' and 'universally recognised', indicates that Judge Moore was following a limited comparative methodology, drawing from the domestic forum. The norm is described as an 'elementary conception', as 'fundamental' and as 'peremptory'.[51] These terms suggest that the type of General Principle referred to here is a true principle, rather than a rule, with natural law leanings: yet bound by a positivist methodology.

C. *Mavrommatis Jerusalem Concessions*

Having upheld Britain's objection in relation to Mavrommatis' contracts in respect of Jaffa, the question of the contracts in respect of the Jerusalem works was reserved for a merits decision.[52] The judgment is interesting for what the Court chose not to address:

> Sir Douglas Hogg asked the court to say that the rules of evidence 'which are established in every civilised jurisprudence, ought to be observed not less but more closely by an international court …' but the actual ruling of the court in this instance did not relate to the rules of evidence in general.[53]

Although the Court was faced with an explicit invitation to consider a rule recognised by 'every civilised jurisprudence' – surely a reference to Article 38(1)(c) – it chose not to do so. This does follow the general trend observed, of the reluctance of the PCIJ to rely on General Principles. Sir Douglas's conception of a general principle, although not addressed by the PCIJ, evinces one drawn from the domestic forum, using comparative methodology.

D. *Polish Upper Silesia* (Preliminary Objections)

This case[54] concerned a nitrate factory in Chorzow, which had been taken over by a delegate of the Polish Government. The German company that had managed the factory brought proceedings against Poland in the Germano-Polish Mixed Arbitral Tribunal in Paris. Germany also commenced PCIJ proceedings against Poland. In the preliminary stage, Poland made objections to the Court's jurisprudence on a number of grounds. One of these was based on the pending

[51] ibid 57–59.

[52] *Mavrommatis Jerusalem Concessions* (n 5).

[53] MO Hudson, 'The Fourth Year of the Permanent Court of International Justice' (1926) 20(1) *American Journal of International Law* 1, 6.

[54] *Certain German Interests in Polish Upper Silesia (Germany v Poland)* (Preliminary Objections) [1925] PCIJ Series A No 6 (*Polish Upper Silesia* (Preliminary Objections)).

action in the Arbitral Tribunal. General Principles were relevant to the Court's judgment on this point in two ways. First, the Court had to decide *when* it could consider the objection: as a preliminary matter, or as defence on the merits? And, second, the Court considered whether the principle of litispendence could bar the claim.

i. Stage of Procedure

The judgment states:

> Is this one of these grounds of defence based on the merits of the case and calculated to cause the judge to refuse the entertain the application, such as are generally called – in French law for instance – by the name of *fins de non-recevoir*? Or is it not rather a genuine objection, directed ... not against the action itself and the legal arguments on which it is based, but against the bringing of the action before the tribunal?
>
> In the case of a municipal court, it would be of some interest to solve this question in order to determine at what stage in the proceedings such a ground of defence might or should be put forward. But, in estimating the value of the alternative submission to the effect that it should suspend judgment in the suit before it, the Court has not to have regard to 'the various codes of procedure and the various legal terminologies' in use in different countries.[55]

The reference to 'the various codes of procedure and the various legal terminologies' in the extract above is a reference back to the PCIJ's decision in the *Mavrommatis Palestine Concessions* case.[56] The Court once again confirmed that when determining its own jurisprudence, it will not draw on a general principle of law drawn from domestic systems to do so. The additional clarification that it would be important for a *municipal* court to do so suggests a reason why – that domestic rules regarding jurisdiction are simply not appropriate for transformation to the international sphere. This seems to be supported by the next paragraph of the judgment:

> Whether this submission should be classified as an 'objection' or as a *fin de non-recevoir*, it is certain that nothing, either in the Statute or Rules which govern the Court's activities, or in the general principles of law, prevents the Court from dealing with it at once ...[57]

There are no General Principles of law in this case because they fail the methodological requirement of appropriateness. Schlesinger points to the inclusion of the phrase 'general principles of law' in the last paragraph as evidence of a practice of international courts to 'expressly or silently resort to procedural and evidentiary principles which are felt to be inherent in all civilized legal systems'.[58]

[55] ibid 19.
[56] *Mavrommatis Palestine Concessions* (n 34).
[57] *Polish Upper Silesia* (Preliminary Objections) (n 54) 19.
[58] Schlesinger, 'Research on the General Principles of Law' (n 9) 736.

In this case, the PCIJ was pointing to an *absence* of a General Principle rather than the presence of one. As such, there is little to be gained from our understanding of the source: except that the type clearly includes procedural norms.

The acceptance of this type of norm, and rejection of its qualification due to appropriateness, is seen more clearly in the PCIJ's consideration of the principle of litispendence.

ii. Litispendence

Litispendence, or *lis pendens*, is a doctrine that bars parallel proceedings from being heard. The plea of litispendence in *Polish Upper Silesia* (Preliminary Objections) was raised only briefly by Poland in comments by counsel.[59] The Court stated that the plea had not been made formally,[60] but went on to consider the issue:

> If, however, the plea were to be examined in accordance with the principles generally accepted in regard to *litispendance*, the Court would undoubtedly arrive at the conclusion that it is not well-founded. It is a much disputed question in the teachings of legal authorities and in the jurisprudence of the principal countries whether the doctrine of *litispendance*, the object of which is to prevent the possibility of conflicting judgments, can be invoked in international relations, in the sense that the judges of one State should, in the absence of a treaty, refuse to entertain any suit already pending before the courts of another State, exactly as they would be bound to do if an action on the same subject had at some previous time been brought in due form before another court of their own country.[61]

The PCIJ thus rejected the application of litispendence in international law on the grounds of appropriateness. Although no reference to Article 38(1)(c) is made explicitly, the reference to jurisprudence of principal countries suggests the principle, if applicable, would be drawn from the domestic forum and transformed to apply internationally. This fits with the development of Article 38(1)(c) and is an illustration of the methodology of comparativism tempered by judicial discretion as to appropriateness.

E. *Polish Upper Silesia* (Merits)

Although the merits stage of the case[62] is also cited for use of General Principles,[63] this is much more ambiguous than the discussion in the preliminary objections.

[59] ibid 225.
[60] *Polish Upper Silesia* (Preliminary Objections) (n 54) 19–20.
[61] ibid 20.
[62] *Polish Upper Silesia* (Merits) (n 6).
[63] Pellet and Müller, 'Article 38' (n 3) 942.

Here, the PCIJ considered the question of the expropriation of the factory at Chorzow, as well as the liquidation of certain rural estates by Poland. Germany argued that both actions were in breach of the German-Polish Convention of Upper Silesia as constructed in the context of the Treaty of Versailles.[64] Pellet and Müller suggest that the Court interpreted part of the Convention between Germany and Poland 'in light of general principles of law'.[65] The Court stated:

> Further, there can be no doubt that the expropriation allowed under Head III of the Convention is a derogation from the rules generally applied in regard to the treatment of the foreigners and the principle of respect for vested rights. As this derogation itself is strictly in the nature of an exception, it is permissible to conclude that no further derogation is allowed.[66]

The phrase 'rules generally applied' is the only possible linkage to General Principles: the Court does not otherwise indicate which source these rules are based on. While 'generally applied' could mean generally in the sense of applied widely, or by many countries (and thus supporting the construction of this phrase as meaning General Principles), it could also mean generally in the sense of usually, or ordinarily applied by other tribunals. If the latter is the case, the phrase means no more than the norms of international law usually applied to the treatment of foreigners. As such, this is more chaff – a reference that could equally be to norms of customary international law.

F. *Mosul Boundary Case*

In this Advisory Opinion,[67] the PCIJ was asked questions by the Council of the League of Nations about the nature and procedure of decisions made by the Council in accordance with provisions of the Treaty of Lausanne.[68] The PCIJ held that unanimity was required for a decision by members of the Council: but this unanimity did *not* include the parties to the dispute.[69] In doing so, the Court stated that '[t]he well-known rule that no one can be judge in his own suit holds good'.[70] Although the Court made no mention of Article 38(1)(c), this case is still cited as an example of the recognition of a General Principle.[71] While the phrase 'well-known rule' could refer to a principle recognised by nations, there

[64] *Polish Upper Silesia* (Merits) (n 6) 12.

[65] Pellet and Müller, 'Article 38' (n 3) 942.

[66] *Polish Upper Silesia* (Merits) (n 6) 22.

[67] *Article 3, Paragraph 2, of the Treaty of Lausanne (Frontier between Turkey and Iraq)* (Advisory Opinion) [1925] PCIJ Series B No 12 (*Mosul Boundary Case*).

[68] ibid 6–7.

[69] ibid 31–32.

[70] ibid 32.

[71] See, eg, I Brownlie, *Principles of Public International Law*, 7th edn (Oxford University Press, 2008) 18; Cheng, *General Principles of Law* (n 23) 280.

is no other textual support for this conclusion. The judgment does illustrate the ongoing lack of distinction between the terms 'rule' and 'principle'.

G. *SS Lotus*

In this case,[72] the PCIJ considered the international legal ramifications of the collision between the Turkish steamer *Boz-Kourt* and the French steamer *Lotus*. The judgment of the Court did not refer to Article 38(1)(c). Nonetheless, this case is cited by various scholars as being instructional in informing various aspects about General Principles – namely, the requirement for universal acceptance,[73] the method of ascertaining such principles[74] and their place as a source of international law.[75] There is also a possible reference to General Principles in the dissenting judgment of Judge Loder.

i. Universal Acceptance

It is suggested that the PCIJ's language in this decision can be read as suggesting that a General Principle must be universally accepted by nations.[76] The Court reflected upon Article 15 of the Convention of Lausanne,[77] which provided that 'all questions of jurisdiction shall ... be decided in accordance with the principles of international law'.[78] The Court stated, in reference to the words 'principles of international law', that 'Now the Court considers that the words "principles of international law", as ordinarily used, can only mean international law as it is applied between all nations belonging to the community of States.'[79]

Bassiouni argues that this statement does not require a General Principle to be universal, rather:

> The court's finding can be explained by reason of the very principle which was found to be universal. That principle, territoriality of criminal jurisdiction, is indeed universal in its recognition and application. Had the facts of the case been different, the court likely would not have suggested a requirement of universality. This writer's conclusion is that the court did not intend to posit a test of universality for 'General Principles' but merely ascertained it in this instance.[80]

While Bassiouni may be correct, in that the Court's language was influenced by the nature of the principle it was examining, there are two alternative

[72] *SS Lotus* (n 14).
[73] Bassiouni, 'A Functional Approach' (n 38) 788.
[74] ibid 794.
[75] Pellet and Müller, 'Article 38' (n 3) 928.
[76] Bassiouni, 'A Functional Approach' (n 38) 788.
[77] Convention of Lausanne (1923) 28 LNTS 152.
[78] *SS Lotus* (n 14) 16.
[79] ibid.
[80] Bassiouni, 'A Functional Approach' (n 38) 788.

constructions. First, there is no indication that the 'principles of international law' incorporated in Article 15 of the Convention of Lausanne were intended, or considered, to be the same as General Principles. Indeed, following the Court's discussion, the principles are referred to as 'the principles which are in force between all independent nations'[81] and the 'principles of general international law relating to jurisdiction'.[82] This language is much more in line with the type of language previously used in international documents to indicate international law generally, rather than a General Principle.[83] Further, this language is used by other commentators to argue that the Court was actually attempting to restrict 'principles of international law' to only include custom and conventional law.[84]

Second, even if 'principles of international law' *are* taken to be General Principles, the passage does not suggest that a principle must be universally recognised to *be* a General Principle, but rather that once recognised, a General Principle will be binding on all nations. Further, the reference by the Court in respect of criminal jurisdiction is not to all nations but to 'all *systems* of law'.[85] The requirement that a General Principle be common to all systems of law is significantly different from its being accepted universally by all national legal systems. Therefore, in as much as the Court can be taken to be referring to General Principles (which is doubtful), it requires only that these norms be accepted across all systems of law, not universally within all nations.

ii. Methodology

Bassiouni argues that the decision of the Court indicates *methodology*: 'the case is important because it instructs one on how to ascertain if a "General Principle" exists'.[86] The section of the judgment cited by Bassiouni in support of this statement sets out the steps the Court took to find whether a 'principle of international law' existed pursuant to Article 15 of the Convention of Lausanne. The first reservation to the reliance on this extract is the same as already enunciated: there is nothing in the decision of the Court to suggest that 'principles of international law' are General Principles and, to the contrary, the court's treatment of such principles is more consistent with expressions of general international law. Accordingly, it would seem that the steps the PCIJ took to determine whether a 'principle of international law' existed do not provide any guidance as to the general methodology of General Principles.

[81] *SS Lotus* (n 14) 17.

[82] ibid.

[83] See discussion in ch 2; See further L Goldschmidt, 'International Arbitral Procedure' (1874) 6 *Revue de droit international et de Législation Comparée* 421, tr in JB Scott (ed), *Resolutions of the Institute of International Law dealing with the Law of Nations* (Oxford University Press, 1916) 205, 228; Convention (I) on Pacific Settlement of International Disputes (n 12), Art 48.

[84] Pellet and Müller, 'Article 38' (n 3) 925.

[85] *SS Lotus* (n 14) 20 (emphasis added).

[86] Bassiouni, 'A Functional Approach' (n 38) 794.

The second problem with reliance on the PCIJ's statement lies in the so-called steps. The Court states:

> [I]n fulfillment of its task of itself ascertaining what international law is, it has not confined itself to a consideration of the arguments put forward, but has included in its researches all precedents, teachings and facts to which it had access and which might possibly have revealed the existence of one of the principles of international law contemplated in the special agreement.[87]

This paragraph is less of an indication of how to ascertain if principles exist, and more of a reliance on subsidiary means set out in Article 38(1)(d), as well as indicating a willingness of the Court to go beyond the arguments of the parties.

iii. General Principles as a Source of Law

Pellet and Müller also reference this case as being important for the Court's actions in focusing on the voluntary nature of international law:

> [T]he PCIJ pretended to limit international law to conventions and customs emanating from the 'free will' of States and considered that 'the words "principles of international law", as ordinarily used can only mean international law as it is applied between all nations belonging to the community of States'. This might have been an attempt, by a Court led by blind adherence to voluntarism, to deprive the general principles mentioned in para 1(c) of any specifity.[88]

This conclusion does not necessarily follow: if General Principles are a binding source of law, they will be included in 'international law as it is applied between all nations'. General Principles are only excluded from such a formulation if they are considered non-binding, and thus not applied to nations.

However, the argument does find more support in the Dissenting Opinion of Judge Altamira in the case, who denied that municipal legislation can ever be the basis of a norm of international law. Altamira states that exceptions to jurisdiction must be 'exceptions recognized by international law', which is those exceptions that have 'their origins in relations between sovereign States, either in the form of a treaty or of international custom'.[89] Thus General Principles are excluded from this consent-based, positivist view of international law. Judge Altamira argued that custom 'must by its nature be positive in character',[90] and any customary rules 'must be positively supported by acts' that are of an international character.[91] In regard to domestic laws, Altamira argued:

> It follows that the municipal legislation of different countries, as it does not by its nature belong to the domain of international law, is not capable of creating an

[87] *SS Lotus* (n 14) 31.
[88] Pellet and Müller, 'Article 38' (n 3) 925–26.
[89] *SS Lotus* (n 14) 96 (Dissenting Opinion of Judge Altamira).
[90] ibid.
[91] ibid.

> international custom, still less a law. Of course it … encroaches upon a domain which is practically speaking international. But it cannot simply on this ground be held to possess a character placing it on the same plane as conventions of international custom.[92]

Thus General Principles are excluded from this strict, volunteeristic view of international law. As recognised by Pellet and Müller, such a view is inconsistent with the work of the Committee of Jurists in drafting the article.[93] This is interesting, as Judge Altamira was the Japanese delegate to the Advisory Committee,[94] although his participation in the discussion on General Principles was minimal.[95] The dissent is valuable, however, in identifying the problem with using municipal laws as a basis for custom – it conflates the sources, bringing what is considered evidence of Article 38(1)(c) into the discussion of customary international law.

iv. Logical Principles of Law

The final consideration of the *SS Lotus* is the Dissenting Opinion of Judge Loder. Before his appointment to the PCIJ, Loder was the Dutch delegate to the Advisory Committee of Jurists.[96] Unlike Altamira, Loder had participated in the discussion on General Principles, seeing it as the duty of the PCIJ to 'develop law, "ripen" customs and principles universally recognized and to crystallize them into positive rules; in other words to establish an international jurisprudence'.[97] Loder viewed the inclusion of General Principles as a way of achieving this duty.[98] He supported Descamp's original, natural law formulation of General Principles.[99] In his Opinion, Judge Loder referred to a 'fundamental consequence' of state sovereignty:

> The fundamental consequence of their independence and sovereignty is that no municipal law, in the particular case under consideration no criminal law, can apply or have binding effect outside the national territory. This fundamental truth, which is not custom but the direct and inevitable consequence of its premise, is a logical principle of law, and is a postulate upon which the mutual independence of States rests.[100]

[92] ibid.
[93] Pellet and Müller, 'Article 38' (n 3) 926. See discussion in ch 2.
[94] See ch 2.
[95] Permanent Court of International Justice: Advisory Committee of Jurists, *Procès-verbaux of the Proceedings of the Committee* (Van Langenhuysen Brothers, 1920), 13th Meeting, 308.
[96] See ch 2.
[97] Permanent Court of International Justice: Advisory Committee of Jurists, *Procès-verbaux* (n 94) 294.
[98] ibid.
[99] ibid.
[100] *SS Lotus* (n 14) 35 (Dissenting Opinion of Judge Loder).

Such a 'logical principle' could fit a conception of General Principles as inductive principles, derived from the fundamental precepts of international law. Unlike other conceptions of 'fundamental principles' however, Loder saw this principle as being capable of being overridden by either treaty or custom.[101] Importantly, however, Loder did not contextualise this logical principle as a General Principle: given his role in the Advisory Committee of Jurists, it would seem such reference would be natural if this was, in fact, what Loder was relying on.

Loder's discussion referred to the norm as a 'fundamental principle', a 'logical principle' and a 'well-established rule',[102] showing again the lack of interchangeability of the rule/principle distinction.

H. *Chorzów Factory*

This case concerned the same nitrate factory and factual matrix surrounding it as was considered in *Polish Upper Silesia* (section II.E). Having been successful in arguing that Poland breached international law in appropriating the factory, Germany brought a new action claiming reparation from Poland for the damage suffered by two German companies. The judgments in *Chorzów Factory* (jurisdiction and merits)[103] are commonly cited as support for the existence of a General Principle relating to the obligation to make reparation for international wrongs.[104] The case has also been cited for other General Principles: the principle *nullus commodum capere de sua injure propria* (a party cannot take advantage of its own wrong),[105] and a principle relating to the content of reparation.[106]

i. Obligation to Make Reparation

This principle is sourced from the merits judgment. It is argued that this principle is one of the 'procedural and administrative rules which are inherent in the

[101] ibid.

[102] ibid.

[103] *Factory at Chorzów (Claim for Indemnity) (Germany v Poland)* (Jurisdiction) [1927] PCIJ Series A No 9 (*Chorzów Factory* (Jurisdiction)); *Chorzów Factory* (Merits) (n 1).

[104] Cheng, *General Principles of Law* (n 23) 169; H Waldock, 'General Course on International Law' (1962) 106 *The Collected Courses of the Hague Academy of International Law* 44, 54; Brownlie, *Principles* (n 71) 18; M Bogdan, 'General Principles of Law and the Problem of Lacunae in the Law of Nations' (1977) 46 *Nordisk Tidsskrift International Relations* 37, 44–45; M Shaw, *International Law*, 2nd edn (Cambridge University Press, 1986) 81.

[105] Waldock, 'General Course on International Law' (n 103) 54; Cheng, *General Principles of Law* (n 23) 149; Brownlie, *Principles* (n 70) 17; Bassiouni, 'A Functional Approach' (n 38) 793–94.

[106] Cheng, *General Principles of Law* (n 23) 50–51.

concept of every legal system',[107] and thus 'must form part of international law because it is a system of law'.[108] The PCIJ identified three questions before it:

> It follows from the foregoing that the application is designed to obtain, in favour of Germany, reparation the amount of which is determined by the damage suffered by the Oberschlesische and Bayerische [the German companies]. Three fundamental questions arise:
>
> (1) The existence of the obligation to make reparation.
> (2) The existence of the damage which must serve as a basis for the calculation of the amount of indemnity.
> (3) The extent of this damage.[109]

It is the Court's answer to the first question that has been used as support for the general principle relating to reparation. However, the language of the Court in considering the existence of this obligation does not necessarily indicate that the obligation exists under Article 38(1)(c):

> As regards the first point, the Court observes that it is a principle of international law, and even a general conception of law, that any breach of an engagement involves an obligation to make reparation. In Judgment No 8, when deciding on the jurisdiction derived by it from Article 23 of the Geneva Convention, the Court has already said that reparation is the indispensable complement of a failure to apply a convention, and there is no necessity for this to be stated in the convention itself. The existence of the principle establishing the obligation to make reparation, as an element of positive international law, has moreover never been disputed in the course of the proceedings in the various cases concerning the Chorzów factory.[110]

The obligation is thus described as a 'principle of international law' and even a 'general conception of law', and as 'an element of positive international law'. The Court also refers back to its earlier judgment, where the obligation is described as an 'indispensable complement of a failure to apply a convention'.[111] Each of these descriptions and their implications for the characterisation of the obligation as a General Principle will be dealt with.

a. Principle/General Conception

In accordance with earlier discussion, 'principle of international law' was often used to refer to general international law. In this context, the words 'general conception of law' may then be a reference to General Principles. This interpretation is supported by Michael Bogdan's argument that this is an instance

[107] ibid.
[108] ibid.
[109] ibid 29.
[110] ibid.
[111] *Chorzów Factory* (Jurisdiction) (n 102) 21.

where the PCIJ refers to the General Principle 'but simultaneously states that there is also a rule of customary international law leading to the same result'.[112] In this case, it is argued, General Principles are irrelevant for filling lacunae, because 'the applied rule had, according to the court, basis also in the customary law of nations'.[113] Again we see the looseness of language in regard to principles/rules. The term 'general conception', however, suggests an abstracted norm of law, which would tend more towards principle than rule on the principle/rule scale.

b. Indispensable Complement

The term 'indispensable complement' is a reference to a passage from the jurisdiction stage of the case:

> It is a principle of international law that the breach of an engagement involves an obligation to make reparation in an adequate form. Reparation therefore is the indispensable complement of a failure to apply a convention and there is no necessity for this to be stated in the convention itself.[114]

The 'indispensable complement' is based on logical induction from the nature of a breach of law, rather than concerns of state practice and *opinio juris*. It seems, then, to fit within a conception of General Principles as logically deduced principles, inherent within the international legal system. This would fit with Judge Loder's view of a logical principle in *SS Lotus*; but as in *SS Lotus*, any clear link between such logically deduced principles and Article 38(1)(c) is absent.

c. Element of Positive International Law

The final description of the principle characterises it as an 'element of positive international law'. There are two possible ways to interpret this statement. The first is that it supports the view that the Court was really discussing a norm of custom all along. This seems consistent with the timing of this case following from the *SS Lotus*, where General Principles were marginalised by at least one dissenting judge, and arguably the Court as a whole, as not being part of positive international law. Alternatively, if the Court was actually referring to a General Principle, it suggests that the source *can* be viewed consistently with a positivist legal framework. This view finds support in the inclusion of 'general conception' at the start of the passage – if this does not refer to a General Principle, it seems redundant.

[112] Bogdan, 'General Principles' (n 103) 44.
[113] ibid 45.
[114] *Chorzów Factory* (Jurisdiction) (n 102) 21.

ii. No One Can Take Advantage of Their Own Wrong

The second General Principle stated to be contained in the *Chorzów Factory* judgment is the maxim that no one can take advantage of their own wrong. The relevant passage is from the judgement of the Court in the jurisdiction phase of the case:

> It is, moreover, a principle generally accepted in the jurisprudence of international arbitration, as well as by municipal courts, that one Party cannot avail himself of the fact that the other has not fulfilled some obligation or has not had recourse to some means of redress, if the former Party has, by some illegal act, prevented the latter from fulfilling the obligation in question, or from having recourse to the tribunal which would have been open, to him.[115]

Although this maxim is cited as a General Principle, there is no explicit indication that the Court was referring to Article 38(1)(c) as the source. The principle is 'generally accepted' in 'jurisprudence of international arbitration' and by municipal courts. Acceptance in international arbitration does not reveal the source of the maxim: while decisions of international tribunals can act as a subsidiary source, informing the content of a norm of international law, they are not norm-creating in themselves.[116] The reference to municipal courts does give more indication as to the source of the principle: general acceptance by national courts may well be evidence of a General Principle. By referring to *both* international courts and municipal courts, however, the methodology employed by Court is less clear.[117] In this way, the 'vague and cryptic formulas'[118] seem to apply to this maxim: it cannot be said that the maxim was actually recognised as a General Principle

iii. Content of Reparations for an Illegal Act

Finally, Bin Cheng cites the *Chorzów Factory* judgment as support for a General Principle relating to reparation for an illegal act: 'if the taking is unlawful, the State may, in the first place, be called upon to restore the property and at the same time to repair any damage not covered by the restitution'.[119] The relevant passage from the judgment sets out what such reparation must consist of – 'reparation must, as far as possible, wipe out all consequences of the illegal act'[120] – and that 'restitution in kind … the award, if need be, of damages for loss sustained which would not be covered by restitution in kind … should serve to determine the amount of compensation'.[121]

[115] *Chorzów Factory* (Jurisdiction) (n 102) 31.
[116] G Schwarzenbeger, *International Law as applied by International Courts and Tribunals*, vol 1, 3rd edn (Stevens and Sons, 1957) 26–27.
[117] This is repeated in some judgments of the ICJ: see chs 4 and 5.
[118] Pellet and Müller, 'Article 38' (n 3) 929.
[119] Cheng, *General Principles of Law* (n 23) 50.
[120] *Chorzów Factory* (Merits) (n 1) 47.
[121] ibid.

The content of the principle is as Bin Cheng sets out: the Court describes it as 'a principle which seems to be established by international practice and in particular by the decisions of arbitral tribunals'.[122] Again, the reference to arbitral tribunals is not particularly helpful in discerning the source of the principle; the reference to 'international practice' could suggest state practice: that is, the Court here is referring to a principle of custom, not a General Principle.

Thus overall the highest that can be said for the use of Article 38(1)(c) in *Chorzów Factory* is that the case shows an ongoing lack of distinction between principles and rules; and a continued lack of specificity delineating between sources of international law. Any more conclusive findings regarding General Principles as a source of law from the case is an overreach.

I. *Jurisdiction of the Courts of Danzig*

The Council of the League of Nations asked the PCIJ to advise whether a decision made by the High Commissions of the League of Nations at Danzig, that the Danzig Courts did not have jurisdiction over a claim brought against the Polish Railways Administration, was correct.[123] The PCIJ held that the decision was not legally well founded. In so doing, it examined a suggested argument that the Danzig Court could not consider provisions of an international agreement between Danzig and Poland, referred to as the *Beamtenabkommen*, because Poland had not implemented provisions of the *Beamtenabkommen* in its domestic laws, despite being required to do so by the agreement. The Court observed that this argument was untenable, because 'Poland could not avail herself of an objection which … would amount to relying upon the non-fulfilment of an obligation imposed upon her by an international engagement'.[124]

This statement is cited by Bin Cheng as support for the General Principle *nullus commodum capere de sua injuria propria* (no one can be allowed to take advantage of his own wrong), alongside the judgment of the Court in the *Chorzów Factory*.[125] While the statement in *Chorzów Factory* at least contained the phrase the 'principle generally accepted', there is no indication in the *Jurisdiction of the Courts of Danzig* that the rule is based on Article 38(1)(c). The only possible link is perhaps the enunciation of the same rule in *Chorzów Factory* one year earlier. As explained in section II.H, however, the link to General Principles in that case is also very unclear.

[122] ibid.

[123] *Jurisdiction of the Courts of Danzig (Pecuniary Claims of Danzig Railway Officials who have Passed into the Polish Service, against the Polish Railways Administration)* (Advisory Opinion) [1928] PCIJ Series B No 15 (*Jurisdiction of the Courts of Danzig*).

[124] ibid 26–27.

[125] Cheng, *General Principles of Law* (n 23) 149.

J. *Interpretation of Judgments Nos 7 and 8 (The Chorzów Factory)*

In this case,[126] the PCIJ was asked by Germany to interpret the previous judgments given in *Certain Polish Upper Silesia* and the *Chorzów Factory* cases. This was done pursuant to Article 60 of the Statute of the PCIJ, which states 'The judgment is final and without appeal. In the event of dispute as to the meaning or scope of the judgment, the Court shall construe it upon the request of any party.'[127]

The Dissenting Opinion of Judge Anzilotti contains the first explicit reference to Article 38(1)(c) in the jurisprudence of the PCIJ. Anzilotti considered whether the question before the Court was one of interpretation of previous judgments or rather a new, substantive question to be determined in pending proceedings, and found the latter to be true.[128] In doing so, Anzilotti stated:

> In coming to this conclusion, I have relied upon principles obtaining in civil procedure; this I feel justified in doing for the following reasons:
>
> ... [I]t appears to me that if there be a case in which it is legitimate to have recourse, in the absence of conventions and custom, to 'the general principles of law recognized by civilised nations', mentioned in No 3 of Article 38 of the Statute, that case is assuredly the present one. Not without reason was the binding effect of *res judicata* expressly mentioned by the Committee of Jurists entrusted with the preparation of a plan for the establishment of a Permanent Court of International Justice, amongst the principles included in the above-mentioned article (Minutes, p 335).[129]

Accordingly, Judge Anzilotti supports a conception of General Principles filling lacunae in international law – to be referred to where convention and custom cannot assist. The type is clearly procedural. Further, by reference to civil procedure, Anzilotti is drawing from the domestic forum, although any evidence of an explicit comparative methodology is not apparent.

K. *Brazilian Loans*

From 1907–09, Brazil paid certain constructors for their work in Brazilian bonds equivalent to certain sums of francs. Some of these bonds were subsequently sold to a French company. A question arose as to how to value the bond – Brazil argued for a value against the 'paper franc', the currency of France, while France (on behalf of its companies) argued for the higher valued 'gold franc'.

[126] *Interpretation of Judgments Nos 7 and 8* (n 15).

[127] ibid 10; Statute of the Permanent Court of International Justice contained in Protocol of Signature of the Statute of the Permanent Court of International Justice (opened for signature 16 December 1920, entered into force 1 September 1921) 200 LNTS 494, Art 60.

[128] *Interpretation of Judgments Nos 7 and 8* (n 15) 27 (Dissenting Opinion of Judge Anzilotti).

[129] ibid.

The case[130] is cited as support for the application of the General Principles *contra preferentem*[131] and *jura novit curia*.[132]

i. Contra Preferentum

In construing the amount and nature of interest to be paid on the loans, the Court stated 'moreover, there is a familiar rule for the construction of instruments that, where they are found to be ambiguous, they should be taken *contra proferentem*'.[133] It is asserted that this is an instance of the court's applying a General Principle.[134] There is no reference made by the Court to Article 38(1)(c), or to the source of the 'familiar rule'. Accordingly, the conclusion that this is an instance of Article 38(1)(c)'s being applied cannot be justified.

ii. Jura Novit Curia

The Court stated in its judgment 'the Court ... is a tribunal of international law, and ... is deemed to know what this law is'.[135] Bin Cheng describes this as a 'recognition of a well-known principle of judicial procedure in municipal law: *jura novit curia*'.[136] The principle of *jura novit curia* – the court knows the law – is an established maxim of civil law countries, and is arguably recognised in common law countries (although the extent of this is contested).[137] Bin Cheng would thus see this as a General Principle drawing on domestic legal systems. Again, however, the Court does not indicate on what source it is basing the rule. Even though the rule may be enshrined in domestic legal systems, without explicit reference to these systems as the basis for the inclusion of the rule at international law,[138] we cannot conclude that the Court was referring to a General Principle in this case; or even if it was, that it was basing such a principle on domestic systems. It may instead be a 'general tenet' deduced from 'legal logic',[139] similar to those examined in *SS Lotus* and *Chorzów Factory*.[140]

[130] *Payment in Gold of Brazilian Federal Loans Contracted in France (France and Brazil)* (Merits) [1929] PCIJ Series A No 21 (*Brazilian Loans*).

[131] Cassese, *International Law* (n 10) 192; Bassiouni, 'A Functional Approach' (n 38) 795.

[132] Cheng, *General Principles of Law* (n 23) 299; Schlesinger, 'Research on the General Principles of Law' (n 9) 736.

[133] *Brazilian Loans* (n 130) 114.

[134] Cassese, *International Law* (n 10) 192; Bassiouni, 'A Functional Approach' (n 38) 795.

[135] *Brazilian Loans* (n 130) 124.

[136] Cheng, *General Principles of Law* (n 23) 299.

[137] M Derlén, *Multilingual Interpretation of European Union Law* (Kluwer Law International, 2009) 315.

[138] Cf *Free Zones of Upper Savoy and the District of Gex (France and Switzerland)* (Judgment) [1932] PCIJ Series A/B No 46, 202 (Dissenting Opinion of Judge Dreyfus) (*Free Zones of Upper Savoy*), discussed in section II.O.

[139] Cassese, *International Law* (n 10) 192.

[140] Although, as seen in ch 7, some commentators would classify these as falling under the auspices of General Principles. See also the Separate and Dissenting Opinions of Judge Cançado Trindade discussed in ch 5.

L. *Interpretation of the Greco-Turkish Agreement*

In this Advisory Opinion,[141] the PCIJ was asked to interpret an arbitral provision contained in a 1926 bilateral treaty between Greece and Turkey. The case is cited as support for the General Principle that a body is competent to determine its own jurisdiction.[142] The provision allowed a Mixed Commission to refer certain questions to arbitration: the PCIJ was asked which body should determine whether the question was eligible. In doing so, it stated that

> it is clear – having regard amongst other things to the principle that, as a general rule, any body possessing jurisdictional powers has the right in the first place itself to determine the extent of its jurisdiction – that questions affecting the extent of the jurisdiction of the Mixed Commission must be settled by the Commission itself without action by any other body being necessary.[143]

The PCIJ thus framed the question as one of competence: 'The right of reference can, however, only belong to the Mixed Commission; for it is a matter of determining the extent of its own competence.'[144] There is no doubt that the principle of jurisdictional competence is accepted at international law,[145] but it is less clear that the source of this is Article 38(1)(c). Bin Cheng does not justify his inclusion of the norm as a General Principle in his text, and it seems the only explicit linkage is the use of the term 'general rule' in the passage quoted above. To rely on 'general rule' to state with certainty that the norm is in fact a General Principle is more than simply 'daring',[146] especially given the explicit power of the PCIJ at least to determine its own jurisdiction was enshrined in its statute.[147] Sir Robert Jennings, however, views this principle as 'one of the few clear examples of those "general principles of law"'.[148] Jennings points to the acceptance of this principle 'for international tribunals generally', as well as its French form, *compétence de la compétence*.[149] While Jennings may well be correct (and remembering that Jennings does not see much value in Article 38(1)(c),[150] and any recognition of such a General Principle is rare),

[141] *Interpretation of the Greco-Turkish Agreement of December 1st 1926 (Final Protocol, Article IV)* (Advisory Opinion) [1928] PCIJ Series B No 16.

[142] Cheng, *General Principles of Law* (n 23) 276; Bassiouni, 'A Functional Approach' (n 38) 793; Schlesinger, 'Research on the General Principles of Law' (n 9) 736.

[143] *Interpretation of the Greco-Turkish Agreement* (n 141) 20.

[144] ibid 21.

[145] CF Amerasinghe, *Jurisdiction of International Tribunals* (Martinus Nijhoff, 2003) 134; MSM Amr, *The Role of the International Court of Justice as the Principal Judicial Organ of the United Nations* (Kluwer Law International, 2003) 103.

[146] Pellet and Müller, 'Article 38' (n 3) 929.

[147] Statute of the Permanent Court of Justice (n 127), Art 36.

[148] R Jennings, 'Introduction' in A Zimmerman, C Tomuschat, and K Oellers-Frahm (eds), *The Statute of the International Court of Justice: A Commentary* (Oxford University Press, 2006) 3, 8.

[149] ibid.

[150] R Jennings, 'The Identification of International Law' in B Cheng (ed), *International Law: Teaching and Practice* (Stevens & Sons, 1982) 3, 4.

these views over 50 years after the decision cannot retroactively stamp the use in *this* case as a General Principle. Even if the PCIJ were truly referring to a General Principle, there is no insight given to any of the sides of the tetrahedral framework.

M. *Greco-Bulgarian Communities*

In this Advisory Opinion,[151] the PCIJ was asked to interpret certain provisions of the 1919 Greco-Bulgarian Convention on emigration. The case is cited by Bassiouni as support for the General Principle that municipal law cannot prevail over conflicting treaty provisions.[152] The relevant passage from the judgment reads, 'it is a generally accepted principle of international law that in the relations between Powers who are contracting Parties to a treaty, the provisions of municipal law cannot prevail over those of the treaty'.[153]

The only words linking this rule to Article 38(1)(c) occur in the description 'generally accepted principle of international law', which could apply to an (already accepted) customary norm. Indeed the norm itself is the rule that states cannot, on the international stage, rely on municipal law to excuse non-performance of a treaty. This was subsequently codified in the Vienna Convention on the Law of Treaties (VCLT),[154] and is generally viewed as having its origin in customary international law.[155] Unlike estoppel, discussed subsequently,[156] there is no historical suggestion that the original introduction of this rule to international law was through General Principles.

N. *Polish Nationals in Danzig*

Similar to *Greco-Bulgarian Communities*, *Polish Nationals in Danzig*[157] is cited as support for the General Principle that a state cannot rely on its domestic law to escape international obligations.[158] In this case, the PCIJ was asked what laws

[151] *Interpretation of the Convention between Greece and Bulgaria Respecting Reciprocal Emigration, Signed at Neuilly-sur-Seine on November 27th, 1919 (Question of the 'Communities')* (Advisory Opinion) [1930] PCIJ Series B No 17 (*Greco-Bulgarian Communities*).

[152] Bassiouni, 'A Functional Approach' (n 38) 795.

[153] *Greco-Bulgarian Communities* (n 151) 32.

[154] Vienna Convention on the Law of Treaties [1974] ATS 2, Art 27; AB Boczek, *International Law: A Dictionary* (Scarecrow Press, 2005) 13.

[155] K Schmalenbach, 'Internal Law and Observance of Treaties' in O Dörr and K Schmalenbach (eds), *Vienna Convention on the Law of Treaties: A Commentary* (Springer, 2012) 453, 454.

[156] See discussion in section II.P in relation to *Legal Status of Eastern Greenland (Denmark v Norway)* (Merits) [1933] PCIJ Series A/B No 53 (*Eastern Greenland*).

[157] *Treatment of Polish Nationals and Other Persons of Polish Origin or Speech in the Danzig Territory* (Advisory Opinion) [1932] PCIJ Series A/B No 44 (*Polish Nationals in Danzig*).

[158] Cheng, *General Principles of Law* (n 23) 171; Bassiouni, 'A Functional Approach' (n 38) 795.

governed the treatment of Polish nationals in Danzig, and to interpret certain provisions of the Treaty of Versailles and the Convention of Paris. The PCIJ stated:

> It should … be observed that, while on the one hand, according to generally accepted principles, a State cannot rely, as against another State, on the provisions of the latter's Constitution, but only on international law and international obligations duly accepted, on the other hand and conversely, a State cannot adduce as against another State its own Constitution with a view to evading obligations incumbent upon it under international law or treaties in force.[159]

As with *Greco-Bulgarian Communities*, any link to Article 38(1)(c) must lie in the use of the phrase 'generally accepted principles'. As there, the norm in question is accepted now as one of custom, codified in the VCLT. Accordingly, any attempt to classify this as a General Principle seems unmerited.

O. *Free Zones of Upper Savoy*

This case[160] is cited as support for the application of General Principles of abuses of rights in the context of the treaty obligations,[161] and *jura novit curia*.[162] It is possible that the Dissenting Opinion of Judge Dreyfus contains a General Principle regarding jurisdiction.

i. Abuses of Rights

The relevant principle is that 'every right must be exercised honestly and loyally'.[163] The passage in the judgment of the Court relied upon in support of this dealt with a treaty obligation held by France concerning zones on its borders with Switzerland. In holding that France had the sovereign right to establish a police presence at the border for tax purposes, the Court stated:

> A reservation must be made as regards the case of abuses of a right, since it is certain that France must not evade the obligation to maintain the zones by erecting a customs barrier under the guise of a control cordon. But an abuse cannot be presumed by the Court.[164]

While the Court applied the doctrine of abuses of rights, there is nothing in the judgment to suggest it did so as an application of a General Principle. Rather,

[159] *Polish Nationals in Danzig* (n 157) 24.
[160] *Free Zones of Upper Savoy* (n 138) 202.
[161] Brownlie, *Principles* (n 70) 18; Cheng, *General Principles of Law* (n 23) 123.
[162] Schlesinger, 'Research on the General Principles of Law' (n 9) 736.
[163] Cheng, *General Principles of Law* (n 23) 123.
[164] *Free Zones of Upper Savoy* (n 138) 167.

the all-too-familiar conclusion is that the Court generally stated that the rule applied in international law, without any indication of the source of the rule.

ii. Jura Novit Curia

Bin Cheng cites *Free Zones of Upper Savoy* as an example of *jura novit curia* as a General Principle.[165] The relevant passage in the judgment states:

> From a general point of view, it cannot be lightly admitted that the Court, whose function it is to declare the law, can be called upon to choose between two or more constructions determined beforehand by the Parties, none of which may correspond to the opinion at which it may arrive. Unless otherwise expressly provided, it must be presumed that the Court enjoys the freedom which normally appertains to it, and that it is able, if such its opinion, not only to accept one or other of the two propositions, but also to reject them both.[166]

As above, no indication is given by the Court to the source of the rule applied. The phrase 'general point of view' perhaps indicates a reference to General Principles, but this is a weak link at best.

iii. Jurisdiction

The Dissenting Opinion of Judge Dreyfus refers to a principle of jurisdiction that could be considered a reference to a General Principle:

> It has always appeared necessary in all jurisdictions – it is a principle of general application with which they may in no circumstances dispense – that, within the limit of the legal or regulation quorum, judges who are called upon to give a final decision shall have sat in the case from the beginning of the oral proceedings down to the pronouncement of that decision.[167]

Although no explicit reference is made to Article 38(1)(c), it would seem that this is the source of the rule relied upon in this passage. The justification given for the application is the presence of the rule 'in all jurisdictions' – that is, a recognition of the rule by nations. If this is the case then there are some implications for the nature of General Principles. First, it could be argued that Judge Dreyfus' application favours a comparative approach, in that the rule is recognised in 'all jurisdictions' – however, there is no explicit consideration of, or comparison of, the rule's manifestation in different municipal systems. This could simply be an example of a judge's recognising the comparative basis of the source without undertaking a comparative study (perhaps, again, basing the rule on a 'hunch'[168]) of the particular rule. Second, the rule itself also seems to

[165] Cheng, *General Principles of Law* (n 23) 299.
[166] *Free Zones of Upper Savoy* (n 138) 138.
[167] ibid 202 (Dissenting Opinion of Judge Dreyfus).
[168] Schlesinger, 'Research on the General Principles of Law' (n 9) 734.

be logically deduced from the requirements of the legal system – it has 'always appeared necessary'. This judgment can be read as an indication of how logically deduced principles can fit within a framework of comparativism: they are in domestic legal systems because they are necessary to that system; such principles then become General Principles because of their inclusion in many domestic legal systems. Thus while the nature of the rule (being essential) is the reason *why* it is contained in many systems, it is not the nature *directly* that elevates the rule to a General Principle. Viewed in this way, those logically deduced rules and principles can be seen simply as a subset of General Principles, still following a comparative methodology.[169]

P. *Eastern Greenland*

This case[170] is cited for the equitable principles of estoppel and acquiescence being General Principles,[171] or alternatively the more specific principle *allegans non contraria est audiens*.[172] In the passage relied upon, the Court stated:

> In accepting these bilateral and multilateral agreements as binding upon herself, Norway reaffirmed that she recognized the whole of Greenland as Danish; and thereby she has debarred herself from contesting Danish sovereignty over the whole of Greenland, and, in consequence, from proceeding to occupy any part of it.[173]

The content of this passage demonstrates the application of estoppel at international law, but there is no indication given by the Court as to the source of the norm. The link made to a General Principle seems to be due to its content. In 1927, five years prior to the decision, Lauterpacht declared estoppel 'recognised by all systems of private law' and concluded it was a General Principle.[174] Estoppel itself is undoubtedly a domestic concept[175] that now applies in the

[169] This approach was also taken by judges in the ICJ: *Fisheries Case (United Kingdom v Norway)* [1951] ICJ Rep 116, 147–48, 148 (Individual Opinion of Judge Alvarez); *Interhandel (Switzerland v United States of America) (Preliminary Objections)* [1959] ICJ Rep 6, 116–17 (Dissenting Opinion of Judge Lauterpacht); *Right of Passage over Indian Territory (Portugal v India)* (Merits) [1960] ICJ Rep 6, 136 (Separate Opinion of Judge Koo); *South-West Africa (Ethiopia v South Africa; Liberia v South Africa)* (Preliminary Objections) [1962] ICJ Rep 319, 577–78 (Dissenting Opinion of Judge Van Wyk); *North Sea Continental Shelf (Federal Republic of Germany v Denmark; Federal Republic of Germany v the Netherlands)* [1969] ICJ Rep 3, 135 (Separate Opinion of Judge Ammoun); *Sovereignty over Pulau Ligitan and Pulau Sipidan (Indonesia v Malaysia)* [2002] ICJ Rep 625, 705–06 (Dissenting Opinion of Judge ad hoc Franck). See further discussion in chs 4 and 5.

[170] *Eastern Greenland* (n 157).

[171] Brownlie, *Principles* (n 70) 18; Bassiouni, 'A Functional Approach' (n 38) 796.

[172] Cheng, *General Principles of Law* (n 23) 145.

[173] *Eastern Greenland* (n 157) 68–69.

[174] H Lauterpacht, *Private Law Sources and Analogies of International Law* (Longmans, Green and Co, 1927) 204.

[175] W Friedmann, 'The Uses of "General Principles" in the Development of International Law' (1963) 57 *American Journal of International Law* 279, 288.

international sphere. The question is how it became elevated to the status of an international norm? In 1958, MacGibbon identified debate over whether estoppel was customary or a General Principle.[176] He concluded that, at that time, it was at least a General Principle but may not have reached customary status.[177] This view was supported by other commentators writing contemporaneously.[178] By 1969, estoppel was increasingly being accepted as a norm of custom.[179] Accordingly, although the PCIJ did not state it was relying on a General Principle, the temporal context supports the suggestion that estoppel was seen this way in the 1930s, and was not accepted as a norm of custom until at least 30 years later. Lacking further elaboration, however, the judgment is of little help in determining anything about the nature of source.

Q. *Oscar Chinn Case*

Bin Cheng cites the Separate Opinion of Judge Anzilotti[180] as an application of the General Principle of self-preservation, and as informing the content of the necessity exception to that principle.[181] In considering the question of necessity, Anzilotti made several statements about the application of the principle: 'necessity may observe the non-observance of international relations' and 'the plea of necessity … implies the impossibility of proceeding by any other method than the one contrary to law'.

While Anzilotti's statements inform the content of the rule of necessity at international law, there is nothing to indicate upon which source this rule is based. Accordingly, it seems unjustified to claim that this is an application of a General Principle. Indeed, later jurisdiction of the ICJ accepted necessity as customary international law,[182] codified by articles of the International Law Commission.[183] Although these developments are over 60 years after the decision in point, they suggest that the principle of necessity may not have been a General Principle but is better understood as a customary norm.

[176] IC MacGibbon, 'Estoppel in International Law' (1958) 7(3) *International and Comparative Law Quarterly* 468.

[177] ibid 470.

[178] DW Bowett, 'Estoppel before International Tribunals and its Relation to Acquiescence' (1957) 33 *British Yearbook of International Law* 176, 176.

[179] A D'Amato, 'Consent, Estoppel, and Reasonableness: Three Challenges to Universal International Law' (1969) 10 *Virginia Journal of International Law* 1, 10–11.

[180] *Oscar Chinn Case (Britain v Belgium)* (Merits) [1934] PCIJ Series A/B No 63, 113 (Separate Opinion of Judge Anzilotti).

[181] Cheng, *General Principles of Law* (n 23) 71–73.

[182] *Gabčíkovo-Nagymaros Project (Hungary v Slovakia)* (Merits) [1997] ICJ Rep 7, 40.

[183] ILC, *Articles on Responsibility of States for Internationally Wrongful Acts* (12 December 2001) UN Doc A/RES/56/83, Art 25; M Fitzmaurice, 'Necessity in International Environmental Law' (2010) 41 *Netherlands Yearbook of International Law* 159, 181.

R. *Lighthouses Case*

The Separate Opinion of Judge Séfériadès in the *Lighthouses Case*[184] is cited as authority for the interaction of the General Principle of good faith with the law of treaties.[185] This book further argues that Judge Séfériadès applied the principle of *nemo dat* as a General Principle.[186]

i. Good Faith

Judge Séfériadès stated that 'Contracting parties are always assumed to be acting honestly and in good faith. That is a legal principle, which is recognized in private law and cannot be ignored in international law.'[187]

No reference is made to Article 38(1)(c). However, by the statement that the legal principle is 'recognized in private law', it would seem that Séfériadès was taking a rule recognised in private, municipal systems and applying it to the international sphere. In this way, it can be seen as taking a rule from *in foro domestico* and, by virtue of its acceptance by nations, elevating it to an international norm through use of Article 38(1)(c). The *methodology* then is seen as comparative, drawing from domestic legal systems.

ii. Nemo Dat

In considering whether a contract between a French firm and the (then) Ottoman Government was binding upon Greece, Judge Séfériadès stated:

> There is a general principle of law which must not be lost sight of in the case we are considering; it is summed up in five words: *Nemo dat quod non habet.*[188]
>
> That principle has served as the basis of several modern codes (eg Art 1599 of the French Civil Code; Art 1459 of the Italian Civil Code; Art 1507 of the Netherlands Code) ...[189]

This reference is clearly alluding to Article 38(1)(c), by the use of the phrase 'general principle of law' and the explicit consideration of domestic legislation as the source of the rule. Although not a comprehensive study of domestic laws, the comparison of the French, Italian and Dutch Codes suggests a comparative approach to the source, founding the General Principle on rules found *in foro domestico*. The *type* of the norm is also significant – *nemo dat* is a substantial rule of law, rather than a procedural regulation.

[184] *Lighthouses Case (France v Greece)* (Merits) [1934] PCIJ Series A/B No 62 (*Lighthouses Case*).

[185] Cheng, *General Principles of Law* (n 23) 106; Bassiouni, 'A Functional Approach' (n 38) 794–95; Schlesinger, 'Research on the General Principles of Law' (n 9) 736.

[186] *Lighthouses Case* (n 184) 49 (Separate Opinion of Judge Séfériadès).

[187] ibid 47.

[188] ibid 49.

[189] ibid 49–50.

S. *Consistency of Certain Danzig Legislative Decrees*

This case[190] is included in this chapter because, although no General Principle was relied upon by the Court or in the individual Opinions, the Individual Opinion of Judge Anzilotti contains comments about the nature of the sources listed in Article 38. He stated:

> Article 38 of Statute, which states the sources of law to be applied by the Court, only mentions international treaties or custom and the elements subsidiary to these two sources, to be applied if both of them are lacking.[191]

Accordingly, Anzilotti viewed Article 38(1)(c) as a source subsidiary to treaties and custom, and only to be applied when neither treaty nor custom exists. The second part of this proposal is entirely consistent with the idea of General Principles filling lacunae in international law, as explained by the Committee of Jurists. The first part, however, seems to be inconsistent with the work of the Committee: the idea of ranking the sources was explicitly rejected.[192] Further, this paragraph would seem to rank Article 38(1)(c) parallel in importance with Article 38(1)(d), both as 'elements subsidiary' to the first two sources. This cannot be the case, as Article 38(1)(d) is not a material source of international law but rather informs the content of norms discovered through the other sources. Anzilotti's statement cannot be read as suggesting that Article 38(1)(c) fulfils the same interpretative role as Article 38(1)(d), otherwise the statement 'to be applied if both of them are lacking' does not make sense – only a norm-creating source could be applied in the absence of treaty and custom.

T. *River Meuse*

This case[193] concerned a dispute between the Netherlands and Belgium over a treaty governing the use and division of the River Meuse, which straddles both nations.[194] This case is generally cited as an example of estoppel existing as a General Principle,[195] and for the principle *inademplenti non est adimplendum.*[196] Bin Cheng further relies on the case as informing the content of the General

[190] *Consistency of Certain Danzig Legislative Decrees with the Constitution of the Free City* (Advisory Opinion) [1935] PCIJ Series A/B No 65 41 (*Consistency of Certain Danzig Legislative Decrees*).

[191] ibid 61 (Separate Opinion of Judge Anzilotti).

[192] See ch 2.

[193] *River Meuse* (n 16).

[194] ibid 9–10.

[195] D Harris, *Cases and Materials on International Law*, 5th edn (Sweet & Maxwell, 1998) 50; Cheng, *General Principles of Law* (n 23) 141–42; Cassese, *International Law* (n 10) 192.

[196] Cassese, *International Law* (n 10) 192; J Ruda, 'The Opinions of Judge Dionsio Anzilotti at the Permanent Court of International Justice' (1992) 3 *European Journal of International*

Principle of good faith in the formation of treaties, specifically looking to the reasonable intentions of the contracting parties.[197]

i. Estoppel

Bin Cheng states that '[i]n the *Meuse Case* it was held that, where two States were bound by the same treaty obligations, State A could not complain of an act by State B which it itself had set an example in the past'.[198] This is an instance of the principle *allegans non contraria est*, a more specific form of the general notion of estoppel at international law.

In its judgment, the Court considered a complaint made by the Netherlands about the construction of a lock by Belgium, and compared the offending features with features on a lock constructed by the Netherlands under the same treaty obligation. The Court relevantly held, 'In these circumstances, the Court finds it difficult to admit that the Netherlands are now warranted in complaining of the construction and operation of a lock of which they themselves set an example in the past.'[199]

Although this is an instance of the Court's applying the equitable principle, there is no evidence that the principle was applied as a General Principle. However, the general remarks made in section II.P on the origins of estoppel in international law apply here.

There is more support in the Separate Opinion of Judge Hudson. In considering the position of the two locks, Hudson found the positions to be the same:

> [I]f the discharge of lock-water … by one of these locks is in accordance with the Treaty it is equally so with respect to the other lock; if such discharge is a violation of the Treaty as to one lock, it is a violation also as to the other lock.[200]

In determining the situation, Hudson looked to equity, finding justification in Article 38(1)(c):

> Article 38 of the Statute expressly directs the application of 'general principles of law recognized by civilized nations', and in more than one nation principles of equity have an established place in the legal system … It must be concluded therefore, that under Article 38 of the Statute … the Court has some freedom to consider principles of equity as part of the international law which it must apply.[201]

Law 100, 104–05; cf J Crawford and S Olleson, 'The Exception of Non-performance: Links between the Law of Treaties and the Law of State Responsibility' (2000) 21 *Australian Yearbook of International Law* 55, 56.

197 Cheng, *General Principles of Law* (n 23) 106.

198 ibid 142.

199 *River Meuse* (n 16) 25.

200 ibid 75 (Separate Opinion of Judge Hudson).

201 ibid 76–77.

Hudson then determined the relevant equitable principle to be:

> [T]hat where two parties have assumed an identical or a reciprocal obligation, one party which is engaged in a continuing non-performance of that obligation should not be permitted to take advantage of a similar non-performance of that obligation by the other party …[202]

This is a principle similar in content to that relied upon by the Court in its judgment, as discussed above. Unlike the Court, however, Hudson provided the means by which he ascertained this General Principle:

> The principle finds expression in the so-called maxims of equity which exercised great influence in the creative period of the development of the Anglo-American law … A very similar principle was received into Roman Law … [The principle] was the basis of Articles 320 and 322 of the German Civil Code.[203]

Finally, Hudson cautioned that 'the general principle is one of which an international tribunal should make a very sparing application',[204] but 'in a proper case, and with scrupulous regard for the limitations which are necessary, a tribunal bound by international law ought not to shrink from applying a principle of such obvious fairness'.[205]

There are several points we can draw from these passages in regard to the nature of General Principles. First, Hudson employed a comparative-type approach to ascertaining the principle – although he did not employ a wide-ranging study of the laws of different nations, he referenced both common and civil law systems. Second, Hudson clearly saw the origin of the General Principle in the municipal laws of nations. Third, although the justification for the use of the principle was mostly focused on its incorporation in municipal systems, the use of the term 'of such obvious fairness' in encouraging international tribunals to apply the principles suggests its content may also be important – a more natural law approach to the source. Thus the decision impacts on the *jurisprudence* and *methodology* of the source.

ii. Inadimplenti Non Est Adimplendum

In his Dissenting Opinion, Judge Anzilotti wrote:

> I am convinced that the principle underlying this submission (*inadimplenti non est adimplendum*) is so just, so equitable, so universally recognized that it must be applied in international relations also. In any case, it is one of these 'general principles of law

[202] ibid 77.
[203] ibid.
[204] ibid.
[205] ibid.

> recognized by civilized nations' which the Court applies in virtue of Article 38 of its Statute.[206]

The principle *inadimplenti non est adimplendum* is a form of the exception of non-performance to obligations, which 'allows a state to withhold performance of an obligation when another state has not performed an obligation of its own'.[207]

Anzilotti described the principle as 'so just, so equitable' and 'so universally recognized'. It is not completely clear, however, whether it is these qualities that render it a General Principle in Anzilotti's eyes. If, however, we are to take it that validity is derived because it is just, equitable and universally recognised, there seem to be elements of natural law: the content of the principle (just, equitable) is determinative of its status as a norm. A comparative element is also arguably present: 'universal recognition' suggests recognition by differing systems. However this 'universal recognition' is not based on any comparative study of systems, nor are any examples offered of its incorporation in municipal systems. In this way, perhaps, the principle is recognised less by comparative methodology and more as a 'hunch',[208] based on the civil systems with which Anzilotti was familiar.

iii. Good Faith

Finally, Bin Cheng also refers to Judge Anzilotti's Dissenting Opinion as informing the content of the General Principle of good faith in treaty relations, specifically that 'contracting parties [cannot] be presumed to have intended anything which would, under the circumstances, have been unreasonable'.[209]

While Anzilotti rejected a construction of an article of the Treaty on the grounds that 'it would be going beyond the reasonable intentions of the Parties',[210] there is nothing in his Opinion to suggest that he did so on the basis that this is a General Principle.

U. *Lighthouses in Crete and Samoa*

Although titled separately from the *Lighthouses Case*, this case concerned the same factual background between France and Greece.[211] After the Court's judgment in 1934, France and Greece returned to the PCIJ by way of another, new,

[206] ibid 50 (Dissenting Opinion of Judge Anzilotti).
[207] Crawford and Olleson, 'The Exception of Non-performance' (n 196) 62.
[208] Schlesinger, 'Research on the General Principles of Law' (n 9) 734.
[209] Cheng, *General Principles of Law* (n 23) 106.
[210] *River Meuse* (n 16) 47 (Dissenting Opinion of Judge Anzilotti).
[211] *Lighthouses in Crete and Samoa* (n 18).

special agreement, to ask the Court to consider the applicability of its 1934 judgment to specific lighthouses situated in Crete and Samoa.[212] The Separate Opinion of Judge Séfériadès contains an explicit reference to General Principles. Judge Séfériadès was considering the construction of the word 'detached' within a treaty between France and Greece, and which party such a construction should favour. Séfériadès stated:

> [I]n accordance with a general principle which is unanimously accepted by the doctrine of international law, all treaties 'stipulating servitudes should be interpreted restrictively, so that the servitude, which is an exceptional right attaching to the territory of a foreign State, may limit the sovereignty of the said State as little as possible.' That is, indeed a general principle of law recognized by all civilized nations, and it is one of the general principles which the Court is obliged to apply in virtue of Article 38 of its Statute.[213]

Judge Séfériadès found support for this principle in the French Civil Code.[214] Although this is a reference to Article 38(1)(c), the judgment does not shed much light on the nature of the source. Judge Séfériadès describes the principle as 'recognized by all civilized nations' – which could be a reference to the comparative method, or could simply be a re-echoing of the wording of Article 38(1)(c). Certainly, no comparative study is undertaken – save the reference to the French Civil Code, no reference is made to the specific acceptance of the principle in any municipal system. This is in comparison to the General Principle of *nemo dat* referred to by Judge Séfériadès in the earlier *Lighthouses Case*, where Séfériadès referred to three different domestic Codes, which each incorporated the principle.[215]

V. *Panevezys-Saldutiskis Railway*

This case[216] concerned the seizure of a railway line by Lithuania from an Estonian company. Lithuania argued that Estonia had failed to exhaust local remedies before bringing the case to the PCIJ.[217] In his Dissenting Opinion, Judge Van Eysinga discussed the application of the local remedies rule. Van Eysinga stated:

> It has been said that since the Court, under Article 38 of the Statute of the Court must apply the general principles of law recognized by civilized nations, it must apply the local remedies rule. This obligation is not denied.[218]

[212] ibid 94.
[213] ibid 137–38 (Separate Opinion of Judge Séfériadès).
[214] ibid 138.
[215] *Lighthouses Case* (n 184) 49–50 (Separate Opinion of Judge Séfériadès).
[216] *Panevezys-Saldutiskis Railway* (n 19).
[217] ibid 6.
[218] ibid 40 (Dissenting Opinion of Judge Van Eysinga).

Prior to this statement, Judge Van Eysinga traced the development of the local remedies rule, describing it as 'a rule of conduct which has been observed for a very long time'[219] and making mention of several arbitration treaties and conventions that contained the rule.[220] As such, the only basis for recognition of the rule by nations given by Judge Van Eysinga is recognition at an international level, not in domestic rules. This follows the nature of the rule itself – it would seem unlikely that a national law, internal in nature, could sensibly refer to the exhaustion of local remedies, which deals with external, international disputes. In this case, then, the acceptance of the General Principle by Van Eysinga must be on the basis of a rule in the international sphere. The methodology draws from the international forum rather than the domestic.

W. *Electricity Company of Sofia and Bulgaria*

This case concerned an action brought by Belgium against Bulgaria concerning tax applied by Bulgaria on the Electricity Company of Sofia and Bulgaria. The company was taken from a Belgian company during World War I, and Belgium was given rights to restitution against Bulgaria as a result.[221] Belgium claimed that the tax imposed by Bulgaria distorted the value of that restitution. The case contained a preliminary objections phase, interim protection order and merits phase. The Interim Protection Order[222] in this case is cited as support for a General Principle[223] that

> parties to a case must abstain from any measure capable of exercising a prejudicial effect in regard to the execution of the decision to be given and, in general, not allow any step of any kind to be taken which might aggravate or extend the dispute.[224]

It could also be argued that Judge Hudson applied a General Principle that the later intentions of Parties prevail over their earlier intentions, in his Dissenting Opinion in the Preliminary Objection phase.[225]

i. Prejudicial Effect

In this case, the Court justified its right to order an interim protection order by reference to the prejudicial effect principle.[226] The Court described the principle

[219] ibid 36.
[220] ibid 37–38.
[221] *Electricity Company of Sofia and Bulgaria (Belgium v Bulgaria)* (Preliminary Objection) [1939] PCIJ Series A/B No 77 64, 69–70 (*Electricity Company* (Preliminary Objection)).
[222] *Electricity Company* (Interim Protection Order) (n 4).
[223] Brownlie, *Principles* (n 70) 18; Bassiouni, 'A Functional Approach' (n 38) 796.
[224] *Electricity Company* (Interim Protection Order) (n 4) 199.
[225] *Electricity Company* (Preliminary Objection) (n 221) 125 (Dissenting Opinion of Hudson J).
[226] *Electricity Company* (Interim Protection Order) (n 4) 199.

as a 'principle universally accepted by international tribunals'[227] and 'laid down in many Conventions'.[228] However, the characterisation of this rule as a General Principle is tenuous. The fact that the principle was 'accepted by international tribunals' and existed in convention does not indicate it is a General Principle: this statement could equally be constructed as referring to a norm of custom. Further, the Court had the power to order an interim protection order by virtue of its own Statute[229] and Rules,[230] a fact the Court recognised.[231] Accordingly, the statement by the Court seems to be more likely an interpretation of its Statute and Rules rather than a finding of a General Principle.[232]

ii. Later v Earlier Intentions

In his Dissenting Judgment, Judge Hudson considered discrepancies between two texts between the parties to the dispute. Hudson stated:

> Called upon to choose which of the two texts is to govern in this case, the Court must apply a general principle of law, and it must say that the expression of the Parties' intention which is the later in point of time should prevail over that which is the earlier.[233]

Although Hudson describes the rule as a 'general principle of law', there is no other indication that the source of the rule is in fact Article 38(1)(c). If this is the case, there is almost nothing to be drawn from the judgment with regard to the nature of this source: it is entirely unclear what basis Judge Hudson had for declaring this rule to be a General Principle. It is clear the principle is being applied as binding, but nothing more can be gained from the text.

III. CONCLUSION

Although the judgments of the PCIJ are used to support a variety of General Principles, it can be seen that, in most cases, the Court either states a general rule with no indication as to the source of the rule, or uses language that could equally be constructed as referring to a customary basis for the rule, rather than a founding in Article 38(1)(c). The wheat is very much integrated with the chaff in the way these cases are used – it is unfortunate they are still cited as support for General Principles, for they do not add to the understanding of the

[227] ibid.
[228] ibid.
[229] Statute of the Permanent Court of International Justice (n 127), Art 41(1).
[230] Permanent Court of International Justice, *Rules of the Court* (adopted 24 March 1922), Art 57.
[231] *Electricity Company (Interim Protection Order)* (n 4) 199.
[232] This follows the same trend as commentary on *Mavrommatis Palestine Concessions* (n 34).
[233] *Electricity Company (Interim Protection Order)* (n 4) 125 (Dissenting Opinion of Judge Hudson).

source. Rather the opposite is true – by referring to such vague and amorphous statements as examples of General Principles, the source itself loses clarity. By insisting on precision when referring to instances of General Principles, we will be able to build a clear model of how the source operates.

The confusion is not helped in this instance by the practice of the Court itself – while Judge Anzilotti accepted General Principles as gap-fillers,[234] General Principles are also used in conjunction with custom (thus making lacunae irrelevant),[235] constructed in a way that suggests they are a subsidiary source,[236] or entirely ignored by the Court.[237]

Of those cases and judgments that can be seen as referring to General Principles, the following conclusions can be made.

A. Function

With one exception,[238] General Principles are considered binding. The use of General Principles to fill lacunae suggests they are used only when convention and custom are silent.

B. Methodology

Although it is argued by scholars that some of the PCIJ judgments can be seen as a rejection of the comparative methodology, analysis suggests that any rejection was only in the specific instance of the particular case and rule in question, and cannot be extended to a more general statement.[239] Indeed, several of the judgments that employ General Principles do so on a comparative basis.[240]

Some of the judgments that consider the source of the laws that make up general principles favour an *in foro domestico* approach,[241] while others draw rules from the international sphere.[242]

[234] *Consistency of Certain Danzig Legislative Decrees* (n 191) 61 (Dissenting Opinion of Judge Anzilotti); *Interpretation of Judgments Nos 7 and 8* (n 15) 27 (Dissenting Opinion of Judge Anzilotti).

[235] *Chorzów Factory* (Merits) (n 1) 29.

[236] *Consistency of Certain Danzig Legislative Decrees* (n 191) 61 (Dissenting Opinion of Judge Anzilotti).

[237] *Mavrommatis Jerusalem Concessions* (n 5).

[238] *SS Lotus* (n 14) 96 (Dissenting Opinion of Judge Altamira).

[239] *Mavrommatis Palestine Concessions* (n 35) see discussion in section II.B.

[240] ibid 59 (Dissenting Opinion of Judge Moore); *Lighthouses Case* (n 185) 49–50 (Separate Opinion of Judge Séfériadès).

[241] *River Meuse* (n 16) 75 (Separate Opinion of Judge Hudson); *Lighthouses Cases* (n 185) 49–50 (Separate Opinion of Judge Séfériadès).

[242] *Panevezys-Saldutiskis Railway* (n 217) 37–38 (Dissenting Opinion of Judge Van Eysinga).

C. Type

Any distinction between rules and principles is not observed in the text of the judgments – both terms are used interchangeably. Further, although some of the General Principles referred to are procedural in nature, non-procedural norms are also discussed as General Principles. There is no suggestion in any of the cases that the source is necessarily limited to procedural norms.

D. Jurisprudential Legitimacy

Some conceptions provide for a comparative methodology but could also be constructed as requiring a content-based approach to validity as well, thus tempering a positivist rule of recognition with a legitimacy grounded in natural law.[243]

The most striking thing to draw from this chapter is although the PCIJ *itself* refers to principles that are logical deductions from international law, these are not contextualised as being part of General Principles.[244] Rather, it is the work of commentators who have subsequently categorised these cases as instances of General Principles, and in a self-perpetuating cycle, declared General Principles to include such norms. Or, to view it from the other direction of the process, to a legal commentator with a hammer, truly some PCIJ cases are a nail.

[243] *Mavrommatis Palestine Concessions* (n 35) 57–59 (Dissenting Opinion of Judge Moore); River Meuse (n 16) 50 (Dissenting Opinion of Judge Anzilotti); *Free Zones of Upper Savoy* (n 140) 202 (Dissenting Opinion of Judge Dreyfus).

[244] See, eg, *SS Lotus* (n 14) 35 (Dissenting Opinion of Judge Loder); *Chorzów Factory* (Jurisdiction) (n 104) 21.

4

Development of Article 38(1)(c): 1945–91

I. INTRODUCTION

THIS CHAPTER CONSIDERS the development of the law surrounding Article 38(1)(c) after the work of the Permanent Court of Justice (PCIJ), from 1945 to 1991. This consists, first, of the introduction of the source into the Statute of the International Court of Justice (ICJ) and, second, the treatment of the source by the ICJ in the period from 1949 to 1991. Chapter 5 will address the treatment of the source by the ICJ from 1992–2019. The reason for this seemingly arbitrary division is threefold: first, out of pure necessity to give the reader a break from the 61 judgments discussed in these two chapters.[1] Second, the time periods chosen reflect a natural division in the use of the Court. Those in chapter 4 are the post-World War II cases and many cases arising out of decolonisation following UN General Assembly Resolution 1514.[2] The cases in chapter 5 are the post-Cold War cases, and reflect a wider use of the Court by a more diverse international community.[3] Finally, there is a trend in the consideration of General Principles by individual judges, whereby judges build a line of judicial commentary through a series of Separate or Dissenting Opinions. The first instance of this trend is seen in chapter 4, with four Opinions of Judge Lauterpacht,[4]

[1] Though not intended, it serendipitously also serves the purpose of avoiding the rather tedious 'AA', 'BB' system of headings, allowing each section to address fewer than 26 judgments, thus fitting within alphabetical constraints!

[2] Declaration on the Granting of Independence to Colonial Countries and Peoples (adopted 14 December 1960) UNGA Res 1514.

[3] See SM Schwebel, 'The Reality of International Adjudication and Arbitration' (2004) 12 *Willamette Journal of International Law and Dispute Resolution* 359; cf EA Posenor, 'The Decline of the International Court of Justice' in S Voigt, M Albert and D Schmidtchen (eds), *International Conflict Resolution* (Mohr Siebeck, 2006) 111.

[4] *Voting Procedure on Questions relating to Reports and Petitions concerning the Territory of South West Africa* (Advisory Opinion) [1955] ICJ Rep 67, 90 (Separate Opinion of Judge Lauterpacht) (*Voting Procedure*); *Certain Norwegian Loans (France v Norway)* (Merits) [1957] ICJ Rep 9, 34 (Separate Opinion of Judge Lauterpacht) (*Certain Norwegian Loans*); *Application of the Convention of 1902 Governing the Guardianship of Infants (Netherlands v Sweden)* (Merits) [1958] ICJ Rep 55, 79 (Separate Opinion of Judge Lauterpacht) (*Guardianship of Infants*); *Interhandel (Switzerland v United States of America)* (Preliminary Objections) [1959] ICJ Rep 6, 95 (Dissenting Opinion of Judge Lauterpacht) (*Interhandel*).

two Opinions of Judge Tanaka,[5] two Opinions of Judge Ammoun,[6] two Opinions of Judge Dillard[7] and two Opinions of Judge Jimenez de Arechaga.[8] The second iteration of this trend – with longer lines of judicial development – is seen in chapter 5, with five Opinions of Judge Weeramantry[9] and 13 Opinions of Judge Cançado Trindade.[10] Dividing the cases in this manner allows these

[5] *South-West Africa Cases (Ethiopia v South Africa; Liberia v South Africa) (Second Phase)* [1966] ICJ Rep 4, 250 (Dissenting Opinion of Judge Tanaka) (*South-West Africa*); *North Sea Continental Shelf (Federal Republic of Germany v Denmark; Federal Republic of Germany v the Netherlands)* [1969] ICJ Rep 3, 171 (Separate Opinion of Judge Tanaka) (*North Sea Continental Shelf*).

[6] *North Sea Continental* Shelf (n 5) 100 (Separate Opinion of Judge Ammoun); *Application for Review of Judgment No 158 of the United Nations Administrative Tribunal* (Advisory Opinion) [1973] ICJ Rep 166, 246 (Dissenting Opinion of Vice President Ammoun) (*Application for Review of Judgment No 158*).

[7] *Legal Consequences for States of the Continued Presence of South Africa in Namibia (South West Africa) notwithstanding Security Council Resolution 276 (1970)* (Advisory Opinion) [1971] ICJ Rep 16, 150 (Separate Opinion of Judge Dillard) (*Legal Consequences for States*); *Appeal Relating to the Jurisdiction of the ICAO Council (India v Pakistan)* (Merits) [1972] ICJ Rep 46, 92 (Separate Opinion of Judge Dillard) (*ICAO Council Appeal*).

[8] *Fisheries Jurisdiction (United Kingdom v Iceland)* (Order) [1972] ICJ 181, 184; *Fisheries Jurisdiction (United Kingdom v Iceland; Federal Republic of Germany v Iceland)* (Order) [1972] ICJ Rep 188, 190 (Joint Dissenting Opinions of Judges Bengzon and Jiménéz de Aréchaga); *Aegean Sea Continental Shelf (Greece v Turkey)* (Interim Protection Measures) [1976] ICJ Rep 3, 15 (Separate Opinion of President Jiménéz de Aréchaga).

[9] *Maritime Delimitation in the Area between Greenland and Jan Mayen (Denmark v Norway)* (Merits) [1993] ICJ Rep 38, 211 (Separate Opinion of Judge Weeramantry); *Application of the Convention on the Prevention and the Punishment of the Crime of Genocide (Bosnia and Herzegovina v Serbia and Montenegro)* (Provisional Measures) [1993] ICJ Rep 325, 370 (Separate Opinion of Judge Weeramantry); *Gabčíkovo-Nagymaros Project (Hungary v Slovakia)* [1997] ICJ Rep 7, 88 (Separate Opinion of Judge Weeramantry); *Land and Maritime Boundary between Cameroon and Nigeria (Cameroon v Nigeria)* (Preliminary Objections) [1998] ICJ Rep 275, 362 (Dissenting Opinion of Vice-President Weeramantry); *Sovereignty over Pulau Ligitan and Pulau Sipadan (Indonesia/Malaysia)* (Application to Intervene) [2001] ICJ Rep 575, 630 (Separate Opinion of Judge Weeramantry).

[10] *Questions relating to the Obligation to Prosecute or Extradite (Belgium v Senegal)* (Order of 28 May 2009) [2009] ICJ Rep 139, 165 (Dissenting Opinion of Judge Cançado Trindade); *Pulp Mills on the River Uruguay (Argentina v Uruguay)* (Merits) [2010] ICJ Rep 14, 135 (Separate Opinion of Judge Cançado Trindade); *Jurisdictional Immunities of the State (Germany v Italy: Greece Intervening)* [2012] ICJ Rep 12, 179 (Dissenting Opinion of Judge Cançado Trindade); *Questions Related to the Obligation to Prosecute or Extradite (Belgium v Senegal)* (Merits) [2012] ICJ Rep 423, 487 (Separate Opinion of Judge Cançado Trindade); *Judgment No 2867 of the Administrative Tribunal of the International Labour Organization upon a Complaint Filed against the International Fund for Agricultural Development* (Advisory Opinion) [2012] ICJ Rep 10, 51;*Ahmadou Sadio Diallo (Republic of Guinea v Democratic Republic of the Congo)* (Compensation) ICJ Rep 2012 ICJ Rep 324, 347 (Separate Opinion of Judge Cançado Trindade); *Certain Activities Carried Out by Nicaragua in the Border Area (Costa Rica v Nicaragua)* (Joinder of Proceedings) [2013] ICJ Rep 166, 172 (Separate Opinion of Judge Cançado Trindade); *Questions relating to the Seizure and Detention of Certain Documents and Data (Timor-Leste v Australia)* (Provisional Measures) [2014] ICJ Rep 147, 167 (Separate Opinion of Judge Cançado Trindade); *Obligation to Negotiate Access to the Pacific Ocean (Bolivia v Chile)* (Preliminary Objection) [2015] ICJ Rep 592, para 1 (Separate Opinion of Judge Cançado Trindade); *Obligations Concerning Negotiations Relating to Cessation of the Nuclear Arms Race and to Nuclear Disarmament (Marshall Islands v Pakistan)* (Jurisdiction and Admissibility) [2016] ICJ Rep 255, 321 (Dissenting Opinion of Judge Cançado Trindade); *Sovereign Rights and Maritime Spaces in the Caribbean Sea (Nicaragua v Colombia)* (Preliminary Objections) [2016] ICJ Rep 4, 44 (Separate Opinion of Judge Cançado Trindade); *Jadhav Case (India v Pakistan)*

lines of judicial philosophy to be analysed in their context.[11] Consistent with the tetrahedral framework established in chapter 1, the *function*, *methodology*, *type* and *jurisprudential legitimacy* of General Principles will be examined for both chapters 4 and 5.

II. HISTORICAL DEVELOPMENT: PCIJ TO ICJ

After the collapse of the League of Nations, Article 38(1)(c) was adopted from the PCIJ Statute to the newly formed ICJ Statute. The ICJ Statute was nonetheless a new international treaty, and hence regard must be had to the preparatory materials for that treaty. The starting point is with the Informal Inter-Allied Committee on the Future of the Permanent Court of International Justice ('Inter-Allied Committee'), formed from experts from 11 countries.[12] The Inter-Allied Committee was, as the name suggests, an informal panel, and its findings were not intended to be binding.[13] When Germany invaded the Netherlands in 1940, the judges of the PCIJ were forced into exile in Geneva.[14] Those who could return home did so, and the Court was effectively non-operational.[15] However, the British judge, Sir Cecil Hurst, and the legal adviser to the British Foreign Office, Sir William Malkin, were keen for the Court to be re-established once hostilities had ceased.[16] Malkin continued agitating for a meeting among the Allied Powers to discuss a new Court, and by 1943 the British Foreign Office issued invitations to its allies to form an informal committee. The United States did not wish to be part of the committee.[17]

(Provisional Measures) [2017] ICJ Rep 231, 247 (Concurring Opinion of Judge Cançado Trindade); *Sovereign Rights and Maritime Spaces in the Caribbean Sea (Nicaragua v Colombia)* (Counter-Claims) [2017] Rep 289, 330 (Declaration of Judge Cançado Trindade).

[11] The one exception to this is Judge Oda, who has three Opinions discussed in this chapter and one in ch 5: *Continental Shelf (Tunisia v Libyan Arab Jamahiriya)* [1982] ICJ Rep 18, 157 (Dissenting Opinion of Judge Oda) (*Continental Shelf (Tunisia v Libyan Arab Jamahiriya)*); *Military and Paramilitary Activities in and against Nicaragua (Nicaragua v United States of America)* (Merits) [1986] ICJ Rep 14, 212 (Dissenting Opinion of Judge Oda) (*Nicaragua*); *Elettronica Sicula SpA (ELSI) (United States of America v Italy)* [1989] ICJ Rep 15, 83 (Separate Opinion of Judge Oda) (*Elettronica Sicula*); *Kasikili/Sedudu Island (Botswana v Namibia)* (Merits) [1999] ICJ Rep 1045, 1116 (Separate Opinion of Judge Oda).

[12] Belgium, Canada, (the then) Czechoslovakia, Greece, Luxembourg, the Netherlands, New Zealand, Norway, Poland, the United Kingdom and (the then) French National Committee.

[13] MO Hudson, 'The Succession of the International Court of Justice to the Permanent Court of International Justice' (1957) 51(3) *American Journal of International Law* 569, 569–70.

[14] G Marston, 'The London Committee and the Statute of the International Court of Justice' in V Lowe and M Fitzmaurice (eds), *Fifty Years of the International Court of Justice: Essays in Honour of Sir Robert Jennings* (Cambridge University Press, 1996) 40, 40.

[15] ibid.

[16] ibid 41.

[17] ibid.

The Inter-Allied Committee was of the general view that the Statute of the PCIJ had 'worked well'[18] and should be retained as a general structure. This reluctance to enact change can be seen specifically with regard to Article 38, on which the Committee wrote:

> The wording of this provision is open to criticism and it would not be difficult to make suggestions for improving it; but on the whole the difficulties resulting from it do not seem to be a sufficiently serious character to necessitate any change. It seems to have worked well in practice, and we consider that any attempt to alter it would cause more difficulties than it would solve.[19]

Unfortunately for the purposes of this book, the Inter-Allied Committee did not elaborate on the criticism, or any possible improvements to the article. Like most of the discussions surrounding the various courts and tribunals established in the late nineteenth and early twentieth century, much of the debate revolved around the appointment of judges to the Court.[20]

The next step in the progression of the ICJ was the Dumbarton Oaks Proposals, initially between the United States, Great Britain and the (then) USSR, and later between the United States, Great Britain and China.[21] The Proposals, in line with the Inter-Allied Committee, suggested that the new Statute align with the content of the PCIJ Statute.[22] This met with little opposition: even those who did suggest alterations, such as Kelsen, focused on appointment of judges, not the sources of law.[23]

Following the Dumbarton Oaks Proposals, the then leaders of the United States, the United Kingdom and the USSR met at the Yalta Conference, and agreed to form a Commission of Jurists to draft the new ICJ Statute.[24] The Commission of Jurists worked in Washington in April 1945, reporting their conclusions to the San Francisco Conference on International Organisation held in April–June 1945.[25] These shed little light on Article 38(1)(c). As Géza Herczegh states:

> The study of the preparatory material, however, leads to the conclusion that – in contrast to the Committee sitting in the Peace Palace in The Hague in 1920 – the

[18] United Nations, 'Report of the Informal Inter-Allied Committee in the Future of the Permanent Court of International Justice' (1945) 39(1) *American Journal of International Law*, Supplement: Official Documents 1.

[19] ibid 20.

[20] Marston, 'The London Committee' (n 14) 49–50; R Jennings, 'Introduction' in A Zimmerman, C Tomuschat, and K Oellers-Frahm (eds), *The Statute of the International Court of Justice: A Commentary* (Oxford University Press, 2006) 3, 5.

[21] Hudson, 'The Succession of the International Court of Justice' (n 13) 570.

[22] ibid.

[23] H Kelsen, 'The Old and the New League: The Covenant and the Dumbarton Oaks Proposals' (1945) 39(1) *American Journal of International Law* 45, 70–71.

[24] J O'Brien, *International Law* (Routledge-Cavendish, 2001) 26.

[25] ibid.

> many committee meetings in San Francisco devoted surprisingly little attention to the formulation of Article 38.[26]

This view that Article 38 did not need alteration was supported by the proposal of Venezuela at the Conference, which stated that 'the provision of Article 38 … does not give occasion to any fundamental objection',[27] and a report prepared by one of the members of the Committee preparing the ICJ Statute, which stated that 'Article 38 … has given rise to more controversies in doctrine than difficulties in practice'.[28] Accordingly, the Committee 'trusted to the Court to put [Article 38] into operation and has left it without change other than that which appears in the numbering of the provisions of the article'.[29]

There are, however, two important points to be drawn from the preparatory materials for the ICJ Statute. First, discussion occurred as to whether the order in which the Court should apply the sources should be defined in the new Statute.[30] The Committee expressly decided against doing so.[31] Accordingly, as was the case with the PCIJ Statute before it, the ICJ Statute does not indicate the order in which the sources should be considered, or the relevant importance of the sources.

Second, a proposal was made by Chile to insert the phrase 'and especially the principles of international law' into Article 38(1)(c).[32] The proposal was rejected on the grounds that Article 38 had always been regarded 'as carrying an implicit mandate to apply international law',[33] and this was later confirmed by the rewording of the first paragraph of Article 38 to read 'The Court whose function is to decide in accordance with international law such disputes as are submitted to it …'.[34] The final alteration is quite different in meaning from the original proposal submitted by Chile: while the Chilean proposal would have expressly included principles of international law in the same source as general principles of law (thus explicitly stating that Article 38(1)(c) contained principles of municipal law and principles of international law), the insertion of the words into the first paragraph merely confirmed 'the function of the Court to decide disputes submitted to it in accordance with international law'.[35] That is:

> The new wording emphasizes that the Court shall settle disputes on the ground of law, and that it shall apply international law; but no stand is adopted regarding the

[26] G Herczegh, *General Principles of Law and the International Legal Order* (Akadémiai Kiadó, 1969) 17.
[27] ibid 17.
[28] ibid 17–18.
[29] ibid.
[30] ibid 18.
[31] ibid.
[32] ibid 18.
[33] ibid.
[34] ibid.
[35] ibid.

question whether clause 1(c) should be interpreted as to contain the principles of either municipal or international law.[36]

It is argued that by reason of the explicit rejection of the inclusion of 'principles of international law' in Article 38(1)(c), the meaning of General Principles in the unchanged paragraph is principles of municipal law, which are transformed into international norms.[37] Other publicists took the opposing view, with Haraszti stating that 'after the San Francisco Conference there can be no doubt that clause 1(c) of Article 38 comprises the general principles of international law'.[38]

III. CASES

Given the longer period of jurisprudence flowing from the ICJ, it is hardly surprising that more judgments of the Court and individual judges considered Article 38(1)(c) than in the work of the PCIJ. A notable feature of the discussion of General Principles is there is much less chaff than was seen in the PCIJ jurisprudence. Perhaps due to a shift in the way judgments are written – judges at the ICJ seem more ready to refer to sources of law by their Article 38 enumerations, clearly indicating when Article 38(1)(c) is being used[39] – most judgments that are said to refer to General Principles, on construction, do so. Thus, this chapter and the following one are happily able to focus on analysing the wheat rather than the task of finding it in the first place.

The cases below consider, to varying degrees of comprehension, the application of General Principles. Although some unpack the source in much more detail than others, all allow some advancement of the understanding of the source in accordance with the tetrahedral model of *type*, *function*, *methodology* and *jurisprudential legitimacy*. There are other cases that contain references to Article 38(1)(c) or its wording that are not included – these are those that do so

[36] ibid 19.

[37] ibid 20.

[38] G Haraszti, *A nemzetközi bíróság joggyakorlata 1946–1956* (Közgazdasági és Jogi Könyvkiadó, 1958) 18, excerpted in G Herczegh, *General Principles of Law and the International Legal Order* (Akadémiai Kiadó, 1969) 21.

[39] See, eg, *Certain Norwegian Loans* (n 4) 45 (Separate Opinion of Judge Lauterpacht); *South-West Africa* (n 5), 46; *Application for Review of Judgment No 158* (n 6), 247 (Dissenting Opinion of Vice President Ammoun), 284 (Dissenting Opinion of Judge De Castro); *Maritime and Territorial Questions between Qatar and Bahrain (Qatar v Bahrain)* (Merits) [2001] ICJ Rep 40, 381 (Dissenting Opinion of Judge Torres Bernárdez); *Oil Platforms (Islamic Republic of Iran v United States of America) (Merits)* [2003] ICJ Rep 161, 354 (Separate Opinion of Judge Simma); *Application of the Interim Accord of 13 September 1995 (Former Yugoslav Republic of Macedonia v Greece)* [2011] ICJ Rep 644, 700 (Separate Opinion of Judge Simma), 745 (Dissenting Opinion of Judge ad hoc Roucounas); *Certain Activities Carried Out by Nicaragua in the Border Area (Costa Rica v Nicaragua)* and *Construction of a Road in Costa Rica Along the San Juan River (Nicaragua v Costa Rica)* [2015] ICJ 667, 847 (Separate Opinion of Judge ad hoc Dugard).

only by way of analogy,[40] in passing,[41] as included in a reference to an earlier case with no further elaboration,[42] or as part of recitation of the sources of law the Court can consider.[43] These cases do not provide any information about the construction of General Principles as a source of law.

Table 4.1 Consideration of Article 38(1)(c) by the ICJ, 1949–91

Corfu Channel (1949)[44]
International Status of South-West Africa, Separate Opinion of Sir Arnold McNair (1950)
Fisheries Case, Individual Opinion of Judge Alvarez (1951)
Anglo-Iranian Oil Company, Dissenting Opinion of Judge Carneiro (1952)
Effect of Awards of Compensation (1954)
Voting Procedure, Separate Opinion of Judge Lauterpacht (1955)
Certain Norwegian Loans, Separate Opinion of Judge Lauterpacht (1957)
Right of Passage, Dissenting Opinion of Judge Chagla (1957)
Guardianship of Infants (1958)
Separate Opinion of Judge Lauterpacht
Separate Opinion of Judge Quintana
Interhandel, Dissenting Opinion of Judge Lauterpacht (1959)
Right of Passage (1960)
Judgment of the Court
Dissenting Opinion of Judge Quintana
Separate Opinion of Judge Koo
Dissenting Opinion of Judge Fernandes

(continued)

[40] See, eg, *Asylum Case (Colombia v Peru)* [1950] ICJ Rep 266, 369 (Dissenting Opinion of Judge Caicedo Castilla).

[41] See, eg, *Nottebohm Case (Liechtenstein v Guatemala)* (Judgment, Second Phase) [1955] ICJ Rep 4, 57–58 (Dissenting Opinion of Judge ad hoc Guggenheim); *Certain Norwegian Loans* (n 4) 90 (Dissenting Opinion of Judge Read); *Right of Passage over Indian Territory (Portugal v India)* (Preliminary Objections) [1957] ICJ Rep 125, 162 (Dissenting Opinion of Vice-President Badawi), 165 (Dissenting Opinion of Judge Klaestad) (*Right of Passage* (Preliminary Objections)); *Fisheries Jurisdiction (United Kingdom v Iceland)* (Merits) (n 8) 100 (Separate Opinion of Judge De Castro); *South-West Africa (Ethiopia v South Africa; Liberia v South Africa)* (Preliminary Objections) [1962] ICJ Rep 319, 411 (Separate Opinion of Judge Jessup), 449 (Dissenting Opinion of President Winiarski) (*South West Africa* (Preliminary Objections); *Continental Shelf (Libyan Arab Jamahiriya v Malta)* (Application to Intervene) [1984] ICJ Rep 3, 139 (Dissenting Opinion of Judge Schwebel).

[42] See, eg, *Nuclear Tests (Australia v France)* [1974] ICJ Rep 253, 386 (Dissenting Opinion of Judge De Castro).

[43] See, eg, *Reparation for Injuries Suffered in the Service of the United Nations* (Advisory Opinion) [1949] ICJ Rep 174, 219 (Dissenting Opinion of Judge Krylov); though note Krylov maintains General Principles could found 'an affirmative reply' to a substantive international law question.

[44] For length purposes, short names of cases are used in this table. See footnotes for long names. Where the reference is to a Separate or Dissenting Opinion, this is noted. Where this is not noted, the reference is to the judgment of the ICJ itself.

Table 4.1 *(Continued)*

Preah Vihear, Separate Opinion of Vice-President Alfaro (1962)
South West Africa (Preliminary Objections), Dissenting Opinion of Judge Van Wyk (1962)
South-West Africa (1966)
Judgment of the Court
Separate Opinion of Judge Van Wyk
Dissenting Opinion of Judge Read
Dissenting Opinion of Judge Tanaka
Dissenting Opinion of Judge Jessup
North Sea Continental Shelf (1969)
Dissenting Opinion of Judge Tanaka
Separate Opinion of Judge Ammoun
Barcelona Traction (1970)
Judgment of the Court
Separate Opinion of Judge Ammoun
Legal Consequences for States, Separate Opinion of Judge Dillard (1971)
ICAO Council Appeal, Separate Opinion of Judge Dillard (1972)
Fisheries Jurisdiction (Order), Joint Dissenting Opinion of Judges Bengzon and Jimenez De Arechaga (1972)
Application for Review of Judgment No 158 (1973)
Judgment of the Court
Dissenting Opinion of Vice President Ammoun
Dissenting Opinion of Judge De Castro
Aegean Sea Continental Shelf Case, Separate Opinion of President Jimenez de Arechaga (1976)
Continental Shelf (Tunisia/Libyan Arab Jamahiriya), Dissenting Opinion of Judge Oda (1982)
Nicaragua (1986)
Judgment of the Court
Separate Opinion of President Singh
Dissenting Opinion of Judge Oda
Dissenting Opinion of Judge Schwebel
Elettronica Sicula, Separate Opinion of Judge Oda (1989)
UN Privileges and Immunities Convention, Separate Opinion of Judge Evensen (1989)

A. *Corfu Channel*

General Principles were relevant in the first case faced by the newly formed ICJ.[45] Although the reference to Article 38(1)(c) is not explicit, the approach the judgment takes to the source is fundamentally important. *Corfu Channel* is cited as acceptance of a General Principle relating to the admissibility of 'evidence by way of factual inference of circumstantial evidence',[46] as well as an example of concepts of justice and humanity applying at international law as General Principles.[47]

i. Circumstantial Evidence

The Court was considering whether Britain had proved that Albania knew about mine fields laid within Albanian territorial waters.[48] Although the fact that Albania had exclusive control over the waters was not enough to demonstrate prima facie that it knew about the mines,[49] this aspect of control did impact on what evidence Britain could gain to support its claim. In recognition of this position, the Court stated:

> By reason of this exclusive control, the other State, the victim of a breach of international law, is often unable to furnish direct proof of facts giving rise to responsibility. Such a State should be allowed a more liberal recourse to inferences of fact and circumstantial evidence. This indirect evidence is admitted in all systems of law, and its use is recognized by international decisions.[50]

No reference is made explicitly to Article 38(1)(c), or its words. Some publicists take the phrase 'admitted in all systems of law' as indicating this principle of international law is in fact a General Principle,[51] although others state that the Court found this rule as a customary norm of law,[52] or as 'accepted practice ...

[45] *Corfu Channel (United Kingdom of Great Britain and Northern Ireland v Albania)* (Merits) [1949] ICJ Rep 4 (*Corfu Channel*).

[46] FO Raimondo, *General Principles of Law in the Decisions of International Criminal Courts and Tribunals* (Brill, 2008) 28. See also M Shaw, *International Law*, 3rd edn (Grotius Publications, 1991) 84.

[47] U Fastenrath, 'Relative Normativity in International Law' in M Koskenniemi (ed), *Sources of International Law* (Routledge, 2000) 153, 176.

[48] *Corfu Channel* (n 45) 18.

[49] ibid.

[50] ibid.

[51] Raimondo, *General Principles of Law* (n 46) 28–29; G Triggs, *International Law: Contemporary Principles and Practices* (LexisNexis Butterworths, 2006) 88; H Lauterpacht, *The Development of International Law by the International Court* (Stevens and Sons, 1958) 168; B Cheng, *General Principles of Law as applied by International Courts and Tribunals* (Stevens and Sons, 1953) 322.

[52] M Bogdan, 'General Principles of Law and the Problem of Lacunae in the Law of Nations' (1977) 46 *Nordisk Tidsskrift for International Ret* 37, 45.

merely reinforced by the Court's reference to the fact that such evidence was "admitted in all systems of law"'.[53]

At the time of the decision, it was described as 'notable for the extent to which the Court relied upon broad principles of law, apparently deemed to be self-evident and stated without citation of precedent or authority'.[54] In this way, the ICJ continued the regrettable tendency of the PCIJ to state tenets of international law without context or justification.[55] If this is to be taken as a reference to a General Principle, however, it gives tentative support to a comparative methodology, drawing from domestic systems.

ii. General Principles and Natural Law

In discussing the obligation of the Albanian Government to warn others of the minefield, the Court stated:

> The obligations incumbent upon the Albanian authorities consisted in notifying, for the benefit of shipping in general, the existence of a minefield in Albanian territorial waters and in warning the approaching British warships of the imminent danger to which the minefield exposed them. Such obligations are based, not on the Hague Convention of 1907, No VTII, which is applicable in time of war, but on certain general and well-recognized principles, namely: elementary considerations of humanity, even more exacting in peace than in war …[56]

It should first be noted that there is no specific reference to Article 38(1)(c) or its exact wording, but the excerpt has nonetheless been taken to refer to it.[57] '[G]eneral and well-recognized principles' does seem close to the wording of the source – enough, this book argues, to consider this an application of General Principles. The notion of 'elementary considerations of humanity' must be considerations that obtain their validity through their content rather than some objectively ascertainable process; thus tending towards natural law jurisprudential legitimacy.

iii. A Dual Approach to General Principles?

If we take both excerpts from *Corfu Channel* as referring to General Principles, we see that they are, in fact, two different manifestations of the source. The first, indirect evidence, is based on a comparative methodology, looking to domestic

[53] G Schwarzenberger, *International Law as Applied by International Courts and Tribunals*, 3rd edn (Stevens and Sons, 1957) 48.

[54] Q Wright, 'The Corfu Channel Case' (1949) 43(3) *American Journal of International Law* 491, 494.

[55] See ch 3.

[56] *Corfu Channel* (n 45) 22.

[57] Fastenrath, 'Relative Normativity in International Law' (n 47) 176.

forums, but tempered by international acceptance. The second, the elementary considerations of humanity, does not reveal any specific methodology but rather seem to gain validity from its inherent subject matter. Further, the use of the term 'elementary' suggests these General Principles would tend towards true principles: abstract, rather than detailed, and fundamental.

B. *International Status of South West Africa*

Judge McNair considered the role of General Principles in his Separate Opinion to the Advisory Opinion given by the Court in this case.[58] McNair was considering the Mandate over South West Africa, and whether private (municipal) law analogies concerning mandates and trusteeships generally could be used in the context of an international agreement.[59] To this end, McNair stated:

> To what extent is it useful or necessary to examine what may at first sight appear to be relevant analogies in private law systems and draw help and inspiration from them? International law has recruited and continues to recruit many of its rules and institutions from private systems of law. Article 38(1)(c) of the Statute of the Court bears witness that this process is still active, and it will be noted that this article authorizes the Court to 'apply … (c) the general principles of law recognized by civilized nations'. The way in which international law borrows from this source is not by means of importing private law institutions 'lock, stock and barrel', ready-made and fully equipped with a set of rules. It would be difficult to reconcile such a process with the application of 'the general principles of law'.[60]

It is clear that McNair saw the laws that inform General Principles as coming from municipal systems. However, he added a caveat to this, that laws must not be imported 'lock, stock and barrel'. McNair argued that Courts should view municipal laws in this sense as 'as an indication of policy and principles rather than as directly importing these rules and institutions'.[61] Here we have the principle of *appropriateness*. Judicial discretion is employed, to ensure that municipal laws are suitable for – or can be transformed to be suitable for – application on the international plane.

McNair considered General Principles relating to trusteeship, stating:

> Nearly every legal system possesses some institution whereby the property (and sometimes the persons) of those who are not *sui juris*, such as a minor or a lunatic, can be entrusted to some responsible person as a trustee or *tuteur* or *curateur*.[62]

[58] *International Status of South-West Africa* (Advisory Opinion) [1950] ICJ Rep 128 (*International Status of South-West Africa*) 146 (Separate Opinion of Judge McNair).

[59] ibid 148.

[60] ibid.

[61] ibid.

[62] ibid 149.

This suggests a comparative approach to finding General Principles, finding principles common to 'nearly every legal system'. However, it must be noted that the actual comparative study demonstrated in McNair's Opinion is more limited, looking to French, American, English, South African and Australian jurisprudence.[63] Nonetheless, the *methodology* of the source is clear. Further, the *type* of General Principle is a substantive norm of law, rather than procedural.

C. *Fisheries Case*

This case[64] concerned a maritime delimitation disputed between the UK and Norway. In an Individual Opinion, Judge Alvarez discussed General Principles, stating:

> In accordance with uniformly accepted doctrine, international judicial tribunals must, in the absence of principles provided by conventions, or of customary principles on a given question, apply the general principles of law. This doctrine is expressly confirmed in Article 38 of the Statute of the Court.[65]

Alvarez is thus using General Principles to fill a lacuna, resorting to them only when treaty and custom are silent. Alvarez continued in his analysis to argue that the Court was not limited to 'general principles of law recognized by civilized nations'[66] and argued for judicial law making: 'if no principles exist covering a given question, principles must be created to conform to those conditions'.[67] It is unclear from here whether Alvarez intends such law making to be pursuant to Article 38(1)(c) or rather authorised by some other means. References to 'new international law' suggest that it is the latter: a conclusion borne out by reading the Opinion in light of Alvarez's other ICJ opinions.[68] Of interest for this book, however, Alvarez linked his new principles of international law to the 'legal conscience of peoples',[69] arguing that doing so made such principles inherently flexible and evolutionary:

> As a result of the present dynamic character of the life of peoples, the principles of the law of nations are continually being created, and they undergo more or less rapid modification as a result of the great changes occurring in that life.[70]

[63] ibid 148–52.

[64] *Fisheries Case (United Kingdom v Norway)* [1951] ICJ Rep 116 (*Fisheries Case*).

[65] ibid 147 (Individual Opinion of Judge Alvarez).

[66] ibid.

[67] ibid 148.

[68] See M Koskenniemi, *From Apology to Utopia: The Structure of International Legal Argument* (Cambridge University Press, 2005) 212–14.

[69] *Fisheries Case* (n 64) 148 (Individual Opinion of Judge Alvarez).

[70] ibid.

This wording is very similar to natural law conceptions of General Principles. However, Alvarez qualified this description by requiring a more positivist expression of such legal conscience: 'For the principles of law resulting from the juridical conscience of peoples to have any value, they must have a tangible manifestation, that is to say, they must be expressed by authorized bodies.'[71] The tangible manifestation includes, in Alvarez's view, treaty, custom, UN General Assembly resolutions, ICJ decisions, resolutions of international law associations, works of codification commissions, opinions of qualified jurists and 'recent legislation of certain countries'[72] – allowing General Principles to be founded on domestic and international sources.

D. *Anglo-Iranian Oil*

The question at the preliminary objection stage of this case[73] was a construction of Article 36 of the Statute of the ICJ. General Principles were not relied on by the Court but were mentioned in passing in the Dissenting Opinion of Judge Carneiro.[74] Judge Carneiro was discussing the process of naturalisation at international law, and introduced municipal laws of Brazil to illustrate his argument.[75] He justified doing so in terms of General Principles:

> It is inevitable that every-one of us in this Court should retain some trace of his legal education and his former legal activities in his country of origin. This is inevitable, and even justified, because in its composition the Court is to be representative of 'the main forms of civilization and of the principal legal systems of the world', and the Court is to apply 'the general principles of law recognized by civilized nations'.[76]

Judge Carneiro's use of municipal law suggests he viewed General Principles as general principles of municipal law, which can be distilled and transformed into norms of international law. This could arguably support a comparative methodology – although it would be a small and selective comparative study, based on the legal origins of the judges. In linking General Principles with the judicial make-up of the Court, Judge Carneiro revisited an idea raised in the drafting of the Draft Court of Arbitral Justice Convention in 1907.[77]

[71] ibid.
[72] ibid 149.
[73] *Anglo-Iranian Oil Company (United Kingdom v Iran)* (Preliminary Objection) [1952] ICJ 93 (*Anglo-Iranian Oil*).
[74] ibid 151, 161 (Dissenting Opinion of Judge Carneiro).
[75] ibid.
[76] ibid.
[77] See further discussion in ch 7.

E. *Effect of Awards of Compensation*

In this case,[78] the ICJ was asked in its advisory jurisdiction whether the UN General Assembly was bound by awards of the UN Administrative Tribunal. It is cited as an example of the Court's applying the General Principle that 'a judgment passed by a judicial body is *res judicata* and binding upon the parties to the dispute'.[79]

The Court recognised the principle as '[a]ccording to a well-established and generally recognized principle of law'.[80] The wording here is similar to that in *Corfu Channel*, decided five years earlier. Further, *res judicata* was one of the examples given of Article 38(1)(c) by the Advisory Committee of Jurists.[81] Taken together, it seems the Court was referring to a General Principle: however, there are no further indications given on the nature of the source.

F. *Voting Procedure*

In this Advisory Opinion,[82] the ICJ was asked by the UN General Assembly whether its interpretation of the earlier *South-West Africa* case was correct.[83] This is the first of four cases where Judge Lauterpacht brought up General Principles. Lauterpacht also wrote on the source in his extra-curial capacity.[84] In this case, Lauterpacht categorised the principles of good faith and that no one shall be a judge in their own case as General Principles – but with no substantiation or elaboration as to why.[85] The principles in question are, and were at the time, well-established in international law,[86] which perhaps explains the reliance on them without further elaboration. Given this, the only thing that can be deduced is the *type* in this case were true principles rather than detailed rules.

[78] *Effect of Awards of Compensation Made by the United Nations Administrative Tribunal* (Advisory Opinion) [1954] ICJ Rep 47 (*Effect of Awards of Compensation*).

[79] Raimondo, *General Principles of Law* (n 46) 29; Shaw, *International Law* (n 46) 86; Lauterpacht, *The Development of International Law* (n 51) 168.

[80] *Effect of Awards of Compensation* (n 78) 53.

[81] Permanent Court of International Justice: Advisory Committee of Jurists, *Procès-verbaux of the Proceedings of the Committee* (Van Langenhuysen Brothers, 1920), 15th Meeting, 331.

[82] *Voting Procedure* (n 4).

[83] ibid 69.

[84] See, eg, H Lauterpacht, *Private Law Sources and Analogies of International Law* (Longmans, Green and Co, 1927); H Lauterpacht, 'Some Observations on the Prohibition of Non Liquet and the Completeness of the Legal Order' in JHW Verzijl (ed), *Symbolae Verzijl: Présentées au Professeur JHW Verzijl, à l'occasion de son Lxx-ieme anniversaire* (Martinus Nijhoff, 1958) 196.

[85] *Voting Procedure* (n 4) 101–02, 105 (Separate Opinion of Judge Lauterpacht).

[86] See, eg, *Article 3, Paragraph 2, of the Treaty of Lausanne (Frontier between Turkey and Iraq)* (Advisory Opinion) [1925] PCIJ Series B No 12, 67; *Lighthouses Case (France v Greece)* (Merits) [1934] PCIJ Series A/B No 62, 47 (Separate Opinion of Judge Séfériadès).

G. *Certain Norwegian Loans*

A dispute between France and Norway was brought to the Court under Article 36 of the ICJ Statute.[87] The French Government argued that the ICJ did not have jurisdiction by virtue of a reservation made by France on acceptance of Article 36.[88] The reservation allowed France to determine for itself, after a dispute had been brought before the Court pursuant to Article 36, whether the ICJ did in fact have jurisdiction. The effect of the reservation was that France did not accept compulsory jurisdiction until it had agreed in each individual circumstance to do so.[89] The only mention of General Principles in this case was in the Separate Opinion of Judge Lauterpacht,[90] in which they were addressed in much more detail than in the *Voting Procedure* case.

Lauterpacht considered the reservation by France invalid, arguing that it deprived the Court of the right to determine its own jurisdiction (instead giving it to France), and thus forced the Court to act 'in disregard with its own Statute'.[91] In considering a reservation that is 'contrary to the provisions of the Statute of the Court',[92] Lauterpacht used several analogies, one of which mentioned General Principle:

> What would be the position if the Declaration were to make it a condition that … contrary to what is said in Article 38 of its Statute, the Court shall apply only treaties and custom in the sense that it shall not be authorized to apply general principles of law as recognized by civilized States and that if it is unable to base its decision on treaty or custom it shall pronounce a *non liquet*?[93]

Lauterpacht saw General Principles as an alternative, distinct and binding source of international law to custom and treaty, able to fill spaces where neither applied. This judgment must not be read in isolation but against the context of Lauterpacht's earlier extra-curial writing. Lauterpacht had expressed the view that the jurisprudence of General Principles was natural law, and argued it was this natural law quality that meant that General Principles could fill the *lacunae*.[94] Accordingly, the statement quoted is consistent with this natural law understanding of Article 38(1)(c).

Lauterpacht also considered a specific General Principle, discussing whether the reservation was binding in itself (separate from whether it was valid under the ICJ Statute). He held it was not, stating that the principle that 'an undertaking in which the applicant party reserves for itself the exclusive right

[87] *Certain Norwegian Loans* (n 4).
[88] ibid 21.
[89] ibid 44 (Separate Opinion of Judge Lauterpacht).
[90] ibid 34.
[91] ibid 43.
[92] ibid 44.
[93] ibid 45.
[94] Lauterpacht, 'Some Observations' (n 84) 196.

to determine the extent or the very existence of its obligation is not a legal undertaking'[95] was 'self-evident as a matter of juridical principle'[96] and was also a General Principle:

> It is a general principle of law as it results from the legislation and practice of courts in various countries in the matter of contracts and other legal instruments ... Reference may be made here to the position in French law ... It is not desirable to prolong this Opinion by an examination of the English law and of the law of the United States of America on the question.[97]

Although Lauterpacht chose not to expand on the background for the principle, it is clear that he looked to municipal legal systems, employing a comparativist approach, as the basis for its existence as a General Principle. Further, it is also clear that Lauterpacht viewed General Principles as something other than those self-evident juridical principles (or, borrowing language from Judge Weeramantry 40 years later, those principles of 'inescapable logical necessity').[98]

Having found that the French reservation was invalid and non-binding,[99] Lauterpacht then considered what effect that had on the general acceptance of the Court's jurisdiction by France. Lauterpacht considered there were two possible alternatives available – either treating only that part of the reservation invalid but holding wider acceptance of jurisdiction valid, or finding that the entire acceptance was 'tainted with invalidity'.[100]

In discussing the first alternative, Lauterpacht considered the severance of the invalid part of the reservation, and whether a treaty is indivisible or rather whether some provisions may be non-essential and therefore able to be severed.[101] In doing so, Lauterpacht turned again to a General Principle:

> International practice on the subject is not sufficiently abundant to permit a confident attempt at generalization and some help may justifiably be sought in applicable general principles of law as developed in municipal law.[102]

Although Lauterpacht does not expand on this General Principle, we can conclude that the source of General Principle is certainly from domestic systems. While the methodology is not made clear, it would seem consistent with this extract and the earlier use of General Principles, discussed previously, that Lauterpacht would favour a comparative law approach of the various municipal

[95] *Certain Norwegian Loans* (n 4) 44, 49 (Separate Opinion of Judge Lauterpacht).
[96] ibid.
[97] ibid 49–50.
[98] *Gabčíkovo-Nagymaros Project (Hungary v Slovakia)* (Merits) [1997] ICJ Rep 7, 95 (Separate Opinion of Judge Weeramantry), see discussion in ch 5.
[99] *Certain Norwegian Loans* (n 4) 55 (Separate Opinion of Judge Lauterpacht).
[100] ibid.
[101] ibid 56.
[102] ibid.

systems to ascertain the General Principle, although understanding the source to be from a natural law background.

H. *Right of Passage* (Preliminary Objections)

In *Right of Passage* (Preliminary Objections),[103] Portugal based its argument on customary international law and General Principles. In his Dissenting Opinion, Judge Chagla briefly considered the substance of Portugal's claim in light of one of India's preliminary objections. He used the term 'principle of international law' to refer to, first, regional custom and, second, what seems to be a General Principle:

> A principle of international law may also be imported from municipal law where the principle in municipal law is universally recognized and when that principle is not in conflict with any rule of international law itself; and the strongest reliance is placed by Portugal on the principle of municipal law which may be described as an easement of necessity.[104]

The methodology draws from the domestic forum, requiring 'universal' recognition. Chagla further requires appropriateness, arguing the analogy from municipal law to international in this case is 'unsafe' as 'there can be no comparison between private property and territorial sovereignty nor can there be any comparison between a citizen and a sovereign State'.[105]

The *function* of the source set out here is subsidiary, in the sense it is unable to contest any existing rule of custom or treaty.

I. *Guardianship of Infants*

This case[106] concerned a Swedish child protection order over a child of Netherlands nationality living in Sweden. A question arose as to whether a 1902 treaty between Sweden and the Netherlands governed the situation.

i. Judge Lauterpacht

A year after his decision in *Certain Norwegian Loans*, Judge Lauterpacht revisited the question of General Principles in his Separate Opinion in this case. Lauterpacht considered whether the concept of 'public policy' or '*ordre public*' could be considered a General Principle, and reaffirmed the use of a comparative

[103] *Right of Passage* (Preliminary Objections) (n 41).
[104] ibid 177 (Dissenting Opinion of Judge Chagla).
[105] ibid 178.
[106] *Guardianship of Infants* (n 4).

methodology based on the domestic forum. Lauterpacht held that the concept was 'the same in most countries', and that the exact nature of the principle could be evinced 'by reference to the practice and experience of the municipal law of civilised nations'.[107] Unfortunately, the comparative study seems to be assumed in this case, as no reference to any particular domestic law or legal system is made.

ii. Judge Quintana

Ordre public was also considered a General Principle by Judge Quintana, who described the source as one that the ICJ is 'required to apply as a main source of law'.[108] Quintana implicitly suggests a comparative methodology, drawing from decisions of national courts.[109]

Quintana elevates General Principles by reason of their inclusion in Article 38 of the ICJ Statute:

> This means that the application of these principles is the subject of an international undertaking by all Members of the United Nations and by those States which have adhered to the Statute of the Court. *Jus posteriori derogat priori* says the well-known Roman maxim in accordance with which Article 103 of the Charter of the United Nations prescribed that, in the event of a conflict between the obligations imposed on Member-States by the Charter and obligations arising from any other international agreement, it is the former obligations that shall prevail. The national *ordre public* of Sweden consequently prevails over the provisions of the 1902 Convention which governs the guardianship of infants as between that country and the Netherlands.[110]

This slightly tortuous reasoning cannot hold up: for if General Principles are elevated in this way, so must be treaties by virtue of Article 38(1)(a), which would include the 1902 Convention in question.

J. *Interhandel*

In this case,[111] Lauterpacht returned to the issue of reservations to Article 36 declarations accepting the jurisdiction of the ICJ. The United States' Article 36 declaration contained a reservation excluding matters 'essentially within the domestic jurisdiction of the United States of America as determined by the United States of America' from the jurisdiction of the ICJ.[112] While the Court

[107] ibid 92 (Separate Opinion of Judge Lauterpacht).
[108] ibid 107 (Separate Opinion of Judge Quintana).
[109] ibid.
[110] ibid.
[111] *Interhandel* (n 4).
[112] ibid 91 (Dissenting Opinion of Judge Armand-Ugon).

upheld the US objection to jurisdiction on the basis of non-exhaustion of local remedies by Switzerland,[113] Judge Lauterpacht argued that the United States had never validly accepted ICJ jurisdiction due to the self-judging reservation.[114] In doing so he referred back to his judgment in *Certain Norwegian Loans* to explain why the US acceptance of jurisdiction must fail for the invalid reservation:

> In the case concerning Certain Norwegian Loans I gave reasons in my Separate Opinion – which must be read as forming part of the present Opinion – why that question must be answered in the negative. These reasons included the general principle of law governing the subject, namely, the principle that a condition which, having regard to the intention of the party making it, is essential to and goes to the roots of the main obligation, cannot be separated from it. This is not a mere refinement of private law, or of any municipal system thereof, but – as all general principles of law – a maxim based on common sense and equity. A party cannot be held to be bound by an obligation divested of a condition without which that obligation would never have been undertaken.[115]

This passage is based on the reason *for* horizontal generality (ie the commonality between municipal legal systems). It offers the reason for such inclusion being the content of the maxim itself, being based on 'common sense and equity'. This natural law approach is tempered by the comparative methodology adopted by Lauterpacht in *Certain Norwegian Loans*, the reasoning of which he explicitly incorporates into this Opinion in *Interhandel*. Thus, the rule of recognition remains positivist, but the *reason* the maxim can satisfy the rule is based on its content.

K. *Right of Passage* (Merits)

This case[116] concerned the Portuguese colonies of Goa, Daman and Diu, which were situated bordering (and in some case wholly surrounded by) India.[117] Portugal asserted certain rights of passage over Indian Territory to and from its colonies.[118] General Principles are discussed in the Judgment of the Court, as well as in the Dissenting Opinion of Judge Quintana, the Separate Opinion of Judge Koo and the Dissenting Opinion of Judge Fernandes.

[113] ibid 30.
[114] ibid 101 (Dissenting Opinion of Judge Lauterpacht).
[115] ibid 116–17.
[116] *Right of Passage over Indian Territory (Portugal v India)* (Merits) [1960] ICJ Rep 6 (*Right of Passage* (Merits)).
[117] ibid 27.
[118] ibid.

i. Judgment of the Court

The judgment of the Court is used as an example by Pellet and Müller of where the court 'will decline to invoke [general principles] when … other rules exist'.[119] The ICJ concluded that a right of passage did exist in favour of Portugal as a principle of local custom[120] due to established practice between India and Portugal,[121] but stated that, having found a local rule of custom, it would not consider whether such a right would also exist as a general norm of custom or a General Principle:

> Portugal also invokes general international custom, as well as the general principles of law recognized by civilized nations, in support of its claim of a right of passage as formulated by it. Having arrived at the conclusion that the course of dealings between the British and Indian authorities on the one hand and the Portuguese on the other established a practice, well understood between the Parties, by virtue of which Portugal had acquired a right of passage in respect of private persons, civil officials and goods in general, the Court does not consider it necessary to examine whether general international custom or the general principles of law recognized by civilized nations may lead to the same result.[122]

Portugal had presented comparative law research covering 64 national legal systems to the Court in support of its argument of a General Principle.[123] The Court was presented with an opportunity to find a General Principle by comparative methodology drawing from municipal laws (*in foro domestico*) and chose not to do so. This has been pointed to as evidence of the 'subsidiary nature of general principles as a source of international law'.[124]

It can be argued on the contrary that the judgment is simply an application of the general maxim that a specific rule trumps a general rule of law.[125] As much as the Court refused to look to General Principles, it also refused to examine a general, rather than regional, customary norm[126] – to the extent that the judgment shows Article 38(1)(c) is subsidiary, the same argument must be extended to custom. When refusing to consider the rule further, however, the Court grouped General Principles and custom together, rendering the distinction between the sources unclear. It also provides no information as to how a

[119] A Pellet and D Müller, 'Article 38' in A Zimmerman, CJ Tams, K Oellers-Frahm and C Tomuschat (eds), *The Statute of the International Court of Justice: A Commentary*, 3rd edn (Oxford University Press, 2019) 819, 928.
[120] *Right of Passage* (Merits) (n 116) 39.
[121] ibid 40.
[122] ibid 43.
[123] H Thirlway, 'The Law and Procedure of the International Court of Justice 1960–1989' (1989) 60(1) *British Yearbook of International Law* 1, 120; Raimondo, *General Principles of Law* (n 46) 30; Pellet and Müller, 'Article 38' (n 119) 928.
[124] Raimondo, *General Principles of Law* (n 46) 30.
[125] ibid.
[126] The same is true for the Dissenting Opinion of Judge Armand-Ugon: *Right of Passage* (Merits) (n 116) 84.

General Principle could be found, despite the clear comparative methodology adopted by Portugal.

ii. Judge Quintana

Like the Court, Quintana veered away from applying General Principles:

> This method of procedure may be found useful whenever it can save the Court from treading upon uncertain ground. I consider to be uncertain ground the reference in this case to the general principles of law recognized by civilized nations ...[127]

Although Judge Quintana did not wish to apply General Principles, some information can be ascertained from his remarks. He continued:

> This method also avoids consideration of a theory so controversial and vulnerable as the theory of so-called international servitudes. Although the applicant denies this – the question is one of legal terminology – it accepts it by implication when it appeals in support of its claim to the general principles of law.[128]

International servitude alleges an international norm 'by analogy to the civil law institution of servitude, in its substance similar to the common-law institution of easement'.[129] Thus although Quintana felt the principle alleged to be vulnerable, he also considered a reference to 'general principles of law' under Article 38(1)(c) as necessarily being to a principle of domestic legal systems incorporated into international law.

Judge Quintana's reluctance to embrace General Principles in this instance may be explained by the doctrine itself – its being 'so controversial and vulnerable' that the judge did not want to find that such a principle could exist at international law.

iii. Judge Koo

While Judge Koo agreed with the Court that a right of passage was established, he did not agree with the Court's limitation of that passage to civilian people and goods: 'I regret to be unable to concur in excluding from the scope or content of this right the passage of Portuguese armed forces, armed police and arms and ammunition.'[130]

Judge Koo characterised the passage of troops, armed police, arms and ammunition as 'indispensable to the exercise of Portuguese sovereignty'[131] over

[127] *Right of Passage* (Merits) (n 116) 90 (Separate Opinion of Judge Quintana).
[128] ibid.
[129] BA Boczek, *International Law: A Dictionary* (Scarecrow Press, 2005) 247.
[130] *Right of Passage* (Merits) (n 116) 54 (Separate Opinion of Judge Koo).
[131] ibid 66.

the enclaves, and then went on to consider the competing rights between this exercise of Portuguese sovereignty and the exercise of Indian sovereignty over its land:

> The existence of two conflicting rights, however, is not an uncommon phenomenon in international law. In the complexities of intercourse between nations such a situation is often unavoidable. It is, however, not an intractable problem; its solution only calls for mutual adaptation and adjustment. By reference to, and application of, the general principles of law as stipulated in Article 38,1, (c) [sic] of the Statute, as well as to customary international law, similar situations have found solutions in the past.[132]

Judge Koo then referred to a comparative study of municipal law concerning the right of access to enclaved property: 'In municipal law, as disclosed by a comparative study by Professor Max Rheinstein, the right of access to enclaved property is always sanctioned.'[133] It appears that Judge Koo was applying comparative methodology to find a General Principle. Koo expanded on the point:

> Admittedly, there are important distinctions between a right of passage of an international enclave and that of an enclaved land owned by a private individual. But in whatever mould municipal law may be cast, in whatever technical framework it may be installed, in harmony with national tradition or out of preference for a particular legal fiction, the underlying principle of recognition of such a right, in its essence, is the same. It is the principle of justice founded on reason.[134]

The first part of this extract addresses the issue of *appropriateness* – the applicability of municipal law to international law – the issue that prompted Judge McNair to warn against 'importing private law institutions "lock, stock and barrel"'.[135]

The second part suggests, in line with Lauterpacht's earlier judgments, that although General Principles require positivist expression in municipal laws, the *reason* for such horizontal generality lies in the qualities of the norm itself – justice founded on reason. This, however, cannot be determined definitively, as in the next paragraph Judge Koo expands on the justice and reason of the principle but concludes that this is why it is *customary* international law:

> Indeed, in the last analysis, the fact that an enclaved land in municipal law and an enclaved territory in the international domain has always been able to enjoy passage through the surrounding land of another owner or the surrounding territory of another State, is based upon reason and the elementary principle of justice. For such land or territory this transit is a necessity and it is reasonable to provide for this necessity both in municipal law and in customary international law. As the great Dutch jurisconsult, Cornelius van Bynkershoek, has so well said: 'In the law of nations,

[132] ibid.
[133] ibid 66.
[134] ibid 66–67.
[135] *International Status of South-West Africa* (n 58) 146 (Separate Opinion of Judge McNair).

> reason is sovereign …' It is reason which dictates the recognition of a rule of international customary law in application of the principle of justice.[136]

Unfortunately, while this judgment does provide some guidance to the nature and methodology of Article 38(1)(c), this is clouded by the ultimate collation of General Principles with customary international law.

iv. Judge Fernandes

In his Dissenting Opinion,[137] Judge Fernandes disagreed with the Court that local custom in itself was sufficient to settle the case,[138] and so addressed the arguments made by Portugal in regard to General Principles.[139] Fernandes distinguished between two types of General Principles as asserted by Portugal:

> As general principles of law, Portugal invoked two kinds of principle:
>
> a) the principle deriving from a comparison of the municipal laws of civilised nations in the matter of right of access to enclaved property;
>
> b) certain fundamental principles inherent in the very fabric of international law.[140]

With regard to the first principle, Judge Fernandes noted a comparative study filed with the Court showing that 'the laws of all civilized nations recognize the right of access to enclaved property in favour of its owner'.[141] While this would appear to be a straightforward comparative approach to finding General Principles, Fernandes went on to consider what would transform municipal content to the international arena:

> No sort of analogy needs to be drawn between ownership and sovereignty, nor is it necessary to transfer a rule of municipal law to the field of international law. What has to be determined is whether there is not a reason deeply rooted in the legal consciousness of all peoples for admitting, as a logical and practical necessity, the recognition of a right of passage …[142]

Thus the approach in this first instance is finding a principle that is not only present, on a comparative study, in 'the laws of all civilised nations',[143] but also present within the 'legal consciousness of all peoples',[144] which will then become a General Principle. Judge Fernandes found the right of access to enclaved property to be such a principle, stating '[i]f that is not a general principle of law,

[136] *Right of Passage* (Merits) (n 116) 67 (Separate Opinion of Judge Koo).
[137] ibid 123 (Dissenting Opinion of Judge Fernandes).
[138] ibid 153.
[139] ibid 136–40.
[140] Ibid 136.
[141] ibid 179, 136.
[142] ibid 136.
[143] ibid.
[144] ibid.

valid alike in municipal and international law, within the meaning of Article 38 of the Statute of the Court, then no principle will meet the conditions of that Article'.[145] For this first category of General Principles we have two, perhaps competing forms of methodology – one that requires a comparativist approach to the incorporation of general principles within municipal legal systems, and one that looks to the nature of the principle, to ascertain whether it is present in the legal consciousness of peoples. This seems more than the appropriateness required by McNair, and instead harks back to Descamps' original formulation of the source.[146]

The second category of principles discussed by Judge Fernandes conceives of General Principles as juridical truths,[147] or fundamental ordered norms.[148] Although Fernandes described these principles as General Principles in the paragraph set out above, the following discussion indicates less clarity in regard to the exact categorisation:

> Whatever view may be held in regard to these principles, whether they are considered to be emanations of natural law or to be rules of custom, or constitutional principles of the international legal community, or principles directly deduced from the concept of law, or principles agreed to by States because they are members of a legal family, whatever, I say, may be the attitude towards the origin and basis of these principles, all are agreed in accepting their existence and their application as a source of positive law.[149]

Judge Fernandes then referred to these principles in discussion not as General Principles but as 'essential principles',[150] and then later to good faith as 'the most general and the most essential of the general principles of law'.[151] While the quotation excerpted in the paragraph above may seem to indicate that Judge Fernandes is not referencing General Principles in the sense of Article 38(1)(c), Fernandes turned to two publicists to support his approach, both of whom explicitly refer to General Principles as a source of law:

> 'The general principles of law are at the basis of custom and of conventional law. The latter are usually no more than the crystallization of those principles. The concrete rules cannot be to conflict with the principles of which they constitute the application.' (Verdross, *Derecho Internacional Publico* pp 205–206.)

[145] ibid 136.
[146] Permanent Court of International Justice: Advisory Committee of Jurists (n 82), 13th Meeting, 306; see ch 2.
[147] Cheng, *General Principles of Law* (n 51) 24.
[148] G Christenson, 'Jus Cogens: Guarding Interests Fundamental to International Society' (1988) 28 *Virginia Journal of International Law* 585, 587.
[149] *Right of Passage* (Merits) (n 116) 136–37 (Dissenting Opinion of Judge Fernandes).
[150] ibid 137.
[151] ibid 139.

> 'The priority given by Article 38 of the Statute of the Court to conventions and custom in relation to the general principles of law in no way excludes a simultaneous application of those principles and the first two sources of law. It frequently happens that a decision given on the basis of a particular or general convention or of a custom requires recourse to the general principles of law ... A court will have recourse to those principles to fill gaps in the conventional rules or to *interpret* them.' (De Visscher in *Rev de Dr int et de Leg compare* 1933, p 413).
>
> These authorities whom I have just cited strengthen me in my opinion that it was really necessary to have recourse to the general principles, at least for the purpose of properly interpreting the practice established between the Parties.[152]

The reference to these authorities confirms that Judge Fernandes' 'essential principles', and the second category of principles, were being treated as General Principles. The use of these two authorities is interesting in itself, however: on one side, Verdross approaches General Principles as fundamental, able to overturn their crystallised form, be that through treaty or custom. On the other, De Visscher takes an approach that the General Principles are not quite subsidiary to custom and convention but gap-filling and interpretative, rather than fundamental and pre-emptory. The extract from Verdross conceives of General Principles as true principles, while custom and treaty are the concrete rules, the expressions of the principles.

In relation to the judgment at hand, we can say that Judge Fernandes accepted a category of General Principles that was based on the content of those principles, without reference to either the laws of nations or the conscience of peoples (as was required for the first category), although it is unclear whether he viewed these General Principles as superior to, subsidiary to, or equal to the other sources of international law. Some help may be found in an earlier statement in his Opinion, 'the general principles to which I shall refer later constitute true rules of *ius cogens*, over which no special practice can prevail'.[153] If Judge Fernandes did view this second category of General Principles as *jus cogens* norms, then they are clearly superior norms of international law.

We thus have a dual conception of General Principles: on the one hand found through a comparative methodology looking to domestic laws (though tempered by a natural law requirement of validity through the legal consciousness of peoples); on the other, true pre-emptory principles, fundamental and foundational. The rule of recognition for this second category is unclear, but validity may be linked to content. This is similar to the duality evident in the Court's decision in *Corfu Channel*.

[152] ibid 140 citing A Verdross, *Derecho internacional público* (Aguilar, 1957); C de Visscher 'Contribution à l'étude des sources du droit international' (1933) 3 *Revue De Droit International Et De Législation Comparée* 395.

[153] *Right of Passage* (Merits) (n 116) 135 (Dissenting Opinion of Judge Fernandes).

L. *Preah Vihear*

In his Separate Opinion in *Preah Vihear*,[154] Judge Alfaro considered a doctrine of international law that 'a State party to an international litigation is bound by its previous acts or attitude when they are in contradiction with its claims in the litigation'.[155] This doctrine encompasses the more specific doctrine of *allegans contraria non audiendus est*, as well as other forms of estoppel.[156]

In discussing the doctrine, Alfaro did not consider whether the doctrine is part of customary law but stated that it is a General Principle:

> While refraining from discussing the question whether the principle of the binding effect of a State's own acts with regard to rights in dispute with another State is or is not part of customary international law, I have no hesitation in asserting that this principle, known to the world since the days of the Romans, is one of the 'general principles of law recognized by civilized nations' applicable and in fact frequently applied by the International Court of Justice in conformity with Article 38, para I(c) of its Statute.[157]

The Opinion provides a list of cases 'in which the International Court of Justice, the Permanent Court of International Justice or arbitration tribunals have applied or recognized the principle above discussed' as evidence for this view.[158] Of the 23 cases cited by Alfaro,[159] most refer to the principle in question without regard to what source of law created it, or discussion of how the norm was formed – rather the assumption seems to be that the principle is binding at

[154] *Temple of Preah Vihear (Cambodia v Thailand)* (Merits) [1962] ICJ Rep 6 (*Preah Vihear*).
[155] ibid 39 (Separate Opinion of Vice-President Alfaro).
[156] ibid 39–40.
[157] ibid 42–43.
[158] ibid 43.
[159] ibid 43–51. The cases are: *Jurisdiction of the European Commission of the Danube* [1927] PCIJ Series B No 14; *Legal Status of Eastern Greenland (Denmark v Norway)* (Merits) [1933] PCIJ Series A/B No 53; *Payment of Various Serbian Loans Issued in France (France v Kingdom of the Serbs, Croats and Slovenes)* [1929] PCIJ Series A Nos 20–21; *Shufeldt Claim (United States v Guatemala)* (1930) 2 RIAA 1079; *Pious Funds Case (United States v Mexico)* (1902) 9 RIAA 1; *Grisbadarna Case (Norway v Sweden)* (1909) 11 RIAA 155; *Minquiers and Ecrehos (France v United Kingdom)* (Oral Proceedings) [1953] ICJ Rep 10; *Yukon Lumber (Great Britain v United States)* (1913) 6 RIAA 17; *United States v Netherlands (Island of Palmas (or Miangas))* (1928) 2 RIAA 829; *Venezuelan Preferential Case (Germany, Great Britain, Italy, Venezuela et al)* (1904) 9 RIAA 107; *Anglo-Norwegian Fisheries (United Kingdom v Norway)* (Merits) [1951] ICJ Rep 116; *SS 'Lotus' (France and Turkey)* (Merits) [1927] PCIJ Series A No 10; *Russian Indemnity Case* (1912), text contained in G Gregory, 'Judicial Decisions Involving Questions of International Law' (1913) 7(1) *American Journal of International Law* 178; *Landreau Claim (USA v Peru)* (1922) 1 RIAA 347; *The Schooner Mechanic* (1862) 29 RIAA 108; *The SS Lisman (United States v Great Britain)* (1937) 3 RIAA 1767; *Salvador Commercial Co* (1902) 15 RIAA 467; *Factory at Chorzów (Claim for Indemnity) (Germany v Poland)* (Jurisdiction) [1927] PCIJ Series A No 9 (*Chorzów Factory* (Jurisdiction)); *Diversion of Water from the Meuse (Netherlands v Belgium)* (Merits) [1925] PCIJ Series A/B No 70; *Behring Sea Arbitration (United States of America v United Kingdom)* (1893) 28 RIAA 263; *Life-Insurance Claims (United States of America v Germany)* (1924) 7 RIAA 91.

international law and further discussion is unnecessary.[160] Some decisions are made pursuant to 'whatever judgment might be found just and equitable' – arguably not an application of international law rules.[161] One decision of the Hague Court of Arbitration refers explicitly to general principles,[162] but conflated them with custom.[163] Both *Chorzów Factory* (Jurisdiction) and *River Meuse* are cited by Alfaro as support for the principle's existence at international law. *Chorzów Factory* (Jurisdiction) makes no explicit reference to Article 38(1)(c) or its wording.[164] Support is found, however, for the foundation of estoppel in international law in contemporaneous commentary.[165] This is also true for the judgment of the Court in *River Meuse*,[166] although the Separate Opinion of Judge Hudson does make explicit reference to Article 38(1)(c) and gives some clues as to the jurisprudence and methodology of the source.[167]

Consequentially, while it seems clear that Judge Alfaro was correct in arguing that the principle of estoppel (or the more specific rule to which the judge referred) was a norm accepted at international law, the authorities relied upon did not, in the most part, clearly refer to that norm as a General Principle. Unlike the PCIJ in *Chorzów Factory*,[168] Alfaro did not refer to the works of municipal courts. Indeed, Alfaro rejected the domestic versions of estoppel as too different from the international version: 'there is a very substantial difference between the simple and clear-cut rule adopted and applied in the international field and the complicated classification, modalities, species, sub-species and procedural features of the municipal system'.[169] Alfaro instead rested the doctrine entirely on 'as it has been applied in the international sphere'.[170]

It cannot be assumed that this methodology of previous acceptance by international courts was intended by Alfaro to be the methodology for ascertaining a General Principle. Rather, Alfaro was using the jurisprudence as evidence for a previous finding of the norm as a General Principle, in line with common law notions of precedence. Although such practice is increasingly common

[160] See, eg, *Award of the King of Spain (Honduras v Nicaragua)* [1960] ICJ Rep 207, 213, 219; *Jurisdiction of the European Commission of the Danube* [1927] PCIJ Series B No 14, 23; *Serbian Loans Case* PCIJ Series A Nos 20–21, 39; *Shufeldt Claim (United States v Guatemala)* (1930) 2 RIAA 1079, 1094; *Yukon Lumber (Great Britain v United States)* (1913) 6 RIAA 17, 20; *The Schooner Mechanic* (1862) 29 RIAA 108, 114.

[161] *Pious Funds Case (United States v Mexico)* (1902) 9 RIAA 1, 5.

[162] *Russian Indemnity Case* (n 159) 189.

[163] ibid 191, 199.

[164] *Chorzów Factory* (Jurisdiction) (n 159) 31.

[165] See ch 3.

[166] *Diversion of Water from the Meuse (Netherlands v Belgium)* (Merits) [1925] PCIJ Series A/B No 70, 25.

[167] ibid 75–77 (Separate Opinion of Judge Hudson).

[168] *Chorzów Factory* (Jurisdiction) (n 159).

[169] *Preah Vihear* (n 154) 39 (Separate Opinion of Vice-President Alfaro).

[170] ibid.

in the ICJ,[171] it is of little help increasing understanding of the source when the judgments referred to do not consistently employ that source.

M. *South-West Africa* (Preliminary Objections)

The case[172] concerned an application brought against South Africa by Ethiopia and Liberia, alleging that South Africa was breaching its obligations in Namibia (South West Africa). South Africa governed in South West Africa by virtue of a League of Nations Mandate. South Africa challenged jurisdiction, arguing that the Mandate was no longer a 'treaty or convention in force' due to the dissolution of the League of Nations, and thus could not fall under Article 37 of the ICJ's Statute.[173] In his Dissenting Opinion, Judge Van Wyk relied on a General Principle that

> [A]pplicable in the interpretation of all contracts, including treaties, conventions, and other international agreements … one should endeavour to arrive at the true common intention of the parties relative to the agreement in question as it existed at the time agreement was reached.[174]

To establish this principle, Van Wyk turned to legislation from Belgium, the Netherlands, Italy, Germany, Switzerland, Greece, Hungary, Spain, Poland, Egypt, Brazil and Chile, as well as commentary from the United Kingdom.[175] This clearly shows a comparative methodology drawing from the domestic forum, and is one of the more comprehensive studies, extending outside only European systems.[176] Van Wyk indicates the *function* of General Principles as a normative source of international law, rather than a subsidiary source:

> It follows that Opinions of this Court, even if they relate to the same legal issues now being considered, cannot be more than a subsidiary means for the determination of the rules of international law. The general principles of law recognized by civilized nations must always prevail where those principles are in conflict with any views stated in previous decisions of this Court.[177]

Van Wyk also gives a rationale for the horizontal generality: the principle in question is based on 'logic, common sense and long experience', and thus 'it

[171] See W Alschner and D Charlotin, 'The Growing Complexity of the International Court of Justice's Self-Citation Network' (2018) 29(1) *European Journal of International Law* 83.

[172] *South-West Africa* (Preliminary Objections) (n 41).

[173] ibid 326–27.

[174] ibid 577 (Dissenting Opinion of Judge Van Wyk).

[175] ibid 577–78 (Dissenting Opinion of Judge Van Wyk).

[176] Van Wyk also undertakes a more limited comparative study looking to England, Italy, France, the Netherlands and the United States – to support the principle that '[t]he Court will always prefer an interpretation which renders an agreement valid and effective to an interpretation which renders it void and ineffective, provided the former can fairly be said not to be inconsistent with the intention of the parties': ibid 582.

[177] ibid 577 (Dissenting Opinion of Judge Van Wyk).

is not surprising that they are substantially the same in almost all civilized States'.[178] This is similar to Lauterpact's 'maxim of common sense and equity' in *Interhandel*: the content of the General Principle gives reasons as to *why* it is general, but the content does not in itself confer validity on the norm.

N. *South-West Africa*

In the second phase of the case,[179] Liberia and Ethiopia argued that the policy of apartheid maintained in Namibia by South Africa breached the terms of the mandate, and international law generally. General Principles are referred to in this case by the Court, in the Separate Opinion of Judge Van Wyk, the Dissenting Opinion of Judge Read, the Separate Opinion of Judge Tanaka, the Dissenting Opinion of Judge Read and the Dissenting Opinion of Judge Jessup.

i. The Court

The standing of the applicants was an issue, as neither had citizens, nor national interests, involved. Ultimately the ICJ held that neither applicant had the legal right or interest in the subject matter to obtain standing, and accordingly the case was dismissed. In the course of their pleadings the applicants argued that a norm of non-discrimination existed at international law, which granted them standing. The applicants argued that this norm was, among other things, a General Principle under Article 38(1)(c).[180] The Court rejected this argument, stating:

> Looked at in another way moreover, the argument amounts to a plea that the Court should allow the equivalent of an '*actio popularis*', or right resident in any member of a community to take legal action in vindication of a legal interest. But although a right of this kind may be known to certain municipal systems of law, it is not known to international law at present: nor is the Court able to regard it as imported by the 'general principles of law' referred to in Article 38, paragraph 1(c) of its Statute.[181]

This has been interpreted as requiring a legal principle to be 'generally recognized in national law'[182] to be a General Principle: '[i]n other words, recognition by a limited number of national legal systems or by a particular legal family of the world is insufficient; it is necessary for the principle to be recognized by the generality of national legal systems'.[183] This supports a comparative

[178] ibid 579.
[179] *South-West Africa* (n 5).
[180] ibid 292.
[181] ibid 46.
[182] Raimondo, *General Principles of Law* (n 46) 32.
[183] ibid 32.

methodology, drawing from domestic laws, with some minimum (unspecified) level of acceptance necessary for a national law principle to become a General Principle.

It has also been suggested that, regardless of the number of countries that had *actio popularis* within their national laws, the Court would not have upheld it as a General Principle due to the 'radically different nature of judicial jurisdiction' between the national and international spheres.[184] This has not been explained in more detail, however,[185] nor is it supported by the text of the judgment of the Court.

ii. Judge Van Wyk

This point was dealt with briefly in the Separate Opinion of Judge Van Wyk.[186] In discussing the argued norm of non-discrimination with reference to Article 38(1)(c), Van Wyk stated:

> The Applicants next invoked the provisions of Article 38(1)(c) to justify their alleged norm, which they contended should be distilled from the general principles of law recognized by civilized nations. The first fallacy in this contention is that this subsection does not authorize the application of the laws of civilized nations, it limits the Court to 'the general principles of law' of these nations. It certainly does not mean that by legislating on particular domestic matters a majority of civilized nations could compel a minority to introduce similar legislation. If, for example, every State but one were to enact a law prohibiting the manufacture of atomic weapons, or enforcing the enfranchisement of women, the remaining State would not be obliged to bring its laws into conformity with the rest.[187]

Judge Van Wyk questioned the (attempted) transferral of the content of domestic laws to become international binding norms. Part of this is in line with Judge McNair's statement in *International Status of South West Africa*: we look to the generality of the law, rather than importing it wholesale. Judge Van Wyk, however, does not explain the precise distinction between the 'application of the laws of civilized nations' and the '"general principles of law" of these nations'. Help may be found by reference to the principle/rule distinction – *rules* from domestic countries cannot become international law (no matter how many countries enact such a rule) but the *principles* behind those rules can. The problem with this assertion is that the rule/principle distinction is not a dichotomy but a sliding scale.[188] Finding requisite horizontal generality between domestic

[184] Thirlway, 'The Law and Procedure of the ICJ' (n 123) 113.
[185] Raimondo, *General Principles of Law* (n 46) 32.
[186] *South-West Africa* (n 5) 67 (Separate Opinion of Judge Van Wyk).
[187] ibid 170.
[188] J Raz, 'Legal Principles and the Limits of Law' (1972) 81 *Yale Law Journal* 823, 838; R Alexy, *A Theory of Constitutional Rights*, tr Julian Rivers (Oxford University Press, 2002); see ch 7 for further discussion.

laws will necessarily require some level of vertical abstraction – unless every law is identical in wording. Would this natural abstraction be enough to be a General Principle?

The two examples cited show that Van Wyk's objection is based on more than just the *appropriateness* of domestic laws' becoming international norms. Both examples – a ban on atomic weapons production and the enfranchisement of women – can properly be considered suitable for transformation into international norms. Indeed, norms similar or analogous in content already exist – the prohibition on the production of anti-personnel land mines[189] and the existing voting rights granted as human rights at international law.[190]

Van Wyk's distinction is somewhat at odds with his earlier reasoning in the Preliminary Objections phase: there, the rationale for inclusion of a principle in 'nearly all' legal systems was because it was based on 'logic, common sense and long experience' – in other words the desirable, or normatively good, content of the principle explained its horizontal generality. But the same can be said for domestic law created by legislation – why else would (nearly all) states legislate in common on a certain issue if not because the legislators believed the law was inherently desirable?

iii. Judge Read

In his Dissenting Opinion, Judge Read stated that '[i]t is a general principle of law, recognised in national legal systems and by international jurisprudence, that a tribunal must base its decision on the legal rights of the parties'.[191] No further substantiation for the principle was given by Judge Read, and the reference to both national legal systems and international jurisprudence leaves the methodology to establish it very unclear.

iv. Judge Tanaka

Judge Tanaka took the opportunity to analyse Article 38(1)(c) on a theoretical level in his Dissenting Opinion. He began by noting the vague nature of General Principles and the possibility of multiple interpretations.[192] Judge Tanaka argued that General Principles are not restricted to 'private law principles or principles of procedural law'[193] but rather must 'embrace all branches of law'.[194]

[189] See, eg, Convention on the Prohibition of the Use, Stockpiling, Production and Transfer of Anti-Personnel Mines and on their Destruction (adopted 18 September 1997, entered into force 1 March 1999) 2056 UNTS 211.

[190] See, eg, International Covenant on Civil and Political Rights (adopted 16 December 1966, entered into force 23 March 1976) 999 UNTS 171, Art 25.

[191] *South-West Africa* (n 5) 150 (Dissenting Opinion of Judge Read).

[192] *South-West Africa* (n 5) 292 (Dissenting Opinion of Judge Tanaka).

[193] ibid.

[194] ibid.

Tanaka warned, however, that the procedure for adoption should not be 'made mechanically'.[195] He argued that principles suitable to be General Principles must 'not be limited to statutory provisions and institutions of national laws: they must be extended to the fundamental concepts of each branch of law as well as to law in general so far as these can be considered as "recognized by civilized nations"'.[196] The word 'general' in this sense means 'common to all branches of law'.[197] Here we have a clear statement as to the *type* of General Principle (not limited to procedural content) and two ideas as to *methodology* and *jurisprudence*.

It is evident in Tanaka's judgment that he makes a distinction between two types of General Principles: those deriving from common elements between diverse national laws; and those deriving from a principle fundamental in human society. He used the nomenclature of Roman law, calling the former type those of *jus gentium* (the law of nations) and the latter *jus naturale* (natural law).[198] We thus return to the idea of a dual conception of General Principles.

a. Jus Gentium

Tanaka's approach in this first type also reveals a methodology. He made reference to 'comparative law studies' as a basis for a finding of a General Principle in regard to non-discrimination.[199] Judge Tanaka stated that the level of recognition of General Principles required is not recognition by *all* civilised nations.[200] He used an example of 73 per cent of national constitutions containing clauses respecting equality as evidence for recognition of equality as a General Principle.[201] The method of identification is clearly comparativist, looking to the content of municipal systems to find General Principles. Unlike the *jus naturale* category, no explicit link between validity and content is made.

b. Jus Naturale

The natural law aspect of Tanaka's second category is strengthened by his adoption of the notion of 'juridical truth' as employed by Bin Cheng.[202] Bin Cheng argues that General Principles are over-arching norms that exist because of their foundational legal character.[203] Tanaka's conception of General Principles as

[195] ibid 293; *International Status of South-West Africa* (n 58) 148 (Separate Opinion of Judge McNair).
[196] *South-West Africa* (n 5) 293 (Dissenting Opinion of Judge Tanaka).
[197] ibid.
[198] ibid 294.
[199] ibid 293.
[200] ibid 297.
[201] ibid.
[202] Cheng, *General Principles of Law* (n 51) 24; *South-West Africa* (n 5) 293 (Dissenting Opinion of Judge Tanaka).
[203] Cheng, *General Principles of Law* (n 51) 585.

'the fundamental legal concepts of which the legal norms are composed'[204] fits with Bin Cheng's natural law construction. Indeed, Tanaka argued that natural law concepts are inherent in General Principles.[205] He supported this argument by reference to the lack of state consent required for General Principles[206] and the drafting process of the provision, including the opposition to the article from the positivist members of the Committee of Jurists.[207] Like Lauterpacht before him, Judge Tanaka used the historical justification of General Principles being used to fill *lacunae* at international law as evidence of their natural law origins.[208] However, Judge Tanaka did not interpret the jurisprudence of General Principles as wholly natural law-based. Rather, he considered that positivist elements co-exist along with the natural law ones, and stated that the final draft of Article 38(1)(c) was a 'compromise between the two schools'.[209]

This category of General Principles was then employed by Tanka in the context of human rights[210] – rights which States cannot create by themselves.[211] These human rights exist in a 'more-or-less vague form' arising from the existence of humanity.[212] Tanaka argued that such rights exist independently of States, and existed before States.[213] As such the source of these General Principles is natural law.

v. Judge Jessup

In his Dissenting Opinion, Judge Jessup first confirmed that *res judicata* is a General Principle of law (in line with the views of the Advisory Committee of Jurists).[214] However, it is actually in *not* referring to a General Principle that Jessup reveals more about his construction of the source. Jessup undertook an analogy with municipal law to explore standing. After looking to the United States and England, Jessup then stated 'That the law in Italy and in other countries may be different … is not relevant to my argument since I am not seeking by the methods of comparative law to establish a 'general principle of law'.'[215]

This tells us, first, that Jessup sees the methodology of ascertaining General Principles as comparative, drawing from domestic systems and, second, that he

[204] *South-West Africa* (n 5) 293 (Dissenting Opinion of Judge Tanka).
[205] ibid 296.
[206] ibid.
[207] ibid.
[208] ibid 296.
[209] ibid.
[210] ibid 296.
[211] ibid 295.
[212] ibid 294.
[213] ibid 295.
[214] ibid 333 (Dissenting Opinion of Judge Jessup).
[215] ibid 387.

recognised the need for horizontal generality between different systems of law. Third, it provides an example whereby a judge may resort to a municipal law analogy without employing General Principles: it is thus a good reminder that not every municipal law analogy by the ICJ or its judges can be taken as a use of Article 38(1)(c).

O. *North Sea Continental Shelf*

The case[216] concerned a dispute about the delimitation of the continental shelf between Germany and Denmark and Germany and the Netherlands. Germany argued that if the equidistance principle of delineation were applied to its continental shelf, it would produce a harsh effect. Instead, it argued that Article 38(1)(c) and the 'natural law of nations' required that the principle of just and equitable apportionment must supersede the equidistance principle.[217] General Principles were considered briefly in the Dissenting Opinion of Judge Tanaka and Declaration of Judge Bengzon, and in more depth by Judge Ammoun.

i. Judge Tanaka and Judge Bengzon

Judge Tanaka dismissed Germany's argument on delineation, finding that 'the character of "general principles of law" is more notably to be recognized in the principle of equidistance than in the alleged principle of just and equitable apportionment'.[218] This was supported by Judge Bengzon, who in a short declaration stated, 'I agree with my colleagues … that as between these Parties equidistance is the rule for delimitation, which rule may even be derived from the general principles of law'.[219] No more elaboration was given by either judge.

ii. Judge Ammoun

In his Separate Opinion, Judge Ammoun addressed General Principles with respect to the delineation of the continental shelf,[220] stating that they are 'nothing other than the norms common to the different legislations of the world, united by the identity of legal reason therefore, or the *ratio legis*, transposed from the internal legal system to the international legal system'.[221]

[216] *North Sea Continental Shelf* (n 5).
[217] ibid 21 (Judgment of the Court), 193 (Separate Opinion of Judge Tanaka).
[218] ibid 194–95 (Separate Opinion of Judge Tanaka).
[219] ibid 56 (Declaration of Judge Bengzon).
[220] ibid 135 (Separate Opinion of Judge Ammoun).
[221] ibid.

Judge Ammoun was concerned with the term 'civilized nations', arguing this had resulted in a 'Concert of Europe'[222] where previous international courts and tribunals had only looked to European systems of law to draw General Principles.[223] Ammoun supported a comparative approach to finding General Principles, but felt it should be across 'national rules in all latitudes'.[224] This conception was picked up again by Judge Weeramantry nearly 30 years later in *Gabčíkovo-Nagymaros*.[225]

Judge Ammoun then turned to the jurisprudence of the provision, stating that General Principles represent the 'purest moral values'.[226] Ammoun argued that if a principle is recognised by differing nations, it is necessarily a principle devoid of nationalism and must therefore be closer to morality than other principles.[227] He stated, 'the general principles of law are indisputably factors which bring morality into the law of nations, inasmuch as they borrow from the law of the nations principles of the moral order'.[228] Judge Ammoun thus considered the role of General Principles as taking moral rules from municipal systems and transforming these rules into norms of international law. The morality of the content is important, which suggests a natural law conception. This interpretation is confirmed by Ammoun's view that General Principles are inconsistent with a positivist conception of international law.[229]

Ammoun returned to the identification of General Principles, advocating a methodology of looking 'both in time, by going back to legal traditions which have continued up to our own day, and in space, by glancing rapidly over the various national contributions'.[230] He held that equity is a General Principle, and based this on recognition of the principle

> in the law of Western Europe and of Latin America ... in the common law ... in Muslim law ... by the Koran ... in the teaching of the four great jurisconsults of Islam condensed in the Shari'a ... Chinese law ... Soviet law ... Hindu law ... [and] finally the law of the other Asian countries, and of the African countries.[231]

Consistent with Ammoun's earlier statement, the identification methodology is clearly comparativism.

[222] ibid.
[223] ibid.
[224] ibid.
[225] *Gabčíkovo-Nagymaros Project* (n 98) 96 (Separate Opinion of Judge Weeramantry): see discussion in ch 5.
[226] *North Sea Continental Shelf* (n 5) 136 (Separate Opinion of Judge Ammoun).
[227] ibid.
[228] ibid 137.
[229] ibid 136–37.
[230] ibid 137.
[231] ibid 139–40.

Judge Ammoun also considered the principle of acquiescence to be a General Principle, further employing a comparativist methodology:

> Acquiescence flowing from a unilateral legal act, or inferred from the conduct or attitude of the person to whom it is to be opposed – either by application of the concept of estoppel by conduct of Anglo-American equity, or by virtue of the principle of western law that allegans contraria non audiendus est, which has its parallel in Muslim law numbered among the general principles of law accepted by international law as forming part of the law of nations.[232]

Unlike the dual conceptions of General Principles that separate the comparative methodology and the natural law jurisprudence, Ammoun views the source as being able to employ both aspects simultaneously. However, the morality of the law does not seem to *make* the norm valid; rather, it is an inherent consequence that if a law is contained over many different legal systems, the *reason* for its replication is that it must be a good, or moral, law. This idea was first introduced in relation to General Principles by Raoul Fernandes at the Advisory Committee of Jurists.[233] In its more established form, the rule of recognition remains the comparative study of the domestic laws of states, and hence morality is linked to, but not decisive of, validity.

P. *Barcelona Traction*

This case[234] concerned proceedings brought by Belgium against Spain for damage caused to Belgian nationals who were shareholders in the Barcelona Traction, Light and Power Company. It is cited as an example of the Court's recognising the General Principle of limited corporate liability.[235] General Principles are also addressed in the Separate Opinion of Judge Ammoun.

i. Judgment of the Court

In this instance the Court set out that it would draw relevant legal principles from domestic laws:

> In turning now to the international legal aspects of the case, the Court must, as already indicated, start from the fact that the present case essentially involves factors derived from municipal law – the distinction and the community between the company and the shareholder – which the Parties, however widely their interpretations may differ, each take as the point of departure of their reasoning. If the Court were to decide the case in disregard of the relevant institutions of municipal law it

232 ibid 120–21.

233 See ch 2.

234 *Barcelona Traction, Light and Power Company (Belgium v Spain) (Second Phase)* [1970] ICJ Rep 3 (*Barcelona Traction*).

235 Shaw, *International Law* (n 46) 86–87; Triggs, *International Law* (n 51) 88.

> would, without justification, invite serious legal difficulties. It would lose touch with reality, for there are no corresponding institutions of international law to which the Court could resort. Thus the Court has, as indicated, not only to take cognizance of municipal law but also to refer to it. It is to rules generally accepted by municipal legal systems which recognize the limited company whose capital is represented by shares, and not to the municipal law of a particular State, that international law refers. In referring to such rules, the Court cannot modify, still less deform them.[236]

While not an exact use of the wording of Article 38(1)(c), the term 'rules generally accepted by municipal systems' would seem to be a reference to General Principles. This offers a view of the *function* of General Principles: as a gap filler not only where custom and treaty are silent, but also where the very nature of the norm is rooted in domestic rather than international institutions. Later, the notion of 'lifting the veil' of a corporation was recognised in municipal law, and that

> the process of lifting the veil, being an exceptional one admitted by municipal law in respect of an institution of its own making, is equally admissible to play a similar role in international law. It follows that on the international plane also there may in principle be special circumstances which justify the lifting of the veil in the interest of shareholders.[237]

Although the Court referred to the 'wealth of municipal law',[238] it did not give examples of the laws it was relying on, or from which municipal systems they had been drawn. It would, however, tend to indicate a comparative *methodology*.

ii. Judge Ammoun

Judge Ammoun suggested that a General Principle of equity, drawn from national legal systems, could operate only to 'remedy the insufficiencies of international law and fill its *logical* lacunae'.[239] In this case, Ammoun perceived the lacanue not of law but of society: a 'social inefficiency', and thus General Principles could not be relied on.[240] Thus General Principles are subsidiary in the sense they can only be used when the international legal system itself is incomplete.

Q. *Legal Consequences for States*

This Advisory Opinion[241] was initiated by the Security Council, which asked the ICJ to deliberate on the question: 'What are the legal consequences for States of

236 *Barcelona Traction* (n 234) 37.
237 ibid 39.
238 ibid.
239 ibid 332 (Separate Opinion of Judge Ammoun).
240 ibid 333.
241 *Legal Consequences for States* (n 7).

the continued presence of South Africa in Namibia, notwithstanding Security Council Resolution 276(1970)?'[242] One issue the Court had to consider was the mandate granted to South Africa from Great Britain to administer Namibia. The mandate had already been the subject of several court decisions.[243] International concern over the actions of South Africa in Namibia led to General Assembly Resolution 2145 (XXI), in which the General Assembly terminated the mandate. The General Assembly declared that South Africa had 'failed to fulfill its obligations' under the Mandate.[244] In particular, the General Assembly pointed to the failure to ensure the 'moral and material well-being and security' of the indigenous population of Namibia.[245]

Judge Dillard mentioned General Principles fleetingly in his Separate Opinion.[246] While discussing his support for the Court's decision, Dillard discussed the difficulty of interpreting agreements when such agreements are interrupted by unexpected events, 'in this instance the Second World War, the dissolution of the League and the birth of the United Nations'.[247] Against this background, Judge Dillard held that

> whenever a long-term engagement, of whatever nature, is so interrupted, emphasis in attempting a reasonable interpretation and construction of its meaning and the obligations it imposes shifts from a textual analysis to one which stresses the object and purpose of the engagement in light of the total context in which the engagement was located.[248]

Judge Dillard found support for this view in General Principles:

> This generalization can be amply supported by recourse to 'the general principles of law recognized by civilized nations' as revealed in the application of doctrines of impossibility and frustration to long-term engagements.[249]

The doctrines of impossibility and frustration exist, with significant variation,[250] in both common and civil law municipal systems.[251] Judge Dillard's use of these municipal doctrines as support for a General Principle binding at international law, and applicable to international agreements, suggests a comparative-based methodology, drawing on domestic laws, to finding such principles, although this was not made explicit in the judgment.

[242] UNSC Res 284 (29 July 1970) UN Doc S/RES/284.
[243] *South West Africa* (Preliminary Objections) (n 41); *South-West Africa* (n 5).
[244] UNGA Res 2145 (XXI) (27 October 1966).
[245] *Legal Consequences for States* (n 7) 19.
[246] ibid 157 (Separate Opinion of Judge Dillard).
[247] ibid.
[248] ibid.
[249] ibid.
[250] HC Gutteridge, *Comparative Law: An Introduction to the Comparative Method of Legal Study and Research* (Cambridge University Press, 1946) 68; D Vagts, 'Rebus Revisited: Changed Circumstances in Treaty Law' (2004–5) 43(2) *Columbia Journal of Transnational Law* 459, 460.
[251] See Gutteridge, *Comparative Law* (n 250) 68; H Smit, 'Frustration of Contracts: A Comparative Attempt at Consolidation' (1958) 58 *Columbia Law Review* 287.

R. *ICAO Council Appeal*

Two years after his opinion in *Legal Consequences for States*, Judge Dillard revisited General Principles in another Separate Opinion.[252] In this Judge Dillard explicitly linked Article 38(1)(c) with the domestic forum,[253] and turned again to domestic judgments to support his finding of a General Principle. Although there was a clear comparative methodology, it was limited to common law countries, focusing particularly on English jurisprudence.[254] The two judgments together confirm a methodology of comparative study of domestic laws. Further, they show support for a view (unlike Van Wyk in *South West Africa*) that the *content* of municipal laws can be transformed into international law by operation of General Principles.

S. *Fisheries Jurisdiction* (Order)

General Principles were mentioned fleetingly in the Joint Dissenting Opinion of Judges Bengzon and Jiménéz de Aréchaga.[255] The Opinion states that 'to allow the applicant to present new submissions and develop its supporting arguments after the default has occurred would be contrary to the general principles of law recognized in national legislations concerning default proceedings'.[256] Clearly the methodology here is drawing from the domestic forum, and type includes procedural principles.

T. *Application for Review of Judgment No 158*

This case[257] concerned an employment dispute between a former employee of the United Nations Development Program, Mohamad Fasla, and the UN, which went to the UN Administrative Tribunal (UNAT). General Principles were cited by the Court, as well as in the Separate Opinion of Judge Ammoun and the Dissenting Opinion of Judge De Castro.

[252] In *ICAO Council Appeal* (n 7).

[253] ibid 109.

[254] ibid 113–14.

[255] *Fisheries Jurisdiction (United Kingdom v Iceland)* (Order) (n 8); *Fisheries Jurisdiction (United Kingdom v Iceland; Federal Republic of Germany v Iceland)* (Order) (n 8).

[256] *Fisheries Jurisdiction (United Kingdom v Iceland)* (Order) (n 8) 185 (Joint Dissenting Opinion of Judges Bengzon and Jiménéz de Aréchaga); *Fisheries Jurisdiction (United Kingdom v Iceland; Federal Republic of Germany v Iceland)* (Order) (n 8) 191 (Joint Dissenting Opinion of Judges Bengzon and Jiménéz de Aréchaga).

[257] *Application for Review of Judgment No 158* (n 6).

i. The Court

A question arose before the Court about the UN General Assembly Resolution, which attempted to remove the inequality between Member States and the UN Secretary General (who are permitted to make Oral Pleadings before the ICJ) and UN staff members (who are not).[258] The Resolution did so by recommending no oral pleadings in cases arising from UNAT hearings. In addressing this, the ICJ commented:

> But it does not appear to the Court that there is any general principle of law which requires that in review proceedings the interested parties should necessarily have an opportunity to submit oral statements of their case to the review tribunal. General principles of law and the judicial character of the Court do require that, even in advisory proceedings, the interested parties should each have an opportunity, and on a basis of equality, to submit all the elements relevant to the questions which have been referred to the review tribunal. But that condition is fulfilled by the submission of written statements.[259]

Nothing more was said on General Principles: so further than the *type's* including procedural rules or principles, and the fact the Court was willing to consider itself bound by General Principles, nothing more can be gained on the nature of the source.

ii. Dissenting Opinion of Vice President Ammoun

The UN Administrative Tribunal had refused to award reparation. In considering the principle of reparation, Ammoun stated that 'the reparation of injury caused by fault is one, if not indeed the most important, of the principles common to nations in the sense of Article 38, paragraph 1 (c), of the Court's Statute, and one of the traditional bases of law'.[260] Ammoun further held that the payment of costs by the losing party can be considered a General Principle, but acknowledged this was challenged: 'It has been denied in this connection that a practice can be regarded as a general principle of law when it runs counter to the Common Law system and, to a certain extent, the law of the United States of America.'[261]

Ammoun argued in that there was an emerging field of 'common administrative law' administered by international tribunals, which followed 'continental practice'.[262] This seeming adherence to one type of municipal system of law is somewhat puzzling in the context of General Principles and Ammoun's earlier Opinion in *North Sea Continental Shelf*. However, a close reading of

[258] Statute of the Permanent Court of Justice [1921] ATS 5, Art 66(4).
[259] *Application for Review of Judgment No 158* (n 6) 181.
[260] ibid 247 (Dissenting Opinion of Vice President Ammoun).
[261] ibid 249.
[262] ibid.

the Opinion evinces not a rejection of common law per se from the General Principle, but rather an overreliance on *one* system of common law (namely, that of the United States). In the end, Ammoun concludes that the 'obligation on the losing party to bear the costs could be regarded either as a general principle or law in itself … or as an application of the equity principle deriving from Article 38, paragraph 1 (c), of the Statute of the Court'.[263]

The methodology thus looks to domestic systems of law: and the type of General Principle is a specific procedural rule (whether derived itself as a rule or as a result of an application of a more generalised principle of equity).

iii. Judge De Castro

The UNAT had also refused to award reparation for damage to the reputation of Fasla. In a passage that explicitly referenced Article 38(1)(c),[264] Judge De Castro held:

> Moral damage should be compensated according to the general principles of law, and such compensation is the guarantee of human rights. Its importance in law is well known. The United Nations Charter begins with an affirmation of faith in 'fundamental human rights, in the dignity and worth of the human person', a doctrine which is taken further in the Universal Declaration of Human Rights, according to which 'No-one shall be subjected to … attacks upon his honour and reputation' and 'Everyone has the right to the protection of the law against such … attacks'.[265]

The General Principle here is thus drawn from international sources rather than tied to any municipal laws.

U. *Aegean Sea Continental Shelf*

In this case,[266] President Jiménéz de Aréchaga expanded on the rationale for interim protection orders in a Separate Opinion. He did so with reference to General Principles:

> According to general principles of law recognized in municipal systems, and to the well-established jurisprudence of this Court, the essential justification for the impatience of a tribunal in granting relief before it has reached a final decision on its competence and on the merits is that the action of one party 'pendente lite' causes or threatens a damage to the rights of the other, of such a nature that it would not be possible fully to restore those rights, or remedy the infringement thereof, simply by a judgment in its favour.[267]

[263] ibid 250.
[264] ibid 284 (Dissenting Opinion of Judge De Castro).
[265] ibid 291.
[266] *Aegean Sea Continental Shelf (Greece v Turkey)* (Interim Protection Measures) (n 8).
[267] ibid 15–16 (Separate Opinion of President Jiménéz de Aréchaga).

No further elaboration is given. However, it is clear Jiménéz de Aréchaga's conception of General Principles has a methodology drawing from municipal systems.

V. *Continental Shelf (Tunisia v Libyan Arab Jamahiriya)*

This case[268] concerned the delimitation of the continental shelf between Tunisia and Libyan Arab Jamahiriya. In his Dissenting Opinion, Judge Oda disagreed with the Court's finding that the relevant rule for delimitation in this case was 'to be effected in accordance with equitable principles, and taking account of all relevant circumstances'.[269] Oda undertook a lengthy exploration of the history of the United Nations Convention on the Law of the Sea. In exploring the right of the coastal state to exploit offshore resources, Oda stated:

> Without reference to customary international law, a similar conclusion was reached by some who maintained that the competence of the coastal State to regulate the exploitation of natural resources in the offshore submerged lands was now one of the general principles of law recognized by civilized nations, and therefore a rule of existing international law.[270]

No further elaboration was given; however, it is clear that this view sees the *function* of General Principles as binding, and the *type* as including substantive rules. Further, the rule/principle distinction is not observed.

W. *Nicaragua*

i. Judgment of the Court

This case[271] was brought by Nicaragua against the United States of America in relation to acts of violence and force carried out in and against Nicaragua. Nicaragua relied on conventional, customary and general international law in its pleadings.[272] General Principles were addressed in the opinion of the Court in its discussion of conventional law. Both parties and the Court agreed that Article 2(4) of the United Nations Charter, containing the prohibition on the use of force, was identical in content to the customary norm and General Principle on the same subject.[273] This agreement, without elaboration as to how

[268] *Continental Shelf (Tunisia v Libyan Arab Jamahiriya)* (n 11).
[269] ibid 92.
[270] ibid 177 (Dissenting Opinion of Judge Oda).
[271] *Nicaragua* (n 11).
[272] ibid 18–19.
[273] ibid 98–99.

an identical norm of custom and General Principle arose, blurs any distinction between the methodology of these two sources. It does, however, show that the ICJ was comfortable declaring a General Principle with substantive, rather than procedural content.

ii. President Singh

In his Separate Opinion, President Singh discussed the norm banning reprisals involving the use of force.[274] Singh found that this norm existed at general international law as well as under treaty, stating:

> Even if the Charter were not a codification of existing customary law on non-use of force and self-defence, and there were a clear progressive development leading on to the banning of reprisals involving the use of force, it needs to be stated that this developmental aspect, or the precise formulatory aspect, is surely now a part of international law, whether it be categorized as customary or as one of the 'general principles of law recognized by civilized nations'.[275]

The apparent willingness to interchangeably categorise the norm as either customary or a General Principle indicates the lack of clarity as to the exact distinction between these two sources of international law. One implication of using the two sources interchangeably is that they may share the same methodology – that is, the requirements for a rule to become a norm under custom are the same as the requirements for a rule to become a norm under General Principles, and thus it does not matter how the norm is characterised. It seems unlikely that this is what President Singh intended, as it would effectively make General Principles redundant as a source of international law, contrary to the intentions of the Committee of Jurists and the later Inter-Allied Committee. Nonetheless, the grouping of the two norms obfuscates their unique rules of recognition.

iii. Judge Oda

Judge Oda mentioned General Principles briefly in his Dissenting Opinion to confirm their role in preventing the Court from declaring a *non liquet*:

> In the case of international law, the Statute of the Permanent Court of International Justice introduced the clause 'the general principles of law recognized by civilized nations' mainly to avoid a non liquet resulting from the lack of any positive rules.[276]

Here General Principles are subsidiary gap fillers, in that they are only turned to when treaty and custom – the 'positive rules' – are lacking.

[274] ibid 153 (Separate Opinion of President Singh).
[275] ibid.
[276] ibid 237 (Dissenting Opinion of Judge Oda).

iv. Judge Schwebel

Judge Schwebel used the term 'general principle' several times in his Dissenting Opinion. He refers to the extra-curial writing of Lauterpacht, who categorises self-defence as a general principle of law[277] but also discusses self-defence as a norm of custom, and who cites sources describing it as a 'rule of general international law' and a 'general principle of international law'.[278] Schwebel also refers to 'general principles of law' in relation to rights and obligations,[279] but there is no further link to Article 38(1)(c) here.

It is clear that Schwebel is referring to Article 38(1)(c) when he discussed the doctrine of clean hands. Schwebel refers back to the PCIJ *River Meuse* case, and in particular the Opinions of Judges Anzilotti and Huber.[280] Although both judges employed different approaches to General Principles, it seems clear that case was a true use of Article 38(1)(c).[281] Judge Schwebel implicitly endorses the comparative approach taken by Judge Huber,[282] and declares clean hands a 'fundamental general principle of law'.[283]

X. *Elettronica Sicula*

In his Separate Opinion in *Elettronica Sicula*,[284] Judge Oda returned to the judgment in *Barcelona Traction*, using language more explicitly linking the decision to General Principles. Thus, after quoting the Court's reference in that case to 'rules generally accepted by municipal legal systems',[285] Oda describes these as 'general principles' and makes reference to Italian, French, German, Japanese and Swiss domestic laws.[286] Intriguingly, Oda then states:

> That general principle of law concerning the rights or status of shareholders, which underlies not only Italian company law but also the company law of some other civil law countries, may not be altered by any treaty aimed at the protection of investments unless that treaty contains some express provision to that end.[287]

Far from being a subsidiary source, Oda thus sees General Principles as being on a par with treaties, to the point where treaties will only override them by express

[277] ibid 286 (Dissenting Opinion of Judge Schwebel); H Lauterpacht, *The Function of Law in the International Community* (Clarendon Press, 1933) 179.
[278] *Nicaragua* (n 11) 304 (Dissenting Opinion of Judge Schwebel).
[279] ibid 388.
[280] ibid 392–93.
[281] See ch 3.
[282] *Nicaragua* (n 11) 393 (Dissenting Opinion of Judge Schwebel).
[283] ibid 296.
[284] *Elettronica Sicula* (n 11).
[285] *Barcelona Traction* (n 234) 37.
[286] *Elettronica Sicula* (n 11) 84–85 (Separate Opinion of Judge Oda).
[287] ibid 86.

provision. The *methodology* is comparative, but in practice it is limited to only civil law countries.

Y. *UN Privileges and Immunities Convention*

In this case,[288] the ICJ was requested to give an Advisory Opinion by the United Nations Economic and Social Council[289] concerning the applicability of the Convention on the Privileges and Immunities of the United Nations to Dumitru Mazilu, a Romanian national and Special Rapporteur of the Sub-Commission on Prevention of Discrimination and Protection of Minorities. The request was brought after Mazilu alleged that the Romanian Government had prevented him from delivering a human rights report by refusing him a travel permit to leave Romania.[290] The Romanian Government also refused any access to Mazilu by representatives of the United Nations.[291]

Article 38(1)(c) was mentioned in the Separate Opinion of Judge Evensen in his discussion of whether the privileges and immunities under the Convention extended to the family of the person in question.[292] Evensen held that the privileges extended to a 'reasonable extent' to families of UN officials.[293] He held that the 'integrity of a person's family and family life' was protected in international law',[294] and argued that this protection derived both from customary international law and General Principles:

> The integrity of a person's family and family life is a basic human right protected by prevailing principles of international law which derive not only from conventional international law or customary international law but from 'general principles of law recognized by civilized nations'.[295]

While Judge Evensen did not explicitly treat convention, custom and General Principles as interchangeable – as President Singh did in his Separate Opinion in *Nicaragua* – the use of all three sources of international law as giving rise to norms of identical content with no further elaboration as to the process is problematic for the same reasons. These Opinions continue the regrettable trend observed by Bin Cheng in 1953, that the 'line of demarcation between custom and general principles of law recognised by civilised nations is often not very clear'.[296]

[288] *Applicability of Article VI, Section 22 of the Convention on the Privileges and Immunities of the United Nations* (Advisory Opinion) [1989] ICJ Rep 177 (*UN Privileges and Immunities Convention*).

[289] United Nations Economic and Social Council Res 1989/75 (24 May 1989) UN Doc E/RES/1989/4.

[290] *UN Privileges and Immunities Convention* (n 288) 181.

[291] ibid 182.

[292] ibid 210 (Separate Opinion of Judge Evensen).

[293] ibid.

[294] ibid.

[295] ibid 210–11.

[296] Cheng, *General Principles of Law* (n 51) 23.

IV. CONCLUSION

Given the division of ICJ cases between chapters 4 and 5, any interim conclusion here is only partial: based on a chronologically truncated consideration of the source by the Court. Nevertheless, a few brief observations can be made.

A. Conflation of Custom and General Principles

Several cases and Opinions conflate General Principles with customary international law. It is unclear whether this was done because the sources were viewed as similar, positivist sources of international law with similar methodologies, or rather simply as a matter of convenience with little thought towards the doctrinal implications.

It may seem pedantic to insist that General Principles must be recognised explicitly as a different source than customary international law. As the judgments show, however, when General Principles are grouped indiscriminately with custom, either no information is given or ascertainable as to fundamental aspects of their nature, or it could be argued that they are relegated to being interchangeable with custom – rendering them superfluous as a distinctive source of international law. However, the cases all indicate that the *type* of General Principles is not limited to procedural norms – they include substantive international law norms of humanitarian law, the use of force and human rights. This is particularly significant for the judgment in *Nicaragua*, given that the Court as a whole agreed that the content of General Principles includes substantive rules of international law.

B. Application of the Tetrahedral Model

Every use of General Principles saw the *function* as a binding source of law, although some judges limited such function to acting to fill a lacuna left by the absence of treaty or custom,[297] or as unable to exist in conflict with treaty or custom.[298] The *type* of General Principles includes procedural[299] and

[297] eg *Fisheries Case* (n 64) 147 (Individual Opinion of Judge Alvarez); *Certain Norwegian Loans* (n 4) 45 (Separate Opinion of Judge Lauterpacht).

[298] *Right of Passage* (Preliminary Objections) (n 41) 177 (Dissenting Opinion of Judge Chagla).

[299] eg *Effect of Awards of Compensation* (n 78) 53; *Fisheries Jurisdiction (United Kingdom v Iceland)* (Order) (n 8) 185 (Joint Dissenting Opinion of Judges Bengzon and Jimenez De Arechaga); *Fisheries Jurisdiction (United Kingdom v Iceland; Federal Republic of Germany v Iceland)* (Order) (n 8) 191 (Joint Dissenting Opinion of Judges Bengzon and Jimenez De Arechaga); *Application for Review of Judgement No 158* (n 4) 247 (Dissenting Opinion of Vice President Ammoun).

substantive norms.[300] It includes abstract and/or generalised principles[301] and specific rules[302] (although the former was more common). For those judgments that revealed a *methodology*, most employed a (limited) comparative analysis of domestic legal systems.[303] In using the comparative methodology, a criterion of appropriateness is required to ensure the domestic principle can operate on the international level.[304] Most cases did not discuss *jurisprudential legitimacy* – but through those that did, a notion of duality of General Principles began to emerge.

C. The Duality of General Principles

Three intriguing approaches to General Principles show a duality to the source. The first, as seen in *Corfu Channel*, suggests General Principles are capable of embracing both rules of international law derived from a comparative study of municipal systems *and* overarching fundamental principles conferred validity and force by the content of the principle itself.[305] The second, as seen in Lauterpacht's Dissenting Opinion in *Interhandel*, offers a natural law reason for the horizontal generality of a principle (a 'maxim of common sense and equity') but, read in tandem with *Certain Norwegian Loans*, tempers this by a positivist rule of recognition of comparativist methodology looking to domestic legal systems. Variations on this approach were also taken by Judge Alvarez in *Fisheries Case*, Judge Koo in *Right of Passage* (Merits), Judge Van Wyk in *South West Africa* (Preliminary Objections) and Judge Ammoun in *North Sea*

[300] eg *Corfu Channel* (n 45) 22; *International Status of South-West Africa* (n 58) 146 (Separate Opinion of Judge McNair).

[301] eg *Corfu Channel* (n 45) 18; *Application for Review of Judgement No 158* (n 4) 249 (Dissenting Opinion of Vice President Ammoun).

[302] eg *Corfu Channel* (n 45) 22; *Voting Procedure* (n 4) 101–02, 105 (Separate Opinion of Judge Lauterpacht); *Certain Norwegian Loans* (n 4) 44, 49 (Separate Opinion of Judge Lauterpacht); *Interhandel* (n 4) 116–17 (Dissenting Opinion of Judge Lauterpacht); *Preah Vihear* (n 154) 39 (Separate Opinion of Vice-President Alfaro).

[303] eg *International Status of South-West Africa* (n 58) 146 (Separate Opinion of Judge McNair); *Anglo-Iranian Oil* (n 73) 151, 161 (Dissenting Opinion of Judge Carneiro); *Certain Norwegian Loans* (n 4) 49–50, 56 (Separate Opinion of Judge Lauterpacht); *Guardianship of Infants* (n 4) 92 (Separate Opinion of Judge Lauterpacht); *Right of Passage* (Merits) (n 116) 66–67 (Separate Opinion of Judge Koo); *North Sea Continental Shelf* (n 5) 120–21, 135 (Separate Opinion of Judge Ammoun); *Legal Consequences for States* (n 7) 157 (Separate Opinion of Judge Dillard); *ICAO Council Appeal* (n 7) 109 (Separate Opinion of Judge Dillard); *Fisheries Jurisdiction (United Kingdom v Iceland)* (Order) (n 8) 185 (Joint Dissenting Opinion of Judges Bengzon and Jimenez De Arechaga); *Fisheries Jurisdiction (United Kingdom v Iceland; Federal Republic of Germany v Iceland) (Order)* (n 8) 191 (Joint Dissenting Opinion of Judges Bengzon and Jimenez De Arechaga).

[304] *International Status of South-West Africa* (n 58) 148 (Separate Opinion of Judge McNair); *Right of Passage* (Preliminary Objections) (n 41) 177 (Dissenting Opinion of Judge Chagla); *Right of Passage* (Merits) (n 116) 66–67 (Separate Opinion of Judge Koo).

[305] This dual conception is also evident in Judge Fernandes' Dissenting Opinion in *Right of Passage* (Merits) (n 116) and Judge Tanaka's Dissenting Opinion in *South-West Africa* (n 5).

Continental Shelf. In contrast, the third approach is seen in Judge Fernandes' Dissenting Opinion in *Right of Passage* (Merits). Fernandes flips Lauterpacht's and Ammoun's conception of the source, and tempers a comparativist study with a natural law requirement of a 'reason deeply rooted in the legal consciousness of all peoples'[306] for recognising a General Principle. Both Fernandes and Lauterpacht see natural law and positivist elements to General Principles: for Lauterpacht the natural law is the reason *why* the positivist rule of recognition can be fulfilled, while for Fernandes it is an element in the rule of recognition itself, perhaps best characterised by fulfilling the role of appropriateness. As will be seen in chapter 5, these dual conceptions of General Principle find support in later judgments of the ICJ.

[306] *Right of Passage* (Merits) (n 116) 136 (Dissenting Opinion of Judge Fernandes).

5

Development of Article 38(1)(c) by the ICJ: 1992–2019

I. INTRODUCTION

IN THE 27 years this chapter spans, there are 33 International Court of Justice (ICJ) Judgments, Declarations and Opinions that, on construction, reference General Principles. Of these, 18 are the individual contributions of Judge Weeramantry and Judge Cançado Trindade, who discussed General Principles in five and 13 Separate or Dissenting Opinions respectively.[1] As such,

[1] *Maritime Delimitation in the Area between Greenland and Jan Mayen (Denmark v Norway)* (Merits) [1993] ICJ Rep 38, 211 (Separate Opinion of Judge Weeramantry) (*Greenland and Jan Mayen*); *Application of the Convention on the Prevention and the Punishment of the Crime of Genocide (Bosnia and Herzegovina v Serbia and Montenegro)* (Provisional Measures) [1993] ICJ Rep 325, 370 (Separate Opinion of Judge Weeramantry) (*Application of the Genocide Convention* (Provisional Measures)); *Gabčíkovo-Nagymaros Project (Hungary v Slovakia)* [1997] ICJ Rep 7, 88 (Separate Opinion of Judge Weeramantry) (*Gabčíkovo-Nagymaros Project*); *Land and Maritime Boundary between Cameroon and Nigeria (Cameroon v Nigeria)* (Preliminary Objections) [1998] ICJ Rep 275, 362 (Dissenting Opinion of Vice-President Weeramantry) (*Land and Maritime Boundary* (Preliminary Objections)); *Sovereignty over Pulau Ligitan and Pulau Sipadan (Indonesia/Malaysia)* (Application to Intervene) [2001] ICJ Rep 575, 630 (Separate Opinion of Judge Weeramantry) (*Pulau Ligitan and Pulau Sipadan* (Application to Intervene)); *Questions relating to the Obligation to Prosecute or Extradite (Belgium v Senegal)* (Order of 28 May 2009) [2009] ICJ Rep 139, 165 (Dissenting Opinion of Judge Cançado Trindade) (*Obligation to Prosecute or Extradite* (Provisional Measures)); *Pulp Mills on the River Uruguay (Argentina v Uruguay)* (Merits) [2010] ICJ Rep 14, 135 (Separate Opinion of Judge Cançado Trindade) (*Pulp Mills*); *Jurisdictional Immunities of the State (Germany v Italy: Greece Intervening)* [2012] ICJ Rep 12, 179 (Dissenting Opinion of Judge Cançado Trindade) (*Jurisdictional Immunities of the State*); *Questions Related to the Obligation to Prosecute or Extradite (Belgium v Senegal)* (Merits) [2012] ICJ Rep 423, 487 (Separate Opinion of Judge Cançado Trindade) (*Obligation to Prosecute or Extradite* (Merits)); *Judgment No 2867 of the Administrative Tribunal of the International Labour Organization upon a Complaint Filed against the International Fund for Agricultural Development* (Advisory Opinion) [2012] ICJ Reports 2012 10, 51 (Separate Opinion of Judge Cançado Trindade) (*Judgment No 2867 of the Administrative Tribunal of the ILO*); *Ahmadou Sadio Diallo (Republic of Guinea v Democratic Republic of the Congo)* (Compensation) ICJ Rep 2012 ICJ Rep 324, 347 (Separate Opinion of Judge Cançado Trindade) (*Diallo* (Compensation)); *Certain Activities Carried Out by Nicaragua in the Border Area (Costa Rica v Nicaragua)* (Joinder of Proceedings) [2013] ICJ Rep 166, 172 (Separate Opinion of Judge Cançado Trindade) (*Certain Activities* (Joinder of Proceedings)); *Questions relating to the Seizure and Detention of Certain Documents and Data (Timor-Leste v Australia)* (Provisional Measures) [2014] ICJ Rep 147, 167 (Separate Opinion of Judge Cançado Trindade) (*Documents and Data* (Provisional Measures)); *Obligation to Negotiate Access to the*

to ensure cohesive analysis, this chapter will first address the references to General Principles by the Court and other judges, and then turn to the jurisprudence of Judges Weeramantry and Cançado Trindade.

As with chapter 4, there are some cases that mention Article 38(1)(c) that are not included for analysis here. These are those cases that do so in passing[2] or as part of a recitation of the Article 38 sources.[3]

Table 5.1 Consideration of Article 38(1)(c) by the ICJ: 1992–2019

Category	Cases
Relevant Cases (except for the Separate and Dissenting Opinions of Judges Weeramantry and Cançado Trindade)	*Aerial Incident at Lockerbie* (Provisional Measures), Dissenting Opinions of Judge El-Kosheri and Judge Ranjeva (1992)[4] *Certain Phosphate Lands in Nauru*, Separate Opinion of Judge Shahabuddeen (1992) *Territorial Dispute*, Separate Opinion of Judge Ajibola (1994) *Threat or Use of Nuclear Weapons* (1996) Declaration of Judge Herczgh Dissenting Opinion of Vice-President Schwebel Dissenting Opinions of Judges Shahabuddeen and Koroma[5] Separate Opinion of Judge Fleischhauer

(continued)

Pacific Ocean (Bolivia v Chile) (Preliminary Objection) [2015] ICJ Rep 592, para 1 (Separate Opinion of Judge Cançado Trindade) (*Access to the Pacific Ocean*); *Obligations Concerning Negotiations Relating to Cessation of the Nuclear Arms Race and to Nuclear Disarmament (Marshall Islands v India)* (Jurisdiction and Admissibility) [2016] ICJ Rep 255, 321 (Dissenting Opinion of Judge Cançado Trindade) (*Nuclear Arms and Disarmament*); *Sovereign Rights and Maritime Spaces in the Caribbean Sea (Nicaragua v Colombia)* (Preliminary Objections) [2016] ICJ Rep 4, 44 (Separate Opinion of Judge Cançado Trindade) (*Sovereign Rights and Maritime Spaces* (Preliminary Objections)); *Jadhav Case (India v Pakistan)* (Provisional Measures) [2017] ICJ Rep 231, 247 (Concurring Opinion of Judge Cançado Trindade (*Jadhav Case*); *Sovereign Rights and Maritime Spaces in the Caribbean Sea (Nicaragua v Colombia)* (Counter-Claims) [2017] Rep 289, 330 (Declaration of Judge Cançado Trindade) (*Sovereign Rights and Maritime Spaces* (Counter-Claims)).

[2] *Legality of the Threat or Use of Nuclear Weapons* (Advisory Opinion) [1996] ICJ Rep 226, 530 (Dissenting Opinion of Judge Weeramantry) (*Threat or Use of Nuclear Weapons*); *Request for Interpretation of the Judgment of 11 June 1998 in the Case Concerning the Land and Maritime Boundary between Cameroon and Nigeria (Cameroon v Nigeria)* (Preliminary Objections) [1999] ICJ Rep 31, 36; *Ahmadou Sadio Diallo (Republic of Guinea v Democratic Republic of the Congo)* [2010] ICJ Rep 639, 773 (Separate Opinion of Judge Cançado Trindade).

[3] *East Timor (Portugal v Australia)* [1995] ICJ Rep 90, 194 (Dissenting Opinion of Judge Weeramantry) 283 (Separate Opinion of Judge Ajibola); *Request for an Examination of the Situation in accordance with Paragraph 63 of the Court's Judgment of 20 December 1974 in the Nuclear Tests (New Zealand v France) Case* [1995] ICJ Rep 288, 359 (Dissenting Opinion of Judge Weeramantry); *Land and Maritime Boundary between Cameroon and Nigeria (Cameroon v Nigeria: Equatorial Guinea intervening)* [2002] ICJ Rep 303, 474 (Dissenting Opinion of Judge Koroma).

[4] For length purposes, short names of cases are used in this table. See footnotes for long names. Where the reference is to a Separate or Dissenting Opinion, this is noted. Where this is not noted, the reference is to the judgment of the ICJ itself.

[5] While the Opinions of Judge Shahabuddeen and Korama are briefly discussed for completeness, note that on construction these are *not* uses of General Principles in the Art 38(1)(c) sense.

Table 5.1 *(Continued)*

Category	Cases
	Application of the Genocide Convention (Preliminary Objections), Dissenting Opinion of Judge ad hoc Kreća (1996) *Aerial Incident at Lockerbie* (Preliminary Objections), Dissenting Opinion of President Schwebel (1998) *Oil Platforms* (Order), Dissenting Opinion of Judge Rigaux (1998) *Kasikili/Sedudu Island*, Separate Opinion of Judge Oda (1999) *Aerial Incident of 10 August 1999*, Dissenting Opinion of Judge Al-Khasawneh (2000) *Maritime Delimitation and Territorial Questions*, Dissenting Opinion of Judge Torres Bernárdez (2001) *Arrest Warrant Case*, Dissenting Opinion of Judge Van den Wyngaert (2002) *Pulau Ligitan and Pulau Sipadan*, Dissenting Opinion of Judge ad hoc Franck (2002) *Oil Platforms* (Merits), Separate Opinion of Judge Simma (2003) *Avena and Other Mexican Nationals* (2004) *Application of the Genocide Convention* (Judgment), Separate Opinion of Judge Owada (2007) *Application of the Interim Accord* (2011) Separate Opinion of Judge Simma Dissenting Opinion of Judge ad hoc Roucounas *Jurisdictional Immunities of the State*, Separate Opinion of Judge Bennouna (2012) *Construction of a Road*, Separate Opinion of Judge ad hoc Dugard (2015) *Delimitation of the Continental Shelf between Nicaragua and Colombia* (2016) Judgment of the Court Separate Opinion of Judge Owada Separate Opinion of Judge Greenwood
Contributions of Judge Weeramantry	*Greenland and Jan Mayen*, Separate Opinion (1993) *Application of the Genocide Convention* (Provisional Measures), Separate Opinion (1993) *Gabčíkovo-Nagymaros Project*, Separate Opinion (1997) *Land and Maritime Boundary* (Preliminary Objections), Dissenting Opinion (1998) *Pulau Ligitan and Pulau Sipadan* (Application to Intervene), Separate Opinion (2001)

(continued)

Table 5.1 *(Continued)*

Category	Cases
Contributions of Judge Cançado Trindade	*Obligation to Prosecute or Extradite* (Provisional Measures), Dissenting Opinion (2009) *Pulp Mills*, Separate Opinion (2010) *Jurisdictional Immunities of the State*, Dissenting Opinion (2012) *Obligation to Prosecute or Extradite* (Merits), Separate Opinion (2012) *Judgment No 2867 of the Administrative Tribunal of the ILO*, Separate Opinion (2012) *Diallo* (Compensation), Separate Opinion (2012) *Certain Activities (Joinder)/Construction of a Road* (Joinder), Separate Opinion (2013) *Documents and Data* (Provisional Measures), Separate Opinion (2014) *Access to the Pacific Ocean*, Separate Opinion (2015) *Nuclear Arms and Disarmament*, Dissenting Opinion (2016) *Sovereign Rights and Maritime Spaces* (Preliminary Objections), Separate Opinion (2016) *Jadhav Case*, Concurring Opinion (2017) *Sovereign Rights and Maritime Spaces* (Counter-Claims), Declaration (2017)

II. CASES (EXCEPT FOR THE SEPARATE AND DISSENTING OPINIONS OF JUDGES WEERAMANTRY AND CANÇADO TRINDADE)

A. *Aerial Incident at Lockerbie* (Provisional Measures)

This case[6] arose from the 1988 bombing of Pan Am flight 103. Libya alleged that the indictment of two Libyan nationals over the bombing was a breach of the Montreal Convention. The Dissenting Opinions of Judge El-Kosheri and Judge Ranjeva both briefly addressed General Principles at the provisional measures stage.

i. Judge El-Kosheri

Judge El-Kosheri discussed the rule against bias and concluded that the operation of this principle meant the suspects of the Lockerbie bombing could not receive a fair trial in Libya.[7] In support, El-Kosheri relied on 'fundamental legal

[6] *Questions of Interpretation and Application of 1971 Montreal Convention Arising from Aerial Incident at Lockerbie (Libyan Arab Jamahiriya v United Kingdom)* (Provisional Measures) [1992] ICJ Rep 3 (*Aerial Incident at Lockerbie* (Provisional Measures)).

[7] ibid 112 (Dissenting Opinion of Judge El-Kosheri).

principles, deeply rooted in the legal traditions of the major systems, particularly Islamic law'.[8] Although the only substantiation given for this statement was the extra-curial writing of Weeramantry,[9] it is clear that El-Kosheri was looking to domestic laws as the basis for the principle. Further, it follows the example of Judge Ammoun in *North Sea Continental Shelf* to include religious legal systems in the methodology of finding a General Principle.[10]

ii. Judge Ranjeva

Judge Ranjeva explicitly referred to General Principles in his Dissenting Opinion. The mention, however, is fleeting – Ranjeva suggests that one conception of the Respondent's argument would be contrary to the '"general principles of law recognized by civilized nations", principles founded upon the equality of States and their equal ability to ensure that obligations under international law are fulfilled'.[11] This is possibly a General Principle drawing from the international forum – in particular, being drawn from other international principles or norms.

B. *Certain Phosphate Lands in Nauru*

Nauru brought an action against Australia regarding phosphate mines mined by Australia before Nauru's independence.[12] Australia raised several objections, including that the obligation owed was joint, pursuant to the Administrating Agreement between Australia, New Zealand and the United Kingdom.[13]

In considering whether Nauru could bring an action against only one of the three obligated parties, Judge Shahabuddeen turned to principles of municipal law to find a General Principle.[14] Shahabuddeen first considered English law principles on the subject,[15] noting that a plaintiff is not barred from choosing to sue only one of several joint contractors.[16] Although Shahabuddeen only considered common law in any depth, he did make mention of other legal systems:

> It does not appear to me that recourse to municipal law, in so far as I have been able to explore it, yields any satisfactory analogies supportive of the suggested existence

[8] ibid.
[9] ibid.
[10] *North Sea Continental Shelf (Federal Republic of Germany v Denmark; Federal Republic of Germany v the Netherlands)* [1969] ICJ Rep 3 (*North Sea Continental Shelf*); see discussion in ch 4.
[11] *Aerial Incident at Lockerbie* (Provisional Measures) (n 6) 72 (Dissenting Opinion of Judge Ranjeva).
[12] *Certain Phosphate Lands in Nauru (Nauru v Australia)* (Preliminary Objections) [1992] ICJ 240 (*Certain Phosphate Lands in Nauru*).
[13] ibid 258–59.
[14] ibid 287 (Separate Opinion of Judge Shahabuddeen).
[15] ibid 287.
[16] ibid 289.

> of any rule of international law precluding the present action on the ground that the obligation was joint. On balance, the general trend of the references given by the Parties to non-Anglo-Saxon legal systems is not, I believe, at variance with this conclusion.[17]

Clearly Shahabuddeen saw General Principles as being drawn from the domestic forum and, although he did not discuss his reasoning any further, a comparative methodology across 'Anglo-Saxon' and 'non-Anglo-Saxon' legal systems.

C. *Territorial Dispute*

This case concerned a border dispute between Libyan Arab Jamahiriya and the Republic of Chad.[18] In his Separate Opinion, Judge Ajibola agreed with the decision of the Court that the 1955 Treaty of Friendship and Good Neighbourliness set out the relevant border. He then explored what application other 'principles like acquiescence, estoppel, recognition and *uti possideti juris* could possibly play in this matter'.[19] Both the discussions on estoppel and *uti possidetis* contain possible General Principles.

i. Estoppel

On estoppel, Ajibola stated:

> [E]stoppel in international law is a developing principle that it may be difficult to classify at this moment, either as forming part of customary international law or as belonging to the general principles of international law.[20]

Although the wording Ajibola employs is not the exact wording of General Principles,[21] his subsequent reference to estoppel as a provision of both customary and civil law systems[22] could suggest an intentional reference to Article 38(1)(c). If so, this Opinion groups together custom and General Principles: the issues with conflating custom and General Principles as discussed in chapter 4 also apply here.

[17] ibid.

[18] *Territorial Dispute (Libyan Arab Jamahiriya v Chad)* (Merits) [1994] ICJ Rep 6 (*Territorial Dispute*).

[19] ibid 77 (Separate Opinion of Judge Ajibola).

[20] ibid.

[21] Although it is a rewording used in the work of some publicists as well in the later Opinions of Judge Cançado Trindade: see discussion in section IV. See also, eg, W Riphagen 'General Principles of Law' in A Cassese and JHH Weiler (eds), *Change and Stability in International Law Making* (Walter de Gruyter, 1988) 33, 34; MC Bassiouni 'A Functional Approach to "General Principles of International Law"' (1990) 11 *Michigan Journal of International Law* 768, 772; S Kadelbach and T Kleinlein, 'International Law – a Constitution for Mankind? An attempt at Re-appraisal with an Analysis' (2007) 50 *German Yearbook of International Law* 303, 337.

[22] *Territorial Dispute* (n 18) 77 (Separate Opinion of Judge Ajibola).

ii. Uti Possidetis

The principle or rule of *uti possidetis* fixes 'the territorial heritage of new States at the moment of independence'.[23] Judge Ajibola seemed to suggest it is a General Principle, stating that '[i]n their dissenting opinions in the case of Sovereignty over Certain Frontier Land … both Judges Armand-Ugon and Moreno Quintana agreed that the *uti possidetis* principle should be treated as a general principle of law'.[24] Neither Judge Armand-Ugon nor Quintana used the phrase: Armand-Ugon describes it as 'the principle of *uti possidetis*'[25] and Moreno Quintana as 'the well-known principle of *uti possidetis*'.[26] Ajibola also suggested the ICJ had accepted *uti posseditis* as a general principle of law in the *Frontier Dispute*[27] case between Burkina Faso and Mali.[28] In that case, the Chamber of the ICJ applied the principle to the dispute, explaining 'the principle is not a special rule which pertains solely to one specific system of international law. It is a general principle, which is logically connected with the phenomenon of the obtaining of independence, wherever it occurs.'[29]

The phrase 'general principle' is the only arguable link to Article 38(1)(c): Ajibola added the words 'of law' in this later Opinion, strengthening the link to Article 38(1)(c). It is unclear what source of law the Chamber of the ICJ viewed *uti posseditis* as stemming from. If it *was* a General Principle, it would be one drawn not from the domestic forum but rather as a logical deduction from the legal system itself. It can also be noted that both Judge Ajibola and the ICJ Chamber used the terms 'rule' and 'principle' interchangeably in their discussions, demonstrating again the lack of delimitation between the two terms.

D. *Threat or Use of Nuclear Weapons*

In *Threat or Use of Nuclear Weapons*,[30] the United Nations General Assembly asked the Court to advise on the question, 'Is the threat or use of nuclear weapons in any circumstance permitted under international law?'[31] The Court ultimately held that the use of nuclear weapons needed to be 'compatible with the requirements of the international law applicable in armed conflict particularly those of the principles and rules of international humanitarian law'.[32]

[23] MN Shaw, 'The Heritage of States: The Principle of *Uti Possidetis Juris* Today' (1996) 67(1) *British Yearbook of International Law* 75, 76.

[24] *Territorial Dispute* (n 18) 88 (Separate Opinion of Judge Ajibola).

[25] *Sovereignty over Certain Frontier Land (Belgium v Netherlands)* [1959] ICJ Rep 209, 240 (Dissenting Opinion of Judge Armand-Ugon).

[26] ibid 255 (Dissenting Opinion of Judge Moreno Quintana).

[27] *Frontier Dispute (Burkina Faso v Mali)* [1986] ICJ Rep 554.

[28] *Territorial Dispute* (n 18) 88 (Separate Opinion of Judge Ajibola).

[29] *Frontier Dispute (Burkina Faso v Mali)* (n 27) 565.

[30] *Threat or Use of Nuclear Weapons* (n 2).

[31] ibid 228.

[32] ibid 266.

However, the Court also concluded that although the use of nuclear weapons would generally breach these principles, it was unable to conclusively state whether nuclear weapons would be lawful or unlawful in 'an extreme circumstance of self-defence in which the very survival of a State would be at stake'.[33] General Principles were engaged with in the face of this apparent *non liquet* by several Judges, and substantively for the principle of self-defence (or protection from self-abandonment) by Judge Fleischhauer.

i. Non Liquet

While many of the Court's findings were unanimous, paragraph 2(e) of the *dispositif* was split with seven votes for and seven votes against: it was only President Bedjaoui's presiding vote that allowed it to carry. The contentious part was the second paragraph, which declared the Court unable to conclude definitively on whether use of nuclear weapons could ever be legal. Several judges took exception to this, pointing to General Principles as a way of resolving a *non liquet* before the Court. Judge Herczgh stated:

> In my view, however, in the present state of international law it would have been possible to formulate in the Advisory Opinion a more specific reply to the General Assembly's request, one less burdened with uncertainty and reticence. In the fields where certain acts are not totally and universally prohibited 'as such', the application of the general principles of law makes it possible to regulate the behaviour of subjects of the international legal order, obliging or authorizing them, as the case may be, to act or refrain from acting in one way or another.[34]

Vice-President Schwebel expressly linked the historical development of General Principles with the role of filling lacuna:

> Indeed, the drafters of the Statute of the Permanent Court of International Justice crafted the provisions of Article 38 of its Statute – provisions which Article 38 of the Statute of this Court maintains – in order, in the words of the President of the Advisory Committee of Jurists, to avoid 'especially the blind alley of *non liquet*'. To do so, they adopted the Root-Phillimore proposal to empower the Court to apply not only international conventions and international custom but 'the general principles of law recognized by civilized nations'.[35]

In this context, Judge Shahabuddeen also seemingly refer to Article 38(1)(c), although with less precise terminology:

> The circumstance that there is no 'comprehensive and universal prohibition of the threat or use of nuclear weapons as such' in customary or conventional international

[33] ibid 266.
[34] ibid 275 (Declaration of Judge Herczgh).
[35] ibid 323 (Dissenting Opinion of Vice President Schwebel).

> law does not conclude the question whether the threat or use of such weapons is lawful; more general principles have to be consulted.[36]

While this construction of 'general principles' as an alternative to custom and convention seems to fit Article 38(1)(c) – and the use by Judge Herczgh and Vice-President Schwebel – the 'general principles' Shahabuddeen was referring to actually comprised an application of the doctrine of permissibility from the *Lotus* decision. Shahabuddeen describes this as the '*Lotus* principle' and discusses four possible conceptions of it.[37] The 'general' principles here are thus drawn from international jurisprudence.[38] If this is a true use of Article 38(1)(c), it suggests a non-comparativist methodology using international judgments as the source of the norm. However, it would seem Shahabuddeen is really employing international legal development by reference to previous cases[39] rather than actually utilising General Principles. The same argument is made by Judge Koroma, who states that the Court, in solving a *non liquet*, will refer to 'the principles of international law, to equity and to its own jurisprudence in order to define and settle the legal issues referred to it'.[40] While this is an accurate statement of what the ICJ has historically done, such approaches are neither grounded in nor justified by Article 38(1)(c), and cannot be taken as referring to General Principles in this sense.

ii. Judge Fleischhauer

In his Separate Opinion, Judge Fleischhauer considered how the rules of humanitarian law and rules governing armed conflict often clash.[41] His solution was to look to the 'smallest common denominator' between the rules to see if a compromise could be reached.[42] Fleischhauer argued that although humanitarian law in general prohibited the use of nuclear weapons, an exception existed in extreme cases of self-defence. In these situations a country could resort to nuclear weapons as a last resort to protect its very existence from an aggressor state.[43] Fleischhauer justified this conclusion by reference to a substantive General Principle:

> The same result is reached if, in the absence of a conventional or a customary rule for the conciliation of the conflicting legal principles and rules, it is accepted that

[36] ibid 377 (Dissenting Opinion of Judge Shahabuddeen).

[37] ibid 391–95 (Dissenting Opinion of Judge Shahabuddeen), referring to *SS 'Lotus' (France v Turkey)* [1927] PCIJ Series A No 10, 16.

[38] Judge Shahabudeen also draws on a number of other PCIJ/ICJ cases in his discussion. See ibid 391–95.

[39] See generally on this trend W Alschner and D Charlotin, 'The Growing Complexity of the International Court of Justice's Self-Citation Network' (2018) 29(1) *European Journal of International Law* 83; see also discussion in ch 4.

[40] *Threat or Use of Nuclear Weapons* (n 2) 576 (Dissenting Opinion of Judge Koroma).

[41] ibid 308 (Separate Opinion of Judge Fleischhauer).

[42] ibid.

[43] ibid.

> the third category of law which the Court has to apply by virtue of Article 38 of its Statute, that is, the general principles of law recognized in all legal systems contains a principle to the effect that no legal system is entitled to demand the self-abandonment, the suicide, of one of its subjects.[44]

This slight rephrasing of the actual words of Article 38(1)(c) – 'general principles of law recognized by civilized nations' – to the words used by Fleischhauer – 'general principles of law recognized in all legal systems'[45] – provides an indication that the judge viewed the methodology of ascertaining General Principles as comparativist: General Principles exist at international law if found in municipal legal systems. This is confirmed by the next line: 'Much can be said, in my view, in favour of the applicability of such a principle in all modern legal systems and consequently also in international law.'[46] If a principle exists in a certain number of municipal legal systems (for Judge Fleischhauer, it seems this number might be all – although this seems impractical) it is a General Principle, existing in the international sphere.

E. *Application of the Genocide Convention* (Preliminary Objections)

This case[47] was brought by Bosnia-Herzegovina against the Former Republic of Yugoslavia (FRY). Bosnia-Herzegovina accused FRY of breaching the Convention on the Crime and Punishment of Genocide.[48] The FRY's third preliminary objection was that Bosnia-Herzegovina did not succeed to the Convention of the Prevention and Punishment of the Crime of Genocide upon its declaration of independence.[49] The Court held that it was not necessary to determine whether Bosnia-Herzegovina succeeded to the Convention or joined it at a later date to rule on the Court's jurisdiction in the matter.[50] Judge Kreća, the judge ad hoc from the FRY, dissented on this point, and argued that Bosnia-Herzegovina could not have succeeded to the Convention, as it had illegally seceded from the Socialist Federal Republic of Yugoslavia.[51]

Kreća discussed this alleged illegality of secession at some length in his Dissenting Opinion. He stated:

> On the other hand, an explicit condemnation of secession can be found in the general principles of law recognized by civilized nations as a formal source of international

[44] ibid 308–09.
[45] ibid 308.
[46] ibid 309.
[47] *Application of the Convention on the Prevention and the Punishment of the Crime of Genocide (Bosnia and Herzegovina v Serbia and Montenegro)* (Preliminary Objections) [1996] ICJ Rep 595 (*Application of the Genocide Convention* (Preliminary Objections)).
[48] ibid 617.
[49] ibid 605.
[50] ibid 612.
[51] ibid 752 (Dissenting Opinion of Judge Kreća).

> law pursuant to Article 38(1)(c) of the Statute of the International Court of Justice. Secession is deemed to be a most serious crime by the national legislations of civilized nations. More particularly, an inside assault on the territorial integrity of a country or an attempted assault, including preparatory actions, are categorized as one of the gravest of crimes in virtually all the criminal codes of civilized nations.[52]

The Court did not agree with Kreća's characterisation of secession, or his conclusion that secession was illegal at international law.[53] Regardless of the legal validity of Kreća's conclusions, it is clear that he used a comparative methodology, looking to the municipal laws of nations, to identify a substantive rule as a General Principle.

F. *Aerial Incident at Lockerbie* (Preliminary Objections)

Following from the provisional measures stage discussed in section II.A, the United States and the United Kingdom raised preliminary objections to jurisdiction and admissibility,[54] which were rejected by the Court.[55] President Schwebel dissented, arguing that United Nations Security Council (UNSC) resolutions governing the situation rendered Libya's claims moot.[56] In doing so, Schwebel explored whether the ICJ can exercise judicial review of UNSC resolutions. As well as considering the past jurisprudence of the ICJ and the text and *travaux préparatoires* of the UN Charter, Schwebel looked to whether a General Principle could found a power of judicial review:

> It would not be a development drawn from the general principles of law. Judicial review, in varying forms, is found in a number of democratic polities, most famously that of the United States, where it was developed by the Supreme Court itself. But it is by no means a universal or even general principle of government or law. It is hardly found outside the democratic world and is not uniformly found in it. Where it exists internationally, as in the European Union, it is expressly provided for by treaty in specific terms. The United Nations is far from being a government, or an international organization comparable in its integration to the European Union, and it is not democratic.[57]

[52] ibid 754.

[53] ibid 610–11 (Judgment of the Court).

[54] *Questions of Interpretation and Application of the Montreal Convention arising from the Aerial Incident at Lockerbie (Libyan Arab Jamahiriya v United Kingdom)* (Preliminary Objections) [1998] ICJ Rep 115; *Questions of Interpretation and Application of the Montreal Convention arising from the Aerial Incident at Lockerbie (Libyan Arab Jamahiriya v United States of America)* (Preliminary Objections) [1998] ICJ Rep 115. As the judgments are identical, subsequent citations of the short title *Aerial Incident at Lockerbie* (Preliminary Objections) are to both, with pinpoints to each case.

[55] *Aerial Incident at Lockerbie* (Preliminary Objections) (n 54) 30–31, 135–36.

[56] ibid 71, 162 (Dissenting Opinion of President Schwebel).

[57] ibid 80, 171.

While Schwebel denied the existence of such a General Principle, his analysis reveals a comparative methodology, drawing from domestic law and requiring some degree of uniformity across different political and legal systems. Schwebel also recognises the need for appropriateness: as the principle is one unique to democratic governments, it is not suitable for transformation to the (non-democratic, non-governmental) system of the United Nations.

G. *Oil Platforms* (Order)

This Order dealt with dealt with the admissibility of a counter-claim made by the United States against Iran.[58] In considering the law surrounding counter-claims in the ICJ, Judge Rigaux stated:

> The notions of counter-claim and connection used in Article 80 of the Rules of Court are borrowed from the vocabulary of the municipal law of procedure. This raises the question whether the Court could rely on general principles of law developed from convergent practice in municipal systems. That would appear to have deserved more painstaking examination. Here are a few examples taken from French law, Belgian law and the law of the European Communities.[59]

Rigaux then went on to consider provisions of the French New Code of Civil Procedure, and the Belgian Judicial Code.[60] In the end, Judge Rigaux did not find a General Principle definitively existed, rather identifying three 'municipal law solutions' that 'the Court could learn from'.[61]

The passage indicates a (limited) comparative approach drawing from the domestic forum, albeit muddied by the inclusion of multinational treaties between European nations.[62]

H. *Kasikili/Sedudu Island*

In this case,[63] the ICJ was asked to determine the boundary around Kasikili/Sedudu Island, which would determine whether the sovereignty of the island inhered with Botswana or Namibia. In a special agreement, the two parties requested the Court to judge the dispute, taking into account both an Anglo-German treaty from 1890 and the 'rules and principles of international law'.

[58] *Oil Platforms (Islamic Republic of Iran v United States of America)* (Order of 10 March 1988) [1998] ICJ Rep 190 (*Oil Platforms* (Order)).

[59] ibid 230.

[60] ibid 230–32.

[61] ibid 234.

[62] ibid 232–33.

[63] *Kasikili/Sedudu Island (Botswana v Namibia)* (Merits) [1999] ICJ Rep 1045 (*Kasikili/Sedudu Island*).

Although in the *compromis* the rules and principles of international law were explicitly interpreted by the parties as meaning Article 38(1) as a whole,[64] Judge Oda, in his Separate Opinion, stated that the parties interpreted 'rules and principles' as General Principles,[65] and proceeded on that basis:

> The Court is requested 'to determine ... on the basis of the [1890] Anglo-German Treaty ... and the rules and principles of international law' (*compromis*, Art I). The words 'rules and principles of international law' are understood by the Parties to mean 'those [as] set forth in the provisions of Article 38, paragraph 1, of the Statute of the International Court of Justice; (*compromis*, Art III), namely, 'the general principles of law recognized by civilized nations' (Statute, Art 38, para 1).[66]

Judge Oda continued to restrict the interpretation of Article 38(1) to a consideration of Article 38(1)(c) alone,[67] without justifying the omission of convention or custom. On this basis he argued that the Anglo-German Treaty and General Principles were mutually exclusionary basis of law, and the Court could not rely on both of them.[68] Oda outlined the legal conclusions that would result from relying on the Anglo-German Treaty as the basis for the decision and then, alternatively, turned to the outcome of relying on General Principles.

Judge Oda considered one possible General Principle – the doctrine of prescription.[69] Oda did not explain why he considered the doctrine of prescription to be a General Principle, but agreed with the Court that no active prescription of the island could be shown on the facts of the case.[70] The Court itself did not specify that it was discussing the doctrine of prescription under the auspices of General Principles, or elaborate on how the doctrine became a norm of international law.[71] Rather, it was assumed that the doctrine existed at international law, and discussion centred on whether as a matter of fact active prescription had actually occurred.[72] Judge Oda did not turn to any other possible General Principles, stating 'I see no reference in the arguments of the Parties to this element [of additional general principles]. I find no reason to take "the rules and principles of international law" as a basis for the Court's determination.'[73]

Although Judge Oda devoted the first few paragraphs of his judgment to why General Principles cannot be considered concurrently with the Anglo-German Treaty, he abandoned any examination of the operation and application of General Principles. Given that Oda construed the parties' special agreement as

[64] ibid 1050.
[65] ibid 1120–21 (Separate Opinion of Judge Oda).
[66] ibid 1120.
[67] ibid 1121.
[68] ibid 1121.
[69] ibid 1132.
[70] ibid.
[71] ibid 1103.
[72] ibid 1103–06.
[73] ibid 1132.

specifically asking the Court to deliberate on the basis of General Principles, his Separate Opinion would have been a prime opportunity for such analysis.[74] It is more likely that the restriction of Article III of the *compromis* to Article 38(1)(c) of the Statute of the Court, rather than Article 38(1) as the *compromis* provided,[75] was a misconstruction, a theory backed up by its lack of citation in jurists' writings on the case or on General Principles more broadly.[76] If this is the case then the judgment is of understandably little help in ascertaining the nature of Article 38(1)(c).

I. *Aerial Incident of 10 August 1999*

In *Aerial Incident of 10 August 1999*,[77] Judge Al-Khasawneh considered a General Principle of separability of treaty provisions in his Dissenting Opinion.[78] In doing so, Al-Khasawneh looked to Indian law as 'an example from one of the major systems of law',[79] as well as Islamic law and Roman law.[80] Judge Al-Khasawneh consciously limited his comparative survey, stating:

> [I]t is unnecessary to delve in like fashion into similar concepts found in other major systems of law. It is reasonable to expect that the solutions devised by those systems would not be radically different from that decision.[81]

Nonetheless, it is clear the methodology is comparative, drawing from national legal systems – including religious systems, as did Judge El-Kosheri in *Aerial Incident at Lockerbie* and Judge Ammoun in *North Sea Continental Shelf*.[82]

J. *Maritime and Territorial Questions*

This case[83] concerned a sovereignty dispute between Qatar and Bahrain. The ICJ had to consider, among other factors, the effect of a decision made by Great Britain in 1939 (as both Bahrain and Qatar were British Protectorates at the

[74] Especially given he did so on three previous occasions: see ch 4.

[75] *Kasikili/Sedudu Island* (n 63) 1050 (Separate Opinion of Judge Oda).

[76] See, eg, M Shaw and M Evans, 'Case Concerning Kasikili/Sedudu Island (Botswana/Namibia)' (2000) 49(4) *The International and Comparative Law Quarterly* 964; A Pellet and D Müller, 'Article 38' in A Zimmerman, CJ Tams, K Oellers-Frahm and C Tomuschat (eds), *The Statute of the International Court of Justice: A Commentary,* 3rd edn (Oxford University Press, 2019) 819; I Brownlie, *Principles of Public International Law*, 7th edn (Oxford University Press, 2008) 17–18.

[77] *Aerial Incident of 10 August 1999 (Pakistan v India)* (Jurisdiction) [2000] ICJ Rep 12 (*Aerial Incident of 10 August 1999*).

[78] ibid 53–54 (Dissenting Opinion of Judge Al-Khasawneh).

[79] ibid 54.

[80] ibid 57.

[81] ibid.

[82] *North Sea Continental Shelf* (n 10); see discussion in ch 4.

[83] *Maritime and Territorial Questions between Qatar and Bahrain (Qatar v Bahrain)* (Merits) [2001] ICJ Rep 40 (*Maritime and Territorial Questions*).

time), which awarded sovereignty over the Hawar Islands to Bahrain. While the Court held the decision was binding on Qatar and Bahrain,[84] Judge Torres Bernárdez disagreed. He argued that the decision was invalid because it was incongruous, inconsistent and arbitrary:

> Internal inconsistency and arbitrariness, as well as incongruity, are in law a cause or ground which may affect the essential validity and, therefore, the applicability of the decision concerned. This is recognized in the various legal systems of the world to the point of being a general principle of law (Art 38 of the Court's Statute).[85]

Although Torres Bernárdez did not elaborate on *which* legal systems he was drawing from, it is clear he was relying on a principle of domestic administrative law, using an implied comparative methodology drawing from the domestic forum.

K. *Arrest Warrant Case*

In 2000, Belgium issued an arrest warrant for Abdulaye Yerodia Ndombasi, the then Foreign Minister of the Democratic Republic of Congo (DRC).[86] The DRC complained, among other things, that the warrant violated Yerodia's diplomatic immunity.[87] The Court held that there was no relevant exception to immunity in this case.[88]

The Belgian ad hoc judge, Judge Van den Wyngaert, dissented on this point. In doing so, he criticised the Court for failing to consider General Principles:

> Questions concerning international accountability for war crimes and crimes against humanity and that were not addressed by the International Court of Justice include the following. Can international accountability for such crimes be considered to be a general principle of law in the sense of Article 38 of the Court's Statute?[89]

Unfortunately, Van den Wyngaert did not elaborate on whether such a General Principle could or did exist.

L. *Pulau Ligitan and Pulau Sipadan*

This case[90] concerned a dispute over the sovereignty of two islands, Ligitan and Sipidan. While the Court concluded that sovereignty lay with Malaysia, Judge

[84] ibid 146.
[85] ibid 381 (Dissenting Opinion of Judge Torres Bernárdez).
[86] *Arrest Warrant of 11 April 2000 (Democratic Republic of the Congo v Belgium)* (Merits) [2002] ICJ Rep 3 (*Arrest Warrant Case*) 9.
[87] ibid 10.
[88] ibid 33.
[89] ibid 156 (Dissenting Opinion of Judge Van den Wyngaert).
[90] *Sovereignty over Pulau Ligitan and Pulau Sipidan (Indonesia v Malaysia)* [2002] ICJ Rep 625 (*Pulau Ligitan and Pulau Sipidan*).

Franck as the ad hoc judge for Indonesia disagreed. In his Dissenting Opinion, Franck relied on a legal presumption that

> when States negotiate a boundary allocating or confirming their respective areas of sovereignty over territories, these shall be presumed to have intended to resolve all outstanding and potentially disputatious claims in the area in question, subject only to convincing evidence to the contrary.[91]

Franck found support for this presumption in the writing of several jurists, including Bin Cheng, who classified the presumption as a General Principle.[92] Franck stated:

> Presumptions are necessary and well-established aspects both of common and civil law and cannot but be a part of the fabric of public international law. They capture the common experience of persons everywhere that make inferences an essential part of rational thought and action. As such, they are often captured in legal maxims recognized across diverse legal systems.[93]

Here the General Principle is drawn from domestic systems using a (limited) comparative methodology. The horizontal generality of the principle is explained by its content's being the 'common experience of persons everywhere': this follows the approach of Judge Lauterpacht in *Interhandel* and Judge Ammoun in *North Sea Continental Shelf*.[94]

M. *Oil Platforms* (Merits)

After the admissibility of the US counter-claim was dealt with by order (see section II.G), its substance was considered as part of the merits phase of the case.[95] Although the Court did not address General Principles, the Separate Opinion of Judge Simma did.[96] Simma considered the US counter-claim, and in particular the apportionment of responsibility between Iran and Iraq for damage caused to the economic environment by the Iran–Iraq war.[97] In this context, Simma turned to General Principles:

> In order to find a solution to our dilemma, I have engaged in some research in comparative law to see whether anything resembling a 'general principle of law' within the meaning of Article 38, paragraph 1 *(c)*, of the Statute of the Court can be

[91] ibid 706 (Dissenting Opinion of Judge ad hoc Franck).

[92] ibid 705.

[93] ibid.

[94] *Interhandel (Switzerland v United States of America)* (Preliminary Objections) [1959] ICJ Rep 6 (*Interhandel*); *North Sea Continental Shelf* (n 10); see ch 4.

[95] *Oil Platforms (Islamic Republic of Iran v United States of America)* (Merits) [2003] ICJ Rep 161 (*Oil Platforms* (Merits)).

[96] ibid 331 (Separate Opinion of Judge Simma).

[97] ibid 354.

> developed from solutions arrived at in domestic law to come to terms with the problem of multiple tortfeasors. I submit that we find ourselves here in what I would call a textbook situation calling for such an exercise in legal analogy. To state its result forthwith: research into various common law jurisdictions as well as French, Swiss and German tort law indicates that the question has been taken up and solved by these legal systems with a consistency that is striking.[98]

Clearly Simma engaged a comparative *methodology*, looking to various municipal laws from both common and civil law jurisdictions – the domestic forum. Although Simma describes his comparative study as 'admittedly modest',[99] he nonetheless finds in it support for holding that a principle of tort law (joint and several liability) is a General Principle, binding at international law.[100]

N. *Application of the Genocide Convention* (Judgment)

Judge Owada's Separate Opinion in the 2007 judgment in this case[101] makes brief reference to General Principles. In the context of *res judicata*, Owada says that 'The statement contained in Article 60 of the Statute has been interpreted as the practical embodiment within the Statute of the rule of *res judicata* as "a general principle of law recognized by civilized nations".'[102]

Owada refers to the work of the Advisory Committee to confirm that *res judicata* is a General Principle.[103] However, his discussion on *res judicata* proceeded on the basis of Article 60 of the Court's Statute rather than as a General Principle, and thus is of no further help in construing the source itself.

O. *Application of the Interim Accord*

This case[104] concerned the interpretation of an accord between the then Former Yugoslav Republic of Macedonia (FYR Macedonia) and Greece, designed to allow the FYR Macedonia to join international organisations despite Greece's ongoing objection to its name.[105] Greece argued that it had not breached the accord and, in the alternative, any possible wrongful conduct was precluded

[98] ibid 354.
[99] ibid 358.
[100] ibid.
[101] *Application of the Convention on the Prevention and Punishment of the Crime of Genocide (Bosnia and Herzegovina v Serbia and Montenegro)* (Judgment) [2007] ICJ Rep 47 (*Application of the Genocide Convention* (Judgment)).
[102] ibid 289 (Separate Opinion of Judge Owada).
[103] ibid.
[104] *Application of the Interim Accord of 13 September 1995 (Former Yugoslav Republic of Macedonia v Greece)* [2011] ICJ Rep 644 (*Application of the Interim Accord*).
[105] The name dispute was settled in 2018 when the FRY Macedonia agreed to the name 'Republic of North Macedonia'.

by a 'general principle of international law' of *exceptio non adimpleti contractus*.[106] The Court held that as no breach of the accord relevant to the doctrine had been demonstrated, there was no need to consider whether it actually existed at international law.[107]

i. Judge Simma

In his Separate Opinion, Judge Simma considered the doctrine. Although the pleadings of the parties and the judgment of the Court referred to it as a 'general principle of international law', Simma clarified it to be a General Principle under Article 38(1)(c):

> The functional synallagma thus confirmed to be applicable also in international law has its historical roots in the law of contracts of most legal systems. Its genealogy can be traced back to the ancient Roman law foundations of the civil law tradition (the Roman *bonae fidei judicia*), as well as to early English contract law concepts of reciprocity in dependent obligations or mutual promises, the doctrine of consideration, and breach of condition. According to what is probably the majority view in international legal doctrine, the widespread acceptance of the principle in the main legal traditions of the civil and common law systems allows to recognize it as a general principle of law under Article 38, paragraph 1 *(c)*, of the Court's Statute.[108]

In conformity with Simma's earlier Separate Opinion in *Oil Platforms*, this evinces a comparative methodology drawing from domestic legal systems. Again, Simma restricts the type of legal systems in his survey to common and civil law systems. Simma also recognises the need for *appropriateness*:

> The question is, of course, the transferability of such a concept developed *in foro domestico* to the international legal plane, respectively the amendments that it will have to undergo in order for such a general principle to be able to play a constructive role also at the international level.[109]

Here, there is some room for judicial discretion, to allow amendments to transform the principle from domestic to international operation.

ii. Judge ad hoc Roucounas

Judge ad hoc Roucounas also briefly considered the *exceptio non adimpleti contractus* doctrine, stating that it

> expresses a principle so just and so equitable … that it can be found in one form or another in every legal system. It is the corollary of reciprocity and synallagmatic agreements. It follows that Article 60 of the Vienna Convention on the Law

[106] *Application of the Interim Accord* (n 104) 680.
[107] ibid 690–91.
[108] ibid 700 (Separate Opinion of Judge Simma).
[109] ibid.

> of Treaties is not the sole form of expression of the exception. As a defence to the non-performance of an obligation, it is a general principle of law, as enshrined in Article 38, paragraph 1 (c), of the Statute of the Court.[110]

Two points can be derived from this: first, Roucounas saw the justness of the principle as the reason for its horizontal generality, in line with Judge ad hoc Franck in *Pulua Ligitan and Pulua Sipidan*, Judge Lauterpacht in *Interhandel*[111] and Judge Ammoun in *North Sea Continental Shelf*.[112] Second, although not explicit, the phrase 'every legal system' seems to suggest a comparative methodology drawing from domestic legal systems.

P. *Jurisdictional Immunities of the State*

In this case,[113] Judge Bennouna argued for a link between state responsibility and state immunity.[114] Bennouna argued that as Germany had accepted the unlawfulness of its conduct towards former Italian war interns, Germany must also take responsibility in the form of compensation.[115] If not, then Germany should not be able to rely on state immunity to avoid suit in Italy's courts. In making this link, Bennouna referred to the ICJ's decision in *Corfu Channel*:

> It is by taking account of all those elements, and their mutually complementary nature, that the Court can help to ensure the unity of international law in the service of international justice. That primordial function cannot be confined within a narrow, formalistic approach, which considers immunity alone, *stricto sensu*, without concern for the victims of international crimes seeking justice. It could be considered that an 'interstitial norm', as expressed by Vaughan Lowe ... would enable the establishment of a link between the law of immunities and the law of State responsibility. This could be done by invoking general principles of law, as the Court did in the *Corfu Channel* case, where it referred to 'elementary considerations of humanity' as a link between human rights and international humanitarian law.[116]

Lowe distinguishes between 'primary norms' of international law, as 'the rules that mandate or forbid or permit certain activities',[117] and the 'interstitial norms', as those 'operating in the interstices between those primary norms'.[118] Such norms do not have normative force but 'operate by modifying

[110] ibid 745 (Dissenting Opinion of Judge ad hoc Roucuonas).
[111] See discussion in ch 4.
[112] *North Sea Continental Shelf* (n 10); see discussion in ch 4.
[113] *Jurisdictional Immunities of the State* (n 1).
[114] ibid 173 (Separate Opinion of Judge Bennouna).
[115] ibid 174.
[116] ibid 176–77, referring to *Corfu Channel (United Kingdom of Great Britain and Northern Ireland v Albania)* (Merits) [1949] ICJ Rep 4 (*Corfu Channel*).
[117] V Lowe, 'The Politics of Law-making: Are the Method and Character of Norm Creation Changing?' in M Byers (ed), *The Role of Law in International Politics: Essays in International Relations and International Law* (Oxford University Press, 2000) 207, 213.
[118] ibid.

the normative effect of other, primary norms of international law'.[119] Although Bennouna anchors such norms in Article 38(1)(c), Lowe does not: 'interstitial norms are not generated by the same processes as the traditional "primary" norms of international law … They simply "emerge" from within the international legal system.'[120] Bennouna's link to General Principle is buoyed by one of Lowe's examples – Judge Weeramnaty's treatment of sustainable development in his Separate Opinon in *Gabçikovo-Nagymaros*.[121] However, it is clear that Lowe is describing a phenomena of legal reasoning that is not tied to a specific source; rather it is an explanation of the *way* judges apply the rules of international law where no clear solution exists. While such interstitial norms may be able to be justified on the basis of General Principles, there is no requirement to do so. Thus while the *type* of General Principle may include these broad principles that modify customary or treaty rules, we cannot say that this is the only type.

Q. *Construction of a Road*

In his Separate Opinion in *Construction of a Road*,[122] Judge ad hoc Dugard discussed the meaning of the term 'general international law' as used in *Pulp Mills*. Dugard queried whether a General Principle could ever *found* an international cause of action:

> As the term 'general international law' does not appear in the sources of international law listed in Article 38 (1) of the Court's Statute there will inevitably be some debate about the precise meaning to be attached to the term. 'General international law' cannot be equated with 'general principles of law recognized by civilized nations' referred to in Article 38 (1) *(c)* in the present context as the Court has accepted the obligation to conduct an environmental impact assessment as an obligation that gives rise to a cause of action. Were the term to be interpreted as synonymous with 'general principles of law' the question would be raised whether such a 'general principle of law' might found a cause of action and require the Court to enter this jurisprudential minefield.[123]

Judge ad hoc Dugard acknowledged that 'a general principle of law might give rise to a cause of action cannot be discounted', with reference to the *Chorzów Factory* case,[124] but contrasted this against *Mavrommatis Jerusalem*

[119] ibid.
[120] ibid 219.
[121] ibid 215–16. See section III.C for further discussion.
[122] *Certain Activities Carried Out by Nicaragua in the Border Area (Costa Rica v Nicaragua)* and *Construction of a Road in Costa Rica Along the San Juan River (Nicaragua v Costa Rica)* [2015] ICJ 667 (*Construction of a Road*).
[123] ibid 847 (Separate Opinion of Judge ad hoc Dugard).
[124] ibid, referring to *Factory at Chorzów (Claim for Indemnity) (Germany v Poland)* (Merits) [1928] PCIJ Series A No 17, 29.

Concessions, where the Permanent Court of International Justice (PCIJ) chose not to use General Principles.[125] It is nonetheless clear that Judge ad hoc Dugard sees General Principles as mostly secondary, in that they are either rules of procedure or used as a defence.[126]

The contention regarding the term 'general international law' seems undue, as it has long been used to refer to intentional law that binds all States.[127] Some publicists have questioned whether it also includes treaties.[128] Dugard considers the term to include General Principles:

> Possibly it includes general international conventions, particularly those that codify principles of international law; and widely accepted judicial decisions, particularly decisions of the International Court of Justice. Certainly it includes both customary international law and general principles of law within the meaning of Article 38 (1) *(c)* and *(d)* of the Court's Statute.[129]

This view accords with that of the International Law Commission.[130]

R. *Question of the Delimitation of the Continental Shelf between Nicaragua and Colombia*

General Principles were addressed briefly in the context of the principle of *res judicata* in this case.[131] The Court confirmed that *res judicata* is a 'general principle of law',[132] and Judge Owada expressly linked it to the Dissenting Opinion of Judge Anzilotti in the PCIJ case of *Interpretation of Judgments Nos 7 and 8*.[133] Judge Greenwood expanded on the source of the principle further: 'Although the doctrine of *res judicata* has its origins in the general principles of law … it is now firmly established in the jurisprudence of the Court.'[134]

[125] ibid 847–48, referring to *Mavrommatis Jerusalem Concessions (Greece v Britain)* (Merits) [1925] PCIJ Series A No 5, 30; see ch 3.

[126] ibid.

[127] See, eg, A Verdross, 'General International Law and the United Nations Charter' (1954) 30 *International Affairs* 342.

[128] See, eg, G Tunkin, 'Is General International Law Customary Law Only?' (1993) 4 *European Journal of International Law* 534. Tunkin ultimately concluded that it did, but makes no reference to General Principles: ibid at 541. This is in contrast with Verdross, who explicitly includes General Principles as part of 'general international law': Verdross, 'General International Law' (n 127) 342.

[129] *Construction of a Road* (n 122) 848.

[130] ILC, *First Report on General Principles of Law* (29 April–7 June and 8 July–9 August 2019) UN Doc A/CN.4/732, para 162.

[131] *Question of the Delimitation of the Continental Shelf between Nicaragua and Colombia beyond 200 Nautical Miles from the Nicaraguan Coast (Nicaragua v Colombia)* [2016] ICJ Rep 101 (*Question of the Delimitation of the Continental Shelf between Nicaragua and Colombia*).

[132] ibid 125.

[133] ibid 163 (Separate Opinion of Judge Owada) referring to *Interpretation of Judgments Nos 7 and 8 (The Chorzów Factory) (Germany v Poland)* (Interpretation) [1927] PCIJ Series A No 13, 5; see ch 3.

[134] ibid 177 (Separate Opinion of Judge Greenwood).

Greenwood treated the principle as an *international* principle, rather than still being a general principle pursuant to Article 38(1)(c):

> It is therefore unnecessary to examine the not inconsiderable differences which exist between different national legal systems regarding the concept of *res judicata* … It is the principle of *res judicata* in international law, in particular as developed in the jurisprudence of the Court, which has to be applied.[135]

In this way, Greenwood is explicitly following the practice of relying on precedence in the ICJ rather than one of the Article 38 sources.[136]

III. CONTRIBUTIONS OF JUDGE WEERAMANTRY

A. *Greenland and Jan Mayen*

In June 1993, Judge Weeramantry delivered a Separate Opinion in *Greenland and Jan Mayen*,[137] beginning an eight-year exploration of Article 38(1)(c). Weeramantry considered the application of equity in international law in some depth, including as a General Principle.[138] Weeramantry set out three classifications of General Principles identified by Oscar Schachter:

> (1) The principles of municipal law 'recognized by civilized nations'.
> (2) General principles of law 'derived from the specific nature of the international community'.
> (3) Principles 'intrinsic to the idea of law and basic to all legal systems'.[139]

It is unclear whether Weeramantry accepted all of these 'general principles of law' as true expressions of Article 38(1)(c), but he did argue that all categories allow for the consideration of equity in international law. Further, he approved Schwarzenberger's view that General Principles 'opened a new channel through which concepts of natural law could be received into international law',[140] and saw equity as doing this.[141]

Thus Weeramantry saw Article 38(1)(c) as capable of supporting natural law norms. It is unclear whether these norms become General Principles because

[135] ibid 178.

[136] This was done on a more implicit basis by Judges Shahabuddeen and Koroma in *Threat or Use of Nuclear Weapons* (n 2). See discussion in section II.D.i. See also Alschner and Charlotin, 'The Growing Complexity' (n 39).

[137] *Greenland and Jan Mayen* (n 1).

[138] ibid 236–38 (Separate Opinion of Judge Weeramantry).

[139] O Schachter, *International Law in Theory and Practice* (Martinus Nijhoff, 1991) 50; *Greenland and Jan Mayen* (n 1) 237 (Separate Opinion of Judge Weeramantry).

[140] G Schwarzenberger, 'Introduction' in B Cheng, *General Principles of Law as Applied by International Courts and Tribunals* (Stevens and Sons Ltd 1953) xi.

[141] *Greenland and Jan Mayen* (n 1) 238 (Separate Opinion of Judge Weeramantry).

of their content, or whether they must also satisfy a comparative methodology drawing on domestic laws.[142] Schachter's first category (but not necessarily the second or third) tends towards a comparative methodology. Weeramantry's later discussion of a broader concept of equity in this Opinion does, however, employ a comparative methodology, looking to indigenous practices.[143]

B. *Application of the Genocide Convention* (Provisional Measures)

Following *Jan Mayen*, Weeramantry fleetingly referred to General Principles three months later in his Separate Opinion in this provisional measures stage of the *Genocide Convention* case.[144] In discussing the binding nature of interlocutory measures, Weeramantry stated:

> This argument is taken yet further by other scholars who argue that the binding nature of interlocutory injunctions and similar measures is a rule universally recognized and as such may even be considered to be a 'general principle of law recognized by civilized nations' under Article 38(1)(c) of the Court's Statute.[145]

In support of this, Weeramantry cited Jerome Elkind, who has published on interim protection measures and General Principles,[146] and Elkind's reliance on 'Anglo-American, Roman, Soviet and Hindu law'.[147] While this seems to evince a comparative methodology, Weeramantry does not expand on the point further, and it is not material to his conclusion.

C. *Gabčíkovo-Nagymaros Project*

In this case,[148] a question arose to whether Hungary could validly rely on environmental concerns to justify repudiation of the treaty between itself and Slovakia. In his Separate Opinion, Vice-President Weeramantry considered the so-called 'concept' of sustainable development to be a normative principle of international law, a view not shared by the Court.[149]

Weeramantry rested the existence of such a principle on several foundations: first, as a necessary compromise between the twin principles of environmental protection and development;[150] second, as a principle contained in treaties,

142 ibid 237.
143 ibid 275–77 (Separate Opinion of Judge Weermantry).
144 *Application of the Genocide Convention* (Provisional Measures) (n 1).
145 ibid 378 (Separate Opinion of Judge Weeramantry).
146 JB Elkind, *Interim Protection: A Functional Approach* (Martinus Nijhoff, 1981).
147 *Application of the Genocide Convention* (Provisional Measures) (n 1) 378 (Separate Opinion of Judge Weeramantry).
148 *Gabčíkovo-Nagymaros Project* (n 1).
149 ibid 88 (Separate Opinion of Vice-President Weeramantry).
150 ibid 89.

regional documents, foundation documents of international organisations, state practice, and other various hard and soft international law instruments;[151] and, third, as a General Principle.[152] It must be noted that Weeramantry's discussion of the principle is not overly concerned as to *which* source is being relied upon – it is referred to as customary before the discussion of it as a General Principle[153] – consideration was focused more on establishing that sustainable development was binding at international law. The first conception of sustainable development as a necessary compromise between competing principles – 'part of modern international law by reason … of its inescapable logical necessity'[154] – could well fit into a conception of General Principles as inherent principles of law, capable of logical deduction.

It is clear, however, that in considering the historical development of sustainable development, Weeramantry turns to General Principles. The analysis considers environmental practice in ancient civilisations, focusing on evidence of ancient irrigation systems[155] and customary environmental practices in traditional indigenous cultures.[156] In justifying the inclusion of these examples as evidence of a principle of law, Weeramantry stated:

> Living law which is daily observed by members of the community, and compliance with which is so axiomatic that it is taken for granted, is not deprived of the character of law by the extraneous test and standard of reduction to writing … Moreover, when the Statute of the Court described the sources of international law as including the 'general principles of law recognized by civilized nations' it expressly opened a door to the entry of such principles into modern international law.[157]

Four points can be made from this judgment. First, while the methodology is comparative, Weeramantry's use of general principles based on 'living law' is novel. This approach looks to domestic forums, but is not restricted to formalised written law of states. This has implications for the consideration of *which* and *what type* of legal systems can support a General Principle. Tied further into this are considerations of the term 'civilized' in international law generally, and in Article 38(1)(c) specifically. Indeed, Weeramantry recognises this specifically with reference to the work of Sir Robert Jennings:

> It seems to the writer, indeed, that at the present juncture in the development of the international legal system it may be more important to stress the imperative need to develop international law to comprehend within itself the rich diversity of cultures, civilizations and legal traditions.[158]

[151] ibid 93.
[152] ibid 110.
[153] ibid 95.
[154] ibid.
[155] ibid 98–106.
[156] ibid 107–08.
[157] ibid 109–10.
[158] R Jennings, 'Universal International Law in a Multicultural World' in TMC Asser Instituut (ed), *International Law and the Grotian Heritage: A Commemorative Colloquium on the Occasion*

Second, Weeramantry also justifies looking to non-traditional[159] legal societies by virtue of Article 9 of the ICJ Statute:

> Especially where this Court is concerned, 'the essence of true universality' of the institution is captured in the language of Article 9 of the Statute of the International Court of Justice which requires the 'representation of the *main forms of civilization* and of the principal legal systems of the world' (emphasis added). The struggle for the insertion of the italicized words in the Court's Statute was a hard one, led by the Japanese representative, Mr Adatci, and, since this concept has thus been integrated into the structure and the Statute of the Court, I see the Court as being charged with a duty to draw upon the wisdom of the world's several civilizations, where such a course can enrich its insights into the matter before it. The Court cannot afford to be monocultural, especially where it is entering newly developing areas of law.[160]

Although not made explicitly clear by Weeramantry, by justifying his use of living law by reference *both* to Article 38(1)(c) and Article 9 of the ICJ Statute, an implicit link is made between the judicial make-up of the Court and General Principles.

Third, it seems that the principle of sustainable development discussed by Weeramantry is a true principle on the rule/principle scale. It is one that 'assists with the balancing'[161] of other norms, rather than setting down a concrete rule. It is also abstract, extracted from practices relating to irrigation,[162] religious texts,[163] and general indigenous approaches to land ownership and cultivation.[164] Thus the principle extracted necessarily lacks specificity, and rather operates as a true principle.

Fourth, unlike his opinion in *Jan Mayen* four years earlier, Weeramantry does not explicitly link General Principles with natural law.

D. *Land and Maritime Boundary* (Preliminary Objections)

A year after *Gabčikovo-Nagymaros*, Weeramantry turned again to General Principles in the context of Article 36(2) declarations.[165] Weeramantry noted

of the Fourth Centenary of the Birth of Hugo Grotius (TMC Asser Instituut, 1985) 195, cited in *Gabčíkovo-Nagymaros Project* (n 1) 96 (Separate Opinion of Judge Weeramantry).

[159] These could be also described as Chthonic Legal Societies: see ch 8. Although Weeramantry describes them as 'traditional', they are termed non-traditional here to distinguish them from *written* legal systems, which are more usually considered by the ICJ.

[160] *Gabčíkovo-Nagymaros Project* (n 1) 97 (Separate Opinion of Judge Weeramantry).

[161] ibid 97.

[162] ibid 98–106.

[163] ibid 102, 108.

[164] ibid 107.

[165] *Land and Maritime Boundary* (Preliminary Objections) (n 1).

that although the question was one of international law, the sphere was 'the law of consensual obligations', and notably the principle of offer and acceptance, which is 'accepted by most legal systems, with the rarest of exceptions. This principle is accepted alike by the Anglo-American law and the Romanistic legal systems.'[166] Weeramantry thus drew the principle from a comparative use of domestic legal systems.

This methodological approach is strengthened by Weeramantry's use of a comparative study on the formation of contracts, written by Rudolf Schlesinger specifically to assist the ICJ in determining General Principles under Article 38(1)(c).[167] It marks the first time a judge explicitly made use of a comparative study conducted outside the auspices of the case (as opposed to those provided by parties in pleadings) to found a General Principle.

E. *Pulau Ligitan and Pulau Sipadan* (Application to Intervene)

This judgment[168] concerned an application by the Philippines to intervene in the case between Indonesia and Malaysia. Acting as Judge ad hoc for Malaysia, Judge Weeramantry considered principles of intervention sourced from domestic laws in his Separate Opinion.[169] In doing so, Weeramantry did not rely on intervention as a General Principle as such, instead looking to a process of 'comparison and contrast' with domestic laws to 'throw much light' onto the international rules.[170]

Weeramantry did raise the issue of General Principles, however, noting that '[i]t is an interesting question whether the principles relating to intervention … are part of the general principles imported into the corpus of international law by Article 38(1)(c) of the Statute'.[171] Weeramantry did not answer the question, but his use of material in this case confirms his approach from *Gabčikovo-Nagymaros* – using a comparative methodology and looking to a wide range of legal systems.[172] Weeramantry also offers a view of how a General Principle and treaty may interact. In this case, the relevant provision was Article 62 of the ICJ Statute. If a General Principle of intervention existed, it would be able to 'be invoked for clarifying the terms of Article 62'.[173] Thus it would not overrule the treaty but rather provide guidance to its interpretation.

[166] ibid 368–69 (Dissenting Opinion of Vice-President Weeramantry).
[167] ibid 369–70.
[168] *Pulau Ligitan and Pulau Sipadan* (Application to Intervene) (n 1).
[169] ibid 634 (Separate Opinion of Judge ad hoc Weeramantry).
[170] ibid.
[171] ibid 636.
[172] ibid 635.
[173] ibid 636.

IV. CONTRIBUTIONS OF JUDGE CANÇADO-TRINDADE

In volume alone, Judge Cançado-Trindade's contributions to the development and understanding of Article 38(1)(c) are unparalleled. The 13 Separate and Dissenting Opinions in this section span an eight-year period, beginning in the first year of Cançado Trindade's service. They have been selected for analysis in this section as the most relevant for aiding in the construction of General Principles as a source of law.[174] As the judge was re-elected in 2018 for a further nine years, it is highly likely that the judgments discussed in this book will not encompass the full contribution of Cançado Trindade to General Principles.

There are several threads that are common throughout the judgments. Perhaps most dominant is Cançado Trindade's background as Judge, Vice-President and President of the Inter-American Court of Human Rights (IACtHR). Cançado Trindade leans heavily and explicitly on Latin American traditions of law in his construction of General Principles. Other common themes are the explicit characterisation of General Principles as a natural law doctrine, comprising foundational principles.

A. *Obligation to Prosecute or Extradite* (Provisional Measures)

This case[175] concerned Belgium's attempt to prosecute Hissène Habré, the former President of Chad. Belgium alleged that Senegal, in neither prosecuting nor extraditing Habré, was in breach of its obligations under the Convention Against Torture[176] and customary international law. In the provisional measures stage, Belgium sought orders to ensure that Senegal kept Habré under the 'the control and surveillance of the judicial authorities of Senegal'.[177] In discussing provisional measures, Cançado Trindade stated:

> Their generalized use at both national and international levels has led a contemporary doctrinal trend to consider such measures as equivalent to a true *general*

[174] This section contains those Opinions that, on construction, refer to General Principles. There are other Opinions of Judge Cançado Trindade that use the phrase 'general principle of law' but where it is unclear whether this is in the sense of Art 38(1)(c), which have not been included in this section. See, eg, *Application of the Convention on the Prevention and Punishment of the Crime of Genocide (Croatia v Serbia)* [2015] ICJ Rep 3, 372 (Separate Opinion of Judge Cançado Trindade); *Questions relating to the Seizure and Detention of Certain Documents and Data (Timor-Leste v Australia)* (Request for Modification) [2015] ICJ Rep 556, para 6 (Separate Opinion of Judge Cançado Trindade). Opinions that refer to General Principles in passing but do not expand on the source further have also been omitted. See, eg, *Certain Activities Carried Out by Nicaragua in the Border Area (Costa Rica v Nicaragua) and Construction of a Road in Costa Rica along the San Juan River (Nicaragua v Costa Rica)* (Judgment) [2015] ICJ Rep 665, paras 4, 68 (Separate Opinion of Judge Cançado Trindade).

[175] *Obligation to Prosecute or Extradite* (Provisional Measures) (n 1).

[176] Convention against Torture and Other Cruel, Inhuman or Degrading Treatment or Punishment (adopted 10 December 1984, entered into force 26 June 1987) 1465 UNTS 85.

[177] *Obligation to Prosecute or Extradite* (Provisional Measures) (n 1) 142.

> *principle of law*, common to virtually all national legal systems, and endorsed by the practice of national, arbitral, and international tribunals.[178]

This conception sees General Principles in a dual manner – drawn from national legal systems in a comparative fashion, but then *endorsed* by activity at the national and international levels. This first discussion of General Principles by Cançado Trindade lacks the link to morality and natural law that is so pervasive in his later Opinions.

B. *Pulp Mills*

The second exploration of General Principles by Cançado Trindade is his most comprehensive to date.[179] Despite both Argentina and Uruguay invoking General Principles, the Court did not refer to them.[180] Cançado Trindade, however, embarked on a lengthy exploration of General Principles relating to international environmental law, focusing on the principles of prevention and the precautionary principle.[181] He identified two areas of contention in respect of General Principles: whether they are drawn only from the domestic forum or include principles 'identified also at international law level';[182] and whether, if drawn from the international level, they are 'those of general international law or whether they comprise also those principles which are proper to the domain of international law'.[183] Cançado Trindade addressed the work of the Advisory Committee of Jurists, as well as selected cases before the PCIJ and the ICJ and contemporaneous writing of publicists, before concluding that General Principles *can* be drawn from the international level,[184] and are not limited to general international law but can relate to specific areas of international law (such as international environmental law).[185]

Cançado Trindade's discussion can be set out under the established tetrahedral framework of function, jurisprudential legitimacy, methodology and type.

i. Function

It is clear that Cançado Trindade sees the *function* of General Principles as a binding, distinct source of international law:

> [M]y own understanding is in the sense that general principles of law – of domestic or international manifestation – stand as a category of their own, conceptually

[178] ibid 170 (Dissenting Opinion of Judge Cançado Trindade).
[179] *Pulp Mills* (n 1).
[180] ibid para 5 (Separate Opinion of Judge Cançado Trindade).
[181] ibid para 6.
[182] ibid.
[183] ibid.
[184] ibid para 28.
[185] ibid para 48.

distinct from customary or conventional international law, in the list of 'formal' sources under Article 38 of the ICJ Statute.[186]

ii. Jurisprudential Legitimacy

Although Cançado Trindade follows the introduction of the source through the Advisory Committee's discussions, including the compromise between Descamps' natural law conception and the more positivist position espoused by Root,[187] he nonetheless sees General Principles as being *intrinsically* valid:

> [E]ven if such invocations or references did not exist, general principles would still be there, at the origins and foundations of any legal system; in my perception, there cannot be any legal system without them. They cannot be overlooked by the ICJ.[188]

Not only does Cançado Trindade found the validity of General Principles in something more that their position in the Statute,[189] he further sees them as *fundamental* to any legal system. They are inherent, and foundational. Later in the judgment, Cançado Trindade describes General Principles as 'guiding principles of general content … they differ from the norms and rules of positive international law, and transcend them'.[190] They emanate from 'human conscience, from the universal juridical conscience'.[191] Thus Cançado Trindade clearly sees General Principles as having a natural law jurisprudence: this position remains consistent throughout his subsequent Opinions.

iii. Methodology

Cançado Trindade views General Principles as being drawn from both the domestic and the international forums. Cançado Trindade justifies this by noting that although Root and Phillimore were eager to restrict General Principles to those found in the domestic forum, Descamps and Fernandes 'pursued to the identification of the principles of international law'.[192] While the Advisory Committee was split between these two camps, it was more on the natural/positivist divide, rather than the domestic/international forum. Indeed, Descamps did not advocate looking to international materials in support of General Principles but rather the 'conscience of mankind'.[193] Further, the compromise

[186] ibid para 19.
[187] ibid para 11; see discussion in ch 2.
[188] *Pulp Mills* (n 1) para 18 (Separate Opinion of Judge Cançado Trindade).
[189] A view supported by the historical development of the source pre-Advisory Committee of Jurists; see ch 2.
[190] *Pulp Mills* (n 1) para 39 (Separate Opinion of Judge Cançado Trindade).
[191] ibid para 52.
[192] ibid para 26.
[193] See ch 2.

reached in the Root-Phillimore plan seems to firmly ground General Principles within the domestic forum. Cançado Trindade, however, argues:

> To hold this view inescapable seems to amount to a static, and dogmatic position, which requires demonstration. It does not appear persuasive to me at all. In our days, given the extraordinary development of the law of nations, there is epistemologically no reason not to have recourse to general principles of law as recognized in domestic as well as international law.[194]

To deviate from the source as intended in this manner could be an example of judicial discretion, the very thing Root and Phillimore were eager to avoid.[195] Cançado Trindade further supports his view by the work of four publicists writing in the early to mid-twentieth century.[196] Three of the four are French publicists (Jules Basdevant, Frede Castburg and Charles Rosseau), perhaps indicative of the common law/'continental' split on this matter, identified by Phillimore in 1920.[197]

Although Cançado Trindade is clear that in his view that General Principles can be drawn from international law, the methodology of doing so is not completely clear. In considering the principle of prevention, Cançado Trindade refers to the writings of Plato and Aristotle,[198] to the Stockholm and Rio Declarations,[199] the World Charter for Nature and the United Nations Convention on the Law of Non-Navigational Uses of International Watercourses.[200] In establishing the precautionary principle, Cançado Trindade refers to decisions of the ICJ,[201] the writings of Socrates[202] and various international conventions.[203] The international forum is being used as a repository from which to *draw* principles (as opposed to deductions form international rules), but there is no clear guidance on how to select or assess the weight of the various international materials.

iv. Type

Cançado Trindade sees General Principles as true principles: 'A principle is not the same as a norm of a rule: these latter are inspired in the former and abide by them.'[204] This is in keeping with the conception of General Principles as fundamental and foundational.

[194] *Pulp Mills* (n 1) para 27 (Separate Opinion of Judge Cançado Trindade).
[195] See ch 2.
[196] ibid paras 30–34.
[197] W Phillimore, 'Scheme for the Permanent Court of International Justice' (1920) 6 *Transactions of the Grotius Society* 89, 94; see ch 2.
[198] *Pulp Mills* (n 1) paras 56–58 (Separate Opinion of Judge Cançado Trindade).
[199] ibid para 59.
[200] ibid para 60.
[201] ibid paras 63–64, 66.
[202] ibid para 75.
[203] ibid para 93.
[204] ibid para 17.

Further, Cançado Trindade takes mentions of 'general principles of international law' by the World Courts (and in particular by the PCIJ) to be instances of General Principles.[205] This cannot be presumed,[206] particularly given the historical tendency of referring to customary law as 'principles of international law'.[207] The reasoning is also somewhat circular – if we assume that General Principles include international principles, 'general principles of international law' fit within the source, and can be taken to properly refer to it; because the Courts have used the term 'general principles of international law' to refer to Article 38(1)(c), the source *must* encompass principles of international law. Finally, Cançado Trindade recognises that practice of the World Courts has recognised both procedural and substantive General Principles.[208]

Following Cançado Trindade's Separate Opinion in *Pulp Mills*, he made reference to 'general principles of law' without explicit links to Article 38(1)(c) in four Opinions. In context, it seems these are the same natural law General Principles as Cançado Trindade sets out in *Pulp Mills*. They are principles 'of international law, emanating from natural law';[209] they have 'fundamental human values underlying them';[210] and they are linked with *jus cogens*, which comprises 'general principles of law enshrining common and superior values shared by the international community as a whole'.[211] Further, General Principles include the principles of the proper administration of justice[212] and reparation for injury.[213] Cançado Trindade returned to General Principles in more detail in 2013 in his Separate Opinion in the joinder of proceedings between *Certain Activities* and *Construction of a Road*.

C. *Certain Activities* (Joinder)/*Construction of a Road* (Joinder)

In 2010, Costa Rica brought a case against Nicaragua alleging Nicaragua illegally entered into Costa Rican territory and breached several international treaties and obligations owed towards it. In 2011, Nicaragua brought a case against Costa Rica in connection with alleged environmental damage and

[205] ibid paras 20–21.

[206] See generally ch 2.

[207] See ch 1.

[208] *Pulp Mills* (n 1) paras 24–25 (Separate Opinion of Judge Cançado Trindade); although note for some of the judgments referred to it is questionable whether Art 38(1)(c) was truly being invoked by the Courts.

[209] *Jurisdictional Immunities of the State* (n 1) 192 (Dissenting Opinion of Judge Cançado Trindade).

[210] *Obligation to Prosecute or Extradite* (Merits) (n 1) 523–24 (Separate Opinion of Judge Cançado Trindade).

[211] ibid 557–58.

[212] *Judgment No 2867 of the Administrative Tribunal of the ILO* (n 1), 90 (Separate Opinion of Judge Cançado Trindade).

[213] *Diallo* (Compensation) (n 1) 359, 366 (Separate Opinion of Judge Cançado Trindade).

violations of sovereignty stemming from Costa Rica's construction of a road along the border between the two countries. In 2013, the ICJ joined the two proceedings.[214] In doing so, the ICJ did not rely on General Principles; however, in his Separate Opinion, Judge Cançado Trindade did. Cançado Trindade's use of General Principles in this case is consistent with his earlier Opinion in *Pulp Mills*.

First, General Principles are a natural law source, 'captured by human conscience'.[215] For Cançado Trindade, positivists 'do not feel at ease with general principles of law; they thus keep on trying, repetitiously and in vain, to minimize their presence and relevance'.[216] Second, Cançado Trindade once more sees General Principles as both domestic and international,[217] and sometimes uniquely international: 'International legal procedure has a specificity and a dynamics of its own, and general principles of law applicable therein are not to be assumed to be identical, in operation, to those sedimented in national legal systems.'[218] Third, they are true principles, indispensably forming the 'substratum of the national and international legal orders'.[219]

This view of General Principles as natural law *international* principles was repeated in *Documents and Data* (Provisional Measures), where Cançado Trindade referred to the principle of the 'juridical equality of States' as a General Principle which embodies the 'objective idea of justice'.[220]

D. *Access to the Pacific Ocean*

Bolivia is a landlocked country in South America. In 2013 it filed proceedings against Chile, alleging Chile was under an obligation to negotiate in good faith to allow Bolivia access to the Pacific Ocean.[221] The Court dismissed Chile's preliminary objection to jurisdiction, and did not rely on General Principles. In his Separate Opinion, Judge Cançado Trindade once more explored the relevance of General Principles to the case, excerpting his dictum from *Certain Activities* (Joinder)/*Construction of a Road* (Joinder) to emphasise that General Principles are 'not only those principles acknowledged in national legal systems,

[214] *Certain Activities* (Joinder of Proceedings) (n 1); *Construction of a Road in Costa Rica along the San Juan River (Nicaragua v Costa Rica)* (Joinder of Proceedings) [2013] ICJ Rep 184. Although the cases have separate citations, the content of the Separate Opinions is identical.

[215] *Certain Activities* (Joinder of Proceedings) (n 1), 177 (Separate Opinion of Judge Cançado Trindade). Indeed, for Cançado Trindade, human conscience is the 'ultimate material conscience' and the 'ultimate juridical source of international law' itself: see Separate Opinion, ibid, fn 14.

[216] ibid 178.

[217] ibid 181.

[218] ibid 178.

[219] ibid 181.

[220] *Documents and Data* (Provisional Measures) (n 1) 184 (Separate Opinion of Judge Cançado Trindade).

[221] *Access to the Pacific Ocean* (n 1).

but likewise the general principles of international law'.[222] In the context of general principles of procedural international law, Cançado Trindade emphasised their foundational and fundamental nature:

> General principles are always present and relevant, at substantive and procedural levels. Such principles orient the interpretation and application of legal norms. They rest on the foundations of any legal system, which is made to operate on the basis of fundamental principles. Ultimately, without principles there is truly no legal system.[223]

Cançado Trindade referred to a number of previous cases as also setting out General Principles, some of which simply refer to a 'principle' without any further link to Article 38(1)(c).[224] While such an approach has also been adopted by some academic commentators, it is one that cannot be justified. The term 'principle' is often used to refer to principles of customary international law; any attempt to declare a case discussing General Principles in the Article 38(1)(c) sense solely because of the word 'principle', does so without taking this context into account.

E. *Nuclear Arms and Disarmament*

In 2014 the Marshall Islands filed actions against nine states[225] it identified as possessing nuclear weapons, alleging a failure of an international obligation to negotiate for the cessation of the nuclear arms race and disarmament.[226] In the present case, India objected to the jurisdiction and admissibility of the case brought against it. The ICJ agreed, dismissing the action for lack of a dispute.[227] In dissent, Judge Cançado Trindade confirmed the role of General Principles in filling lacuna: 'Even if there was a "gap" in the law of nations in relation to nuclear weapons, which there is not, it is possible to fill it by resorting to general principles of law.'[228] In keeping with his earlier Opinion, Cançado Trindade also rejects a positivist conception of General Principles, and stresses their foundational position:

> The general principles of law (prima principia), in my perception, confer upon the (national and international) legal order its ineluctable axiological dimension. Notwithstanding, legal positivism and political 'realism', in their characteristic subservience to power, incur [*sic*] into their basic mistake of minimizing those

[222] ibid para 40 (Separate Opinion of Judge Cançado Trindade).
[223] ibid para 23.
[224] ibid paras 37–38 (Separate Opinion of Judge Cançado Trindade).
[225] *Nuclear Arms and Disarmament* (n 1). The states were China, the Democratic People's Republic of Korea, France, India, Israel, Pakistan, the Russian Federation, the United Kingdom of Great Britain and Northern Ireland, and the United States of America.
[226] ibid 266.
[227] ibid 277.
[228] ibid 396 (Dissenting Opinion of Judge Cançado Trindade).

> principles, which lie in the foundations of any legal system, and which inform and conform the norms and the action pursuant to them, in the search for the realization of justice. Whenever that minimization of principles has prevailed the consequences have been disastrous.[229]

F. *Sovereign Rights and Maritime Spaces* (Preliminary Objections)

Nicaragua brought an action against Colombia alleging that it had failed to respect the territorial sovereignty of Nicaragua over zones that were subject to an earlier ICJ case.[230] Nicaragua rested jurisdiction on the Pact of Bogotá, and in the alternative in the inherent jurisdiction of the Court as the issue arose from the earlier judgment.[231] As the ICJ found it had jurisdiction under the Pact of Bogotá, it did not consider the issue of inherent jurisdiction.[232]

Although Judge Cançado Trindade voted with the Court that there was 'no need' to consider inherent powers, he nonetheless devoted his Separate Opinion to doing so. Drawing on his own jurisprudence from his time as a judge at the IACtHR, Cançado Trindade linked inherent juridical powers to General Principles, namely the principle of *jura novit curia*.[233] In line with his earlier Opinions, Cançado Trindade draws support for this General Principle not from domestic systems but from use by international tribunals – namely the International Criminal Tribunal for Rwanda, the International Criminal Tribunal for the Former Yugoslavia, the International Criminal Court, the Special Tribunal for Lebanon and the International Tribunal for the Law of the Sea.[234]

Cançado Trindade also reiterates his view of General Principles as oppositional to positivist conceptions of international law. They are 'precepts which ensue from natural reason, and are deeply-rooted in natural law thinking'[235] and, in Cançado Trindade's eyes, a remedy to international law's 'undue reliance on State voluntarism'.[236]

***

These two threads – the use of the IACtHR and the view of General Principles as natural law – are also seen in the last two Opinions considered in this section. In the Provisional Measures phase of the *Jadhav Case*,[237] Cançado Trindade

229 ibid 435.
230 *Sovereign Rights and Maritime Spaces* (Preliminary Objections) (n 1).
231 ibid 13.
232 ibid 43.
233 ibid 61 (Separate Opinion of Judge Cançado Trindade).
234 ibid 61–63.
235 ibid 57.
236 ibid.
237 *Jadhav Case* (n 1).

once again drew upon his previous judgments in the IACtHR.[238] He positioned General Principles as 'those [principles] which are endowed with a true fundamental character',[239] 'wherefrom norms and rules emanate and wherein they find their meaning'.[240] In a slight departure from some of the earlier cases, in *Jadhav*, Cançado Trindade sees General Principles as both international and those in 'comparative domestic law'.[241] In the counter-claim in *Sovereign Rights and Maritime Spaces*,[242] Cançado Trindade notes that Latin American jurisprudence and international legal thinking has 'always remained attentive to the importance of general principles of international law, reckoning that conscience (recta ratio) stands well above the "will", faithfully in line with the longstanding jusnaturalist international legal thinking'.[243]

V. CONCLUSION

Taking all the cases in chapters 4 and 5 together, the schism noted in commentary about General Principles belies a surprisingly coherent treatment of the source by the ICJ. In terms of function, the source is seen as binding, with explicit recognition of its gap-filling status.[244] A few judges support a higher conception of General Principles, as encompassing *jus cogens*[245] or 'transcending' positive international law.[246] The type of General Principle varies, embracing abstract principles and specific rules such as norms relating to property rights and trusteeships,[247] naturalisation,[248] frustration,[249] secession,[250] sustainable development[251] and the formation of contracts.[252]

[238] ibid 258 (Concurring Opinion of Judge Cançado Trindade).
[239] ibid.
[240] ibid.
[241] ibid.
[242] *Sovereign Rights and Maritime Spaces* (Counter-Claims) (n 1).
[243] ibid 335 (Declaration of Judge Cançado Trindade).
[244] See, eg, *Threat or Use of Nuclear Weapons* (n 2) 275 (Declaration of Judge Herczgh), 323 (Dissenting Opinion of Vice President Schwebel); *Nuclear Arms and Disarmament* (n 1) 396 (Dissenting Opinion of Judge Cançado Trindade).
[245] *Right of Passage over Indian Territory (Portugal v India)* (Merits) [1960] ICJ Rep 6, 135 (Dissenting Opinion of Judge Fernandes) (*Right of Passage* (Merits)).
[246] *Pulp Mills* (n 1) para 39 (Separate Opinion of Judge Cançado Trindade).
[247] *International Status of South-West Africa* (Advisory Opinion) [1950] ICJ Rep 128, 149 (Separate Opinion of Judge McNair) (*International Status of South-West Africa*).
[248] *Anglo-Iranian Oil Company (United Kingdom v Iran)* (Preliminary Objection) [1952] ICJ 93, 161 (Dissenting Opinion of Judge Carneiro) (*Anglo-Iranian Oil Company*).
[249] *Legal Consequences for States of the Continued Presence of South Africa in Namibia (South West Africa) notwithstanding Security Council Resolution 276 (1970)* (Advisory Opinion) [1971] ICJ Rep 16, 157 (Separate Opinion of Judge Dillard) (*Legal Consequences for States*).
[250] *Application of the Genocide Convention* (Preliminary Objections) (n 45) 754 (Dissenting Opinion of Judge Kreća).
[251] *Gabčíkovo-Nagymaros Project* (n 1) 109–10 (Separate Opinion of Judge Weeramantry).
[252] *Land and Maritime Boundary* (Preliminary Objections) (n 1) 369–70 (Separate Opinion of Judge Weeramantry).

Coherence in methodology is even more striking. Where a judgment or Opinion evinces an ascertainable methodology, it is overwhelmingly comparative,[253] drawing from the domestic forum,[254] although both the scope

[253] See, eg, *Corfu Channel* (n 116) 18 (on the matter of indirect evidence); *International Status of South-West Africa* (n 246) 148–52 (Separate Opinion of Judge McNair); *Certain Norwegian Loans (France v Norway)* (Merits) [1957] ICJ Rep 9, 49 (Separate Opinion of Judge Lauterpacht) (*Certain Norwegian Loans*); *Application of the Convention of 1902 Governing the Guardianship of Infants (Netherlands v Sweden)* (Merits) [1958] ICJ Rep 55, 92 (Separate Opinion of Judge Lauterpacht), 107 (Separate Opinion of Judge Quintana) (*Guardianship of Infants*); *South-West Africa (Ethiopia v South Africa; Liberia v South Africa)* (Preliminary Objections) [1962] ICJ Rep 319, 577–78 (Dissenting Opinion of Judge Van Wyk) (*South West Africa* (Preliminary Objections)); *South-West Africa Cases (Ethiopia v South Africa; Liberia v South Africa) (Second Phase)* [1966] ICJ Rep 4, 292–93 (Dissenting Opinion of Judge Tanaka), 378 (Dissenting Opinion of Judge Jessup) (*South West Africa*); *North Sea Continental Shelf* (n 10) 135 (Separate Opinion of Judge Ammoun); *Barcelona Traction, Light and Power Company (Belgium v Spain) (Second Phase)* [1970] ICJ Rep 3, 39 (*Barcelona Traction*); *Legal Consequences for States* (n 249) 157 (Separate Opinion of Judge Dillard); *Appeal Relating to the Jurisdiction of the ICAO Council (India v Pakistan)* (Merits) [1972] ICJ Rep 46, 109–14 (Separate Opinion of Judge Dillard) (*ICAO Council Appeal*); *Elettronica Sicula SpA (ELSI) (United States of America v Italy)* [1989] ICJ Rep 15, 84–85 (Separate Opinion of Judge Oda) (*Elettronica Sicula*); *Certain Phosphate Lands in Nauru* (n 12), 287–89 (Separate Opinion of Judge Shahabuddeen); *Threat or Use of Nuclear Weapons* (n 2) 308 (Separate Opinion of Judge Fleischhauer); *Application of the Genocide Convention* (Preliminary Objections) (n 47) 752–54 ((Dissenting Opinion of Judge Kreća); *Aerial Incident at Lockerbie* (Preliminary Objections) (n 54) 80,171 (Dissenting Opinion of President Schwebel); *Oil Platforms* (Merits) (n 95) 354–58 (Separate Opinion of Judge Simma); *Application of the Interim Accord* (n 104) 700 (Separate Opinion of Judge Simma); *Gabčíkovo-Nagymaros Project* (n 1) 107–10 (Separate Opinion of Vice-President Weeramantry); *Land and Maritime Boundary* (Preliminary Objections) (n 1) 368–69, 369–70 (Dissenting Opinion of Vice-President Weeramantry); *Pulau Ligitan and Pulau Sipadan* (Application to Intervene) (n 1), 635 (Separate Opinion of Judge ad hoc Weeramantry).

[254] *Corfu Channel* (n 116) 18; *International Status of South-West Africa* (n 246) 148–52 (Separate Opinion of Judge McNair); *Anglo-Iranian Oil Company* (n 247) 161 (Dissenting Opinion of Judge Carneiro); *Certain Norwegian Loans* (n 253) 49 (Separate Opinion of Judge Lauterpacht); *Right of Passage over Indian Territory (Portugal v India)* (Preliminary Objections) [1957] ICJ Rep 125, 177 (Dissenting Opinion of Judge Chagla); *Guardianship of Infants* (n 253) 92 (Separate Opinion of Judge Lauterpacht); 107 (Separate Opinion of Judge Quintana); *South-West Africa* (Preliminary Objections) (n 253) 577–78 (Dissenting Opinion of Judge Van Wyk); *South-West Africa Cases* (n 253) 292–93 (Dissenting Opinion of Judge Tanaka) (but also recognised natural law GP), 378 (Dissenting Opinion of Judge Jessup) *North Sea Continental Shelf* (n 10) 135 (Separate Opinion of Judge Ammoun); *Barcelona Traction* (n 252) 37; *Legal Consequences for States* (n 249) 157 (Separate Opinion of Jude Dillard); *ICAO Council Appeal* (n 253) 109–14 (Separate Opinion of Judge Dillard); *Fisheries Jurisdiction (United Kingdom v Iceland)* (Order) [1972] ICJ 181, 185; *Fisheries Jurisdiction (United Kingdom v Iceland; Federal Republic of Germany v Iceland)* (Order) [1972] ICJ Rep 188, 191 (Joint Dissenting Opinions of Judges Bengzon and Jimenez de Arechaga); *Aegean Sea Continental Shelf (Greece v Turkey)* (Interim Protection Measures) [1976] ICJ Rep 3, 15–16 (Separate Opinion of President Jiménéz de Aréchaga); *Elettronica Sicula* (n 253) 84–85 (Separate Opinion of Judge Oda); *Aerial Incident at Lockerbie* (Provisional Measures) (n 6) 112 (Dissenting Opinion of Judge El-Kosheri); *Certain Phosphate Lands in Nauru* (n 12), 287–89 (Separate Opinion of Judge Shahabuddeen); *Threat or Use of Nuclear Weapons* (n 2) 308 (Separate Opinion of Judge Fleischhauer); *Aerial Incident at Lockerbie* (Preliminary Objections) (n 54) 80,171 (Dissenting Opinion of President Schwebel); *Aerial Incident of 10 August 1999* (n 77) 53–54 (Dissenting Opinion of Judge Al-Khasawneh); *Maritime and Territorial Questions* (n 83) 381 (Dissenting Opinion of Judge Torres Bernárdez); *Pulau Ligitan and Pulau Sipidan* (n 90) 705–06 (Dissenting Opinion of Judge ad hoc Franck); *Oil Platforms* (Merits) (n 95) 354–58 (Separate Opinion of Judge Simma);

and variety of legal systems selected for comparison often leads much to be desired. Nonetheless, there are some variances. Five Opinions support (or arguably support) General Principles as logical deductions from international law.[255] The methodology here is categorisicm, the forum international. In contrast, another line of judgments employ a comparative methodology but extend the forum to include international sources such as UN General Assembly Resolutions,[256] and international declarations and treaties.[257]

Few judges discuss jurisprudential legitimacy explicitly, the notable exception being Judge Cançado Trindade – he,[258] and others[259] see General Principles as natural law creatures, although sometimes as an addition to positivist General Principles.[260] However most judgments employ the comparativist methodology as an implicit positivist rule of recognition, albeit without sharp definitional limits as to what that rule actually is.

In some cases, as seen in the conclusion to Chapter 4, a more sophisticated relationship between the positivist rule of recognition and the natural law elements of the source emerges. Most commonly, this seen in a recognition that the *reason* for horizontal generality of a General Principle in domestic legal systems is the inherent normative desirableness of that rule or principle.[261]

Application of the Interim Accord (n 104) 700 (Separate Opinion of Judge Simma); *Gabčíkovo-Nagymaros Project* (n 1) 107–10 (Separate Opinion of Vice-President Weeramantry); *Land and Maritime Boundary* (Preliminary Objections) (n 1) 368–69, 369–70 (Dissenting Opinion of Vice-President Weeramantry); *Pulau Ligitan and Pulau Sipadan* (Application to Intervene) (n 1) 635 (Separate Opinion of Judge ad hoc Weeramantry).

[255] *Right of Passage* (Merits) (n 245) 136–40 (Dissenting Opinion of Judge Fernandes); *Aerial Incident at Lockerbie* (Provisional Measures) (n 6) 72 (Dissenting Opinion of Judge Ranjeva); *Territorial Dispute* (n 18) 88 (Separate Opinion of Judge Ajibola) (though unclear); *Documents and Data* (Provisional Measures) (n 1) 184 (Separate Opinion of Judge Cançado Trindade); *Access to the Pacific Ocean* (n 1) para 23 (Separate Opinion of Judge Cançado Trindade).

[256] *Fisheries Case (United Kingdom v Norway)* [1951] ICJ Rep 116, 147–48 (Individual Opinion of Judge Alvarez) (*Fisheries Case*).

[257] *Application for Review of Judgment No 158 of the United Nations Administrative Tribunal* (Advisory Opinion) [1973] ICJ Rep 166, 291 (Dissenting Opinion of Judge De Castro); *Pulp Mills* (n 1) paras 56–93 (Separate Opinion of Judge Cançado Trindade).

[258] *Pulp Mills* (n 1) paras 39, 52 (Separate Opinion of Judge Cançado Trindade); *Jurisdictional Immunities of the State* (n 1) 192 (Dissenting Opinion of Judge Cançado Trindade); *Obligation to Prosecute or Extradite* (Merits) (n 1) 523–24, 557–58 (Separate Opinion of Judge Cançado Trindade); *Certain Activities* (Joinder of Proceedings) (n 1), 177–78 (Separate Opinion of Judge Cançado Trindade); *Documents and Data* (Provisional Measures) (n 1) 184 (Separate Opinion of Judge Cançado Trindade); *Nuclear Arms and Disarmament* (n 1) 435 (Dissenting Opinion of Judge Cançado Trindade); *Sovereign Rights and Maritime Spaces* (Preliminary Objections) (n 1) 57 (Separate Opinion of Judge Cançado Trindade); *Jadhav Case* (n 1) 258 (Concurring Opinion of Judge Cançado Trindade); *Sovereign Rights and Maritime Spaces* (Counter-Claims) (n 1) 335 (Declaration of Judge Cançado Trindade).

[259] *Right of Passage* (Merits) (n 245) 136–40 (Dissenting Opinion of Judge Fernandes).

[260] *South-West Africa Cases* (n 253) 293 (Dissenting Opinion of Judge Tanaka).

[261] *Fisheries Case* (n 256) 147–48 148 (Individual Opinion of Judge Alvarez); *Interhandel* (n 94), 116–17 (Dissenting Opinion of Judge Lauterpacht); *Right of Passage* (Merits) (n 245) 136 (Separate

The rule of recognition remains positivist, objective and ascertainable but the theory recognises the *type* of General Principle will most likely have some link to 'reason', 'common sense', 'equity' or something else considered necessary or desirable. In contrast, Judge Fernandes links the normative desirableness to fulfilling the criteria of appropriateness.[262] Appropriateness is dealt with by others by being fulfilled by international acceptance of the principle.[263]

Opinion of Judge Koo); *South-West Africa* (Preliminary Objections) (n 253) 577–78 (Dissenting Opinion of Judge Van Wyk); *North Sea Continental Shelf* (n 10) 135 (Separate Opinion of Judge Ammoun); *Pulau Ligitan and Pulau Sipidan* (n 90) 705–06 (Dissenting Opinion of Judge ad hoc Franck).

262 *Right of Passage* (Merits) (n 245) 136 (Dissenting Opinion of Judge Fernandes).

263 *Corfu Channel* (n 116) 18; *Obligation to Prosecute or Extradite* (Provisional Measures) (n 1) 170 (Dissenting Opinion of Judge Cançado Trindade).

6

General Principles in Other Courts and Tribunals

I. INTRODUCTION

ALTHOUGH GENERAL PRINCIPLES as a source of law first found its expression in the Statute of the Permanent Court of International Justice (PCIJ) (and continues to be codified in the Statute of the International Court of Justice (ICJ)), the use of the source is not limited to the World Courts. This chapter looks to discussion of General Principles in other international and regional courts and tribunals. There are certain limitations to be noted. First, a clear distinction between General Principles in the Article 38(1)(c) sense and other amorphous and undefined general principles of international law must be maintained. As was seen in the previous chapters, a bright-line distinction is not always present, even in the PCIJ and the ICJ: this is even more true when turning to other courts and tribunals.

Second, this chapter does not purport to be a comprehensive analysis – it is an overview of selected international and regional jurisprudence relating to General Principles. A note of debt must be expressed to others who have done extensive work on General Principles in the distinct contexts of international criminal law, international investment law and international trade law. This chapter does not seek to recreate this work already done, but rather to contextualise it against the historical development of the source and treatment by the PCIJ and ICJ in general international law.

The third limitation is from which courts and tribunals to draw the selected cases. The immediate qualifier must be those bodies with the jurisdiction to consider international law. Thus although some domestic courts do consider international law, the focus in this chapter is on international and regional bodies. Specifically, this chapter identifies four main areas of international law that are adjudicated by bodies competent to consider General Principles. These are: international criminal law (looking to decisions of the International Criminal Tribunal for the Former Yugoslavia (ICTY), the International Criminal Tribunal for Rwanda (ICTR) and the International Criminal Court (ICC)); international economic law (looking to decisions of the World Trade Organisation (WTO), General Agreement on Tariffs and Trade (GATT) panels and selected investment arbitrations); the law of the sea (looking to decisions of the International

Tribunal for the Law of the Sea (ITLOS)); and, finally, the work of selected regional bodies, which will be considered with reference to General Principles. The case law of the Iran-US and US-Mexico arbitral tribunals will not be examined, as neither tribunal really applies General Principles in the Article 38(1)(c) sense.[1] Reference to 'general principles of law' by the Iran-US tribunal, while *influenced* by Article 38(1)(c), is best understood as a creature specific to that tribunal, fused from several sources,[2] while the US-Mexican tribunal considered 'principles of international law, justice and equity'.[3]

II. INTERNATIONAL CRIMINAL TRIBUNALS

General Principles have had a long history of use in international criminal law. The Nuremberg Tribunal drew its procedural rules from 'general principles recognized in different legal systems in the absence of a clearly articulated legal standard'.[4] The Draft Code of Crimes against the Peace and Security of Mankind, adopted by the International Law Commission in 1996,[5] sets out that the admissibility of defences shall be determined 'in accordance with the general principles of law'.[6]

The recent increase in international criminal tribunals, and the creation of the ICC, has seen commentary on the use of General Principles in international criminal law.[7] In considering this commentary and the cases, care must be had in two areas. First, as noted in section I, it is important to ensure that the so-called 'general principles' discussed are actually the same source

[1] Although note that the work of such bodies has been included in other volumes on General Principles. See, eg, CT Kotuby Jr and LA Sobota, *General Principles of Law and International Due Process: Principles and Norms Applicable in Transnational Disputes* (Oxford University Press, 2017).

[2] G Hanessian, 'General Principles of Law in the Iran-US Claims Tribunal' (1989) 27(2) *Columbia Journal of Transnational Law* 309, 311–12, 317–18.

[3] General Claims Convention (United States-Mexico) (signed 8 September 1923, entered into force 1 March 1924) TS 678, Art 1.

[4] V Morris and MP Scharf, *An Insider's Guide to The International Criminal Tribunal for the Former Yugoslavia*, vol 1 (Brill-Nijhoff, 1995) 9.

[5] ILC, 'Draft Code of Crimes against the Peace and Security of Mankind' (6 May–26 July 1996) UN Doc A/CN.4/L.532 ('Draft Code of Crimes').

[6] ibid Art 14.

[7] See, eg, N Jain, 'Judicial Lawmaking and General Principles of Law in International Criminal Law' (2016) 57 *Harvard International Law Journal* 111; N Jain, 'Comparative International Law at the ICTY: The General Principles Experiment' (2015) 109(3) *American Journal of International Law* 486; KS Gallant, *The Principle of Legality in International and Comparative Criminal Law* (Cambridge University Press, 2009); FO Raimondo, *General Principles of Law in the Decisions of International Criminal Courts and Tribunals* (Martinus Nijhoff, 2008); A Cassese, *International Criminal Law*, 2nd edn (Oxford University Press, 2008); A Cassese, 'Balancing the Prosecution of Crimes against Humanity and Non-Retroactivity of Criminal Law' (2006) 4 *Journal of International Criminal Justice* 410; G Boas and WA Schabas (eds), *International Criminal Law Developments in the Case Law of the ICTY* (Leiden, 2003).

of law as those General Principles set out in Article 38(1)(c). As will be seen, only one subset of general principles discussed by the ICTY are comparable to Article 38(1)(c). Second, some commentary reveals in-built assumptions: for example, Raimondo defines General Principles as 'legal principles generally recognized in national law',[8] which presupposes the appropriate forum for ascertaining General Principles is domestic.

A. International Criminal Tribunal for the Former Yugoslavia

The ICTY was a temporary body, established by the United Nations Security Council (UNSC) in 1993[9] to prosecute certain crimes committed in the Former Yugoslavia.[10] The ICTY's mandate existed from 1993 to 2017. It was expressly authorised to apply 'general principles of law' with regard to the pardon and commutation of sentences[11] and rules of evidence.[12] A third authorisation with regard to defences was confirmed by the UN Secretary-General in his Report to the Security Council on the formation of the ICTY:[13]

> [The ICTY] will have to decide on various personal defences which may absolve a person of individual criminal responsibility, such as minimum age or mental incapacity, drawing upon the general principles of law recognized by all nations.[14]

The inclusion of the words 'recognized by all nations' in the Secretary-General's Report, in contrast to the first two authorisations cited above, makes the reference very similar in wording to General Principles in the sense of Article 38(1)(c). Virginia Morris and Michael P Scharf also draw a link between the establishment of the Rules of Procedure and Evidence[15] and General Principles:

> The participation of all of the judges in the elaboration and adoption of the rules ensured consideration of the general principles of criminal procedure and evidence recognized in the different legal systems represented by the judges.[16]

[8] Raimondo, *General Principles of Law* (n 7) 1.

[9] Morris and Scharf, *An Insider's Guide* (n 4) 46–47; A Cassese, 'The ICTY: A Living and Vital Reality' (2004) 2 *Journal of International Criminal Justice* 585, 585.

[10] G Feinberg, 'The International Criminal Tribunal for the Former Yugoslavia: The Establishment and Evaluation of a Unique Concept in International Justice Administration' (2006) 2 *War Crimes, Genocide and Crimes Against Humanity* 87, 88–89.

[11] UNSC Res 827 (1993) UN Doc S/RES/827 (ICTY Statute), Art 28.

[12] ICTY, 'International Criminal Tribunal for the Former Yugoslavia Rules of Procedure and Evidence' (11 February 1994) UN Doc IT/32 (ICTY RPE) r 89(c); Raimondo, *General Principles of Law* (n 7) 86; Morris and Scharf, *An Insider's Guide* (n 5) 259.

[13] UNSC, 'Report of the Secretary-General Pursuant to Paragraph 2 of the Security Council Resolution 808' (3 May 1993) UN Doc S/25704 (Report of the Secretary-General); Raimondo, *General Principles of Law* (n 7) 84.

[14] Report of the Secretary-General (n 13) para 34; Raimondo, *General Principles of Law* (n 7) 85.

[15] ICTY RPE (n 12).

[16] Morris and Scharf, *An Insider's Guide* (n 4) 177.

This link between the nationality of judges and General Principles has been made before[17] and is discussed further in chapter 7 of this book.

i. Classification of General Principles

In addition to the explicit mentions of General Principles outlined in section II.A, the ICTY has considered 'general principles of law' in a broader context. This application is not always identical to Article 38(1)(c). A good starting point for considering these various 'general principles of law', and their applicability to discussions on General Principles generally, is contained in the 2000 decision of the Trial Chamber in *Prosecutor v Kupreskić*.[18] The Chamber stated:

> [A]ny time the Statute does not regulate a specific matter, and the Report of the Secretary-General does not prove to be of any assistance in the interpretation of the Statute, it falls to the International Tribunal to draw upon (i) rules of customary international law or (ii) general principles of international criminal law; or, lacking such principles, (iii) general principles of criminal law common to the major legal systems of the world; or, lacking such principles, (iv) general principles of law consonant with the basic requirements of international justice.[19]

Of these conceptions of general principles of law, the third – 'general principles of criminal law common to the major legal systems of the world' – is most in line with Article 38(1)(c). The wording used, however, presupposes a methodology: comparative study of domestic laws. Those principles set out in the fourth category also pose a challenge. Are they a subset of General Principles, or something else? The 'basic requirements of international justice' seems to suggest a more natural law foundation. They are an alternative to the comparative methodology, but they may still fit within some conceptions of Article 38(1)(c). Is the existence of these two categories another expression of the duality of General Principles?

The second category, the 'general principles of international criminal law', is said to be currently 'embedded in the international legal system',[20] and can be deduced by induction from the international legal order.[21] Antonio Cassese, the presiding judge in the decision, later elaborated on this category extra-curially, stating it included 'principles specific to criminal law, such as the principles of legality, and of specificity, the presumption of innocence, the principles of the equality of arms, etc'.[22]

[17] See ch 2; M Virally, 'The Sources of International Law' in M Sørenson (ed), *Manual of Public International Law* (St Martin's Press, 1968) 116, 146; see also PE Corbett, 'The Search for General Principles of Law' (1961) 47(5) *Virginia Law Review* 811, 824; GJH van Hoof, *Rethinking the Sources of International Law* (Kluwer Publishing, 1983) 142–43.

[18] *Prosecutor v Kupreskić et al* (Judgment) ICTY-95-16, T Ch III (14 January 2000) (*Kupreskić*).

[19] ibid para 591.

[20] Raimondo, *General Principles of Law* (n 7) 170.

[21] Cassese, *International Criminal Law* (n 7) 21.

[22] ibid 20.

However, as Raimondo points out, these principles 'have a common origin and are similar in content and scope to the "general principles of criminal law common to the major legal systems of the world"'.[23] In particular it has been argued that the principle of legality is a General Principle.[24] Raimondo argues that the difference is

> that while recourse to international jurisprudence and comparative law is the appropriate method for arriving at the former [the general principles of criminal law common to the major legal systems of the world], the latter [the general principles of international criminal law] may be identified in conventional and customary rules of international law (in particular, in international human rights instruments).[25]

Thus although the 'general principles of international criminal law' *may* be instances of General Principles, they may equally be found in customary international law or treaties. They are based on already existing norms of international law[26] – though note, some such international instruments can *also* found General Principles.[27]

Given this foundation of two types of potential General Principles, the analysis of cases following will follow the tetrahedral framework with some modifications. First, *function* is briefly considered. Second, *methodology* and *jurisprudential legitimacy* are considered together, as there is substantial overlap between the two categories in the ICTY judgments. Third, the *type* of General Principle will also be considered.

ii. Function

The function of General Principles through the ICTY jurisprudence is fairly clear – although usually used where custom is lacking, they are always considered binding. The interplay between General Principles and custom was considered in more depth by Judge Shahabuddeen, in his Separate Declaration to the Appeals Chamber judgment in *Furundžija*.[28]

As discussed in chapter 5 of this work, Judge Shahabuddeen considered General Principles in his Separate Opinion to the 1992 case of *Phosphate Lands in Nauru*.[29] In that case, Shahabuddeen employed a comparative methodology,

[23] Raimondo, *General Principles of Law* (n 7) 170.

[24] Gallant, *The Principle of Legality* (n 7) 298.

[25] Raimondo, *General Principles of Law* (n 7) 170–171.

[26] Cassese, *International Criminal Law* (n 7) 14–5, 21; Raimondo (n 7) 171.

[27] *Fisheries Case (United Kingdom v Norway)* [1951] ICJ Rep 116, 147–48 (Individual Opinion of Judge Alvarez); *Application for Review of Judgment No 158 of the United Nations Administrative Tribunal* (Advisory Opinion) [1973] ICJ Rep 166, 291 (Dissenting Opinion of Judge De Castro); *Pulp Mills on the River Uruguay (Argentina v Uruguay)* (Merits) [2010] ICJ Rep 14, 135 (Separate Opinion of Judge Cançado Trindade) paras 56–93 (Separate Opinion of Judge Cançado Trindade). See further discussion in ch 7.

[28] *Prosecutor v Furundžija* (Judgment, Declaration of Judge Shahabuddeen) ICTY-95-17/1-A, App Ch (21 July 2000) (*Furundžija* (Shahabuddeen Declaration)).

[29] *Certain Phosphate Lands in Nauru (Nauru v Australia)* (Preliminary Objections) [1992] ICJ 240 (*Certain Phosphate Lands in Nauru*).

looking to municipal laws.[30] Eight years later, in *Furundžija*, Shahabuddeen considered the principle of impartiality. This is contained within the ICTY's Statute itself,[31] and so the Court was not concerned with its basis in international law beyond the Statute. Shahabuddeen argued that that the principle was a General Principle, resting this on the writings of publicists including Bin Cheng and Fitzmaurice.[32] Leaving aside whether impartiality is a General Principle or not, Shahabuddeen's comments are informative for the interaction between General Principles and custom. Shahabuddeen stated, citing Rosenne, that 'a new rule of customary international law may override a general principle, or add to it, or subtract from it, or otherwise qualify it'.[33]

Thus while Shahabuddeen sees General Principles as binding, they are subsidiary in the sense that they are able to be overridden by competing norms of custom.

iii. Methodology and Jurisprudential Legitimacy

The identification of the two different categories of 'general principles' dictates a methodology – those principles in category 3 will most likely be found by way of comparativism. In contrast, those principles in category 4 are not explicitly linked to any methodology. In this way, the examination of ICTY jurisprudence is necessarily different from that of the PCIJ and ICJ.

a. Comparativism

Those principles under the third category are found using comparative analysis of domestic jurisprudence. Examples can be seen in the discussion of *non bis in idem* by the Trial Chamber in the preliminary decision in *Tadić*,[34] the discussion on *unus testis, nullus testis* in the Opinion and Judgment in *Tadić*,[35] and the discussions on penalties for crimes against humanity by the Trial Chamber in *Erdemovic*.[36] Further examples are seen in two cases where the Appeals Chamber failed to find a General Principle following comparative analysis of domestic laws, due to a lack of horizontal generality.[37]

[30] ibid, 287–89 (Separate Opinion of Judge Shahabuddeen).

[31] ICTY Statute (n 11) Art 13(1); *Furundžija* (Shahabuddeen Declaration) (n 28) para 256.

[32] *Furundžija* (Shahabuddeen Declaration) (n 28) para 256; B Cheng, *General Principles of Law as Applied by International Courts and Tribunals* (Cambridge University Press, 1953) ch 13; GG Fitzmaurice, *The Law and Procedure of the International Court of Justice*, vol 2 (Grotius Publications Limited, 1986) 627, 676.

[33] *Furundžija* (Shahabuddeen Declaration) (n 28) para 257; S Rosenne, *The Law and Practice of the International Court, 1920–1966*, vol 3 (Brill Nijhoff, 1997) 1606.

[34] *Prosecutor v Tadić* (Decision on the Defence Motion on the Principle of Non Bis in Idem) ICTY-94-1-T, T Ch II (14 November 1995) para 9.

[35] *Prosecutor v Tadić* (Opinion and Judgment) ICTY-94-1-T, T Ch II (7 May 1997) paras 535–39.

[36] *Prosecutor v Erdemovic* (Sentencing Judgment) ICTY-96-22-T, T Ch 1 (29 November 1996) paras 19, 26.

[37] *Prosecutor v Šainović* (Judgment) ICTY-05-87-A (23 January 2014) paras 1644–45 (*Šainović*); *Prosecutor v Delić* (Decision on the Outcome of Proceedings) ICTY-04-83-A (29 June 2010) (*Delić*); see also Jain, 'Comparative International Law' (n 7) 489.

As was the case with judgments from the PCIJ and ICJ, some of the ICTY decisions utilised a very limited comparative methodology,[38] and have been criticised by publicists for this.[39] There are, however, also examples of more comprehensive comparative studies, such as the analysis of 30 national legal systems in the Joint Opinion of Judges McDonald and Vohrah in the Appeals Chamber in *Erdemovic*,[40] the analysis of 33 national legal systems by the Trial Chamber in *Kunurac*[41] and the analysis of 34 national legal systems by the Appeals Chamber in *Šainović*.[42]

In *Furundžija*,[43] the Trial Chamber, in defining the elements of rape, found that – along with treaty and custom – the 'general principles of international criminal law' or the 'general principles of international law' were of no avail.[44] The Trial Chamber instead considered the 'principles of criminal law common to the major legal systems of the world'.[45] Thus the Court expressly distinguished between 'general principles of international law' and General Principles.[46] The work of the Court in *Furundžija* seems explicitly to be addressed to General Principles in the sense of Article 38(1)(c). It emphasised the need to look to different legal systems, not just different national laws, in ascertaining General Principles:

> [R]eference should not be made to one national legal system only, say that of common-law or that of civil-law States. Rather, international courts must draw upon the general concepts and legal institutions common to all the major legal systems of the world.[47]

The Appeal Chamber in *Tadić*[48] confirmed this approach seven months later, stating that to rely on a General Principle, 'it would be necessary to show that,

[38] See, eg, *Prosecutor v Tadić* (Decision on the Defence Motion for Interlocutory Appeal on Jurisdiction) ICTY-94-1-AR72, App Ch (2 October 1995) para 6 (Separate Opinion of Judge Sidwa) (*Tadić* (Jurisdiction)); *Prosecutor v Erdemovic* (Sentencing Judgment) ICTY-96-22-T Ch 1 (29 November 1996) paras 19, 26; *Prosecutor v Limaj et al* (Judgment) ICTY-95-16-T (14 January 2000) para 3 (Declaration of Judge Shahabuddeen).

[39] See, eg, Raimondo, *General Principles of Law* (n 7) 96; A Nollkaemper, 'Decisions of National Courts as Sources of International Law: An Analysis of the Practice of the ICTY' in G Boas and W Schabas (eds), *International Criminal Law Developments in the Case-law of the ICTY* (Leiden, 2003) 277, 289; A Cassese, *International Criminal Law* (n 7) 24; Jain, 'Comparative International Law' (n 7) 486, 490.

[40] *Prosecutor v Erdemovic* (Judgment) ICTY-96-22-A, App CH (7 October 1997) para 57 (Joint Separate Opinion of Judge McDonald and Judge Vohrah) (*Erdemovic*).

[41] *Prosecutor v Kunarac et al* (Judgment) ICTY-96-23-T and IT-96-23/1-T (22 February 2001) (*Kunarac*).

[42] *Šainović* (n 37) paras 1644–45.

[43] *Prosecutor v Furundžija* (Judgment) ICTY-85-17/1-T, T Ch II (10 December 1998) (*Furundžija*).

[44] ibid para 177.

[45] ibid.

[46] Though the trial chamber did return to a 'general principle of international law' of human dignity to assess, in light of inconsistent domestic laws, whether forcible oral penetration rose to the level of rape: ibid para 183. In light of the earlier distinction at para 177, this cannot be read as stating that this general principle of international law is also a General Principle in the Art 38(1)(c) sense. For a contrary view, see Jain, 'Comparative International Law' (n 7) 488.

[47] *Furundžija* (n 43) para 178.

[48] *Prosecutor v Tadić* (Judgment) ICTY-94-1-A (15 July 1999) (*Tadić* (Judgment)).

in any case, the major legal systems of the world take the same approach to this notion'.[49] In general, the main legal families recognised in decisions of the ICTY are civil and common law,[50] although there has been recognition of 'other states' (in that instance, Japan, China, Morocco, Somalia and Ethiopia),[51] and of China.[52] In practice, the national laws considered by the ICTY are generally European-centred.[53]

The decisions indicate that universal acceptance of a General Principle is not required[54] – although *Tadić* did call for 'most, if not all countries',[55] but modified that statement with a reference to 'the major legal systems'.[56] The Appeal Chamber in *Prosecutor v Šainović* adopted the *Tadic* approach without the modifier of 'in any case':

> [U]nder the doctrine of general principles of law recognised by nations, national legislation and case law may be relied upon as a source of international principles or rules in limited situations. Such reliance, however, is permissible only where it is shown that most, if not all, countries accept and adopt the same approach to the notion at issue. More specifically, it would be necessary to show that the major legal systems of the world take the same approach to that notion.[57]

In *Šainović*, the Appeals Chamber found that the inconsistency within and between major legal systems meant no General Principle regarding the concept of 'specific direction' in the context of aiding and abetting existed.[58]

b. International Principles

In contrast to the cases discussed in section II.A.iii.a, some of the judgments turn to international materials to establish General Principles. Thus the Appeals Chamber in *Tadić* found a principle that courts must be established by law in international human rights treaties.[59] Raimondo argues that this is sufficient, because 'the identification of general principles of law that have crystallised in conventional human rights law does not require comparative law research'.[60]

[49] ibid para 225.
[50] Raimondo, *General Principles of Law* (n 7) 179.
[51] *Erdemovic* (n 40) para 57 (Joint Separate Opinion of Judge McDonald and Judge Vohrah).
[52] *Prosecutor v Tadić* (Appeals Judgment on Allegations of Contempt against Prior Consul, Milan Vujin) ICTY-94-1-A-AR77, App Ch (27 February 2001) para 17 (*Tadić* (Appeal of Vujin)).
[53] See, eg, *Prosecutor v Delalic et al* (Judgment) Case No IT-96-21-A App Ch (20 February 2001) paras 575–88 (*Delalic*); *Prosecutor v Nikolic* (Sentencing Judgment) ICTY-94-2-S, T Ch II (18 December 2003) §163; *Delić* (n 37) paras 11–13; but see *Šainović* (n 37) paras 1644–45 which considered mostly non-European countries.
[54] *Kunarac* (n 41) para 439.
[55] *Tadić* (Judgment) (n 48) para 225.
[56] ibid.
[57] *Šainović* (n 37) para 1643.
[58] ibid paras 1644–45.
[59] *Tadić* (Jurisdiction) (n 38) para 352.
[60] Raimondo, *General Principles of Law* (n 7) 89.

This rests on a conception that the 'general principles of international criminal law', the first category identified in Kupreskić,[61] *are* true General Principles.[62] Other cases rely on both domestic and international materials in their discussion of General Principles.[63]

c. Justice

The fourth category from *Kupreskić*,[64], brings a different methodology: rather than base a General Principle on its acceptance in municipal legal systems, it is based on its content – being 'just' – and hence brings in natural law jurisprudential legitimacy. The operation of this category of General Principle is seen in the Separate and Dissenting Opinion of Judge Stephen in *Erdemovic*. Stephen relied on the defence of duress[65] – a defence recognised in civil law but not in common law.[66] Stephen justified this 'as a matter of simple justice'.[67] Hence, even though a comparative study would *not* find a General Principle, the content of the norm is enough to make it a General Principle.

A link between morality and General Principles was also made by the Appeals Chamber in *Delalic*.[68] The issue being considered was whether those crimes contained in Article 3 of the ICTY Statute contravened the principle of legality. The Appeals Chamber stated:

> It is universally acknowledged that the acts … are wrongful and shock the conscience of civilised people and thus are, in the language of Article 15(2) of the ICCPR 'criminal according to the general principles of law recognised by civilised nations'.[69]

This formulation harks back to Descamps' original formulation of Article 38(1)(c) – the 'conscience of civilised people' is much like the 'conscience of mankind'. Accordingly, natural law elements are again raised. A comparative methodology, however, remains to an extent. The Appeals Chamber cited with approval the statement of the Trial Chamber that '[i]t is undeniable that acts such as murder, torture, rape and inhuman treatment are criminal according to "general principles of law" recognised by all legal systems'.[70] The phrase 'recognised by all legal systems' indicates that the legality of the General Principle was not founded solely on the 'conscience of civilised people'.

[61] *Kupreskić* (n 18) para 591; see discussion in section II.A.i.

[62] ibid 170. As was seen in ch 5, and is discussed in ch 7, the role of international materials in the ascertainment of General Principles is not settled.

[63] *Prosecutor v Nikolić* (Sentencing Judgment) ICTY-94-2-S, T Ch II (18 December 2003) para 163; *Kupreskić* (n 18) paras 687–92.

[64] *Kupreskić* (n 18) para 591; see discussion in section II.A.i.

[65] *Erdemovic* (n 40) paras 25–26.

[66] Raimondo, *General Principles of Law* (n 7) 101.

[67] *Erdemovic* (n 40) para 26.

[68] *Delalic* (n 53).

[69] ibid para 173.

[70] ibid para 179.

d. Discretion

A link between the preceding section and judicial discretion can also be made. This is seen particularly in the Trial Chamber decision in *Kupreskić*. The matter at hand was the misclassification of facts by the Prosecutor. The Trial Chamber sought to find a General Principle on how to procedurally deal with this.[71] It could not find the requisite commonality, and instead turned to 'a general principle of law consonant with the fundamental features and the basic requirements of international criminal practice'.[72] This seems to be in line with the fourth category identified earlier in *Kupreskić* and the approach of Judge Stephen in *Erdemovic* one year later.

One of the principles that the Trial Chamber in *Kupreskić* identified in this manner was that the ICTY must be able to exercise all its powers 'necessary for them to fulfill their mission efficiently and in the interests of justice'.[73] With this as justification, the Trial Chamber then developed procedural guidelines to cover the situation.[74] Raimondo criticises these as being 'not real general principles of law, but judge made law'.[75] This is certainly an instance of judicial discretion, but does it follow that it is not a 'real' General Principle? This reveals a flaw in the fourth category of *Kupreskić* – it invites judicial discretion, which is incompatible with the historical development of General Principles as a source of law.[76]

Discretion is also considered in Judge Shahabuddeen's declaration in *Furundžija*. The discussion here is also related to the rule/principle question, as well as the jurisprudence and methodology of the source. Shahabuddeen viewed General Principles as true principles, being 'general propositions … which express the essential qualities of juridical truth itself'[77] and 'an expression … of socially realisable morality'.[78] Shahabuddeen saw General Principles as resting only loosely on a comparative methodology,[79] being less of a generalisation of municipal laws and more 'particularizations of a common underlying sense of what is just in the circumstances'.[80] They represent a *common* underlying sense, so maintain horizontal generality, but these General Principles also have vertical generality – they are not a specific rule. They are linked with notions of morality,

[71] *Kupreskić* (n 18) para 728.
[72] ibid para 738.
[73] ibid para 739.
[74] ibid para 742.
[75] Raimondo, *General Principles of Law* (n 7) 124.
[76] See discussion in ch 2.
[77] *Furundžija* (Shahabuddeen Declaration) (n 28) para 260; Cheng, *General Principles of Law* (n 32) 24.
[78] *Furundžija* (Shahabuddeen Declaration) (n 28) para 260.
[79] Cf *Certain Phosphate Lands in Nauru* (n 29).
[80] *Furundžija* (Shahabuddeen Declaration) (n 28) para 260; Rosenne, *Law and Practice* (n 33) 1605.

truth and justice. Because of this vertical generality – the abstract nature of such principles – discretion may be an issue:

> Because such a principle is broad, the necessity for interpreting it whenever it is applied is inescapable. But the function of the interpretation is limited: if it exceeds the proper needs of the case, the spectre of an imperial judiciary arises. On the international plane, that is even more unacceptable than it is on the national.[81]

The framework in chapter 1 set out issues of discretion in the *identification* of a General Principle in the absence of an identifiable rule of recognition. Here, Shahabuddeen highlights a new concern – where an identified principle is of a very broad application, discretion is inevitable, to apply it to a particular circumstance. This is an example of guided discretion – a choice between different applications of the General Principle. Shahabuddeen refers to the choice as the 'correct interpretation'[82] – which is consistent with Dworkinian guided discretion, looking to find the 'right' solution.[83]

e. Appropriateness

The ICTY has maintained the requirement set out by Judge McNair in *International Status of South-West Africa* that General Principles must be appropriate to be international principles.[84] In some cases, such as in *Tadić* (Jurisdiction), this has necessitated applying the General Principle differently at the international level than at the municipal level.[85] *Kupreskić* warns that 'it will always be necessary to bear in mind the dangers of wholesale incorporation of principles of national law into the unique system of international criminal law'.[86] The Trial Chamber in *Furundžija* stated that by taking account of the

> specificity of international criminal law proceedings when utilising national law notions … a mechanical importation or transposition from national law into international criminal law is avoided, as well as the attendant distortions of the unique traits of such proceedings.[87]

Nonetheless, the use of domestic provisions on the definition of rape in *Furundžija* shows the appropriateness of domestic criminal law provisions as a basis for international criminal law.[88]

[81] *Furundžija* (Shahabuddeen Declaration) (n 28) para 261.
[82] ibid para 262.
[83] R Dworkin 'Law's Ambitions for Itself' (1985) 71 *Virginia Law Review* 173, 175.
[84] *International Status of South-West Africa* (Advisory Opinion) [1950] ICJ Rep 128, 148 (Separate Opinion of Judge McNair) (*International Status of South-West Africa*).
[85] *Tadić (Jurisdiction)* (n 38) para 43.
[86] *Kupreskić* (n 18) para 677.
[87] *Furundžija* (n 43) para 178.
[88] ibid paras 177–81.

iv. Type

a. Principles/Rules

There is inconsistent practice in the ICTY regarding where General Principles sit on the principle/rule scale. On the one hand, *Kunurac* emphasised the role of the source was to

> disclose 'general concepts and legal institutions' ... [I]n considering these national legal systems the Trial Chamber does not conduct a survey of the major legal systems of the world in order to identify a specific legal provision ... but to consider, from an examination of national systems generally, whether it is possible to identify certain basic principles ...[89]

This clearly indicates an approach that looks to principles rather than rules. The Trial Chamber in *Kunurac*, however, rests this passage in part on the language used in *Furundžija* of 'common denominators'.[90] Examining *Furundžija*, it appears the Trial Chamber in that case was *not* stating the need for principles rather than rules, but rather establishing that in order to find commonality between different municipal laws, 'in spite of inevitable discrepancies',[91] some degree of abstraction is necessary:

> Rather, international courts must draw upon the general concepts and legal institutions common to all the major legal systems of the world. This presupposes a process of identification of the common denominators in these legal systems so as to pinpoint the basic notions they share.[92]

These basic notions could easily encompass a rule rather than a principle. Indeed the finding by the Trial Chamber in *Furundžija* is a rule of some specificity:

> [M]ost legal systems in the common and civil law worlds consider rape to be the forcible sexual penetration of the human body by the penis or the forcible insertion of any other object into either the vagina or the anus.[93]

Other cases do not distinguish between principles and rules but use the terms interchangeably. Thus the Appeals Chamber in *Tadić* (Judgment) refers to General Principles as 'international principles or rules'.[94] Other General Principles are specific so they must be considered rules, such as the notion of reciprocal speciality found by the Trial Chamber in *Kupreskić*. The Trial Chamber based the General Principle on decisions of municipal courts.[95] These have been criticised as being 'too detailed and precise to be considered abstractions of legal rules'

[89] *Kunarac* (n 41) para 439.
[90] ibid para 439.
[91] *Furundžija* (n 43) para 181.
[92] ibid para 178.
[93] ibid para 181.
[94] *Tadić* (Judgment) (n 48) para 225.
[95] *Kupreskić* (n 18) paras 681, 685.

and so are not a true General Principle.[96] Such criticism is only valid if we accept that General Principles are *true* principles and cannot be rules.

B. International Criminal Tribunal for Rwanda

The ICTR, like the ICTY, was a temporary international criminal tribunal. It was established in 1994 to judge cases arising from the Rwandan genocide, and its mandate ran until 2015. The provisions for the ICTR to consider General Principles are much the same as for the ICTY.[97] Unlike the ICTY, however, there is no case in the ICTR jurisprudence that differentiates between 'general principles of international criminal law' and 'general principles of criminal law common to the major legal systems of the world'.

While some ICTR decisions refer to General Principles,[98] this is often done in passing[99] or asserts the existence of a General Principle with no further substantiation.[100] The decision in *Karemera*[101] is interesting, as it seems to suggest that contrary national practice is not inconsistent with a General Principle:

> Furthermore, the submission that a number of national jurisdictions prohibit the practice of witness proofing does not, in the view of the Appeals Chamber, make such practice incompatible with … the general principles of law.[102]

This is at odds with much of the established jurisprudence on General Principles, and the earlier ICC *Dyilo* decision.[103] It is explained, however, by reference to the ICTR Rules of Procedure and Evidence (ICTR RPE), which state:

> Rule 89: General Provisions
>
> (A) The rules of evidence set forth in this Section shall govern the proceedings before the Chambers. The Chambers shall not be bound by national rules of evidence.

[96] Raimondo, *General Principles of Law* (n 7) 122.

[97] ibid 143–44.

[98] ibid 144; *Prosecutor v Akayesu* (Judgment) ICTR-96-4-T, T Ch 1 (2 September 1998) (*Akayesu*); *Barayagwiza v Prosecutor, Decision* (Prosecutor's Request for Review or Reconsideration) ICTR-97-19-AR72, App Ch (31 March 2000) (*Barayagwiza*); *Kambanda v The Prosecutor* (Judgment) ICTR-97-23-A App Ch (19 October 2000) (*Kambanda*).

[99] *Akayesu* (n 98) paras 471, 501.

[100] *Barayagwiza* (n 98) para 19 (Declaration of Judge Nieto-Navia); *Kambanda* (n 96) para 98; *Prosecutor v Nzabonimana* (Decision on Third Defence Motion for the Admission of a Written Statement and accompanying Documents) ICTR-98-44D-T, T Ch III (19 October 2001) para 26 (*Nzabonimana*); *Prosecutor v Nshogoza* (Decision on Defence Request for Order for Cooperation of the Republic of Rwanda and the United Republic of Tanzania) ICTR-07-91-T, T Ch II (28 July 2009) para 10 (*Nshogoza*).

[101] *Prosecutor v Karemera et al* (Decision on Interlocutory Appeal regarding Witness Proofing) ICTR-98-44-AR73.8, A Ch (11 May 2007) (*Karemera*).

[102] ibid para 11.

[103] *Situation in the Democratic Republic of the Congo in the Case of Prosecutor v Thomas Lubanga Dyilo*, (Decision on Witness Familiarisation and Proofing) Case No ICC-01/04-01/06, PT Ch I (8 November 2006) (*Dyilo* (Witness Proofing)).

(B) In cases not otherwise provided for in this Section, a Chamber shall apply rules of evidence which will best favour a fair determination of the matter before it and are consonant with the spirit of the Statute and the general principles of law.[104]

One reading of the Rules themselves divorces General Principles from national laws to an extent, by the close juxtaposition of Rule 89(A) and 89(B).[105] Thus this judgment is better viewed as limited to the specific circumstances of the ICTR, rather than being indicative of the nature of General Principles more broadly. Even so, the Appeals Chamber in *Karemera* did consider some national laws as support for the principle.[106] The impact of Rule 89 is also seen in *Ndindabahizi*,[107] where the Trial Chamber was content to rest so-called 'general principles' of the assessment of evidence on prior jurisprudence of the ICTY, with no reference to municipal laws.[108]

There are a few cases of the ICTR that indicate a comparative methodology. In *Bagosora*, the Trial Chamber referred to the 'general principles of law articulated in divergent national legal systems';[109] in *Semanza*, the Trial Chamber undertakes an extremely brief look at common law jurisdictions, finding civil law jurisdictions irrelevant on questions relating to adversarial processes;[110] and the Joint Separate Opinion of Judges Tieya and Nieto-Navia in *Kanyabashi* referred to 'certain general principles of law, recognised by all major legal systems'.[111]

Although we cannot derive anything about the *jurisprudential legitimacy* of the source from the cases considered, we can ascertain the *type* of General Principle. Many are evidential, due to the operation of Article 89 of the ICTR RPE. Some include very specific rules, such as 'an Advocate should not certify documents in a case in which he appears as Counsel'.[112] Others are true principles, such as *non bis in idem*[113] and *res judicata*.[114]

[104] ICTR, 'International Criminal Tribunal for Rwanda Rules of Procedure and Evidence' (29 June 1995) UN Doc ITR/3/REV.1, Art 89 (ICTR RPE).

[105] Although an identical provision is contained at Art 89 of the ICTY Rules of Procedure and Evidence, this does not seem to have impacted on the consideration of General Principles by that tribunal in the same way.

[106] Although only the practice of the United States was explicitly mentioned: *Karemera* (n 99) para 11.

[107] *Prosecutor v Ndindabahizi* (Judgment and Sentencing) ICTR-2001-71-I, T Ch I (15 July 2004) (*Ndindabahizi*).

[108] ibid para 23.

[109] *Prosecutor v Bagosora* (Decision on Certification of Appeal concerning Will-Say Statements of Witnesses DBQ, DP and DA) ICTR-98-41-T, T Ch I (5 December 2003) para 10 (*Bagosora*).

[110] *Prosecutor v Semanza* (Decision on Defence Motion for Leave to Call Rejoinder Witnesses) ICTR-97-20-T Trial Chamber III (30 April 2002) para 4 (*Semanza*).

[111] *Kanyabashi v Prosecutor* (Interlocutory Appeal) ICTR-96-15-A, App Ch (3 June 1999) para 20 (Joint and Separate Opinion of Judge Tieya and Judge Nieto-Navia) (*Kanyabashi*).

[112] *Nzabonimana* (n 100) 26.

[113] *Nshogoza* (n 100) para 10.

[114] *Barayagwiza* (n 98) para 19.

C. International Criminal Court

The Statute of the International Criminal Court came into force on 1 July 2002. Under Article 21(1)(c) of its Statute, the ICC is authorised to apply general principles, but only after applying 'applicable treaties and the principles and rules of international law':[115]

> (c) Failing that, general principles of law derived by the Court from national laws of legal systems of the world including, as appropriate, the national laws of States that would normally exercise jurisdiction over the crime, provided that those principles are not inconsistent with this Statute and with international law and internationally recognized norms and standards.[116]

Unlike Article 38(1) of the ICJ Statute, General Principles are explicitly subsidiary to treaties and customary international law in the ICC Statute. The methodology is prescribed by the ICC Statute, and is comparative, based *in foro domestico*. Accordingly, to the extent to which the ICC employs this methodology can only be reflective of the strictures of its own Statute. Pellet equates Article 21(1)(c) of the ICC Statute with Article 38(1)(c) of the ICJ Statute, but argues that the ICC 'defines [the source] better and more precisely'.[117] In this manner, Article 21(1)(c) of the ICC Statute 'indicates that those principles are 'derived by the Court from national laws of legal systems of the world', which 'dispels all uncertainty to their nature'.[118] This presupposes, however, that this *is* the correct meaning of Article 38(1)(c) – a meaning that does not sit well with, for example, the Separate and Dissenting Opinions of Judge Cançado Trindade in the ICJ,[119] or those publicists who see General Principles as foundational deductions from the international legal order itself.[120] It also sits at odds with the categories from *Kupreskić*, and in particular the suggestion that General Principles can be evidenced by international materials alone.[121]

An example of the comparative methodology utilised by the ICC is found in two decisions in the *Dyilo* prosecution in 2006. In the Judgment on Application

[115] 'Rome Statute of the International Criminal Court', UN Diplomatic Conference of Plenipotentiaries on the Establishment of an International Criminal Court (Rome 15 June–17 July 1998) UN Doc A/CONF.183/9 (ICC Statute), Art 21(1)(b).

[116] ibid Art 21(1)(c).

[117] A Pellet, 'Applicable Law' in A Cassese, P Gaeta and JRWD Jones (eds), *The Rome Statute of the International Criminal Court: A Commentary*, vol 2 (Oxford University Press, 2002) 1051, 1073.

[118] ibid 1073.

[119] See ch 5.

[120] See, eg, W Riphagen 'General Principles of Law' in A Cassese and JHH Weiler (eds), *Change and Stability in International Law-Making* (Walter de Gruyter, 1988) 33, 34; S Kadelbach and T Kleinlein, 'International Law – a Constitution for Mankind? An attempt at re-appraisal with an analysis' (2007) 50 *German Yearbook of International Law* 303, 337; M Biddulph and D Newman, 'A Contextualized Account of General Principles of International Law' (2014) 26(2) *Pace International Law Review* 286. See further ch 7.

[121] Cassese, *International Criminal Law* (n 7) 14–15, 21; Raimondo, *General Principles of Law* (n 7) 171.

for Extraordinary Review, the Pre-Trial Chamber had previously denied leave to appeal against a decision allowing victims to participate in the proceedings.[122] The Prosecutor applied for a review of this decision. Such a review was not provided for in either the ICC Statute or the ICC Rules of Procedure and Evidence.[123] The Prosecutor argued that was a lacuna that should be filled by an Article 21(1)(c) general principle.[124] In making this argument the Prosecutor referred to 22 nations from three legal families – common law,[125] civil law[126] and Islamic law.[127] This comparative study has been criticised for its lack of any legal system from Africa.[128] The Appeals Chamber denied the request on two grounds, finding against both the existence of a general principle[129] and the notion of a lacuna on the point.[130]

In finding against a general principle, the Court grouped its criticisms within the three legal systems. Thus, in terms of civil systems, the Court referred to the contrary practice of France and Germany, as well as inconsistent practice within those countries that did allow review of decisions.[131] The Court found that the common law practice of review of lower court decisions could not apply to the ICC, as the pre-trial Chamber was not an inferior court analogous to the court structure within the United Kingdom.[132] Finally, the Pre-Trial Chamber found no consistent practice within the three Islamic Law countries.[133] From this we can draw the importance of having consistent practice *within* a legal tradition, as well as *between* legal traditions. Further, in rejecting the analogy to the common law process of review, the ICC was exercising judgment on the *appropriateness* of the principle in question.

A comparative study was also undertaken in the *Dyilo* decision on witness proofing.[134] In this case, the Pre-Trial Chamber looked to the laws of 10 nations with regard to witness proofing.[135] There was a strong European-Western focus to the countries selected, with one from South America, one from Africa and no Asian legal systems considered.[136] Argued comparative general principles under

[122] *Prosecutor v Dyilo* (Judgment on the Prosecutor's Application for Extraordinary Review of Pre-Trial Chamber I's 31 March 2006 Decision Denying Leave to Appeal) ICC-01/04-01/06 PT Ch 1 (13 July 2006) (*Dyilo* (Judgment on Application for Extraordinary Review)).

[123] ibid para 3.

[124] ibid para 5.

[125] Australia, Canada, Sierra Leone, the United Kingdom and the United States: ibid para 28.

[126] Argentina, Chile, Ecuador, El Salvador, Finland, Germany, Mexico, Portugal, Spain, Guatemala, Honduras, Nicaragua, Panama, Uruguay: ibid para 26.

[127] Malaysia, Singapore and the Philippines: ibid para 31.

[128] Raimondo, *General Principles of Law* (n 7) 155.

[129] *Dyilo* (Judgment on Application for Extraordinary Review) (n 122) para 32.

[130] ibid para 39.

[131] ibid para 27.

[132] ibid para 30.

[133] ibid para 31.

[134] *Dyilo* (Witness Proofing) (n 103).

[135] ibid para 37.

[136] The national legal systems considered were Australia, Belgium, Brazil, England and Wales, France, Germany, Ghana, Scotland, Spain and the USA.

Article 21(1)(c) have also been rejected by the ICC for lack of representation of systems and for having too few legal systems cited.[137]

The judgments that do deal with Article 21(1)(c) of the ICC Statute employ a comparative approach, as they must under the wording of that provision. While the limited nature of the provision limits the usefulness of the ICC cases in commenting more generally about General Principles in the Article 38(1)(c) sense, these cases do provide a modern example of comparative study. Although the legal systems considered are not completely representative (the exclusion of African and Asian legal systems respectively), they are certainly less Eurocentric than previous courts' and tribunals' studies have been.

III. INTERNATIONAL ECONOMIC LAW

A. World Trade Organisation

The WTO was established in 1995 to administer the trade agreements of its members.[138] The WTO has a compulsory dispute settlement system, which is a two-stage process.[139] Complaints are first heard by ad hoc Panels, created at the request of WTO members.[140] After the report of the Panel, members have the right of appeal to the permanent Appellate Body.[141] Importantly, Panel members are not required to have legal qualifications,[142] and although Appellate Body members must possess 'demonstrated expertise in law, international trade and the subject matter of the covered agreements generally',[143] in practice only the small minority have law degrees or judicial experience.[144] I argue elsewhere that this has contributed to a culture of 'siloisation' of WTO law, where general international law is not well integrated into consideration of the WTO treaties.[145]

[137] MM deGuzman, 'Article 21, Applicable Law' in O Triffiter and K Ambos (eds), *The Rome Statute of the International Criminal Court: A Commentary*, 3rd edn (Beck/Hart, 2016) 932, 944.

[138] Marrakesh Agreement Establishing the World Trade Organization (opened for signature 15 April 1994, entered into force 1 January 1995) 1867 UNTS 3.

[139] Marrakesh Agreement Establishing the World Trade Organization (opened for signature 15 April 1994, entered into force 1 January 1995) 1867 UNTS 3, annex 2 (*Understanding on Rules and Procedures Governing the Settlement of Disputes*) 1869 UNTS 401 (*DSU*).

[140] V Hughes, 'WTO Dispute Settlement: An Overview' in A Mitchell (ed), *Challenges and Prospects for the WTO* (Cameron May, 2005) 23, 28.

[141] *DSU* (n 139) Arts 16(4), 17(1). At the time of writing the Appellate Body is functionally crippled by ongoing US refusal to appoint new members. See I Saunders, 'Populism, Backlash and the Ongoing Use of the World Trade Organization Dispute Settlement System: State Responses to the Appellate Body Crisis' (2020) 35 *Maryland Journal of International Law* (forthcoming).

[142] *DSU* (n 139) Art 8(1).

[143] ibid Art 17(3).

[144] J Pauwelyn, 'Who Decides Matters: The Legitimacy Capital of WTO Adjudicators versus ICSID Arbitrators' in N Grossman et al (eds), *Legitimacy and International Courts* (Cambridge University Press, 2018) 216, 221–22.

[145] See I Saunders, 'Navigating the backlash: Re-integrating WTO and Public International Law?' (2020) 38 *Australian Yearbook of International Law* 134.

In line with this general trend, although it has been suggested that General Principles (along with customary international law) could have a larger role to play in future WTO jurisprudence,[146] specific discussion of General Principles by WTO tribunals is, for now, scarce.

Andrew Mitchell has identified decisions where WTO Tribunals have considered principles such as good faith,[147] proportionality[148] and due process,[149] which could be General Principles (but which could also be principles of custom). Reference to such principles is usually made without explicit reference to their source.[150] Where principles are explicitly referred to as 'general principles of law', no discussion of the source or elaboration of how the principle is found is usually given,[151] or decisions rely on previous decisions of international courts with no further discussion of the source.[152] Other decisions conflate General Principles and custom, and fail to distinguish between the sources.[153]

In some instances, members make explicit reference to General Principles in their submission but the WTO body does not decide on that point. In *EC Measures Concerning Meat and Meat Products (Hormones)*,[154] submissions were made by members on the precautionary principle. The European Communities submitted that the principle was 'a general customary rule of international law or at least a general principle of law',[155] while Canada took a more cautious approach, viewing it as 'an *emerging* principle of international law, which may in the future crystallize into one of the "general principles of law recognized by civilized nations", within the meaning of Article 38(1)(c) of the *Statute of the International Court of Justice*'.[156] The Appellate Body chose not to determine whether a General Principle of the precautionary principle existed,

[146] A Mitchell 'The Legal Basis for using Principles in WTO Disputes' (2007) 10 *Journal of International Economic Law* 1, 18.

[147] See generally A Mitchell, 'Good Faith in WTO Dispute Settlement' (2006) 7(2) *Melbourne Journal of International Law* 339.

[148] See generally A Mitchell, 'Proportionality and Remedies in WTO Disputes' (2007) 17(5) *European Journal of International Law* 985.

[149] A Mitchell, 'Due Process in WTO Disputes' in R Yerxa and B Wilson (eds), *Key Issues in WTO Dispute Settlement: The First Ten Years* (Cambridge University Press, 2005) 144.

[150] See, eg, Mitchell, 'Good Faith' (n 147) 351; Mitchell, 'Proportionality' (n 148) 986.

[151] See, eg, *United States – Continued Dumping and Subsidy Offset Act of 2000*, Appellate Body Report (adopted 27 January 2003) WT/DS217/AB/R, WT/DS234/AB/R, AB-2002-7, para 297; *United States – Import Prohibition of Certain Shrimp and Shrimp Products*, Panel Report (adopted 6 November 1998) WT/DS58/R, 98-1710, para 7.14.

[152] *India – Measures Affecting the Automotive Sector*, Panel Report, (adopted 5 April 2002) WT/DS146/R, WT/DS175/R, para 4.55.

[153] *United States – Definitive Anti-Dumping and Countervailing Duties on Certain Products from China*, Appellate Body Report (adopted 25 March 2011) WT/DS379/AB/R, AB-2010-3, paras 36, 38, 305, 308, 309.

[154] *EC Measures Concerning Meat and Meat Products (Hormones)*, Appellate Body Report (adopted 13 February 1998) WT/DS26/AB/R, WT/DS48/AB/R, AB-1997-4 (*EC Measures (Hormones)*).

[155] ibid para 16.

[156] ibid para 62.

stating 'we consider, however, that it is unnecessary, and probably imprudent for the Appellate Body in this appeal to take a position on this important, but abstract, question'.[157]

Similarly in *Guatemala – Definitive Anti-Dumping Measures on Grey Portland Cement from Mexico*,[158] Guatemala argued that a delay in giving notification under the Anti-Dumping Agreement should be considered a 'harmless error'.[159] The Guatemalan submissions argued that the doctrine of harmless error was a General Principle, and made reference to laws in Australia, the United States, Namibia, Spain, Canada, Guatemala and Mexico.[160] This was a comparative approach to General Principles, based on the domestic forum. The Panel recognised the submission in its findings, stating 'Guatemala refers to certain Member's practice in civil and criminal proceedings in this regard',[161] but held 'we do not consider that the concept of "harmless error" as presented by Guatemala has attained the status of a general principle of public international law'.[162] No further elaboration on why the Panel held this view was given.

B. GATT Panels

Prior to the establishment of the WTO in 1995, international trade law was regulated by the GATT. Disputes under the GATT were resolved by ad hoc panel decisions, which required consensus of members in each dispute to form the panel and adopt the report of the panel.[163] General Principles were considered by the GATT Panel in *US Hot-Rolled Lead and Bismuth*.[164]

In this dispute, the Panel was invited by the European Community to consider General Principles in an attempt to find an alternative to the standard of 'reasonableness'. The Panel summarised the EC's argument:

> This approach is embedded in Art 38 of the Statute of the International Court of Justice whereby the general principles of law recognized by civilized nations figure among the recognized sources of international law. These are principles generally applied and common to national legal systems of the United Nations members …[165]

[157] ibid para 123.

[158] *Guatemala – Definitive Anti-Dumping Measures on Grey Portland Cement from Mexico*, Panel Report (adopted 17 November 2000) WT/DS156/R, 00-4282 (*Guatemala – Cement II*).

[159] ibid para 6.383.

[160] ibid paras 6.384–6.387.

[161] ibid para 8.21.

[162] ibid para 8.22.

[163] BM Hoekman and PC Mavroidis, *The World Trade Organisation: Law, Economics and Politics* (Routledge, 2007) 77.

[164] *United States – Imposition of Countervailing Duties on Certain Hot-Rolled Lead and Bismuth Carbon Steel Products Originating in France, Germany and the United Kingdom*, Panel Report (adopted 7 June 1994) SCN/185 (*US Hot-Rolled Lead and Bismuth*).

[165] ibid para 95.

This approach involves a comparativist methodology, rooted in the domestic forum. The idea of 'civilized' has been replaced by 'United Nations members'. However, the GATT Panel did not consider this argument in any more depth, and continued to use the standard of reasonableness, stating:

> The Panel was not persuaded that the concepts suggested by the EC performed this function better than the concepts used in certain previous panel reports [reasonableness]. In any event, the Panel was of the view that the criteria for a review by a panel of factual assessments by domestic investigating authorities against the requirements of the Agreement could not be based on a simple transposition of standards applied in domestic administrative law of signatories.[166]

The characterisation of General Principle as a 'simple transposition of [domestic] standards' ignores approaches that transpose and transform domestic principles so they can operate effectively on the international level, conscious of not importing them 'lock, stock and barrel'.[167] A simplistic reduction of General Principles to a straight transition from domestic to international with no adaptation or alteration restricts the source of law to make it less reflexive, flexible and, ultimately, less appealing.

Ultimately, the treatment of General Principles by both GATT panels and the WTO dispute settlement system represents promise unfulfilled. This is not surprising given the general reluctance of both bodies to engage with international law outside the confines of the trade law treaty system more generally.

C. International Investment Arbitrations

The use of General Principles in international investment arbitration varies, in part because of the differing ways tribunals are empowered (or not) to utilise the source.[168] Moreover, there remains some controversy as to whether investment arbitral tribunals (IATs) are really using General Principles in the Article 38(1)(c) sense, or rather determining for themselves 'what counts as a source and how its content is determined'.[169]

Recent works have examined General Principles in international investment arbitrations in far more detail than this book can provide.[170] However, a few key observations employing the tetrahedral framework of analysis can be made.

[166] ibid para 371.

[167] *International Status of South-West Africa* (n 84) 148 (Separate Opinion of Judge McNair).

[168] For an overview, see P Dumberry, *A Guide to General Principles of Law in International Investment* (Oxford University Press, 2020) ch 2.

[169] SW Schill, 'Sources of International Investment Law: Multilateralization, Arbitral Precedent, Comparativism, Soft Law' in S Besson and J d'Aspremont (eds), *The Oxford Handbook on the Sources of International Law* (Oxford University Press, 2017) 1096, 1113; cf Dumberry, *A Guide* (n 168) 14.

[170] See especially Dumberry, *A Guide* (n 168). See also CT Kotuby Jr and LA Sobota, *General Principles of Law and International Due Process* (Oxford University Press, 2017); A Gattini, A Tanzi and F Fontanelli (eds), *General Principles of Law and International Investment Arbitration* (Brill, 2018).

First, General Principles have a binding *function*, on a par with custom and treaties,[171] but are often used only in the absence of custom or treaty.[172] Further, although some IAT decisions explicitly separate out General Principles from custom,[173] many do not.[174] As seen in chapters 3–5, this conflation also occurs in judgments and Opinions of the PCIJ and ICJ, and is similarly unhelpful in this context: it reveals nothing about the *source* of General Principles itself.

Second, the debate about whether the *methodology* of General Principles draws solely from the domestic forum or can also include international principles (as seen in the ICJ)[175] is also present in investment arbitration cases.[176] Two sub-points must be made on this. First, when IATs have drawn General Principles from the domestic forum, the same limitations as to selection of *which* forum (tending towards European and Western States) seen in the PCIJ and ICJ jurisprudence are often present.[177] Second, the vexed question of terminology arises with respect to the international forum. Dumberry rightfully distinguishes between the 'general principles of *international law*' (that is, those principles general to international law itself) and the 'general principles of *international* law' (that is, those General Principles drawn from the international forum).[178] As set out in chapter 5 of this book, the former are simply the international norms that bind all states, which encompass custom, (all) General Principles and (some) treaties.[179] The latter are General Principles with a methodology drawing from the international rather than, or in addition to, the domestic forum. However, with a few exceptions,[180] it is not always clear that IATs (or commentators) take heed of the same nuanced approach. The practice of establishing a General Principle by reference to other courts and tribunals (also seen in judgment of the ICJ)[181] muddies the water further. When an IAT rests

[171] See, eg, *Inceysa Vallisoletana SL v El Salvador* (Award of 2 August 2006) ICSID Case No ARB/03/26, para 226.

[172] See, eg, *Merrill & Ring Forestry L.=P v Canada* (Award of 31 March 2010) UNCITRAL para 187.

[173] ibid paras 185–87.

[174] Dumberry, *A Guide* (n 168).

[175] And particularly in the judgments of Judge Cançado Trindade: see ch 5.

[176] Dumberry, *A Guide* (n 168) 29–42; A Gattini, A Tanzi and F Fontanelli, 'Under the Hood of Investment Arbitration: General Principles of Law' in A Gattini, A Tanzi and F Fontanelli (eds), *General Principles of Law and International Investment Arbitration* (Brill, 2018) 3.

[177] Even cases praised for comparative methodology are limited to European countries: see *Total v Argentina* (Decision on Liability) ICSID Case No ARB/04/1 (21 December 2010) para 127; Dumberry, *A Guide* (n 168) 106–07.

[178] Dumberry, *A Guide* (n 168) 30.

[179] See, eg, A Verdross, 'General International Law and the United Nations Charter' (1954) 30 *International Affairs* 342, 342; ILC, *First Report on General Principles of Law* (29 April–7 June and 8 July–9 August 2019) UN Doc A/CN.4/732, para 162.

[180] Such as *Texaco Overseas Petroleum Co (TOPCO) v Government of the Libyan Arab Republic* (Award) (1978) 17 *ILM* 1, 21.

[181] See, eg, *Legality of the Threat or Use of Nuclear Weapons* (Advisory Opinion) [1996] ICJ Rep 226, 391–95 (Dissenting Opinion of Judge Shahabuddeen), 576 (Dissenting Opinion of Judge Koroma).

a General Principle on decisions of the ICJ or another tribunal, is this truly a general principle of *international* law, or is it simply relying on previous recognition of a General Principle?[182]

Third, the *type* of General Principle considered by IATs includes procedural and substantive norms, from private and public law.[183]

Finally, IATs themselves do not explore overmuch the *jurisprudential legitimacy* of the source. However, the classification of certain cases as instances of General Principles by commentators reveals inherent assumptions about the source. For example, the decision in the *Abu Dhabi Case* is considered to be an invocation of General Principles by some commentators.[184] The source used by the arbitrator in that case was the 'the principles rooted in the good sense and common practice of the generality of civilized nations'.[185] The addition of good sense has two effects: first, it imported great discretion, with the arbitrator rejecting English laws deemed as 'parochial';[186] second, it imports natural law considerations into the source, presupposing an answer to the question explored in the conclusion to chapter 5, whether the 'logical' or 'common sense' content of General Principles is part of their rule of recognition, or whether it is an implicit reason *behind* horizontal generality but not a necessary constitutive element of the source.

IV. INTERNATIONAL TRIBUNAL FOR THE LAW OF THE SEA

The ITLOS has been in operation since 1997, and case law is subsequently limited. As of 1 August 2020, 29 cases have been submitted to ITLOS.[187] General Principles have been referred to in Separate Opinions,[188] and argued in oral pleading in *Activities in the International Seabed*.[189] Despite arguments in oral pleading, the Tribunal refrained from examining General Principles in its Advisory Opinion.[190]

As with other courts and tribunals, there are instances where judges make references to certain General Principles without further discussion of the source

[182] See, eg, Dumberry, *A Guide* (n 168) 168.

[183] ibid 32–33; *El Paso International Company v Argentina* (Award of 31 October 2011) ICSID Case No ARB/03/15, para 622.

[184] Kobuty Jr and Sobota, *General Principles of Law* (n 170) 32–33.

[185] *Petroleum Development (Trucial Coast) Ltd v Sheikh of Abu Dhabi* (Award) (1951) 18 *ILR* 149.

[186] Kobuty Jr and Sobota, *General Principles of Law* (n 170) 33.

[187] 'ITLOS: List of Cases', available at www.itlos.org/en/cases/list-of-cases/.

[188] *M/V 'Saiga' (No 2) (Saint Vincent and the Grenadines v Guinea)* (Provisional Measures, Order of 11 March 1998, Sep Op Laing) ITLOS Reports 1998, fn 5.

[189] *Responsibilities and Obligations of States Sponsoring Persons and Entities with respect to Activities in the International Seabed Area (Request for Advisory Opinion Submitted to the Seabed Disputes Chamber)* (Oral Pleading of Donald Anton, International Union for the Conservation of Nature, 16 September 2010) ITLOS Reports 2010, 29.

[190] *Responsibilities and Obligations of States Sponsoring Persons and Entities with Respect to Activities in the Area* (Advisory Opinion of 1 February 2011) ITLOS Reports 2011.

or how the general principle is found – for example, a 'general principle of fairness in international legal proceedings',[191] a 'general principle concerning the consequences of litispendence'[192] and the general principle of good faith.[193] Although Judge Shearer considered the application of the precautionary principle in the *Bluefin Tuna* case, this was not linked explicitly to General Principles.[194]

Judge Cot considered certain 'ethical principles' in his Separate Opinion in *MV Louisa*[195] as General Principles, as they could be found 'all major legal systems of the world'.[196] Evidence for this proposition was founded on codes of conduct drawn from domestic legal systems, but also those from the International Bar Association, the International Law Association and the International Criminal Court.[197]

V. REGIONAL BODIES

A. European Court of Justice: General Principles of EU Law

The Court of Justice of the European Union (CJEU) considers the 'general principles common to the laws of Member States' as a source of law.[198] These principles were considered under the auspices of the European Community (EC) prior to the Treaty of Lisbon, which amalgamated the former EC into the overarching European Union (EU).[199] For clarity, all references in this section will be to the 'EU' and 'EU law', although in most cases the terminology was EC and EC law at the time of the case or publication.

Although similar to General Principles, there are distinct features unique to EU general principles. Rather than being an example of an application of international General Principles, they are analogous but remain a discrete EU body of law. The CJEU derives principles from the laws of Member States, but the content is 'determined by the distinct features of the Community polity'.[200]

[191] *The M/V 'Saiga' (No 2) Case (Saint Vincent and the Grenadines v Guinea)* (Provisional Measures, Order of 6 October 1998, Sep Op Anderson) ITLOS Reports 1998, 5.

[192] *The MOX Plant Case (Ireland v United Kingdom)* (Provisional Measures) (2001, Order of 3 December 2001, Sep Op Treves) ITLOS Reports 2001, para 5.

[193] *The M/V 'Louisa' Case (Saint Vincent and the Grenadines v Kingdom of Spain)* (Merits, Judgment of 28 May 2013, Diss Op Jesus) ITLOS Report 2013, para 45.

[194] *Southern Bluefin Tuna Cases (New Zealand v Japan; Australia v Japan)* (Provisional Measures, Order of 27 August 1999, Sep Op Shearer) ITLOS Reports 1999, 11.

[195] *The M/V 'Louisa' Case (Saint Vincent and the Grenadines v Kingdom of Spain)* (Merits, Judgment of 28 May 2013, Sep Op Cot) ITLOS Report 2013, 6.

[196] ibid para 43.

[197] ibid para 47.

[198] Treaty Establishing the European Community (consolidated) [2002] OJ C325/33, Art 288(2); Treaty on the Functioning of the European Union [2010] OJ C83/47, Art 340.

[199] Treaty of Lisbon [2007] OJ C306/01, Art 2(2).

[200] T Tridimas, *The General Principles of EC Law*, 2nd edn (Oxford University Press, 2007) 4.

The principles are 'extended, narrowed, restated, transformed by a creative and eclectic judicial process'.[201] The EU describes EU general principles as 'non-written sources of European law',[202] to be used in a supplementary manner where the primary written sources cannot assist.[203] There three types of EU general principles. The first are those 'developed by the CJEU', allowing the Court to 'to implement rules in different domains of which the treaties make no mention'.[204] The second, most analogous to General Principles in the Article 38(1)(c) sense, are those 'common to all the national legal systems of the EU countries and compatible with EU objectives'.[205] The third are those 'specific to the EU, even if inspired from principles enshrined in certain national legal systems only'.[206] This tripartite system of general principles means any comparison to Article 38(1)(c) General Principles is potentially misleading, especially as even the most compatible category has the additional qualifier that principles must be compatible with EU objectives. Explicit references to General Principles in the Article 38(1)(c) sense are fleeting, and in footnotes.[207]

There are problems too in the way such general principles are developed. Akehurst argues that the subsequent development of the principle based on citing 'the previous judgments of the Court rather than the national laws on which the principle was originally based'[208] results in principle's being modified so that, in some instances:

> [T]he Court can end up applying a principle in a manner which is contrary to the laws of *all* the member States. At this point the fiction that the Court is applying general principles of law becomes transparently false. What the Court is *really* doing is *creating* law.[209]

This modification of general principles of the EU to become wholly judge-made law does illustrate how reliance on General Principles as a source of law can, in practice, lead to wide-ranging judicial discretion. As has been discussed in previous chapters, the drafters of Article 38(1)(c) explicitly condemned such discretion, and deliberately framed the provision to avoid it. Nonetheless, the phenomenon of resting a General Principle on previous judicial decisions is not limited to the EU.

[201] ibid.

[202] 'The Non-Written Sources of European law: Supplementary Law', available at https://eur-lex.europa.eu/legal-content/EN/TXT/?uri=LEGISSUM:l14533.

[203] ibid.

[204] ibid.

[205] ibid.

[206] ibid.

[207] See, eg, Case C-384/02 *Grøngaard v Bang* (ECJ, 25 May 2004) fn 5; Case C-384/10 *Jan Voogsgeerd v Navimer SA* (ECJ, 8 September 2011) fn 11.

[208] M Akehurst, 'The Application of General Principles of Law by the Court of Justice of the European Communities' (1981) 52 *British Yearbook of International Law* 29, 39.

[209] ibid 40.

Although the CJEU has made extensive use of the EU 'general principles of law', these are often referred to without elaboration as to how the principle has been found.[210] This abruptness was explained by Judge Kutscher, a judge of the CJEU, writing extra-curially:

> It can be assumed that in a court composed of judges from all the member States, important strands of the national legal systems are woven into its judgments, even if the judges may prefer – particularly having regard to the generality of general principles – to limit themselves in this connection to oral discussion during the deliberation and to forego more detailed comparisons of the laws of the member States in the ... judgment. This may explain the terse findings which are frequently found in the ... judgment.[211]

Similarities can be seen between this view and the linking of Article 38(1)(c) to the judicial makeup of the ICJ.[212] As Akehurst points out, the legitimacy of assuming a comprehensive comparative methodology based on the make-up of judges is flawed, due to absences though illness, the operation of judgment by Chamber rather than Full Court, judgments by majority vote, and the fact that 'no judge, however learned, can be an expert on every area of his national law'.[213]

B. European Court of Human Rights

There is one instance of the exact wording of Article 38(1)(c)'s being incorporated into EU law. Article 7 of the European Convention on Human Rights (ECHR) provides for protection against retroactivity with regard to criminal prosecution. Article 7(2) states:

> This article shall not prejudice the trial and punishment of any person for any act or omission which, at the time when it was committed, was criminal according the general principles of law recognised by civilised nations.[214]

The ECHR is adjudicated by the European Court of Human Rights (ECtHR).[215] In *Kolk and Kislyiy v Estonia*,[216] the Court dismissed an application by two

[210] ibid 32.

[211] Court of Justice of the European Communities, *Judicial and Academic Conference, 27–28 September 1976: Reports* (1976) 28–29 (Judge Kutscher).

[212] M Virally 'The Sources of International Law' in M Sørenson (ed), *Manual of Public International Law* (Cambridge University Press, 1968) 116, 146; see also PE Corbett, 'The Search for General Principles of Law' (1961) 47(5) *Virginia Law Review* 811, 824; van Hoof (n 18) 142–43.

[213] Akehurst, 'The Application of General Principles of Law' (n 208) 32, fn 4.

[214] Convention for the Protection of Human Rights and Fundamental Freedoms (European Convention on Human Rights, as amended) (ECHR) Art 7(2).

[215] ibid Art 19.

[216] *Kolk and Kislyiy v Estonia* App nos 23052/04 and 24018/04 (Judgment) (ECtHR, 17 January 2006).

Estonian nationals who alleged they had been tried for crimes against humanity in violation of the non-retroactivity provision in Article 7(1) of the ECHR. The Court held, among other things, that crimes against humanity were criminal at international law due to the operation of a General Principle, and thus covered by Article 7(2). The evidence the Court gave for such a General Principle was the charter of the Nuremberg Military Tribunal and an affirmation of crimes against humanity as 'principles of international law' by a General Assembly resolution.[217] No reference was made to any domestic laws or principles. This decision has been criticised as improperly characterising the prohibition on crimes against humanity as a General Principle. Cassese states:

> [I]n 1949 the proscription of crimes against humanity manifestly did not amount to a general principle of law, let alone to a rule laid down in the legislation of most countries of the world. At that stage, the international criminalization of that category of offences remained at the limited stage of treaty law (Article 6(c) of the Charter of the Nuremberg Tribunal) as well as customary rules …[218]

However, there are arguments that the crimes against humanity at Nuremberg were, in fact, General Principles.[219] The willingness of the ECtHR to consider crimes against humanity as General Principles was also shown in the admissibility decision in *Naletilic v Croatia*.[220] While this goes to a view as to the binding nature of the source, and its capacity to found substantive norms of international law, neither decision elaborates further on how such General Principles are found.

General Principles were considered in the Partly Dissenting Opinion of Judge Pellonpää in *K–HW v Germany*.[221] The case concerned the shooting of East German citizens trying to cross the border into West Germany in 1972. Pellonpää argued that although systematic closing of borders may have been a crime against humanity in 1972, there was no General Principle to support the proposition that the actions of border guards in maintaining the East German border were themselves a crime against humanity at the relevant time.[222] Accordingly, in his view, the action was in violation of Article 7(1) of the ECHR. To justify this finding, Pellonpää looked to a decision of the German Federal Court of Justice, as well as 'general human rights instruments'.[223] Thus the relevant forum was both domestic and international. However, the judgment did not provide any comprehensive methodology beyond this.

[217] ibid.
[218] Cassese, 'Balancing the Prosecution' (n 7) 415.
[219] Gallant, *The Principle of Legality* (n 7) 94, 122–23.
[220] *Naletilic v Croatia* App no 51891/99 (Decision as to Admissibility) (ECtHR, 4 May 2000).
[221] *K–HW v Germany*.App no 37201/97 (Judgment: Merits) (ECtHR, 27 March 2001) (*K–HW v Germany*).
[222] ibid (Partly Dissenting Opinion of Judge Pellonpää, joined by Judge Zupančič).
[223] ibid.

C. Inter-American Court of Human Rights

The Inter-American Court of Human Rights (IACtHR) was established in 1979 and issued its first merits judgment in 1988.[224] It operates much like the ECtHR,[225] hearing complaints of human rights violations from individuals within its Member States. As in the PCIJ and ICJ, much of the jurisprudence of the IACtHR that mentions General Principles does so fleetingly and without justification for the existence of the principles asserted.[226] Often, the assertion of a General Principle rests on a PCIJ or ICJ decision,[227] or international arbitral law,[228] with no further elaboration. An example of this is found in the judgment in *Velásquez Rodríguez*.[229] The Court stated that a General Principle of 'iura novit curia' existed, and based this assertion on the decision of the PCIJ in the *Lotus* decision,[230] as well as the ECtHR case of *Handyside*:[231]

> The Commission did not specifically allege the violation of Article 1 (1) of the Convention, but that does not preclude the Court from applying it. The precept contained therein constitutes the generic basis of the protection of the rights recognized by the Convention and would be applicable, in any case, by virtue of a general principle of law, iura novit curia, on which international jurisprudence has repeatedly relied and under which a court has the power and the duty to apply the juridical provisions relevant to a proceeding, even when the parties do not expressly invoke them.[232]

An identical paragraph is contained within the decision in the *Godinez Cruz Case*.[233] This has been subsequently cited in many judgments, but no further

[224] JL Cavallaro and SE Brewer, 'Reevaluating Regional Human Rights Litigation in the Twenty-First Century: The Case of the Inter-American Court' (2008) 102 *American Journal of International Law* 768, 771.

[225] AAC Trindade, 'The Merits of Coordination of International Courts on Human Rights' (2004) 2(2) *Journal of International Criminal Justice* 309, 309.

[226] See, eg, *Suárez Rosero* (Judgment of 12 November 1997) Inter-American Court of Human Rights Series C No 35, para 77; *Bulacio v Argentina* (Judgment of 18 September 2003) Inter-American Court of Human Rights Series C No 100, para 117–18; *Chaparro Álvarez y Lapo Íñiguez v Ecuador* (Judgment of 21 November 2007) Inter-American Court of Human Rights Series C No 170, para 146.

[227] See, eg, *Loayza Tamayo – Reparations (Art 63(1) of the American Convention on Human Rights)* (Judgment of 27 November 1998) Inter-American Court of Human Rights Series C No 42, para 9 (Judges Cançado Trindade and Abreu-Burelli); *Velásquez Rodríguez* (Judgment of 21 July 1989) Inter-American Court of Human Rights Series C No 7, para 25; *Godínez Cruz* (Judgment of 21 July 1989) Inter-American Court of Human Rights Series C No 8, para 23.

[228] *Aloeboetoe et al – Reparations (Art 63(1) American Convention on Human Rights)* (Judgment of 10 September 1993) Inter-American Court of Human Rights Series C No 15, para 50; *Garrido and Baigorria – Reparations (Art 63(1) American Convention on Human Rights)* (Judgment of 27 August 1998) Inter-American Court of Human Rights Series C No 39, 5, para 48.

[229] *Velásquez Rodríguez* (Judgment of 29 July 1988) Inter-American Court of Human Rights Series Series C No 4 (*Velásquez Rodríguez*).

[230] ibid para 163.

[231] *Handyside v The United Kingdom* (Judgment of 7 December 1976) Series A No 24 ECHR, para 41 (*Handyside*).

[232] *Velásquez Rodríguez* (n 227) para 163.

[233] *Godínez Cruz* (Judgment of 20 January 1989) Inter-American Court of Human Rights Series C No 5, para 172.

explanation of how the General Principle is found or justification for its existence is provided.[234] The relevant section of the *Lotus* judgment reads:

> [The Court] observes that in the fulfillment of its task of itself ascertaining what the international law is, it has not confined itself to a consideration of the arguments put forward, but has included in its researches all precedents, teachings and facts to which it had access and which might possibly have revealed the existence of one of the principles of international law contemplated in the special agreement.[235]

No indication was given by the PCIJ that it viewed its approach as the application of a General Principle. Similarly, in the *Handyside* judgment, the ECtHR stated the general proposition with no reference to General Principles: 'once a case is duly referred to it, the Court may take cognisance of every question of law arising in the course of the proceedings and concerning facts submitted to its examination by a Contracting State or by the Commission'.[236]

Accordingly, although there is a string of jurisprudence in the IACtHR stating that *jura novit curia* is a General Principle, no justification for this assertion is given in the judgments themselves, or found in the jurisprudence referred to by the Court. This is, as a result, of no assistance in ascertaining the nature of General Principles, except that they are viewed as a formal rather than secondary source of law. Rather it shows that the sometimes superficial and cavalier treatment of this source is not limited to the World Courts.

There are judgments of the IACtHR that do examine General Principles in more depth. The Court expressly applied General Principles in the *Aloeboetoe et al*[237] case:

> The ILO Convention No 169 concerning Indigenous and Tribal Peoples in Independent Countries (1989) has not been accepted by Suriname. Furthermore, under international law there is no conventional or customary rule that would indicate who the successors of a person are. Consequently, the Court has no alternative but to apply general principles of law (Art 38(1)(c) of the Statute of the International Court of Justice).
>
> It is a norm common to most legal systems that a person's successors are his or her children. It is also generally accepted that the spouse has a share in the assets acquired during a marriage; some legal systems also grant the spouse inheritance rights along with the children. If there is no spouse or children, private common law recognizes the ascendants as heirs. It is the Court's opinion that these rules, generally accepted

[234] eg *Castillo Petruzzi et al* (Judgment of 30 May 1999) Inter-American Court of Human Rights Series C No 52, para 166, 172; *Durand and Ugarte* (Judgment of 16 August 2000) Inter-American Court of Human Rights Series C No 68, para 76; *Hilaire, Constantine and Benjamin et al vs Trinidad and Tobago* (Judgment of 21 June 2002) Inter-American Court of Human Rights Series C No 94, para 107; *Cantos* (Judgment of 28 November 2002) Inter-American Court of Human Rights Series C No 97, para 58.

[235] *SS 'Lotus' (France and Turkey)* (Merits) [1927] PCIJ Rep Series A No 10, 31.

[236] *Handyside* (n 231) para 41.

[237] *Aloeboetoe et al – Reparations (Art 63(1) American Convention on Human Rights)* (n 228).

> by the community of nations, should be applied in the instant case, in order to determine the victims' successors for purposes of compensation.[238]

The Court employs a limited comparative approach to find the General Principle – looking to 'most legal systems', 'some legal systems' and 'private common law'. The lack of any specifics as to the legal systems makes commenting on the comparative study used impossible. Nonetheless, it is clear that the IACtHR employed a comparative methodology looking to laws from the domestic forum. The IACtHR only applied General Principles in this case after an explicit mention of the lack of custom and treaty law. Thus, although a formal source of international law, the Court treats General Principles as subsidiary to both treaty and custom.

Judge Cançado Trindade discussed General Principles in some depth in his Concurring Opinion in *Juridical Condition and Rights of Undocumented Migrants*,[239] seven years before his Separate Opinion in the *Pulp Mills*.[240] Cançado Trindade considered General Principles as follows:

> Every legal system has fundamental principles which inspire, inform and conform their norms. It is the principles … that, evoking the first causes, sources or origins of the norms and rules, confer cohesion, coherence and legitimacy upon the legal norms and the legal system as a whole. It is the general principles of law (*prima principia*) which confer to the legal order (both national and international) its ineluctable axiological dimension; it is they that reveal the values which inspire the whole legal order and which, ultimately, provide its foundations themselves.[241]

It is clear that Cançado Trindade views these general principles as the most fundamental aspects of law and, further, views them as having natural law origins but constrained by positivist frameworks of interpretation:

> Despite the apparent indifference with which [general principles of law] were treated by legal positivism (always seeking to demonstrate a 'recognition' of such principles in the positive legal order), and despite the lesser attention dispensed to them by the shallow and reductionist legal doctrine of our days, nevertheless we will never be able to prescind from them.[242]

Cançado Trindade views the structure of Article 38(1)(c) in this manner – a positivist limit on the natural law source of General Principles, introduced to assuage concerns of judicial discretion:

> If, in the framework of [international law], one has insisted, in the chapter of the (formal) 'sources' of international law on the general principles 'recognized' *in foro*

[238] ibid para 61–62.

[239] *Juridical Condition and Rights of Undocumented Migrants* (Advisory Opinion OC-18 of 17 September 2003) Inter-American Court of Human Rights Series A No 13 (*Undocumented Migrants*).

[240] *Pulp Mills on the River Uruguay (Argentina v Uruguay)* (Merits) [2010] ICJ Rep 14, 135 (Separate Opinion of Judge Cançado Trindade); see ch 5.

[241] *Undocumented Migrants* (n 239) para 44 (Judge Cançado Trindade).

[242] ibid para 45.

> *domestico*, this was due to an endeavour to proceed with juridical security, as such principles are present in every and any legal system, at national or international levels.[243]

Within Cançado Trindade's conception of General Principles, he identifies a set of 'truly fundamental' principles.[244] These have universal scope and 'an objective character which impose them to the observance of all States'.[245] They do not depend on consent of states but rather are inherent and inalienable in international law.[246] Cançado Trindade links these General Principles with *jus cogens* norms, arguing, 'In fact, it is perfectly possible to visualize the peremptory law (the *jus cogens*) as identified with the general principles of law of material order which are guarantors of the legal order itself, of its unity, integrity and cohesion.'[247]

This view of General Principles encapsulates a natural law jurisprudence. Cançado Trindade concedes a methodology of comparativism required at international law, but suggests such requirements will always be met due to the fundamental nature of General Principles such that they are present in 'every and any legal system'.[248] It is unclear whether in practice Cançado Trindade would resort to a comparative methodology to find such General Principles, or would be content to identify principles based on their content and 'objective character'. Cançado Trindade also identifies a subset of General Principles, those that are so fundamental they amount to *jus cogens* norms. In this instance, it would seem that Cançado Trindade would *not* view General Principles as subsidiary to treaty and custom – as *jus cogens* norms are peremptory. Cançado Trindade reiterated these views on General Principles in later decisions, quoting his own discussion.[249] It is interesting to compare this with Cançado Trindade's later Opinions in the ICJ, where he considered General Principles to be principles of *international* law, as well as being drawn from the domestic forum.[250]

VI. CONCLUSION

There are three key things to draw from the foregoing analysis. The first, as foreshadowed, is that the particular expression of 'general principles' within each Court or Tribunal necessitates, to an extent, the outcome of the tetrahedral model's application. Thus any use of Article 21(1)(c) general principles by the

[243] ibid para 52.
[244] ibid para 53.
[245] ibid.
[246] ibid para 54.
[247] ibid para 58.
[248] ibid para 52.
[249] *'Juvenile Reeducation Institute' v Paraguay* (Preliminary Objections, Merits, Reparations and Costs, 2 September 2004) Inter-American Court of Human Rights Series C No 112, paras 16–18 (Judge Cançado Trindade); *Plan de Sánchez Massacre v Guatemala* (Sentencing Judgment 29 April 2004) Inter-American Court of Human Rights Series C No 105, para 15 (Judge Cançado Trindade).
[250] See ch 5.

ICC will necessarily be comparative, looking to domestic systems. The problem for the ICC is not *whether* the study should be comparative, but whether it has been comparative *enough* – both in scope and selection of system. In the ICTY, this is true for general principles found pursuant to the third category of principles as set out in *Kupreskić*, whereas those found under the fourth category are linked with natural law. General principles of the EU are another creature altogether, and the use of ECJ cases to ascertain elements of Article 38(1)(c) General Principles is deeply problematic.

Second, the cases above illustrate the phenomenon of judicial cross-fertilisation. The link between judges' national backgrounds and General Principles has been made before in this book, and is explored further in chapter 7. In this chapter, however, the impact is seen as judges move between international courts and tribunals, taking their conceptions of General Principles with them. Thus the 'fundamental principles' considered by Judge Cançado Trindade in *Undocumented Migrants* at the IACtHR[251] find clear reflection in the General Principles 'endowed with a true fundamental character' in his Concurring Opinion in the *Jadhav Case*.[252] This same cross-fertilisation is seen with Judge Shahabuddeen, who considered General Principles in *Certain Phosphate Lands in Nauru* at the ICJ in 1992, and in *Furundžija* at the ICTY in 2000. There is (some) consistency between approaches here too: Shahabudeen employed a limited comparative methodology in *Certain Phosphate Lands in Nauru*, but really was looking to find that 'common underlying sense' he refers to in *Furundžija*. It is fair to say Shahabudeen's declaration in *Furundžija* links General Principles explicitly with morality, in contrast to his Separate Opinion in *Certain Phosphate Lands in Nauru*.[253] Such judicial cross-fertilisation has occurred at the WTO (though in the context of international law more generally)[254] – perhaps this is the best prospect of inclusion of General Principles in future WTO jurisprudence.

Finally, there are commonalities with the issues faced in the above cases and those in the PCIJ and ICJ discussed in chapters 3–5. There is no definitive answer as to whether General Principles are limited to being drawn from the domestic forum, or can include international instruments for their genesis. Discretion is an ongoing concern, both in finding a General Principle and in applying the General Principle to a situation. The type is, again, wide-ranging, encompassing true principles and specific rules. Comparative studies are limited, and criticised as such – although in most instances less limited than their PCIJ and ICJ counterparts. As will be seen in the next chapter, many of these issues are also a matter of contention in the commentary on General Principles.

[251] *Undocumented Migrants* (n 239) para 53 (Judge Cançado Trindade).

[252] *Jadhav Case (India v Pakistan)* (Provisional Measures) [2017] ICJ Rep 231, 258 (Concurring Opinion of Judge Cançado Trindade).

[253] *Certain Phosphate Lands in Nauru* (n 29) 287–89 (Separate Opinion of Judge Shahabuddeen).

[254] D McRae, 'International Economic Law and Public International Law: The Past and The Future' (2014) 17(3) *Journal of International Economic Law* 627, 629–30.

7

Commentary in Context

DESPITE INCREASED RECENT attention being paid to General Principles, there is still a lack of coalescence in the literature around fundamental aspects of the source. While some of the lack of clarity relates to legitimate disagreements about aspects of the source, much of it can be traced to a lack of precision surrounding identification of General Principles and their subsequent analysis. Cases are misidentified as being applications of General Principles without justification,[1] or through the use of unsustainable methodologies of identification.[2] Further, discussions of General Principles often import assumptions about the source that are not fully unpacked or interrogated. As Vladimir-Djuro Degan put it, 'most opinions on general principles reflect rather the doctrinal predilections of their authors, rather than a result of the thorough analysis of all the complex aspects of this particular source'.[3]

It is almost de rigueur, when analysing General Principles, to start by listing the different 'categories' or 'functions' of such principles. Examples include Wolfgang Friedmann in 1963,[4] Oscar Schacter in 1991[5] and Robert Kolb in 2016.[6] The content of these lists varies – in itself an indication of the ongoing unsettled nature of the source.[7] However, such lists also demonstrate the need for a systematic framework-based analysis of the source. Without such a framework, the lists often import assumptions as to what a General Principle is

[1] As seen in the 'chaff' discussion in ch 3.

[2] See, eg, M Đorđeska, *General Principles of Law Recognised by Civilised Nations (1922–2018)* (Brill Nijhoff, 2020) 204–06, in particular 'In this study, it sufficed that the Court referred once to the norm as a "principle" for it to be considered as a general principle within the meaning of Article 38(1)(c) of the Court's Statute' (ibid 206).

[3] V Degan, 'General Principles of Law (A Source of General International Law)' (1992) 3 *Finnish Yearbook of International Law* 1, 1.

[4] See W Friedmann, 'The Uses of "General Principles" in the Development of International Law' [1963] *American Journal of International Law* 279.

[5] O Schachter, *International Law in Theory and Practice* (Martinus Nijhoff, 1991) 50.

[6] R Kolb, *Theory of International Law* (Hart Publishing, 2016) 136–44.

[7] For a recent summary of different functions ascribed to General Principles, see U Linderfalk, 'General Principles as Principles of International Legal Pragmatics: The Relevance of Good Faith for the Application of Treaty Law' in M Andenas et al (eds), *General Principles and the Coherence of International Law* (Brill Nijhoff, 2019) 100, 100–01.

(or is not); assumptions that may not actually be supported by the source itself. Taking Schachter's list as an example, the five categories are:

1) The principles of municipal law 'recognized by civilized nations'.
2) General principles of law 'derived from the specific nature of the international community'.
3) Principles 'intrinsic to the idea of law and basic to all legal systems'.
4) Principles 'valid through all kinds of societies in relationships of hierarchy and co-ordination'.
5) Principles of justice founded on 'the very nature of man as a rational and social being'.[8]

Each of these imports a certain meaning: 1) necessitates a positivist methodology that draws from domestic forums, by adding the word 'municipal' to the wording of Article 38(1)(c); 2), on other hand, includes international principles unique to the international system; but are these truly General Principles? And how do they differ from custom?[9] 3) suggests a foundational or normative principle rather than any specific rule – in Schachter's words, a 'substratum of legal postulates';[10] while 4) and 5) explicitly bring in natural law conceptions, and divorce themselves from any link to municipal laws.

Can General Principles be at once positivist and drawn from domestic rules; foundational and underlying and embrace natural law considerations? It seems staggering – and incoherent – that one source of law could encompass so many disparate conceptions. In truth, as was seen in the preceding chapters of this book, while examples of each of Schachter's categories can be found in the cases, it is far less clear that the judge in question was relying on Article 38(1)(c) to use such principles.

Nonetheless, the list illustrates why the framework used by this book is so important to achieve a cohesive understanding of General Principles. It becomes clear that the source cannot support a list of principles that have disparate and often incompatible *functions*, *jurisprudential legitimacy*, *methodologies* and *type*. This chapter considers the views of commentators under this framework by examining five key questions, each of which touches on multiple aspects of the framework:

I. Article 38(1)(c) as a norm-creating source of international law (*function*; *jurisprudential legitimacy*; *methodology*; *type)*
II. The rule/principle distinction (*jurisprudential legitimacy*; *methodology*; *type)*
III. Judicial discretion (*jurisprudential legitimacy*; *methodology)*

[8] Schachter, *International Law in Theory and Practice* (n 5) 50.

[9] Kolb sees such principles as 'part and parcel of customary international law': Kolb, *Theory of International Law* (n 6) 135.

[10] Schachter, *International Law in Theory and Practice* (n 5) 54.

IV. Where are General Principles drawn from? (*methodology*; *type*)
V. Content of General Principles (*jurisprudential legitimacy*; *methodology*; *type*)

I. ARTICLE 38(1)(C) AS A NORM-CREATING SOURCE OF INTERNATIONAL LAW

As has been seen in the earlier chapters of this book, Courts usually do not rely on Article 38(1)(c) to ground their decisions. Such reluctance may suggest the source itself does not give rise to binding norms of international law. This view finds support with some commentators, who see General Principles as a truly subsidiary norm, equivalent to Article 38(1)(d) in potency.[11] However these are a minority, dated[12] and often a relic of the Soviet era.[13]

The more commonly accepted view is that General Principles can form binding norms of international law. This is often limited to situations where treaty or custom are lacking[14] – the role of General Principles as 'gap fillers'[15] – although such limitation can be asserted without substantiation.[16] Some commentators

[11] H Bokor-Szegö 'General Principles of Law' in M Bedjaoui (ed), *International Law: Achievements and Prospects* (Martinus Nijhoff, 1991) 213, 217.

[12] M Virally 'The Sources of International Law' in M Sørenson (ed), *Manual of Public International Law* (St Martin's Press, 1968) 116, 144, 147.

[13] GJH van Hoof, *Rethinking the Sources of International Law* (Kluwer Law and Taxation Publishers, 1983) 132–33; PK Menon, 'Primary, Subsidiary and Other Possible Sources of International Law' (1989) 1 *Sri Lanka Journal of International Law* 113, 125–26; Degan, 'General Principles of Law' (n 3) 2–3.

[14] B Cheng, 'Comments' in HC Gutteridge, 'The Meaning and Scope of Article 38(1)(c) of the Statute of the International Court of Justice' (1952) 38 *Transactions of the Grotius* Society 125, 132; H Lauterpacht, *Private Law Sources and Analogies of International Law* (Archon Books, 1970) viii; G Schwarzenberger and ED Brown, *A Manual of International Law*, 6th edn (Professional Books, 1976) 27; M Bogdan, 'General Principles of Law and the Problem of Lacunae in the Law of Nations' (1977) 46(1) *Nordisk Tidsskrift for International Ret* 37, 44; American Law Institute, *United States of America Restatement (Third) of Foreign Relations Law* (1987) §102(l); JI Charney, 'Universal International Law' (1993) 87 *American Journal of International Law* 529, 534; U Fastenrath, 'Relative Normality in International Law' in M Koskenniemi (ed), *Sources of International Law* (Routledge, 2000) 153, 176; S Hall, 'The Persistent Spectre: Natural Law, International Order and the Limits of Legal Positivism' (2001) 12(2) *European Journal of International* Law 269, 298; D Mitchell, 'The Prohibition of Rape in International Humanitarian Law as a Norm of Jus Cogens: Clarifying the Doctrine' (2005) 15 *Duke Journal of International and Comparative Law* 219, 233; DP Harris, 'Carrying a Good Joke Too Far: Trips and Treaties of Adhesion' (2006) 27 *University of Pennsylvania Journal of International Economic Law* 681, 695; BB Jia, 'The Relations between Treaties and Custom' (2010) 9 *Chinese Journal of International Law* 81, 91; Kolb, *Theory of International Law* (n 6) 138.

[15] See, eg, M Andenas and L Chiussi, 'Cohesion, Convergence and Coherence of International Law' in Andenas et al (eds), *General Principles* (n 7) 10, 14; N Jain, 'Judicial Lawmaking and General Principles of Law in International Criminal Law' (2016) 57(1) *Harvard International Law Journal* 111, 113–14; ILC, *First Report on General Principles of Law* (29 April–7 June and 8 July–9 August 2019) UN Doc A/CN.4/732, para 66(b).

[16] See, eg, Schwarzenberger and Brown, *A Manual* (n 14) 27.

extend this limitation to argue that a General Principle, while binding, will be overridden by a competing norm of custom.[17]

The view that is most consistent with the development and application of the source is that General Principles form binding norms of international law. Although in practice they are often only turned to when rules of custom are absent, legally speaking there is no need for this requirement. This view finds support in commentary,[18] and indeed only this conception can explain the argument that General Principles can encompass *jus cogens* norms.[19]

A. Function Explained by Source Theory

Both the limited and expansive views of General Principles can be analysed in respect of source theory, which seeks to understand the 'history, cause or basis from which law "emerges" so as to 'provide for the law's legitimacy'.[20]

The limited view of the function of Article 38(1)(c) can be justified by viewing the legitimiser of General Principles as its inclusion in the Statutes of the Permanent Court of International Justice (PCIJ) and the International Court of Justice (ICJ). Thus Schwarzenberger argues that Article 38(1)(c) is a 'direct ... product of treaty law', that law being the PCIJ and ICJ Statutes.[21] This view is, in its way, a positivist conception of the source, attempting to reconcile it with ideas of state consent and give it a Kelsian *grundnorm*. Such a view prioritises treaty and custom over General Principles because, as has been discussed in chapter 2 of this book, the introduction of the source by the Advisory Committee of Jurists was viewed by some as fixing the issue of a lacuna in international law – a gap where treaty and custom could not apply.[22]

[17] S Rosenne, *The International Court of Justice: An Essay in Political and Legal Theory* (AW Sijthoff, 1957) 424; V Degan, *Sources of International Law* (Martinus Nijhoff, 1997) 107.

[18] JG Lammers, 'General Principles of Law Recognized by Civilized Nations' in F Kalshoven, PJ Kuyper and JG Lammers (eds), *Essays on the Development of the International Legal Order in Memory of Haro F Van Panhuys* (Sijthoff and Noordhoff, 1980) 53, 65, 69; CT Kotuby Jr and LA Sobota, *General Principles of Law and International Due Process: Principles and Norms Applicable in Transnational Disputes* (Oxford University Press, 2017) 2.

[19] See, eg, H Mosler, *The International Society as a Legal Community* (Springer, 1980) 135; A Cassese 'Discussion' in A Cassese and JHH Weiler (eds), *Change and Stability in International Law Making* (Walter de Gruyter, 1988) 55; MC Bassiouni, 'A Functional Approach to "General Principles of International Law"' (1990) 11 *Michigan Journal of International Law* 768, 779–80; B Simma, 'International Human Rights and General International Law: A Comparative Analysis' (1993) 4(2) *Collected Courses of the Academy of European Law* 153, 226; D Shelton, 'Normative Hierarchy in International Law' (2006) 100 *American Journal of International Law* 291, 299.

[20] M Koskenniemi, 'Introduction' in M Koskenniemi (ed), *Sources of International Law* (Routledge, 2000) xi, xiii.

[21] G Schwarzenberger, *International Law and Order* (Stevens and Sons, 1971) 41.

[22] See the statements of F Hagerup, Permanent Court of International Justice: Advisory Committee of Jurists, *Procès-verbaux of the Proceedings of the Committee* (Van Langenhuysen Brothers, 1920) 13th Meeting, 296.

The problem with this legitimiser is it fails to take into account the considerable use of General Principles as a source of law prior to its inclusion in the PCIJ Statute.

In contrast, Koskenniemi argues that the legitimiser of General Principles is that

> such principles emerge from, or give expression to, values and considerations that are widely shared among the community of States and we feel that in the case of dispute, community values should be enforced on deviant members.[23]

This does not rely on any external creation to give the source its legitimacy. Rather it hints at natural law concerns – the 'community values'. This can also fit with notions of *inherent* morality of General Principles, as suggested by Raoul Fernandes in the Advisory Committee of Jurists,[24] and those judges who see content as the *reason* for horizontal generality.[25] Such a legitimiser puts General Principles on an equal footing with custom and treaty, rather than as subservient to them. This is more in keeping with the historical development of the source.

B. General Principles as Interpreters/General Principles as Unifiers

There is a view that in addition to being a formal source of law, Article 38(1)(c) forms a function as a *subsidiary* source, 'supportive of other sources'.[26] The influence of General Principles on the development of other areas of international law cannot be denied. This can be through implicit influence: Jimenez de Arechaga, a former judge of the ICJ, states 'So general principles of law, though rarely mentioned in the Court's judgments, should not be underestimated as to their influence on the minds and the intellectual processes of judges.'[27] It is also seen in explicit influence as being used to interpret treaties and custom.[28] Robert Kolb gives examples of how General Principles influence both the interpretation

[23] Koskenniemi, 'Introduction' (n 20) xiii.

[24] See the statements of R Fernandes, Permanent Court of International Justice: Advisory Committee of Jurists, *Procès-verbaux of the Proceedings of the Committee* (Van Langenhuysen Brothers, 1920) 15th Meeting, 346.

[25] See, eg, *Fisheries Case (United Kingdom v Norway)* [1951] ICJ Rep 116, 147–48, 148 (Individual Opinion of Judge Alvarez); *Interhandel (Switzerland v United States of America) (Preliminary Objections)* [1959] ICJ Rep 6, 116–17 (Dissenting Opinion of Judge Lauterpacht); *Right of Passage over Indian Territory (Portugal v India)* (Merits) [1960] ICJ Rep 6, 136 (Separate Opinion of Judge Koo); *South-West Africa (Ethiopia v South Africa; Liberia v South Africa)* (Preliminary Objections) [1962] ICJ Rep 319, 577–78 (Dissenting Opinion of Judge Van Wyk); *North Sea Continental Shelf (Federal Republic of Germany v Denmark; Federal Republic of Germany v the Netherlands)* [1969] ICJ Rep 3, 135 (Separate Opinion of Judge Ammoun); *Sovereignty over Pulau Ligitan and Pulau Sipidan (Indonesia v Malaysia)* [2002] ICJ Rep 625, 705–06 (Dissenting Opinion of Judge ad hoc Franck).

[26] American Law Institute, *Restatement (Third)* (n 14) Reporters' Notes 7.

[27] J de Arechaga, 'Discussion' in Cassese and Weiler (eds), *Change and Stability* (n 19) 50.

[28] ILC, *First Report* (n 15) para 66(c), (e).

and development of custom and treaty, such that the latter are interpreted and/or developed to be consistent with broad and overarching applicable General Principles.[29]

While this role is demonstrably true, two things should be noted. First, as seen in chapters 3–6, General Principles may often fall into the category of procedural or interpretative rules, they are not limited to this *type* of content. Second, some literature extends the role of General Principles from that of interpreters to unifiers: Mads Andenas and Ludovica Chiussi argue that General Principles 'operate as a centripetal force by providing a common ground for interaction between clusters and individual bodies of law'.[30] In the same vein, Johann Leiss extends General Principles to 'fill or bridge gaps between different sub-systems of international law'.[31] This view of General Principles as 'the bees of law',[32] cross-pollinating ideas across fragmented sub-systems, necessarily involves a high level of abstraction. Leiss continues, 'General Principles by their very construction and purposes, leave ample room for discretion and choice. Their high level of abstraction leaves extensive discretion to judges when they apply them to different cases.'[33]

The perceived function here thus impacts on type and methodology, assuming authorised discretion and true principles rather than rules. Care must also be taken when considering the application of 'general principles' in sub-fields of international law. As seen in chapter 6 of this work, such references are not always to General Principles in the Article 38(1)(c) sense, but rather to a modified source of law, unique to that system.[34]

II. THE RULE/PRINCIPLE DISTINCTION

There are many views as to the proper distinction (if any) between rules and principles, and these views each have a repercussion on how General Principles should be interpreted.

The distinction given by many commentators is one of generality. In the context of rules and principles of obligation, Raz drew the distinction as '[r]ules prescribe relatively specific acts; principles prescribe highly unspecific actions'.[35] Alexy describes such theories as classifying principles as 'norms of relatively high

[29] Kolb, *Theory of International Law* (n 6) 138.

[30] Andenas and Chiussi, 'Cohesion' (n 15) 33.

[31] J Leiss, 'The Juridical Nature of General Principles' in Andenas et al (eds) *General Principles* (n 7) 79, 91.

[32] R Kolb, 'Principles as Sources of International Law (with special reference to Good Faith)' (2006) 53(1) *Netherlands International Law Review* 1, 27.

[33] Leiss, 'Juridical Nature' (n 31) 93.

[34] This is particularly the case in the International Criminal Court (ICC), the International Criminal Tribunal for the Former Yugoslavia (ICTY) and the European Court of Justice (ECJ).

[35] J Raz, 'Legal Principles and the Limits of Law' (1972) 81 *Yale Law Journal* 823, 838.

generality' and rules as 'norms of relatively low generality'.[36] Such a distinction is one of degree.[37]

In contrast, other theories argue that the difference between rules and principles is qualitative, 'which allows us to distinguish strictly between rules and principles'.[38] Dworkin characterised this 'logical distinction' as that 'rules are applicable in an all-or-nothing fashion',[39] whereas a principle 'states a reason that argues in one direction, but does not necessitate a particular decision'.[40] Rules cannot conflict – rules are either valid or not – but principles can, and do, conflict; the prevailing principle will be the one with the most relative weight.[41] In contrast, Alexy characterises the difference as one of satisfaction: principles can 'be satisfied to varying degrees',[42] while rules are 'norms which are always either fulfilled or not'.[43] Fitzmaurice distinguishes on the basis of function: 'A rule answers the question "what", a principle in effect answers the question "why".'[44] Such distinctions have been applied by commentators to the study of Article 38(1)(c).[45] Finnis views General Principles as more abstract than rules. He states that 'they justify, rather than require, particular rules and determinations and are qualified in their application to particular circumstances by other like principles'.[46] Bogdan argues Article 38(1)(c) 'must be interpreted to mean that only fundamental principles as such, but not their expression in specific legal rules, can be applied'.[47] Kolb argues that it is the 'generality of the principles' that 'puts them beyond the realm of operation of simple rules', being 'filled with normative energy'.[48] In some cases, the distinction is assumed or even defined: thus Bokor-Szegö takes General Principles to be 'principles which effectively characterize the basic features of the legal system in each State and are directly related to the socio-economic system of the State in question'.[49] Degan argues that 'the term "legal principles" is used in doctrine and in international instruments imprecisely and inconsistently',[50] and thus points to two understandings of General Principles, one based on 'the capacity of a judge to

[36] R Alexy, *A Theory of Constitutional Rights*, tr J Rivers (Oxford University Press, 2002) 45.
[37] Raz, 'Legal Principles' (n 35) 838; Alexy, *A Theory* (n 36) 47.
[38] Alexy, *A Theory* (n 36) 47.
[39] R Dworkin, 'The Model of Rules' (1967–68) 35 *University of Chicago Law Review* 14, 25.
[40] ibid 26.
[41] ibid 27.
[42] Alexy, *A Theory* (n 36) 47–48.
[43] ibid 48.
[44] G Fitzmaurice, 'The General Principles of International Law Considered from the Standpoint of the Rule of Law' (1957) 92 *Recueil de Cours* 1, 7.
[45] N Petersen, 'Customary Law without Custom? Rules, Principles and the Role of State Practice in International Norm Creation' (2008) 23 *American University International Law Review* 275, 286–88.
[46] J Finnis, *Natural Law and Natural Rights* (Clarendon Press, 1988) 288.
[47] Bogdan, 'General Principles of Law' (n 14) 48.
[48] R Kolb, 'Principles as Sources of International Law' (n 33) 9.
[49] Bokor-Szegö, 'General Principles of Law' (n 11) 213.
[50] Degan, *Sources of International Law* (n 17) 17.

have recourse to analogy with municipal law' and the other 'fundamental principles of international law of peremptory character and superior to all other legal rules'.[51] The second type is those consistent with an (extreme) understanding of true principles.

Degan's classification illustrates the importance of assessing whether General Principles *are* truly principles, or can contain rules. Depending on the understanding of the term 'principles', an imputation of values surrounding words into the source can lead to necessary (or at least more likely) conclusions about other aspects of the source. If, for example, we take Kolb's view of General Principles (as true principles) as importing value, by their nature as principles, into international law,[52] then a natural law basis would more easily flow from this conception of the source. In another vein, Dworkin's view that '[p]rinciples have a dimension that rules do not – the dimension of weight or importance'[53] would, if applied to Article 38(1)(c), imbue that source with the same weight or importance, thus impacting on the hierarchy of sources.[54] Bokor-Szegö's definition of basic principles linked to a socio-economic system justifies, perhaps, views such as Tunkin's that General Principles can never exist in common between socialist and capitalist states.[55] The question becomes whether we can justify such imputation of values – did the source in its historical development distinguish between rules and principles, and was it intended to impute into General Principles understandings of *principles* as abstract, foundational,[56] fundamental,[57] constitutive[58] and value orientated?[59] To answer this question, attention needs to turn to differing national conceptions of General Principles.

A. 'National' International Law

In the last decade and a half there has been much academic attention given to the influence of 'specific legal cultures … on the understanding of international law'.[60] As Jouannet states:

> [T]here does not exist any global or cosmopolitan vision of international law, but, on the contrary, an inevitable multiplicity of particular national, regional, individual,

[51] ibid 18.

[52] Kolb, 'Principles as Sources of International Law' (n 32) 29.

[53] R Dworkin, *Taking Rights Seriously*, 6th edn (Harvard University Press, 1977) 26.

[54] van Hoof, *Rethinking the Sources* (n 13) 149.

[55] G Tunkin, 'Coexistence and International Law' (1958) 95 *Recuil des Cours* 5, 26.

[56] B Cheng, *General Principles of Law as applied by International Courts and Tribunals* (Cambridge University Press, 1953) 585; G Christenson, 'Jus Cogens: Guarding Interests Fundamental to International Society' (1988) 28 *Virginia Journal of International Law* 585, 587.

[57] JHW Verzijl, *International Law in Historical Perspective*, vol 1 (Brill Nijhoff, 1968) 59.

[58] Bogdan, 'General Principles of Law' (n 14) 48.

[59] Kolb, 'Principles as Sources of International Law' (n 32) 29; Petersen, 'Customary Law without Custom?' (n 45) 288.

[60] S Kadelbach and T Kleinlein, 'International Law – a Constitution for Mankind? An attempt at re-appraisal with an analysis' (2007) 50 *German Yearbook of International Law* 303, 303. See also

> and institutional visions. This is so because the actors in the international arena are conditioned by their own legal cultures ...[61]

In the context of General Principles, these national visions play out in a tendency of commentators from Continental European jurisprudential backgrounds to lean towards viewing General Principles as true principles, distinct from rules.

For example, German views on international law are often associated with a constitutionalist approach,[62] which 'tend[s] to rely on values'.[63] In the view of Kadelbach and Kleinlein, General Principles are best viewed as true principles, which are 'structurally equivalent to statements of value'.[64] This conception imports characteristics into General Principles – in this view, they can only be developed over long periods of time (in contrast with the possibility of instant, or near instant, custom),[65] 'cannot be changed overnight'[66] and, as a corollary of this, are primarily sourced from 'judicial practice'.[67] The influence of national background is also seen in scholars from the French legal tradition, who often construct General Principles as 'latent principles'.[68] As Koskenniemi states, 'We Europeans share this intuition: the international world will be how we are. And we read international law in the image of our domestic legalism ...'.[69]

The point here is not that the 'European' view is incorrect – nor inappropriate – rather that it is but one view of international law. Assuming either that domestic definitions and understandings of terms such as 'principles' apply equally on the international stage, or, more generally, that a norm accepted within one country or community of countries is more broadly universal, can lead to unjustified conclusions – 'the abuses to which the appeal to general norms of supposedly universal standing can lead'.[70] Given this, it is useful to discuss the rule/principle distinction in the context of the historical development of the source.

R Wolfrum, 'Introduction: American-European Dialogue: Different Perceptions of International Law' (2004) 64 *Zeitschrift für ausländisches öffentliches Recht und Völkerrecht* 255; M Koskenniemi, 'International Law in Europe: Between Tradition and Renewal' (2005) 16(1) *European Journal of International Law* 113; P Dupuy, 'Some Reflections on Contemporary International Law and the Appeal to Universal Values: A Response to Martti Koskenniemi' (2005) 16(1) *European Journal of International Law* 131; A Carty, 'Conservative and Progressive Visions in French International Legal Doctrine' (2005) 16(3) *European Journal of International Law* 525; A Orakhelashvili, 'The Idea of European International Law' (2006) 17(2) *European Journal of International Law* 315; A Roberts, *Is International Law International?* (Oxford University Press, 2017).

[61] E Jouannet, 'French and American Perspectives on International Law: Legal Cultures and International Law' (2006) 58 *Maine Law Review* 292, 292.

[62] Kadelbach and Kleinlein, 'International Law – a Constitution for Mankind?' (n 60) 306–07.

[63] ibid 330.

[64] ibid 337.

[65] ibid 338.

[66] ibid 340.

[67] ibid 339.

[68] M Bos, *A Methodology of International Law* (Elsevier Science Publishers, 1984) 100–01.

[69] Koskenniemi, 'International Law in Europe' (n 60) 117.

[70] Dupuy, 'Some Reflections' (n 60) 133.

B. A Temporal Dimension to the Rule/Principle Distinction

i. Pre-PCIJ

As was discussed in chapter 2, a source of law additional to treaty and custom has been included in international conventions, commentaries and other materials since at least 1875. The use of the term 'principle' was not consistent in this early development. The reference to the source in Goldschmidt's commentary on the *Arbitral Procedural Regulations* referred to 'principles' at a domestic level but 'rules' at the international level.[71] The International Prize Court Convention[72] referred to 'general principles of law and equity',[73] and its commentary explicitly linked these principles to judicial discretion[74] (a linkage that may be unavoidable if we take General Principles to be true principles). Where the Prize Court Convention referred to customary international law as the 'rules of international law',[75] the instruments establishing the Permanent Court of Arbitration and the Draft Convention on the Court of Arbitral Justice both referred to customary law as 'principles of international law',[76] signalling confusion between the terms throughout the documents. This interchangabilty of terms continued into the Advisory Committee of Jurists – the source was first introduced as the 'rules of international law' by Descamps,[77] and although this wording was changed to principles, the Committee in its discussion used both terms throughout.[78]

As the terms 'principles' and 'rules' were used interchangeably by the drafters of the PCIJ Statute and in the previous conventions, it is difficult to maintain the argument that 'principles' as used in Article 38(1)(c) connotes some specific philosophical difference from 'rules' such that it excludes various content from being capable of being a General Principle. This is confirmed when considering the jurisprudence of the PCIJ and ICJ on this point.

[71] L Goldschmidt, 'International Arbitral Procedure' (1874) 6 *Revue de droit international et de Législation Comparée* 421, tr in JB Scott (ed), *Resolutions of the Institute of International Law dealing with the Law of Nations* (Oxford University Press, 1916) 228.

[72] Convention Relative to the Creation of an International Prize Court (signed 18 October 1907) 205 CTS 381.

[73] ibid Art 7.

[74] L Renault, 'Report to the Conference from the First Commission on the Draft Convention relative to the Creation of an International Prize Court' in JB Scott (ed), *The Reports to the Hague Conferences of 1899 and 1907* (Clarendon Press, 1917) 758, 769.

[75] Convention Relative to the Creation of an International Prize Court (n 72) Art 7.

[76] Convention (I) on Pacific Settlement of International Disputes (adopted 29 July 1899, entered into force 4 September 1900)) 187 CTS 410, Art 48; Convention (II) on Pacific Settlement of International Disputes (adopted 18 October 1907, entered into force 26 January 1910) 205 CTS 233, Art 73.

[77] Permanent Court of International Justice: Advisory Committee of Jurists, *Procès-verbaux of the Proceedings of the Committee* (Van Langenhuysen Brothers, 1920) 13th Meeting, annex 3.

[78] ibid 14th Meeting, 315 per Ricci-Busatti; 15th Meeting, annex 2 per Fernandes.

ii. PCIJ and ICJ

Once the provision was drafted, one could assume that the language used to discuss the source centred on the *actual* wording of the source, and thus 'principle' would be preferred. This is not the case. Not only is there a general trend by both the PCIJ and the ICJ to continue to use the terms interchangeably, this also occurs with regard to Article 38(1)(c) specifically. Thus, in his Dissenting Opinion in *Panevezy-Saldutiskis Railway*, Judge Van Eysinga recognises an obligation 'that since ... the Court must apply the general principles of law recognized by civilized nations, it must apply the local remedies rule';[79] while Judge Shahabudden, in his Separate Opinion in *Certain Phosphate Lands in Nauru*, makes use of General Principles to discuss a 'rule of international law precluding [Nauru's action against Australia] on the ground that the obligation was joint'.[80]

The confusion surrounding the distinction, if any, between principles and rules in the context of Article 38(1)(c) is exacerbated by commentators who assert the Courts were referring to General Principles when in fact the text does not support such a conclusion, but also the word choice of the Court refers to rules – a 'well known rule',[81] a 'familiar rule'[82] and a 'general rule'.[83] Thus even when the source was *temporally* well-established as using the wording 'principle', the term itself was still being used interchangeably with 'rule'.

C. A Blurred Distinction

A consideration of the use of Article 38(1)(c) reveals applications with such requisite specificity and prescription of content that the relevant norm would fall under a 'rule' on the rule/principles spectrum, even if that specific terminology is not used. For example, the application of limited corporate liability[84] and the admissibility of circumstantial evidence[85] have been discussed as General

[79] *Panevezys-Saldutiskis Railway Case (Estonia v Lithuania)* (Merits) [1939] PCIJ Series A/B No 76, 40 (Dissenting Opinion of Judge Van Eysinga).

[80] *Certain Phosphate Lands in Nauru (Nauru v Australia)* (Preliminary Objections) [1992] ICJ 240, 287 (Separate Opinion of Judge Shuhabuddeen).

[81] *Article 3, Paragraph 2, of the Treaty of Lausanne (Frontier between Turkey and Iraq)* (Advisory Opinion) [1925] PCIJ Series B No 12, 32. Brownlie and Cheng both assert this is recognition of a General Principle by the PCIJ (see ch 3, section II.F).

[82] *Payment in Gold of Brazilian Federal Loans Contracted in France (France and Brazil)* (Merits) [1929] PCIJ Series A No 21, 114. Bassiouni and Cassesse both assert this is recognition of a General Principle by the PCIJ (see ch 3, section II.K).

[83] *Interpretation of the Greco-Turkish Agreement* (Advisory Opinion) [1928] PCIJ Series B No 16, 20. Cheng, Bassiouni and Schlesinger assert this is recognition of a General Principle by the PCIJ (see ch 3, section II.L).

[84] *Barcelona Traction, Light and Power Company (Belgium v Spain)* (Second Phase) [1970] ICJ Rep 3, 39.

[85] *Corfu Channel (United Kingdom of Great Britain and Northern Ireland v. Albania)* (Merits) [1949] ICJ Rep 4, 18.

Principles. Further, the recognition that General Principles echo existing rules contained in treaties and customary international law, such as the prohibition on the use of force[86] and the humanitarian content of the Geneva Conventions,[87] also suggest the source encompasses specific rules as well as abstract principles.

This treatment of the source is entirely consistent with Mendolsen's approach to the matter:

> [A]lthough there is quite a debate among legal theorists as to the difference and hierarchical relation between rules and principles, none of this finds any reflection in the utterances of the ICJ, which tends to treat the two terms as synonymous.[88]

This is also true of other international tribunals – the ICTY has been criticised for referring to customary norms as 'general principles of international law', further muddying the waters.[89]

It is evident that the language of 'rule' and 'principle' has been used in a far from precise manner. Not only is there the unfortunate habit (stretching well into the past) of referring to customary norms as 'principles',[90] leading to potential confusion between Article 38(1)(b) and Article 38(1)(c), but there is also a lack of distinction between 'rules' and 'principles' within discussion of Article 38(1)(c) itself. Accordingly, the treatment of General Principles should recognise that it is unwise to imbue the source with specific theoretical meaning solely on the basis of the inclusion of the word 'principle'. What this means is that a level of abstraction and generality should not be *assumed*. If we do take 'principles' as having a specific theoretical conception distinct from a rule, we are importing concepts into Article 38(1)(c) that are not supported either by the historical development of the source, or by its treatment by the PCIJ and ICJ. Further, by analysing the source with this underlying assumption, we risk limiting its potential application. Thus, Akehurst writes:

> While general principles often exist at a very high level of abstraction, there is no reason why detailed rules which happen to be common to different systems of municipal law should not be applied as general principles of law; the difference between a principle and a rule is only a difference of degree.[91]

[86] *Military and Paramilitary Activities in and against Nicaragua (Nicaragua v United States of America)* (Merits) [1986] ICJ Rep 14, 98–99.

[87] ibid 113.

[88] M Mendelson, 'The International Court of Justice and the sources of international law' in V Lowe and M Fitzmaurice (eds), *Fifty Years of the International Court of Justice: essays in honour of Sir Robert Jennings* (Cambridge University Press, 1996) 63, 80.

[89] R O'Keefe, 'Recourse to the *Ad Hoc* Tribunals to General Principles of Law and Human Rights Law' in M Delmas-Marty (ed), *Les sources du droit international pénal: l'expérience des tribunaux pénaux internationaux et le statut de la Cour pénale internationale* (Société de législation comparée, 2004) 297, 298–99.

[90] This habit is also observable in the Statute of the International Criminal Court: see J Verhoeven, 'Article 21 of the Rome Statute and the Ambiguities of Applicable Law' (2002) 32 *Netherlands Yearbook of International Law* 3, 9.

[91] M Akehurst, 'Equity and General Principles of Law' (1976) 25 *International and Comparative Law Quarterly* 801, 815.

Other commentators follow the path of the World Courts, and treat Article 38(1)(c) as including both rules and principles, using the terms together[92] or interchangeably.[93] Even some commentators who argue for a difference between rules and principles in theory recognise the difference may not be so stark in reality. Where a multitude of common legal rules are found with some common principle behind them, Bogdan does not require the distillation of that principle from the commonly accepted municipal rule only to be reformed into an international rule:

> The particular common legal rule can thus be seen as an expression of the common principle. The existence of such a common principle behind common particular legal rules can normally be presumed and there are thus no reasons why such rules could not be applied by international tribunals directly …[94]

This idea, that the horizontal commonality of the rule presupposes a common principle, leads to the final point to be discussed under the rule/principle distinction – the idea of generality.

D. Generality

'General' is clearly a requirement of Article 38(1)(c). But are we talking about a *vertical* generality, leading to abstraction, and classic 'principles', or are we discussing a *horizontal* generality, requiring representation in many legal systems, and which may encompass specific rules? This discussion impacts on other parts of the framework and issues discussed in this chapter. *Vertical* generality, requiring an abstract principle applied to facts, may lead to judicial discretion, legislating from 'principles to principles'.[95] On the other hand, a requirement of *horizontal* generality leads to a clear predilection for a comparative methodology.

Horizontal generality is fairly straightforward – it is a requirement that the principle be commonly accepted amongst many systems. As will be seen in the discussion on methodology, such a requirement is commonly accepted amongst commentators, and is reflected in the cases. Will horizontal generality be enough, or is a dual generality required?

Vertical generality has been described as the 'fundamental, constitutive function the principle plays within the municipal legal system'.[96] A requirement of vertical generality goes to 'the very character of the legal proposition that

[92] van Hoof, *Rethinking the Sources* (n 13) 140; American Law Institute, *Restatement (Third)* (n 14) §102(l).

[93] Virally, 'The Sources of International Law' (n 12) 144, 146.

[94] Bogdan, 'General Principles of Law' (n 14) 49.

[95] J Stone, 'From Principles to Principles' (1981) 97(2) *The Law Quarterly Review* 224.

[96] Bogdan, 'General Principles of Law' (n 14) 49.

is at stake',[97] and thus links to concepts of morality. Commentators who only require horizontal generality are sometimes criticised for not understanding 'principles' correctly. Thus Mann states, 'it is the generality of the application of the rule [or principle] not the generality of the legal idea underlying it that determines whether or not it is a general principle',[98] reasoning that has been criticised as 'fallacious' and amounting to 'a deliberate twisting of the meaning of words to fit a desired thesis'.[99]

In contrast, Shlesinger has argued that vertical generality cannot be assessed across many systems, and the only way principles can be realised is by assessing the horizontal generality of rules:

> A priori speculation will not help us to ascertain what standards and principles are in fact recognized by the civilized nations of the world; and intuitive insights, however valuable in expounding one's national law, necessarily elude us when we enter an arena which by virtue of its global nature is beyond the experience and intuition of any single men.[100]

This view is consistent with Bogdan's approach to rules and principles, and is the view that is most consistent with the development and use of the source. Vertical generality may *come* from horizontal generality: why else would a common rule or principle be contained in so many legal systems without a generality of the idea itself? However, the legitimising generality is horizontal: vertical generality is a consequence of (or a reason for) horizontal generality but is in itself not a requirement to found a General Principle.

III. JUDICIAL DISCRETION

It is clear from the history of Article 38(1)(c) that it expressly did not authorise discretion. Members of the Committee of Jurists, still scarred from the failure of the Prize Court, laid such failure firmly at the provisions in that Court's statute allowing for judicial law making.[101] The drafts leading up to PCIJ Statute showed two alternatives for the third source of law – one allowing discretion, one not.[102] The latter was chosen. As Verzijl writes, Article 38(1)(c) 'is without

[97] D Kritsiotis, 'On the Possibilities of and for Persistent Objection' (2010) 21 *Duke Journal of Comparative and International Law* 121, 126.

[98] FA Mann, 'Reflections on a Commercial Law of Nations' (1957) 33 *British Yearbook of International Law* 20, 36.

[99] FTF Jalet, 'The Quest for the General Principles of Law Recognised by Civilised Nations: A Study' (1962–1963) 10 *UCLA Law Review* 1041, 1046.

[100] RB Shlesinger, 'The Common Core of Legal Systems: An Emerging Subject of Comparative Study' in KH Nadelmann, AT von Mehren, and JN Hazard (eds), *XXth Century Comparative and Conflicts Law: Legal Essays in Honor of Hessel E Yntema* (AW Sythoff, 1961) 65, 79.

[101] See ch 2.

[102] See ch 2.

any reasonable doubt intended to give the World Court far less freedom than the International Prize Court of 1907 would have enjoyed under the corresponding, very controversial Article 7'.[103] It acts to 'avoid the danger of such cases [of a lacuna] of the judges deciding according to their personal views of right and wrong'.[104] Yet it is a common fear of commentators that Article 38(1)(c) allows 'judge-made law',[105] and this perception is pointed to as reason behind the under-utilisation of the source by the PCIJ and ICJ.[106]

There is an argument for a type of judicial discretion allowable under Article 38(1)(c) – that which has been described as the '"legislative" or "creative" powers which are implicitly entrusted to independent law-determining agencies'.[107] This discretion allows the court to decide 'whether or not, and if so, to what extent, rules or principles derived from municipal law can appropriately be applied to international relations'.[108] Read narrowly, this kind of discretion is a rules-based discretion – 'not discretion in a proper etymological sense'.[109] Judges exercise their judgment, or discretion, to ascertain if a certain rule or principle has fulfilled the criteria in the relevant rule of recognition – in this case, the requirements of Article 38(1)(c). This kind of narrow, strict 'sound discretion'[110] is by no means at odds with the formation of Article 38(1)(c), and is indeed a necessary part of the functioning of any court. However, it has been suggested that judges can use more than this narrow discretion, but what exactly this looks like depends on the *methodology* of the source, and in particular whether a comparative methodology is used or something else.

A. Comparativism, Categoricism and Discretion

The question of methodology really goes to the rule of recognition. What is needed to ascertain a General Principle? Is it a positivistic rule or recognition, centring on *how* the norm is found? Or is there a natural law dimension, requiring consideration of the *content* of the norm itself?

Some commentators tend to be sceptical of the comparative methodology,[111] although others embrace it wholeheartedly.[112] On one hand, there was a flurry

[103] Verzijl, *International Law in Historical Perspective* (n 57) 52.

[104] GA Finch, *The Sources of Modern International Law* (Carnegie Endowment for International Peace, 1937, repr 1971) 97.

[105] Bassiouni, 'A Functional Approach' (n 19) 792. See also R Jennings 'What is International Law and How Do We Tell It When We See It?' in M Koskenniemi (ed), *Sources of International Law* (Routledge, 2000) 59, 71–73.

[106] W Friedmann, *The Changing Structure of International Law* (Stevens and Sons, 1964) 189–90.

[107] van Hoof, *Rethinking the Sources* (n 13) 143.

[108] ibid.

[109] J Edelman, 'Judicial Discretion in Australia' (2000) 19 *Australian Bar Review* 285, 286.

[110] *R v Wilkes* (1770) 4 Burr 2527; Edelman, 'Judicial Discretion in Australia' (n 109) 286.

[111] See, eg, Cheng, 'Comments' (n 14) 130.

[112] Friedmann, 'The Uses of "General Principles"' (n 4) 282; Friedmann, *The Changing Structure of International Law* (n 106) 192; LC Green, 'Comparative Law as a "Source" of International Law'

of comparative study in the late 1950s and 1960s, perpetuated by Schlesinger's project at Cornell University on massing General Principles.[113] These studies called for an inductive, rather than deductive, approach to General Principles, avoiding what Schwarzenberger termed the 'dreamland of deductive speculation' in favour of the 'reality of hard work on raw material waiting for the workman'.[114]

On the other hand, there are earlier formulations of Article 38(1)(c) that reject comparativism, referring instead to overarching norms or juridical truth,[115] a methodology labelled as categoricist.[116] Bin Cheng's reluctance to embrace comparativism is seen even in his joint presentation with Harold Gutteridge, a noted comparativist commentator,[117] where he cautioned against over-reliance on comparativism to find General Principles. Bin Cheng argued that while comparative law can 'fulfill a most valuable function in checking whether a particular principle, deduced from one single system of law … possesses "ecumenical validity"',[118] he warned that 'the general principles of law should not … be regarded as a kind of mathematical highest common factor of municipal law of all countries'.[119] More recently, Pellet and Müller argued that the PCIJ rejected a comparative approach towards General Principles in *Mavrommatis Palestine Concessions*.[120] As discussed in chapter 2, this is not the only viable interpretation of the Courts' failure to invoke General Principles in that case.

Bin Cheng's reluctance to embrace a purely comparative methodology is clearly tied to his conception of Article 38(1)(c) as constituting true principles with vertical generality, valid because of their content and position in legal systems – 'the common foundation of every system of law'.[121] Accordingly, in his view, the *main* methodology is internal deduction from a legal system – comparative law merely furnishes a way of checking that the principle has sufficient

(1967–1968) 42 *Tulane Law Review* 52, 66; Akehurst, 'Equity and General Principles of Law' (n 91) 814; Bogdan, 'General Principles of Law' (n 14) 49; LJ Maki, 'General Principles of Human Rights Law Recognized by All Nations: Freedom from Arbitrary Arrest and Detention' (1980) 10 *California Western International Law Journal* 272, 275.

[113] See, eg, R Schlesinger, 'Research on the General Principles of Law Recognised by Civilised Nations' (1957) 51 *The American Journal of International Law* 734; JN Hazard, 'The General Principles of Law' (1958) 52 *The American Journal of International Law* 91, 91–92; Schlesinger, 'The Common Core of Legal Systems' (n 100).

[114] G Schwarzenberger, 'The Inductive Approach to International Law' (1947) 60 *Harvard Law Review* 539, 562.

[115] Cheng, *General Principles of Law* (n 56) 24.

[116] CA Ford, 'Judicial Discretion in International Jurisprudence, Article 38(1)(c) and General Principles of Law' (1994) 5 *Duke Journal of Comparative and International Law* 35, 72.

[117] HC Gutteridge, *Comparative Law: An Introduction to the Comparative Method of Legal Study and Research* (Cambridge University Press, 1949).

[118] Cheng, 'Comments' (n 14) 130.

[119] ibid.

[120] A Pellet and D Müller, 'Article 38 ' in A Zimmerman, CJ Tams, K Oellers-Frahm and C Tomuschat (eds), *The Statute of the International Court of Justice: A Commentary*, 3rd edn (Oxford University Press, 2019) 819, 928–929.

[121] Cheng, 'Comments' (n 14) 129.

horizontal generality as well. It would seem that comparative law on its own, without the initial first step, would not be appropriate under this view. This categoricist approach to methodology has been criticised for allowing discretion not 'channelled through a careful process of consideration and explanation'.[122] In contrast, Elkind defends Bin Cheng's categoricist approach as a 'systematic theory for identifying general principles'.[123] This theory requires both horizontal generality and that a principle 'must be traced back to the idea of law in a way that is transcendent of the legal system'.[124] Such a method authorises a very loose discretion whereby judges decide whether a principle is truly a 'juridical truth' without any further strictures to be followed. It also clearly brings natural law dimensions to Article 38(1)(c), as it is the *content* of the norm that is important, rather than its presence in municipal legal systems.

In contrast, Gutteridge argues in favour of the application of comparativism to Article 38(1)(c) because it provides an 'objective test', thus limiting a judge 'blindly following the teaching' of commentators[125] – that is, transforming a wide discretion into a more narrow, rule-based discretion. Comparativism provides 'a guarantee against arbitrary decisions on the part of the judges'.[126] It also protects against the problem noted by Jaye Ellis:

> One of the reasons for treating general principles with suspicion is that, too often, the legal reasoning used to identify them simply involves elevating legal rules and concepts with which individual judges are familiar from their own legal education and practice to the level of universal truths, sometimes without any reference to a source at all.[127]

Despite the divide between the opinions of commentators in this matter, the practice by the Courts is fairly one-sided. Where a methodology can be ascertained, it is overwhelmingly comparative (although some of the comparative studies leave much to be desired). Nonetheless, the use of comparativism still leaves room for discretion, in the form of appropriateness.

B. Discretion as to Appropriateness

van Hoof argues that judicial discretion is required for General Principles to determine 'to what extent rules or principles derived from municipal law can *appropriately* be applied to international relations.[128] This could suggest a more

[122] Ford, 'Judicial Discretion in International Jurisprudence' (n 116) 74.
[123] JB Elkind, *Interim Protection: A Functional Approach* (Brill Nijhoff, 1981) 13.
[124] ibid 15.
[125] Gutteridge, *Comparative Law* (n 117) 65.
[126] Virally, 'The Sources of International Law' (n 12) 148.
[127] J Ellis, 'General Principles and Comparative Law' (2011) 22(4) *European Journal of International Law* 949, 965.
[128] van Hoof, *Rethinking the Sources* (n 13) 143.

guided discretion – where judges decide between 'a number of possible alternatives',[129] where laws 'can rule out certain decisions … [but] do not determine any decision as the correct one'.[130] In this sense, the rule of recognition associated with Article 38(1)(c) would act to rule *out* possibilities, acting as a necessary but not sufficient condition, and those rules or principles that fulfilled the requirements (say, comparative methodology of all major legal systems) would require a further validation from the judges – whether such a rule or principle is *appropriate* to become a General Principle, or, in the words of Raz, the correct decision. The problem becomes by what measure a judge assesses appropriateness. In the context of fairness, Thomas Franck argues that judges should reference ideas of 'common sense'.[131] Gerry Simpson argues in response:

> Alas, these notions of community and common sense are contentious enough in relatively homogenous national societies. Any attempt to incorporate such concepts into judicial decisionmaking in the international order is likely to result in the influence of even more egregious biases and ideological preferences than in these domestic systems.[132]

Such a criticism can be made of the categoricist approach to General Principles more broadly: the very idea of what is inherently right or moral chosen without reference to some objective criteria or standard is inherently personal. As Anthony Arend states, '[t]he difficulty with this understanding of general principles is that there do not seem to be universally accepted definitions of concepts such as equity and humanity. Rather, they seem merely to reflect subjective values espoused by certain states'.[133]

If we accept that judges can *choose* whether a principle is appropriate to some external reference then General Principles risk importing the 'egregious biases' observed by Simpson, and the dominance of certain subjective views observed by Arend, into international jurisprudence.

On the other hand, choosing whether a principle is appropriate may just be a matter of whether it can actually function at the international level. It is argued that this is the discretion that McNair required when he warned against importing principles 'lock, stock and barrel'.[134] Similarly, Degan argues that for a rule or principle to be a General Principle, it must be applicable 'in municipal, international, transnational and supranational law'.[135] This requirement is a rules-based discretion – the rule of recognition requiring, first, that the appropriate methodology be met and, second, that the principle be capable of functioning at the international level.

[129] Edelman, 'Judicial Discretion in Australia' (n 109) 286.
[130] Raz, 'Legal Principles' (n 35) 843.
[131] T Franck, *Fairness in International Law and Institutions* (Oxford University Press, 1995).
[132] G Simpson, 'Is International Law Fair?' (1996) 17 *Michigan Journal of International Law* 615, 625.
[133] AC Arend, *Legal Rules and International Society* (Oxford University Press, 1999) 51.
[134] Elkind, *Interim Protection* (n 123) 12.
[135] Degan, *Sources of International Law* (n 17) 103.

Even this fairly simple requirement is subject to changes of understanding over time. Jerome Elkind, writing in 1981, suggested that

> the mere fact that a principle can be found in the vast majority of municipal legal systems or even in all the legal systems of the world is not adequate grounds for treating it as a principle of international law. It may, for instance, be a principle of revenue law or a principle of criminal liability which is simply not appropriate to international law.[136]

In the 40 years since that book was published, issues of criminal liability and taxation (though certainly *raising* revenue remains in the state's domestic forum) have become issues at international law. Principles that in 1981 were thought to be purely domestic continue to be elevated to the international forum, as the world and its law become increasingly globalised. As the American Restatement on International Law asserts:

> Whether a general principle common to national legal systems is appropriate for absorption by international law may depend on the development of international law. For example, there is now substantial international law on human rights, and it is plausible to conclude that a rule against torture is part of international law, since such a principle is common to all major legal systems.[137]

C. A Broader Discretion

The discretion allowed under General Principles is taken further by Kolb, who writes that

> general principles of law may serve as the basis of autonomous legal reasoning. They then serve to free the legal actor from the constraints of positive law and seek in more lofty and general areas a satisfactory solution for the single case submitted to him.[138]

In this manner, Kolb argues, a judge may reject relying on a certain rule (in this case, reliance on municipal law in arbitrating a commercial contract between a state and a private actor) in favour of 'recourse to the general principles of good faith, of good will and of equity'.[139] Thus judges may *reject* a certain approach in favour of a General Principle. There are two problems with this approach.

First, it seems to directly contradict the work of the Advisory Committee of Jurists in ensuring that judges would not exercise wide discretion in applying General Principles.[140] It falls foul of Schwarzenberger's warning that:

> Legal maxims, however useful for didactic purposes are neither a substitute for comparative research nor, by themselves, evidence of any general principle of law.

[136] Elkind, *Interim Protection* (n 123) 12.
[137] American Law Institute, *Restatement (Third)* (n 14) Reporters' Notes 7.
[138] Kolb, 'Principles as Sources of International Law' (n 32) 34.
[139] ibid.
[140] See ch 2.

> They are inherently suspect of providing a spurious cover for illegitimate efforts at law making in disguise.[141]

It should be noted that Kolb does not attempt to cover 'law making in disguise'; rather he argues that 'The Court, in fact, developed during many years a whole body of case-law on all these questions, and it had recourse to a wealth of rules it deduced more or less directly from the general idea of equity.'[142] And further that

> the Court has in effect developed the law, or to say it more bluntly: that it legislated. And this legislation took place under the auspices of a general principle, 'equity', or 'equitable principles'. Thus, in other words, the principle of 'equity' served here as source of the law.[143]

This kind of judicial law making is the same that was identified by Akehurst as occurring in the ECJ with regard to its use of general principles of law.[144] However, it is not always clear in the history of the PCIJ and the ICJ that the use of equity and equitable principles is in fact under the auspices of Article 38(1)(c).[145] So there are dual concerns here – we may not actually be discussing General Principles in the Article 38(1)(c) sense at all; and if we are, such judicial legislative activity is in direct contradiction with the intentions of the Advisory Committee of Jurists.

The second problem is the actual methodology for finding these General Principles alluded to is entirely unclear. Rather, Kolb writes of them as 'great principles' not limited to the category of 'general principles of law'.[146] In a later publication, and referring explicitly to Article 38(1)(c), Kolb admits that while General Principles can be used to adapt international law to new circumstances, 'one must not exaggerate this function. The judge is not legislator, and he or she cannot simply re-invent law as he or she sees fit.'[147]

To suggest that judges have a 'creative' function in the context of rules-based discretion in relation to General Principles (and more widely to all law) is no doubt correct. This rules-based discretion can cover both the appropriate methodology being fulfilled and the appropriate nature of the principle, such that it can practically apply at the international arena. Any argument, though, that extends this discretion to a more guided discretion, or even to the extreme of judicial legislation, is at odds with the constraints of Article 38(1)(c).

[141] G Schwarzenberger, *International Law as Applied by International Courts and Tribunals*, vol 1, 3rd edn (Stevens and Sons, 1957) 43.

[142] Kolb, 'Principles as Sources of International Law' (n 32) 10.

[143] ibid 11.

[144] M Akehurst, 'The Application of General Principles of Law by the Court of Justice of the European Communities' (1981) 52 *British Yearbook of International Law* 29, 40.

[145] See generally chs 3 and 4.

[146] Kolb, 'Principles as Sources of International Law' (n 32) 9.

[147] Kolb, *The Theory of International Law* (n 6) 142.

D. Nationality, Judicial Discretion and Methodology

As with commentators, the national background of judges necessarily influences the way they view international law. Indeed, the requirement of different national backgrounds of judges on the ICJ[148] is pointed to as a way of ensuring that one specific national view of international law is not preferred or given undue importance. As has been seen, a link has been made between this requirement and General Principles in the development of the source, and in cases. This link is also made by several commentators.[149] Virally argues that instead of a comparative study of 'all municipal systems of law', the

> International Court proceeds in a more pragmatic fashion, and is satisfied with a coincidence of opinion amongst its own judges. Such a method affords sufficient safeguards, the judges having been elected so as to ensure 'the representation of the main forms of civilization and the principal legal systems of the world' …[150]

The problem with depending solely on 'coincidence of opinion' between judges without wider comparative support is it runs the risk of losing the 'objective test by which [the judge] can measure the justice of a principle which [the judge] believes to be the correct one',[151] replacing it with a more subjective consensus between individuals. Although Article 9 of the ICJ Statute requires that judges as whole represent 'the main forms of civilization and of the principal legal systems of the world',[152] it is dangerous to suggest that the nationality of 15 judges is necessarily representative of the 193 UN Member States. Not only do issues with legal systems as representatives of legal families arise,[153] in practice the ICJ judiciary is dominated by certain countries,[154] including the five permanent UN Security Council members (P5).[155] Indeed, by 1951 an 'unwritten rule' had emerged that the P5 would always have a seat on the Court.[156]

Further, historical records show that nominations by the United States and the United Kingdom were heavily influenced by the goal of protecting their (Western) interests: a 1975 leaked US Department of State memo stressed the need to 'achieve the most western orientated bench possible'.[157] Such assessment

[148] Statute of the International Court of Justice [1945] ATS 1, Art 9.

[149] PE Corbett, 'The Search for General Principles of Law' (1961) 47(5) *Virginia Law Review* 811, 824; van Hoof, *Rethinking the Sources* (n 13) 142–43.

[150] Virally, 'The Sources of International Law' (n 12) 146.

[151] Gutteridge, *Comparative Law* (n 117) 65.

[152] Statute of the International Court of Justice [1945] ATS 1, Art 9.

[153] See ch 8.

[154] K Polonskaya, 'Selecting Candidates to the bench of the World Court: (Inevitable) politicization and its consequences' (2020) 33 *Lieden Journal of International Law* 409, 409.

[155] K Keith, 'Challenges to the Independence of the International Judiciary: Reflections on the International Court of Justice' (2017) 30 *Lieden Journal of International Law* 137, 147.

[156] P Sands, 'Global Governance and the International Judiciary: Choosing Our Judges' (2003) 56 *Current Legal Problems* 481, 494. This convention was broken in 2017, when the UK lost 'its' seat to Judge Dalveer Bhandari, the candidate from India.

[157] Polonskaya, 'Selecting Candidates' (n 154), 417.

of candidates was often on racial lines – when considering the 1954 elections, Sir Gerald Fitzmaurice assessed the likelihood of a seat held by a Latin American judge being replaced by one from Asia: '[O]f the two evils, the Latin American is the lesser evil than the Asian.'[158] The so-called 'Commonwealth' seat, held by Canada (Judge Read) and then Australia (Sir Percy Spender), was viewed as a 'white Commonwealth seat' for preference.[159] When judges from non-Western/non-white backgrounds were supported, it was because they were from ex-British colonies,[160] or had graduated from an American university.[161] Although it is to be hoped such attitudes are things of the past, they demonstrate some of the pitfalls with assuming that a politically appointed bench can fairly represent all legal systems. The Western domination of international law is also seen in the development of doctrine surrounding 'civilized nations', discussed in the next section.

IV. WHERE ARE GENERAL PRINCIPLES DRAWN FROM?

A. 'Civilized' Nations

General Principles present an opportunity to embrace the globalisation of international law.[162] This was not always the view of the PCIJ and the ICJ,[163] or of commentators. Indeed, the very concept of 'civilized' necessarily suggests the other; the uncivilised.[164] Early views on international law and civilisation were rife with notions of European superiority and racism. Thus Westlake, writing at the turn of the twentieth century, argued that international society 'is composed of all the States of European blood',[165] and 'understood international law as a tool for ensuring the supremacy of the interests of "peoples of European blood" over those of the inhabitants of the territories they colonized'.[166] Although such extreme views are thankfully (for the most part) relegated to history, writing on General Principles retained a Western-centric flavour for some decades after. As recently as 1965, one commentator described Article 38(1)(c) as encompassing 'principles to be found in the civil law codes and in the Anglo-Saxon

[158] Sands, 'Global Governance' (n 156) 494. The seat, filled by Sir Zalfrullah Khan (Pakistan) in the 1954 election, was described as 'the nigger in the woodpile' by a contemporary of Fitzmaurice in 1960: ibid 497.

[159] ibid 497.

[160] ibid.

[161] Polonskaya, 'Selecting Candidates' (n 154), 418.

[162] This is explored further in ch 8 of this book.

[163] See discussion in chs 3 and 4 in particular.

[164] D Otto, 'Rethinking the "Universality" of Human Rights Law' (1997) 29 *Columbia Human Rights Law Review* 1, 20.

[165] J Westlake, *International Law: Part I* (Cambridge University Press, 1904) 40; Orakhelashvili, 'The Idea of European International Law' (n 60) 315, 320.

[166] Orakhelashvili, 'The Idea of European International Law' (n 60) 320.

common law', with no mention of other legal systems.[167] Friedmann, writing in 1964, recognised the need 'in certain cases' to look to 'some of the non-Western legal systems, such as Muslim or Hindu law', but maintained that in the 'great majority of cases' reference to Western systems would be adequate as Western principles have been 'deliberately adapted by the non-Western systems'.[168] This of course ignores the chthonic and religious traditions that existed in these states before the (often non-voluntary) adaptation of Western laws, and the concept of legal cultures and 'thin' law.[169] The 1976 edition of Schwarzenberger and Brown distinguishes 'civilised' from 'barbarous or savage communities',[170] instead defining it as a 'European, Christian standard of international law, imposed upon other states'.[171] This disagreement over 'civilised' in relation to general principles also impacted the drafting of the International Covenant on Civil and Political Rights,[172] with the proposed wording of (what would be) Article 15(2) being changed in 1952 from the 'general principles of law recognized by civilized nations'[173] to the 'general principles of law recognised by the community of nations',[174] at the instigation of non-Western countries.[175]

More recent writing has minimised the requirement 'civilised'. Bassiouni argues that 'civilised' merely means a member of the United Nations[176] – a requirement fulfilled by 193 states – and stresses the importance of including laws from *all* legal systems, Western and non-Western.[177] Some variations exist – for example, Simma recasts 'civilised' as 'nations committed to human rights'.[178] This definition has the potential to be somewhat self-serving if arguing that General Principles include human rights norms (which Simma does):[179] it is easy to find commonality between laws if your definition excludes those countries without such laws. Mosler argues that 'civilised'

> must in present day circumstances be interpreted as meaning recognition by the international community. This is because the distinction between civilised nations and others has now been replaced by the concept of the sovereign equality of States.[180]

[167] C Fenwick, *International Law*, 4th edn (Appleton-Century-Crofts, 1965) 87.
[168] Friedmann, *The Changing Structure of International Law* (n 106) 195.
[169] Jain, 'Judicial Lawmaking' (n 15) 137. See discussion in ch 8.
[170] Schwarzenberger and Brown, *A Manual* (n 14) 27.
[171] ibid 13.
[172] International Covenant on Civil and Political Rights (adopted 16 December 1966, entered into force 23 March 1976) 999 UNTS 171 (ICCPR).
[173] United Nations Economic and Social Council, 'Report of the Third Session of the Commission on Human Rights' (28 June 1948) UN Doc E/800, Art 14.
[174] ICCPR (n 172) Art 15(2).
[175] KS Gallant, *The Principle of Legality in International and Comparative Criminal Law* (Cambridge University Press, 2009) 189.
[176] Bassiouni, 'A Functional Approach (n 19) 768.
[177] Akehurst 'Equity and General Principles of Law' (n 91) 818–19; Bokor-Szegö, 'General Principles of Law' (n 11) 215; DJ Bederman, *The Spirit of International Law* (University of Georgia Press, 2002) 30.
[178] Simma, 'International Human Rights and General International Law (n 19) 153, 225.
[179] ibid 225–26.
[180] Mosler, *The International Society* (n 19) 122.

Recognition by the 'international community' does not necessarily mean recognition in the municipal law of states. Just as Simma's definition potentially impacts on the type of General Principle, Mosler's understanding could impact on the methodology. Thus in casting off 'civilised' (which must happen), care needs to be taken that the nature of the source is not transformed (at least, not without due justification). A two-stage approach to recognition by the international community is discussed in section IV.III.c. The formulation preferred by the International Law Commission is 'the general principles of law recognized by States'.[181] This maintains the link to domestic systems and the need for recognition without keeping the offensive and exclusionary aspects of 'civilized'; however, it does not necessarily capture non-State based legal systems.[182]

B. Domestic Forum

Some commentators have suggested that national legislation is not an appropriate source from which to draw General Principles;[183] this view is not universal, however, and finds little support in the comparative studies undertaken by judges of the ICJ. Aside from this minor discrepancy in views, it is well accepted by commentators, including former judges of the ICJ,[184] that General Principles can be drawn from municipal laws, both legislative and non-legislative.[185] This also fits in with a comparative approach to the methodology of the source.

[181] ILC, *First Report* (n 15) para 186.

[182] See ch 8. Even where states recognise non-state law, this is often fragmented: see, eg, Z Korofsy, 'Native Title, Sovereignty and the Fragmented Recognition of Indigenous Law and Custom' (2008) 12(1) *Australian Indigenous Law Review* 81.

[183] W Adamkiewicz in HC Gutteridge, 'The Meaning and Scope of Article 38(1)(c) of the Statute of the International Court of Justice' (1952) 38 *Transactions of the Grotius* Society 125, 132.

[184] A El-Erian, 'The International Court of Justice and the Concept of Universality' (1981) 19 *Columbia Journal of Transnational Law* 197, 208–09.

[185] See, eg, Green, 'Comparative Law as a "Source" of International Law' (n 112) 61; Virally, 'The Sources of International Law' (n 12) 144; Schwarzenberger and Brown, *A Manual* (n 14) 40; Akehurst, 'Equity and General Principles of Law' (n 91) 814; Bogdan, 'General Principles of Law' (n 14) 42; Lammers, 'General Principles of Law Recognized by Civilized Nations' (n 18) 56–57; Mosler, *The International Society* (n 19) 122; van Hoof, *Rethinking the Sources* (n 13) 139; A Pellet, 'The Normative Dilemma: Will and Consent in International Law-making' (1988-1989) 12 *Australian Yearbook of International Law* 22, 38; T Meron, *Human Rights and Humanitarian Norms as Customary Law* (Clarendon Press, 1989) 88–89; JI Charney, 'Universal International Law' (1993) 87 *American Journal of International Law* 529, 535; Bederman, *The Spirit of International Law* (n 177) 30; J Hathaway, *The Rights of Refugees under International Law* (Cambridge University Press, 2005) 26; Kolb, *The Theory of International Law* (n 6) 135; E de Wet, 'Sources and the Hierarchy of International Law: The Place of Peremptory Norms and Article 103 of the UN Charter within the Sources of International Law' in S Besson and J d'Aspremont (eds), *The Oxford Handbook on the Sources of International Law* (Oxford University Press, 2017) 625, 627; P d'Argent, 'Sources and the Legality and Validity of International Law: What Makes Law "International"?' in S Besson and J d'Aspremont, *The Oxford Handbook on the Sources of International Law* (Oxford University Press, 2017) 541, 555; P Palchetti, 'The Role of General Principles in Promoting the Development of Customary International Rules' in Andenas et al (eds), *General Principles* (n 7) 47, 48; M Wood, 'Customary International Law and the General Principles of Law Recognized by Civilized Nations' (2019) 21 *International Community Law Review* 307, 317; ILC, *First Report* (n 15) para 230.

Care must be taken, however, that not every use of municipal law by a court or tribunal is labelled as a General Principle. As Degan points out, such reference may be done by an adjudicator by analogy

> to confirm with additional arguments the motives of his judgment which he based on conventional or customary international law. The associations of this kind, resting on principles common to municipal law, can prove to be convincing to the disputing parties, to whom these motives are mainly addressed.[186]

C. General Principles Drawn from International Law

The more contentious question is whether we can also look to the international forum for material on which to base General Principles. This question is made more difficult by the work of some commentators who use imprecise and incorrect language to back their claim. For instance, Bassiouni adds an additional word to the source, labelling Article 38(1)(c) the 'General Principles of *International* Law',[187] asserting that 'the majority of scholars believe that article 38(1)(c) of the Statute of the PCIJ and article 38(1)c) of the ICJ Statute envision or imply that "General Principles" can be identified from two different legal sources – national and international'.[188] He further argues:

> Of course, principles deemed basic to international law can emerge in the international legal context without having a specific counterpart in national legal systems because of the differences that characterize those two legal systems. Indeed, it would be incongruous to think that the framers of article 38 of the PCIJ and ICJ Statutes intended, for example to exclude from 'General Principles of International Law' those principles which emerge from the customary practice of States or from treaties.[189]

The problem with this argument is that the general principles of *international* law can be, and often are, taken to be different from those General Principles found under Article 38(1)(c).[190] They are taken to be general norms of international law, usually customary, already existing and binding at the international level.[191] It does not follow, however, that Article 38(1)(c) General Principles – general principles of law, not general principles of *international* law – must also encompass such norms. This rewording of the source is not restricted to Bassiouni's works.[192]

[186] Degan, *Sources of International Law* (n 17) 101.

[187] Bassiouni, 'A Functional Approach' (n 19) 768 (emphasis added).

[188] ibid 772.

[189] ibid.

[190] See discussion in chs 2, 3 and 4.

[191] Virally, 'The Sources of International Law' (n 12) 144; Bogdan, 'General Principles of Law (n 14) 42; American Law Institute, *Restatement (Third)* (n 14) Reporters' Note 7; O'Keefe, ' Recourse' (n 89) 297, 298–99.

[192] See, eg, W Riphagen 'General Principles of Law' in Cassese and Weiler (eds), *Change and Stability* (n 19) 33, 34; Kadelbach and Kleinlein, 'International Law – a Constitution for Mankind?' (n 60) 337; M Biddulph and D Newman, 'A Contextualized Account of General Principles of International Law' (2014) 26(2) *Pace International Law Review* 286.

Putting aside the issue of rewording, it is apparent that even among those who support a conception of General Principles drawn from international law, there are actually three distinct ways this is envisioned as happening: as a deduction from rules of international law; being drawn from international sources; and as the second step of a two-stage process whereby international materials verify *appropriateness*.

i. General Principles as Deductions from Existing Rules of International Law

Some commentators argue that Article 38(1)(c) allows principles of an international origin by way of analogy from existing norms of international law[193] that 'do not have a parallel in domestic law'.[194]

Although the practice of international law creation by analogy or deduction has certainly been employed by judges of the PCIJ and ICJ, there are four problems with linking such actions with General Principles. First, where judgments have made analogy, or used inductive reasoning from one established rule of international law to find another, there is usually no indication that they are viewing this process as utilising Article 38(1)(c).[195] Thus, while Palchetti points to the *Frontier Dispute* case as an example of this process, as discussed in chapter 5, the ICJ Chamber gave no indication in that case that the term 'general principle' was being used in Article 38(1)(c) sense.[196] There is also a lack of consensus among commentators as to whether this type of deduced principle is, in fact, a General Principle pursuant to Article 38(1)(c).[197]

Second, such an approach to Article 38(1)(c) seems directly at odds with the explicit link to 'recognized by civilized nations' in the Root-Phillimore draft.[198]

Third, it ventures into authorising broad judicial law making (as Palchetti recognises):[199] this is Kolb's judicial legislation, drawn from international rules generally rather than the 'idea of equity'.[200] As discussed, such broad discretion is at odds with the historical development of the source.

Finally, it bypasses the notion of 'recognition' as a constitutive element of Article 38(1)(c). In his 2019 report, the International Law Commission Special Rapporteur on General Principles, Marcelo Vázquez-Bermúde, considered the disparate views on general principles and the international forum, concluding that 'despite the different approaches in the literature, there seems to be agreement on the point that recognition in the sense of Article 38, paragraph 1(c),

[193] Lammers, 'General Principles of Law Recognized by Civilized Nations' (n 18) 57–58.

[194] Palchetti, 'The Role of General Principles' (n 185) 50.

[195] See discussion in chs 3 and 4.

[196] See ch 5.

[197] S Besson, 'Sources of International Human Rights Law: How General is General International Law?' in Besson and d'Aspremont (eds), *The Oxford Handbook* (n 185) 837, 853.

[198] See ch 2.

[199] Palchetti, 'The Role of General Principles' (n 185) 51.

[200] See discussion accompanying n 142; Kolb, 'Principles as Sources of International Law' (n 32) 10.

can take place at the international level, without the need to look at the national legal systems of States'.[201] However, this first category of international General Principles, which allows deduction or analogy from existing rules of international law, does not involve states. The judicial law making, although drawing from norms first established through treaty or custom, bypasses any notion of state recognition for the newly 'found' General Principle. In contrast, the second two categories of international General Principle allow for the element of recognition to be fulfilled.

ii. General Principles Gathered from International Material

Other commentators also support the inclusion of General Principles drawn from international resources into Article 38(1)(c). Simma and Alston argued that the justification for the original limitation of domestic legal systems was 'that such principles were not to be derived from mere speculation; they had rather to be made objective though some sort of general acceptance or recognition by States'.[202] At the time of the PCIJ Statute's being drafted,

> nothing like the multilateral treaty-making and standard-setting machinery of today was in place, and the League of Nations had just been founded; thus the only reliable source of generally recognized principles was domestic jurisprudence. Today, however, new means of objective validation of general principles are available: they can now be accepted in an international setting from the beginning.[203]

Unlike General Principles based on induction from existing principles of international law, this type of international General Principle provides an objective methodology looking to state acceptance of the norm in question. However, instead of drawing that acceptance from municipal laws, it looks for acceptance at the international level – most likely through General Assembly resolutions.[204]

There are two primary criticisms of this view. The first, addressed by Simma and Alston, is the potential conflation of General Principles and custom, especially if both take General Assembly resolutions as evidence (of state practice for the case of custom, and of recognition for the case of General Principles).[205] The authors' answer to that problem is to argue that state practice for custom should *not* include General Assembly resolutions, especially where states may widely accept a norm in the General Assembly setting but simultaneously widely violate it in terms of actual practice.[206] The issue of state practice and custom

[201] ILC, *First Report* (n 15) para 174.

[202] B Simma and P Alston, 'The Sources of Human Rights Law: Custom, Jus Cogens and General Principles' (1988–89) 12 *Australian Yearbook of International Law* 82, 102. See also Simma, 'International Human Rights and General International Law' (n 19) 224.

[203] Simma, 'International Human Rights and General International Law' (n 19) 224–25.

[204] Simma and Alston, 'The Sources of Human Rights Law' (n 202) 102. See also ILC, *First Report* (n 15) para 173.

[205] Simma and Alston, 'The Sources of Human Rights Law' (n 202) 102.

[206] ibid.

in relation to General Principles is discussed further in chapter 8 of this book. The second criticism is related to the idea of wide acceptance coupled with wide violation, and is drawn from Akehurst's rejection of General Assembly resolutions as reliable evidence for General Principles:

> General Assembly resolutions proclaiming the existence of a general principle of law are even less reliable as evidence of the existence of a general principle of law, because there is no guarantee that the laws of States voting for such a resolution are in conformity with the resolution ...[207]

Akehurst gives the example of states that condemned apartheid in various General Assembly resolutions yet 'whose own laws were full of discriminatory provisions'.[208] Despite these criticisms, the Simma and Alston approach (and an earlier version of the theory written by Verdross and Simma[209]) has found support with other commentators.[210] A final point in regards to the Simma and Alston approach is the temporal aspect – while Simma and Alston argue that the 'new means of objective validation' available today means the international forum is appropriate for General Principles, temporal concerns have also impacted on using the *domestic* forum to find General Principles. In particular, the twin advancements of full text database searchability and the Internet have radically transformed access to information. This concept will be explored further in chapter 8.

There are, then, two opposing scenarios under this approach. In the first, a General Principle is based on General Assembly resolutions that are, in fact, representative of state laws and actual state practice. In this case, the utility of finding a General Principle is questionable, as it would seem the requirements of a norm of custom are fulfilled. In the second, a General Principle is based on General Assembly resolutions that, in fact, are *not* representative of state laws and actual state practice. No norm of custom can be found, for there is no state practice to accompany the *opinio juris*. The question here is at what point the domestic violation of a principle recognised by states at the international level countermands that international recognition?

Another perspective comes from Hilary Charlesworth, who argued that allowing General Principles to draw from international systems, rather than national laws, will 'reduce the andocentric influence of statehood'.[211] In this manner, Charlesworth argued that as domestic legal systems are dominated and created by men, and exclude women, drawing General Principles from these

[207] Akehurst, 'Equity and General Principles of Law' (n 95) 818.

[208] ibid.

[209] A Verdross and B Simma, *Universelles Völkerrecht* (Duncker and Humblot, 1976) 311–12.

[210] Lammers, 'General Principles of Law Recognized by Civilized Nations' (n 18) 58–59; Kadelbach and Kleinlein, 'International Law – a Constitution for Mankind?' (n 60) 340; Petersen, 'Customary Law without Custom?' (n 45) 284–86.

[211] H Charlesworth, 'Remarks' in R Lefeber (ed), *Contemporary International Law Issues: Opportunities at a Time of Momentous Change* (Martinus Nijhoff, 1993) 421, 423.

systems risks transposing 'the gender bias of national legal systems to the international plane'.[212]

Any attempt to exclude national laws from General Principles is entirely inconsistent with the historical foundations and development of the source. A better way to avoid this bias may be in the concept of appropriateness. Given the international law instruments regarding gender equality and non-discrimination,[213] it could be argued that any General Principle that does discriminate against women is inherently inappropriate for the international forum. Care must be taken, however – first, by linking appropriateness to the *desirability* of content, rather than the practical workability of the law, we risk placing a subjective standard on General Principles, and encouraging judicial discretion with the risk of 'egregious biases and ideological preferences'.[214] Nonetheless, if we assess such desirability against *objective* measures – in this case, international conventions – this problem is minimised. Second, although egregious discrimination will be easy to ascertain, those principles or rules that are discriminatory in effect rather than on face may be harder to identify.

iii. International Forum as a Measure of Appropriateness

Following the above, it is appropriate to posit a third scenario – where international materials are relevant to the formation of General Principles but only, as Akehurst phrases it, as 'indirect evidence'[215] or for assessing appropriateness. That is, the *primary* forum from which a General Principle can be drawn is the domestic forum, but that in evidence gathering, evidence of municipal laws can be augmented by evidence of international recognition. This approach is in congruence with those judges of the ICJ who have contemplated international materials in their consideration of Article 38(1)(c). Similarly, if a proposed General Principle is inconsistent with objectively ascertainable standards of international law, as evidenced by treaties and other instruments, it will not be appropriate. This approach accords with a suggestion that General Principles should be accepted by the 'international community'. This is thus a two-stage process, first looking to domestic systems and then turning to acceptance of the rule internationally.[216]

[212] ibid 422.

[213] eg Convention on the Elimination of All Forms of Discrimination against Women (adopted 18 December 1979, entered into force 3 September 1981) 1249 UNTS 14; Optional Protocol to the Convention on the Elimination of All Forms of Discrimination against Women (opened for signature on 10 December 1999, entered into force 22 December 2000) 2131 UNTS 83; Council of Europe Convention on Preventing and Combating Violence against Women and Domestic Violence (opened for signature 11 May 2011, entered into force 1 August 2014) CETS No 210.

[214] Simpson, 'Is International Law Fair?' (n 132) 625.

[215] Akehurst, 'Equity and General Principles of Law' (n 91) 818.

[216] C Eggert, 'The Role of Principles and General Principles in the "Constitutional Processes" of International Law' (2019) 66 *Netherlands International Law Review* 197, 208.

V. CONTENT OF GENERAL PRINCIPLES

A. Public/Private Law

In 1933, Sir Hersch Lauterpacht wrote that the 'general principles of law are, in the great majority of cases, in substance co-extensive with the general principles of private law'.[217] Even in that same work, however, Lauterpacht went on to state that the 'general principles of public law are equally applicable. The same may be said of general maxims and principles of jurisprudence.'[218] In his later work, Lauterpacht wrote of General Principles as 'the analogy of all the branches of municipal law, and in particular, of private law'.[219] As was argued by Friedmann in 1964, the changing nature of international law means General Principles cannot be limited to any one sphere of law:

> Many kinds of international activities, formerly taken as a matter of course to be in the sphere of private international relations, have become a matter of public international concern through the participation of public entities – either states or public international organisations – as well as through the transfer of that activity in question.[220]

Sir Robert Jennings echoed a similar sentiment in 1984, albeit with respect to the changing content of international law generally:

> This big change in the content and span of the law, was not the result of doctrinal enlightenment but of actual necessities arising from the juxtaposition of a larger number of States, all of them pushed by modern economic and technological developments into ever-increasing interdependence in ever more matters; matters which therefore imperatively required regulation by international law.[221]

These statements are no less true today. As international law expands, the blurring between private and public law continues, and General Principles can comfortably encompass rules and principles from both areas. Areas once exclusively in the domain of domestic jurisprudence are now regulated by international law: 'powers which formerly fell within the national jurisdiction of States are of international concern and as a result the principles and rules which are derived from the structure of international law have also changed'.[222] The technological

[217] H Lauterpacht, *The Function of Law in the International Community* (Oxford University Press, 1933) 115.

[218] ibid.

[219] H Lauterpacht, 'Some Observations on the Prohibition of "Non Liquet" and the Completeness of Law' in JHW Verzijl (ed), *Symbolae Verzijl: Présentées au Professeur JHW Verzijl, à l'occasion de son Lxx-ieme anniversaire* (Martinus Nijhoff, 1958) 196, 205.

[220] Friedmann, *The Changing Structure of International Law* (n 106) 190. See also Friedmann, 'The Uses of "General Principles"' (n 4) 281.

[221] R Jennings, 'Teachings and Teaching in International Law' in J Makarczyk (ed), *Essays in International Law in Honour of Judge Manfred Lachs* (Brill Nijhoff, 1984) 121, 124.

[222] Mosler, *The International Society* (n 19) 137.

interdependence that Jennings spoke of almost 30 years ago is increasing rapidly. Markus Burgstaller noted in 2005 that 'Science ... has enabled a virtual leap of humanity into many new fields of activity that require regulation. When the consequences of these activities affect more than one state, they demand international regulation.'[223]

B. Procedural/Substantive

It is sometimes said that most of the General Principles referred to by the PCIJ and the ICJ have been procedural in nature.[224] There are three responses to this allegation. The first is almost the 'so what?' argument. Even if this statement were true, such history does not limit the future potential of the source to encompass more substantive areas of international law, nor does it indicate any fundamental limitation to the source. Second, it should be noted that over 20 years ago, the view of General Principles as procedural was considered 'old', with reference being made to 'general principles of law norms with a much stronger substantive content'.[225] This is consistent with the *actual* practice of the ICJ, which has never restricted General Principles to procedural norms, and further has used it to found substantive norms. Third, there are many commentators who support General Principles encompassing more substantive norms of international law,[226] and in particular human rights law.[227]

C. Crimes against Humanity and *Jus Cogens*

There is a question as to whether crimes against humanity, when prosecuted at the Nuremberg trials, were in fact a new norm of international criminal law.[228] It has been suggested that one possible justification for prosecuting these crimes is that they were crimes pursuant to General Principles.[229] This view is

[223] M Burgstaller, *Theories of Compliance with International Law* (Martinus Nijhoff, 2005) 22.

[224] van Hoof, *Rethinking the Sources* (n 13) 145; J Waincymer et al, *WTO Litigation: Procedural Aspects of Formal Dispute Settlement* (Cameron May Ltd, 2002) 501.

[225] JHH Weiler, 'Discussion: The Classical Sources of Law Revisited' in Cassese and Weiler (eds), *Change and Stability* (n 19) 47.

[226] See, eg, Friedmann, *The Changing Structure of International Law* (n 106) 200; Mosler, *The International Society* (n 19) 124; P Tubman, 'National Jurisprudence in International Tribunals' (1995–1996) 28 *New York University Journal of International Law & Politics* 115, 165–73.

[227] See, eg, Simma, 'International Human Rights and General International Law' (n 19) 225–26; A Rosas, 'State Sovereignty and Human Rights: towards a Global Constitutional Project' in D Beetham (ed), *Politics and Human Rights* (John Wiley and Sons Ltd, 1995) 61, 77; Hathaway, *The Rights of Refugees* (n 185) 41; Petersen, 'Customary Law without Custom?' (n 45) 284–86.

[228] A Cassese, 'Crimes against Humanity' in A Cassese, P Gaeta and JRWD Jones (eds), *The Rome Statute of the International Criminal Court*, vol 1 (Oxford University Press, 2002) 353, 354–55.

[229] Gallant, *The Principle of Legality* (n 175) 94.

strengthened by the argument of the French prosecutor at the time, that the crimes were 'punishable under the penal laws of all civilized States'.[230] This view was also supported by the British prosecutor in his closing argument, but never explicitly adopted by the tribunal itself.[231] Nonetheless, the view of General Principles advanced at the Nuremberg trials – being capable of founding crimes against humanity – sees them as norm-creating, substantive in nature and based on a comparative analysis of domestic laws.

Simma and Alston have suggested that General Principles go further than only founding crimes against humanity and could be viewed as the source of *jus cogens* norms:

> [T]he truth of the matter may very well be that *jus cogens* is not international custom as defined in the ICJ Statute at all. The customary law-making process may well be unable to provide logical and sound devices to identify peremptory norms of abstention. Such norms do not (and simply cannot) result from a gradual accretion of State practice eventually accepted as law. Rather, what we witness here is the express articulation of principles in the first instance, *ab initio* or progressively being 'accepted and recognized' as binding and peremptory by the 'international community of States as a whole'. This process does not – or not yet – lead to the emergency of customary law but to the formation of 'general principles of law recognized by civilized nations' in the sense of Article 38 of the ICJ Statute.[232]

Although previous arguments that General Principles encompass *jus cogens* norms view Article 38(1)(c) as a natural law source,[233] Simma and Alston deny such a link is necessary. Their conception of *jus cogens* General Principles 'remains grounded in a consensualist conception of international law'.[234] As support for this consent, Simma and Alston would turn to national laws *and* international materials.[235] Even within such a consensualist conception, natural law considerations must remain – the content of *jus cogens* norms is after all what makes them peremptory.

If we accept General Principles as capable of founding norms of *jus cogens* then, for these norms at least, General Principles would take primacy over conventional and customary international law. This is not a view that has enjoyed support in the jurisprudence of the PCIJ and the ICJ.[236]

[230] ibid.

[231] ibid 122–23.

[232] Simma and Alston, 'The Sources of Human Rights Law' (n 202) 104.

[233] See, eg, *South-West Africa Cases (Ethiopia v South Africa; Liberia v South Africa)* (Second Phase) [1966] ICJ Rep 4 (Dissenting Opinion of Judge Tanaka).

[234] Simma and Alston, 'The Sources of Human Rights Law' (n 202) 105.

[235] ibid 105.

[236] Save for Judge Fernandes and Judge Cançado Trindade: *Right of Passage over Indian Territory (Portugal v India)* (Merits) [1960] ICJ Rep 6, 135 (Dissenting Opinion of Judge Fernandes); *Pulp Mills on the River Uruguay (Argentina v Uruguay)* (Merits) [2010] ICJ Rep 14, para 39 (Separate Opinion of Judge Cançado Trindade).

8

Global General Principles

AS HAS BEEN foreshadowed, the study of General Principles invites discussion of a more global consideration of the issues involved. This is for two reasons. First, there is a greater and growing understanding of the need to discuss models of law outside the traditional bounds that classically make up public international law.[1] Concepts such as the Westphalian model of nation states, and the historical focus on civil and common law systems (both by the Advisory Committee of Jurists itself,[2] and in the application of Article 38(1)(c) by the Permanent Court of International Justice (PCIJ) and the International Court of Justice (ICJ) and other courts and tribunals[3]) must be reconciled with notions of customary or chthonic law that usurp nation-state hierarchies and the reality of a multi-legal system world.[4] Although calls for the recognition of the universality of international law are not new, the embrace of non-Western, non-traditional legal systems has been slow. Thus, although Jennings wrote in 1985 of the 'the imperative need to develop international law to comprehend within itself the rich diversity of cultures, civilizations and legal traditions',[5] recognition of diverse cultures by the ICJ is scarce[6] (although there are instances of such recognition in Separate and Dissenting Opinions).[7]

[1] W Twining, *General Jurisprudence* (Cambridge University Press, 2009) 5–7.

[2] See ch 2: the work of the Advisory Committee was praised by H Lauterpacht for its 'compromise which honours equally the representatives of both Continental and British-American jurisprudence': H Lauterpacht, *Private Law Sources and Analogies of International Law* (Longmans, Green and Co, 1927) ix.

[3] As demonstrated in chs 3–6 of this work.

[4] Twining, *General Jurisprudence* (n 1) 5–7; HP Glenn, *Legal Traditions of the World*, 2nd edn (Oxford University Press, 2004) 69.

[5] R Jennings, 'Universal International Law in a Multicultural World' in TMC Asser Instituut (ed), *International Law and the Grotian Heritage: A Commemorative Colloquium on the Occasion of the Fourth Centenary of the Birth of Hugo Grotius* (TMC Asser Instituut, 1985) 195.

[6] Exceptions include a brief mention of Islam in *United States Diplomatic and Consular Staff in Tehran (United States of America v Iran)* (Merits) [1980] ICJ Rep 3,40.

[7] eg *North Sea Continental Shelf (Federal Republic of Germany v Denmark; Federal Republic of Germany v Netherlands)* (Merits) [1969] ICJ Rep 3, 140 (Separate Opinion of Judge Ammoun) (*North Sea Continental Shelf*); *Aegean Sea Continental Shelf Case (Greece v Turkey)* (Jurisdiction) [1978] ICJ Rep 3, 57 (Separate Opinion of Judge Tarazi); *United States Diplomatic and Consular Staff in Tehran (United States of America v Iran)* (Merits) (n 6) (Separate Opinion of Judge Tarazi); *Arbitral Award of 31 July 1989 (Guinea-Bissau v Senegal)* (Merits) [1991] ICJ Rep 53, 109 (Dissenting Opinion of Judge Weeramantry); *Maritime Delimitation in the Area between Greenland and Jan Mayen (Denmark v Norway)* (Merits) [1993] ICJ Rep 38, 38, fn 2 (Separate Opinion of

Further, even in recent forums, such as the International Criminal Tribunal for the Former Yugoslavia (ICTY), comparative study of legal systems mostly still retains a Western focus.[8] The need to focus on diverse legal systems is supported by third-world approaches to international law (TWAIL)[9] and the recent spread of jurisprudence examining the globalisation or internationalisation of international law.[10]

Second, and more specifically, Article 38(1)(c) itself has always invited study of various legal systems of the world. By expanding such study outside the 'Concert of Europe'[11] we can 'take cognizance of the forced Westernisation of the non-Western world'.[12] Indeed, using General Principles as a truly global source of law will go some way to responding to Emmanuelle Jouannet's criticisms of the Western universality of international law, allowing embrace of the cross-cultural values she identifies:

> Certain values can indeed 'correspond to general characteristics of human beings', thus expressing not merely a cultural, but an anthropological human identity. The dignity of the person, the experience of freedom, the ideal of cooperation are thus common across all cultures, as many of the major historians of cultures and civilizations have remarked; we can find them in medieval Islam just as in the China of Confucius. Different cultures simply have different intellectual or institutional means of expressing and operationalizing them: there exist, for example, many different ways of living the dignity of the person, or of guaranteeing the enjoyment of freedom or equality.[13]

Judge Weeramantry) (*Greenland and Jan Mayen*); *Gabčíkovo-Nagymaros Project (Hungary v Slovakia)* (Merits) [1997] ICJ Rep 7, 107 (Separate Opinion of Judge Weeramantry) (*Gabčíkovo-Nagymaros Project*); *Aerial Incident of 10 August 1999 (Pakistan v India)* (Jurisdiction) [2000] ICJ Rep 12, 57 (Dissenting Opinion of Judge Al-Khasawneh).

[8] See discussion in ch 6.

[9] For an overview of third-world approaches to international law, see JT Gathii, 'The Agenda of Third World Approaches to International Law (TWAIL)' in J Dunoff and M Pollack (eds), *International Legal Theory: Foundations and Frontiers* (Cambridge University Press, forthcoming) available at SSRN at https://ssrn.com/abstract=3304767. See further, eg, BS Chimni, 'Customary International Law: A Third World Perspective' (2018) 112(1) *American Journal of International Law* 1; L Eslava, M Fakhri and V Nesiah (eds), *Bandung, Global History and International Law: Critical Pasts and Pending Futures* (Cambridge University Press, 2017). Though note that recent works on sources of international law have been criticised for a failure to take such approaches into account. See, eg, GF Amin, 'Letter to the Journal: A Marxist and TWAIL Reading of the Oxford Handbook of the Sources of International Law' (2020) 19(1) *Chinese Journal of International Law* 183.

[10] See, eg, A Roberts, *Is International Law International?* (Oxford University Press, 2017); JJ Heckman, RL Nelson and L Cabatingan (eds), *Global Perspectives on the Rule of Law* (Routledge-Cavendish, 2010); C Antons (ed), *Traditional Knowledge, Traditional Cultural Expressions, and Intellectual Property Law in the Asia-Pacific Region* (Kluwer Law International, 2009); Twining, *General Jurisprudence* (n 1); AA An-Na'im, 'Globalization and Jurisprudence: An Islamic Law Perspective' (2005) 54 *Emory Law Journal* 25; PS Berman (ed), *The Globalisation of International Law* (Taylor and Francis, 2005); S Zifcak (ed), *Globalisation and the Rule of Law* (Routledge, 2005); CG Weeramantry, *Universalising International Law* (Martinus Nijhoff, 2004); Glenn, *Legal Traditions* (n 4); W Twining, *Globalisation and Legal Theory* (Cambridge University Press, 2000).

[11] *North Sea Continental Shelf* (n 7) 135 (Separate Opinion of Judge Ammoun).

[12] E Jouannet, 'Universalism and Imperialism: The True-False Paradox of International Law?' (2007) 18(3) *European Journal of International Law* 379, 406–07.

[13] ibid 403.

General Principles, once properly understood, can play a role in larger discussions on globalisation, universality and hegemony of international law. In this context, Dianne Otto argues international law needs to be critically viewed in a transformative manner to 'develop a more contextually-responsive, open-ended and ethically-accountable legal order',[14] and that General Principles are examples of such 'contextually-determined legal standards'.[15] However, to do this, General Principles *must* be truly global in nature, not simply products of Western thought.

The purpose of this chapter is two-fold. The first aim is to identify types of legal systems different from those usually considered in General Principles analysis, and consider how such systems fit with conceptions of General Principles. Second, this chapter looks to jurisprudence and commentary: both from the systems themselves on General Principles, and international jurisprudence that draws on these systems to establish General Principles.

It must be noted from the outset that there are important qualifiers and limitations to this chapter. This is a broad-brush approach to these issues, aimed at sketching an outline rather than comprehensively addressing the legal systems. The amount of jurisprudence alone makes any comprehensive survey well beyond the bounds of this work. As Twining puts it:

> Students coming to Jurisprudence for the first time are often bewildered and daunted by the disorderly profusion of our heritage of legal thought … One leading British student work discusses the ideas of over 100 thinkers, yet in the Preface to the seventh edition the author apologises for not finding room for many other significant figures. On examination it becomes obvious that the work is focused almost entirely on modern Western, mainly Anglo-American, theorising about law. The index does not mention Hindu, Islamic, or Jewish jurisprudence and there are only passing references to Chinese, Japanese, Latin American and African traditions. So this presents only part of the total picture of the heritage of legal theory.[16]

Second, analysis is limited to texts published in English. Many of the texts discussing these issues from non-Western perspectives are inaccessible to this monolingual author. Accordingly, this chapter does not set out to be an exhaustive or comprehensive analysis of global views of international law or of General Principles. Rather it is a stepping stone, to bridge the excellent work being done in these spaces with the discussion of sources, where it is often absent. It argues that 'different' legal systems can, and should, be taken into account when considering General Principles. It is hoped it will act as a springboard for others to take this work forward.

[14] D Otto, 'Rethinking the "Universality" of Human Rights Law' (1997) 29 *Columbia Human Rights Law Review* 1, 43.

[15] ibid 43–44.

[16] Twining, *General Jurisprudence* (n 1) 10; Twining was referring to MDA Freeman, *Lloyd's Introduction to Jurisprudence*, 7th edn (Sweet & Maxwell, 2001) Preface.

I. TYPES OF LEGAL SYSTEMS

The categorisation of the world's legal systems is fluid, and depends on the author's place, both geographically and in history. While some legal systems, such as common, civil and Islamic law, have been consistently identified by studies over the past 40 years,[17] others have either fallen out of favour and political reality (such as the Socialist legal system)[18] or have only been recognised recently (such as chthonic legal systems).[19] In his extensive work on the legal traditions of the world, H Patrick Glenn identifies seven different legal systems – chthonic, Talmudic, civil law, Islamic, common law, Hindu and Asian.[20] Given the focus of much of international law on common and civil law systems, these will not be addressed in this chapter. The five other types of systems will be discussed in turn, broadly grouped into three categories – chthonic, religious (Talmudic, Islamic and Hindu) and Asian legal systems.[21]

A. Chthonic Legal Systems

Glenn uses the term 'chthonic' to identify the traditional or customary legal systems used by indigenous societies.[22] A chthonic legal system is characterised by being the law of people 'who live ecological lives by being chthonic, which means that they live in or in close harmony with the earth'.[23] There are many different chthonic societies in the world, with chthonic groups existing on every inhabited continent. Despite the large number of groups, and the variety within them, there are some features common to chthonic legal systems.

First, the systems focus on orality of law, often with an express rejection of formalisation.[24] Because of the focus on orality, the law is shared among the people: 'The law is vested in a repository in which all, or most, share and

[17] See, eg, D Brierly, *Major Legal Systems* (Stevens and Sons, 1968); R David and D Brierly, *Major Legal Systems in the World Today*, 2nd edn (Free Press, 1978); RA Danner and M-LH Bernal (eds), *Introduction to Foreign Legal Systems* (Oceana Publications, 1994); K Zweigert and H Kötz, *An Introduction to Comparative Law*, 3rd edn (Clarendon Press, 1998); Glenn, *Legal Traditions* (n 4); JN Hazard, 'The General Principles of International Law' (1958) 52(1) *The American Journal of International Law* 91.

[18] Much room was devoted to Socialist Law in texts of the 1950s, 1960s and 1970s. See Hazard, 'The General Principles of International Law' (n 17), 92, 94-96; Brierly, *Major Legal Systems* (n 17) 119–224; David and Brierly, *Major Legal Systems in the World Today* (n 17) 143–280.

[19] Glenn, *Legal Traditions* (n 4) 59–91.

[20] See generally Glenn, *Legal Traditions* (n 4).

[21] This is of course not the only grouping of legal systems or families, but it serves the purpose of this chapter. For an overview of different groupings, see N Jain, 'Comparative International Law at the ICTY: The General Principles Experiment' (2015) 109(3) *American Journal of International Law* 486, 490–92.

[22] Glenn, *Legal Traditions* (n 4) 59. It should be noted that Glenn has reservations as to the use of the words 'indigenous', 'aboriginals' and 'natives' to refer to these groups of people.

[23] ibid 60.

[24] ibid 62.

in which all, or most, may participate.'[25] Those laws that are formalised are mostly done by non-chthonic people.[26] Second, the systems have very few formal structures, although usually a council of elders or sometimes a chief will speak with greater authority.[27] Finally, chthonic law cannot be divorced from all other aspects of chthonic life:

> Chthonic law is thus inextricably interwoven with all the beliefs of chthonic people and is inevitably, and profoundly, infused with all those other beliefs. If there is chthonic law, and there is, you cannot understand it without understanding other things. There is no separation of law and morals, no separation of law and anything else.[28]

This totality of law and society means traditional Western analyses of chthonic legal systems can be flawed, relying on 'basic colonialist assumptions about the nature of law in Indigenous communities'.[29] Western positivist conceptions of legal systems are often not compatible with chthonic legal systems. One example of this is Hart's requirement of a 'rule of change' inherent in the secondary rules of legal systems,[30] a notion Glenn argues is contrary to the 'fundamental legal and moral duty of chthonic law to change nothing in the life of the world'.[31]

Many chthonic legal systems are in fact *hybrid* legal systems (linked but not limited to the effects of colonisation)[32] – for example, the legal system of Afghanistan includes secular, religious and chthonic aspects;[33] similarly, Nigeria's legal system consists of customary, Islamic and common law;[34] customary (chthonic) law and civil law operate side by side in many former French colonies in Africa such as Togo, Benin and Mauritius;[35] although South Africa is considered a common law country, indigenous law is still recognised;[36] within the common law system of Canada, First Nations Law is used as a source of law.[37]

[25] ibid 63.

[26] ibid 63.

[27] ibid 63; but compare the use of customary tribunals in Afghanistan: A Senier, 'Rebuilding the Judicial Sector in Afghanistan: The Role of Customary Law' [2006] *Al Naklah: The Fletcher School Online Journal for issues related to Southwest Asia and Islamic Civilization* 1, 2.

[28] Glenn, *Legal Traditions* (n 4) 69.

[29] C Cunneen and M Schwartz, 'Customary Law, Human Rights and International Law: Some Conceptual Issues' (2005) *Law Reform Commission of Western Australia Background Paper No 11*, 430.

[30] HLA Hart, *The Concept of Law*, 2nd edn (Clarendon Press, 1994) 95.

[31] HP Glenn, 'Doin' the Transsystemic: Legal Systems and Legal Traditions' (2005) 50 *McGill Law Journal* 863, 888.

[32] W Menski, *Comparative Law in a Global Context: The Legal Systems of Asia and Africa*, 2nd edn (Cambridge University Press, 2006) 116.

[33] Senier, 'Rebuilding the Judicial Sector in Afghanistan' (n 27) 1.

[34] AA Oba, 'Religious and Customary Laws in Nigeria' (2011) 25(2) *Emory International Law Review* 881, 882.

[35] MW Prinsloo, 'Recognition and Application of Indigenous Law in Francophone Africa' (1993) 2 *Journal of South African Law* 189, 195–96.

[36] B Harris, 'Indigenous Law in South Africa – Lessons for Australia' (1998) 5 *James Cook University Law Review* 70, 79.

[37] J Borrows, *Recovering Canada: The Resurgence of Indigenous Law* (University of Toronto Press, 2002) 5.

B. Religious Legal Systems

There are three major religion-based legal systems in the world – Talmudic, Islamic and Hindu. All three share certain characteristics, and similarities are particularly strong between the Talmudic and Islamic systems, given their common Abrahamic roots.[38] As with chthonic law, most modern applications of religious systems are pluralistic – for example, common law, Hindu law and Islamic law all operate in India;[39] Israel has secular and Talmudic courts;[40] similarly, Malaysia has both secular and Islamic courts;[41] and, as noted in the preceding section, within Nigeria some states are governed by secular law and others by Islamic law.[42] Other countries, such as Pakistan and Saudi Arabia, have primarily Islamic legal systems.[43] The following is by necessity a brief summary of the broad structure of the three major religious systems.

The basic structure of all the systems is a core set of laws that are divinely inspired. In the Talmudic tradition, this is the first five books of the Hebrew Bible, believed to be the word of God as revealed to Moses, the written *Torah*.[44] In the Islamic tradition, the core set of laws is the *Koran*, believed to be the word of God given directly to the Prophet Muhammad.[45] In the Hindu system, the revelatory text is the *Vedas*,[46] although the identity of who the content was revealed to is unknown.[47]

Following this base text, the systems diverge somewhat. In the Talmudic and Islamic traditions, oral interpretations of the divinely inspired laws were developed. In the Talmudic system, an oral tradition of interpretations of the *Torah* developed over many years.[48] It is believed this tradition began with explanations given by Moses of the revelations in the *Torah*, which were then passed

[38] LA Bambach, 'The Enforceability of Arbitration Decisions made by Muslim Religious Tribunals: Examining the Beth Din Precedent' (2010) 25(2) *Journal of Law and Religion* 379, 380; Oba, 'Religious and Customary Laws in Nigeria' (n 34) 884.

[39] J Goodman, 'Divine Judgment: Judicial Review of Religious Legal Systems in India and Israel' (2009) 32(2) *Hastings International and Comparative Law Review* 477, 483. While Hindu personal laws have been codified to certain extents, Islamic personal laws have largely not been: A Malhotra and R Malhotra, 'Family Law and Religion – The Indian Experience' in BN Patel (ed), *India and International Law*, vol 2 (Martinus Nijhoff, 2008) 487, 489.

[40] A Scolnicov, 'Religious Laws, Religious Courts and Human Rights within Israeli Constitutional Structure' (2006) 4(4) *International Journal of Constitutional Law* 732, 735.

[41] Goodman, 'Divine Judgment' (n 39) 483.

[42] Scolnicov, 'Religious Laws' (n 40) 735.

[43] M Lau, *The Role of Islam in the Legal System of Pakistan* (Martinus Nijhoff, 2006) 211; FE Vogel, *Islamic Law and Legal System: Studies of Saudi Arabia* (Brill, 2000) 3.

[44] Glenn, *Legal Traditions* (n 4) 93; JR Wegner 'Islamic and Talmudic Jurisprudence: The Four Roots of Islamic Law and their Talmudic Counterparts' (1982) 26(1) *American Journal of Legal History* 25, 25.

[45] Glenn, *Legal Traditions* (n 4) 171; Zweigert and Kötz, *An Introduction to Comparative Law* (n 17) 305.

[46] L Rocher, 'Hindu Conceptions of Law' (1978) 29 *Hastings Law Journal* 1283, 1292.

[47] Glenn, *Legal Traditions* (n 4) 274.

[48] Wegner, 'Islamic and Talmudic Jurisprudence' (n 44) 25.

down orally throughout the Jewish people.[49] This oral tradition was finally formalised into writing, and is now referred to as the *Mishnah*.[50] In the Islamic system, the interpretation of the *Koran* stems from the Prophet Muhammad, and the explanations given by him of the *Koran*, known as the *Sunna*.[51] As with the *Mishnah*, the *Sunna* was passed down through generations of Islamic people in an oral tradition.[52] The final part of the Islamic and Talmudic traditions is a third layer of interpretation. Unlike the first two layers, which maintain direct links with divine inspiration or divine messengers, the third level of interpretation recognised is based on the teachings of humans. In the Talmudic system, interpretations of the *Mishnah* were recorded in the form of commentaries. Two separate commentaries were recorded, and they are known as the Jerusalem and Babylonian *Talmud*.[53] The study of Talmudic law then encompasses the *Torah*, the *Mishnah* and the *Talmud*.[54] In the Islamic system, this third level of interpretation is known as the *ijma*, or doctrinal consensus.[55] The totality of Islamic law, known as the *Shari'ah*, consists of the study of the *Koran*, the *Sunna* and *ijma*,[56] and a fourth level known as *qiyas* (or *kiyas*) – the method of reasoning by analogy, creating new rules based on established rules in the first three sources.[57] These are commonly considered to be the four roots of Islamic law.[58] It is argued that there is also a fourth level to Talmudic law, the *heqqes*, also a method of reasoning by analogy, equivalent to the Islamic *qiyas*.[59]

In the Hindu system, the *Vedas* themselves do not identify a specific author (gods or God) or messenger.[60] Interpretations of the *Vedas* first took the form of *sultras*, or *sutras*, developed by Brahman priests, and written texts on law called the *sastras*.[61] The texts of the *sultras* and *sastras* together are known as the *Smriti*,[62] and have an analogous position and authority to that of the

[49] Glenn, *Legal Traditions* (n 4) 94.

[50] DM Feldman, 'The Structure of Jewish Law' in MP Golding (ed), *Jewish Law and Legal Theory* (Dartmouth Publishing Co, 1994) 21, 22; Glenn, *Legal Traditions* (n 4) 95.

[51] Glenn, *Legal Traditions* (n 4) 173–74.

[52] ibid 174; Wegner, 'Islamic and Talmudic Jurisprudence' (n 44) 30.

[53] Feldman, 'The Structure of Jewish Law' (n 50) 23–24; Glenn, *Legal Traditions* (n 4) 95.

[54] M Elon, 'The Legal System of Jewish Law' (1985) 17 *International Law and Politics* 221, 228.

[55] Glenn, *Legal Traditions* (n 4) 174; Zweigert and Kötz, *An Introduction to Comparative Law* (n 17) 308.

[56] Glenn, *Legal Traditions* (n 4) 173.

[57] Zweigert and Kötz, *An Introduction to Comparative Law* (n 17) 308.

[58] Wegner, 'Islamic and Talmudic Jurisprudence' (n 44) 30; BJ Theutenberg, 'Sharia and International Law – the Need of Dialogue' (*Legal Traditions of the World: The concept of Human Rights and its legal implementation – the Arab experience*, Seminar given at the Swedish Institute, Alexandira, November 2006) available at www.theutenberg.se/pdf/LEGAL_TRADITIONS_OF_THE_WORLD.pdf 10.

[59] Wegner, 'Islamic and Talmudic Jurisprudence' (n 44) 31.

[60] Glenn, *Legal Traditions* (n 4) 274.

[61] ibid 275.

[62] VP Nanda and SP Sinha, 'Introduction' in VP Nanda and SP Sinha (eds), *Hindu Law and Legal Theory* (New York University Press, 1996) xi, xiii.

Mishnah and the *Sunna* in the Talmudic and Islamic traditions.[63] Unlike the *Mishnah* and the *Sunna*, however, it is not claimed that the *Smriti* are divine in origination; rather, they are the memories of the sages who heard the divine revelation.[64] Finally, on the third level analogous to the *Talmud* or the *ijma*, the Hindu tradition also encompasses commentaries on the *Smriti*. This third level encompasses many commentaries on the various *sastras*, believed to be written over a millennium.[65]

As well as having a similar overriding structure, the three legal systems also share other factors. First, the primary books (the *Torah*, the *Koran* and the *Vedas*) are not written in legalistic manner. The *Koran* and the *Vedas* are both in verse,[66] while the *Torah* is split into five books of verse/prose.[67] Second, although the law for each system is contained within the structures discussed above, each of the texts at every level contains instructions on matters that would not be considered 'law' in the Western sense. The texts include instructions on dietary matters, religious observance and rituals.[68] As with chthonic legal systems, these are interwoven with the more legalistic aspects of the religious legal systems, 'so that it is almost impossible to delve deeply into any topic of the civil law without having recourse to some text or principle concerning matters of ritual'.[69] Third, and importantly for our discussion, the divine nature of the law means that nothing can challenge the content of the primary text. The *Koran* is 'supremely authoritative, unalterable, comprehensive and the source and touchstone of every legal rule'.[70] Further, 'the combination of divine revelation and human reason is the *only* path to law: such systems deny that law can be created … by human legislation'.[71]

C. Asian Legal Systems

Asian legal systems are varied and diverse.[72] Historically, they have often been grouped together as the 'Orient'[73] or the 'Far East',[74] with little discussion as

[63] Glenn, *Legal Traditions* (n 4) 276.

[64] LR Penna, 'Traditional Asian Approaches: An Indian View' (1980) 9 *Australian Yearbook of International Law* 168, 177.

[65] Glenn, *Legal Traditions* (n 4) 277.

[66] ibid 172, 276.

[67] Genesis, Exodus, Leviticus, Numbers and Deuteronomy.

[68] CG Weeramantry, *Islamic Jurisprudence: An International Perspective* (Palgrave Macmillan, 1988) 5; Elon, 'The Legal System of Jewish Law' (n 54) 222.

[69] S Shilo, 'The Contrast between Mishpat Ivri and Halakhah' (1982) 20(2) *Tradition: A Journal of Orthodox Thought* 91, 92; See also Rocher, 'Hindu Conceptions of Law' (n 46) 1286–87.

[70] Weeramantry, *Islamic Jurisprudence* (n 68) 8.

[71] Wegner, 'Islamic and Talmudic Jurisprudence' (n 44) 28.

[72] EA Black and GF Bell, 'Introduction' in EA Black and GF Bell (eds), *Law and Legal Institutions of Asia* (Cambridge University Press, 2011) 1, 4–5.

[73] Hazard, 'The General Principles of International Law' (n 17) 91.

[74] M Bogdan, 'General Principles of Law and the Problem of Lacunae in the Law of Nations' (1977) 46(1) *Nordisk Tidsskrift for International Ret* 37, 46.

to distinctions between them. Many Asian countries have hybrid legal systems, incorporating varying aspects of chthonic, religious and common or civil law legal systems.[75] Malaysia has secular and Islamic courts;[76] similarly, Islamic and secular law sit side by side in the Philippines.[77] In contrast, while Singapore was pluralistic under British rule, since independence it has limited recognition of chthonic and Islamic law.[78]

There are, however, some elements common to Asian legal systems,[79] most notably that they are inherently pluralistic.[80] In particular, there is a need to recognise the coexistence of formal written law and non-formal custom that exists within most Asian legal systems: it is an 'unquestioned fact of life'.[81] This is often traced to the Confucian concepts of *li* and *fa*.[82] *Fa* is formal law, while *li* is its opposite – the 'denial of the lasting and effective normativity of formal concepts'.[83] The existence of *li* has limited the formal structures of law in Asian countries – many areas of law that exist formally in Western countries do not so exist in Asian countries.[84] Areas of civil regulation are instead covered by the tradition of *li* – the unwritten, persuasive norms.[85] It is 'possible to speak both of the normative richness of life in China while at the same time taking note of the episodic and unreliable character of Chinese (formal) laws'.[86] There are different views as to how far these concepts have spread in Asia – while some publicists argue the limits on formalism are true of all Asian systems,[87] others argue that there is no such thing as a 'Far Eastern Asian Family',[88] and that some countries, such as Japan, are closer to Western legal systems.[89] Nevertheless, any understanding of Asian legal systems must embrace the unwritten along with the written.

[75] Glenn, *Legal Traditions* (n 4) 301; JV Feinerman, 'Introduction to Asian Legal Systems' in RA Danner and MH Bernal (eds), *Introduction to Foreign Legal Systems* (Oceana, 1994) 95, 97, 119–20; Black and Bell, *Law and Legal Institutions of Asia* (n 72) 5.

[76] Goodman, 'Divine Judgment' (n 39) 483.

[77] J Holbrook, 'Legal Hybridity in the Philippines: Lessons in Legal Pluralism from Mindanao and the Sulu Archipelago' (2010) 18 *Tulane Journal of International and Comparative Law* 403, 407–08; MO Mastura, 'Legal Pluralism in the Philippines' (1994) 28(3) *Law and Society Review* 461, 463.

[78] GF Bell, 'Multiculturalism in Law is Legal Pluralism: Lessons from Indonesia, Singapore and Canada' (2006) 2 *Singapore Journal of Legal Studies* 315, 326.

[79] Glenn, *Legal Traditions* (n 4) 308.

[80] AES Tay and P-L Tan, 'Legal Pluralism in East-Asia: Diversity, Unity, Universality' in P-L Tan (ed), *Asian Legal Systems* (Butterworths, 1997) 390, 397.

[81] ibid.

[82] J deLisle, 'China's Approach to International Law: A Historical Perspective' (2000) 94 *Proceedings of the Annual Meeting (American Society of International Law)* 267, 268–69.

[83] Glenn, *Legal Traditions* (n 4) 305.

[84] ibid 309.

[85] ibid 310–11; Feinerman, 'Introduction to Asian Legal Systems' (n 75) 101.

[86] Glenn, *Legal Traditions* (n 4) 310.

[87] ibid 309.

[88] Zweigert and Kötz, *An Introduction to Comparative Law* (n 17) 287.

[89] ibid 299.

II. PERSPECTIVES ON GENERAL PRINCIPLES

The purpose of this section is to identify specific intersections between the legal systems set out in section I and General Principles that may differ from intersections in common and civil law legal systems. While exploring such differences is valuable, it is a mistake to position these legal systems in *opposition* to modern international law. As scholars from these systems emphasise, the Grotian idea of international law is itself Eurocentric:[90] 'ancient cultures hailed basically the same principles, or perhaps rather ideas, that are purported to have been invented by the occidental world'.[91] Thus, as argued by Pemmaraju Rao, 'States belonging to different regions of the world, irrespective of the cultural traditions they symbolize, subscribe to the same basic principles of international law.'[92] Nonetheless, the fact remains that the legal systems discussed in this chapter are often *not* used by courts when determining General Principles: this section sets out ways they *could* be.

A. Chthonic Systems

i. Intersection between Chthonic Systems and International Law

The lack of formality inherent within chthonic systems results in a lack of formal jurisprudential analysis of international law generally, or General Principles specifically within chthonic systems themselves. There is legal scholarship, however, on the interaction of chthonic systems with international law from an external perspective.[93] By examining this scholarship, it becomes clear that chthonic law intersects with international law in several key areas, all related to the fundamental link between chthonic legal systems and the environment. The first area is the protection of the environment in international environmental law, especially in notions of sustainable development.[94] The second is chthonic land rights as part of property rights at international law, and the third is the intersection between chthonic traditional knowledge of biodiversity and plant

[90] N Singh, *India and International Law* (S Chand and Co, 1969) 1–3; Theutenberg, 'Sharia and International Law – the Need of Dialogue' (n 58) 6–7.

[91] BJ Theutenberg, 'Different Trends of the International Legal System of Today' in R Dupey (ed), *The Future of International Law in a Multicultural World* (Martinus Nijhoff, 1984) 261, 265.

[92] PS Rao, 'The Indian Position on Some General Principles of International Law' in BN Patel (ed), *India and International Law*, vol 1 (Martinus Nijhoff, 2005) 33, 33.

[93] See, eg, Antons, *Traditional Knowledge* (n 10); EC Kamau and G Winter (eds), *Genetic Resources, Traditional Knowledge and the Law: Solutions for Access and Benefit Sharing* (Earthscan, 2009).

[94] B Richardson, 'Indigenous Peoples, International Law and Sustainability' (2001) 10 *Review of European Community and International Environmental Law* 1; G Maggio, 'Recognising the Vital Role of Local Communities in International Legal Instruments for Conserving Biodiversity' (1998) 16 *UCLA Journal of Environmental Law and Policy* 179.

resources and intellectual property protection at international law.[95] It is in these areas where chthonic systems could hold great value for the development of General Principles.

ii. Chthonic Legal Systems and 'Nations'

The incorporation of chthonic legal systems into our understanding of Article 38(1)(c) faces a challenge in their compatibility with the phrase 'recognized by civilized nations'. Chthonic legal systems are not the legal systems of nations. Rather, chthonic groups exist within nation states, sometimes with different chthonic groups within the one state,[96] and in other cases one chthonic group existing over national borders.[97] To add to this difficulty, there is also the reality that all chthonic groups today are integrated, to some extent, into the legal system of the nation state in which they are located: 'There are now no chthonic peoples in the world who do not live within a state, which is a non-chthonic construction.'[98] Chthonic societies are thus integrated into wide pluralistic legal traditions. This leaves us with two questions: first, can a model of General Principles look beyond the laws of nation states to the legal systems of peoples *within* those states? And, second, on a practical note, how can we find the principles in chthonic legal systems, given the orality and non-formality of chthonic systems themselves, and the integration of chthonic groups into the formal structures of modern nation states?

Both of these questions can be answered in part by re-visiting the judgment of Judge Weeramantry in his separate decision in *Gabčíkovo-Nagymaros Project*.

[95] B Tobin, 'The Role of Customary Law and Practice in the Protection of Traditional Knowledge Related to Biological Diversity' in Antons (ed), *Traditional Knowledge* (n 10) 127; S Munzer and K Raustiala, 'The Uneasy Case for Intellectual Property Rights in Traditional Knowledge' (2009) 27 *Cardozo Arts and Entertainment Law Journal* 37; T McClellan, 'The Role of International Law in protecting the Traditional Knowledge and Plant Life of Indigenous Peoples' (2001) 19 *Wisconsin International Law Journal* 249; S Pritchard and C Heindow-Dolman, 'Indigenous Peoples and International Law: A Critical Overview' (1998) 3(4) *Australian Indigenous Law Reporter* 473.

[96] For example, the Sami people in Norway, Sweden, Finland and Russia: M Fitzmaurice, 'The Sami People: Current Issues Facing and Indigenous People in the Nordic Region' (1997) 8 *Finnish Yearbook of International Law* 200, 200; Khoe and San people across Angola, Botswana, Namibia, South Africa, Zambia and Zimbabwe, Ju'hoansi in Botswana and Namibia: RK Hitchcock and D Vinding, 'Introduction' in RK Hitchcock and D Vinding (eds), *Indigenous Peoples' Rights in Southern Africa* (International Work Group for Indigenous Affairs, 2004) 8, 9; Haudenosaunee Native Americans in Canada and the United States of America: CYA Trujano, *Indigenous Routes: A Framework of Understanding Indigenous Migration* (International Organization for Migration, 2008) 41; Kumeyaay, Cocopah, Tohono O'odham, Yaqui, Gila River Pima, Yavapai, Ysleta del Sur (Tira) and Kickapoo tribes on the US-Mexican border: S Singleton, 'Not our borders: Indigenous People and the Struggle to Maintain Shared Lives and Cultures in post-9/11 North America' (2009) *Border Policy Research Institute Working Paper No 4*, fn 3.

[97] eg the Ju'Hoansi, Himba, Khoe and San in Namibia: Hitchcock and Vinding, *Indigenous Peoples' Rights in Southern Africa* (n 96) 9; The First Nations, Métis and Inuit in Canada: Government of Canada, 'Indigenous People and Communities', available at www.aadnc-aandc.gc.ca/eng/1100100013785/1304467449155, accessed 11 August 2020.

[98] Glenn, *Legal Traditions* (n 4) 80.

As discussed in chapter 5, Weeramantry found that sustainable development was a General Principle, and rested that on traditional practices.[99] Weeramantry argued that the orality of what he called 'living law' does not deprive those systems of the quality of law:

> By virtue of its representation of the main forms of civilization, this Court constitutes a unique forum for the reflection and the revitalization of those global legal traditions. There were principles ingrained in these civilizations as well as embodied in their *legal systems*, for legal systems include not merely written legal systems but traditional legal systems as well, which modern researchers have shown to be no less legal systems than their written cousins, and in some respects even more sophisticated and finely tuned than the latter.[100]

He further argued that Article 38(1)(c) 'expressly opened a door to the entry of such principles into modern international law'.[101] It is clear from the work of the Committee of Jurists that the inclusion of Article 38(1)(c) in the Statute of the PCIJ was not intended to authorise judicial use of chthonic legal systems[102] – indeed, during that period of active colonisation and Western expansion, recognition of chthonic legal systems as law was not a reality.[103] A better argument may be that our understanding of the phase 'recognized by civilized nations' should reflect a twenty-first-century view of international law and global politics, rather than an early twentieth century one. Just as the word 'civilized' has been implicitly dropped (or at the least made redundant, as all nations are now considered 'civilized')[104] from the understanding of Article 38(1)(c), we can argue Weeramantry's point: that a modern understanding of international law does not restrict itself only to the laws of nation states, and that the lack of formality surrounding chthonic legal systems does not rob them of validity as law.

This can be supported by reference to the growing recognition of non-state actors in international law.[105] As non-governmental organisations (NGOs) are accepted more and more as participants in the international legal system,[106]

[99] *Gabčíkovo-Nagymaros Project* (n 7) 107–08 (Separate Opinion of Judge Weeramantry).

[100] ibid 109.

[101] ibid 110.

[102] See ch 2.

[103] N Lerner, *Group Rights and Discrimination in International Law*, 2nd edn (Martinus Nijhoff, 2003) 29.

[104] A Pellet and D Müller, 'Article 38 ' in A Zimmerman, CJ Tams, K Oellers-Frahm and C Tomuschat (eds), *The Statute of the International Court of Justice: A Commentary*, 3rd edn (Oxford University Press, 2019) 819, 927.

[105] See generally RA Higgot, GRD Underhill and A Bieler (eds), *Non-State Actors and Authority in the Global System* (Routledge, 2003). See also H Charlesworth, 'The Unbearable Lightness of Customary International Law' (1998) 92 *American Society of International Law Proceedings* 44, 45–47; AM Banks, 'The Growing Impact of Non-State Actors on the International and European Legal System' (2003) 5(4) *International Law Forum du Droit International* 293, 294.

[106] See, eg, the role of NGOs in the formation of the Convention on the Prohibition of the Use, Stockpiling, Production and Transfer of Anti-Personnel Mines and on their Destruction (signed 18 September 1997, entered into force 3 March 1999) 2056 UNTS 211: K Anderson, 'The Ottawa Convention Banning Landmines, the Role of International Non-governmental Organizations and the Idea of International Civil Society' (2000) 11 *European Journal of International Law* 91, 92.

the traditional Westphalian conceptions of international law are increasingly challenged. It is no longer nation states that are the only bodies who can contribute to the development of international law. Within this transnational system, it can be argued that there is also room for the recognition of non-state (chthonic) law and legal traditions within international law. This recognition operates in the context of 20 years of international legal recognition of the rights of chthonic people in the form of the Convention concerning Indigenous and Tribal Peoples in Independent Countries,[107] as well as a growing field of jurisprudence recognising the significance of non-state law in international law.[108]

However, to recognise such contributions to the international legal system, we also need to be able to recognise chthonic traditions as law – that is, to agree with Judge Weeramantry that the lack of formalism inherent in these systems does not deprive those systems of the quality of law. While this concept would not have been easily accepted by the drafters of the Statute of the PCIJ, in the modern world it is clear that there is ongoing recognition of the validity of chthonic legal systems. This is shown by the recognition of indigenous courts by domestic legal systems of states,[109] and by the recognition of traditional land, hunting and gathering and fishing rights.[110] Another example of recognition of traditional practices as law is seen Latin American states such as Argentina, which recognises unwritten traditional legal practices as a source of law,[111] provided they fulfil certain criteria.[112] These criteria provide a framework to assess chthonic traditions and award some with the validity of law. The factors are constant and uniform operation, generality of operation, duration of operation, public operation of the custom, government tolerance of the custom and a general conviction that the practice is a legal rule that must be followed.[113] These factors are similar to those that have been established in other domestic laws that recognise traditional custom.

The second question is of a more practical nature: if we accept that chthonic legal systems can have the force of law for the purpose of supporting a General Principle, how, in the absence of codification, do we extract the relevant

[107] Convention Concerning Indigenous and Tribal Peoples in Independent Countries (opened for signature 27 June 1989, entered into force 5 September 1991) ILO No 169.

[108] Twining, *General Jurisprudence* (n 1) 362.

[109] For example, the Village Courts in Papua New Guinea and Indian Tribal Courts in the United States of America: GD Westermark, 'Court is an Arrow: Legal Pluralism in Papua New Guinea' (1986) 25(2) *Ethnology* 131; SD O'Conner, 'Lessons from the Third Sovereign: Indian Tribal Courts' (1997) 33(1) *Tulsa Law Journal* 1.

[110] eg *Mabo v Queensland (No 2)* (1995) 175 CLR 1; See generally S Wiessner, 'Rights and Status of Indigenous Peoples: A Global Comparative and International Legal Analysis' (1999) 12 *Harvard Human Rights Journal* 57.

[111] G Savastano, 'Custom as a Source of Law: Argentinean and Comparative Legal Systems' (2009) 15(3) *ILSA Journal of International and Comparative Law* 651.

[112] ibid 654.

[113] ibid 654–55.

principles from these systems? Judge Weeramantry did so by examining the practice of traditional (chthonic) communities:

> In relation to concern for the environment generally, examples may be cited from nearly every traditional system, ranging from Australasia and the Pacific Islands, through Amerindian and African cultures to those of ancient Europe. When Native American wisdom, with its deep love of nature, ordained that no activity affecting the land should be undertaken without giving thought to its impact on the land for seven generations to come; when African tradition viewed the human community as three-fold – past, present and future – and refused to adopt a one-eyed vision of concentration on the present; when Pacific tradition despised the view of land as merchandise that could be bought and sold like a common article of commerce, and viewed land as a living entity which lived and grew with the people and upon whose sickness and death the people like-wise sickened and died; when Chinese and Japanese culture stressed the need for harmony with nature; and when Aboriginal custom, while maximizing the use of all species of plant and animal life, yet decreed that no land should be used by man to the point where it could not replenish itself, these varied cultures were reflecting the ancient wisdom of the human family which the legal systems of the time and the tribe absorbed, reflected and turned into principles whose legal validity cannot be denied.[114]

The evidence Weeramantry presented in support of these principles is mostly written accounts of the chthonic societies, with one example of evidence being given by a member of the chthonic society.[115] It would have been more helpful for the purposes of this analysis if all the practices Weeramantry included were explicitly backed by evidence – the statements in regard to African, Chinese and Japanese culture in the passage above were not substantiated by references in the judgment.[116]

Nevertheless, the judgment provides an example of how to integrate chthonic legal systems into a more traditional assessment of domestic laws. Instead of looking to statutes and case law, as is the case with the domestic laws of nation states, the practices and traditions as evidenced in (often external) documentation of the chthonic societies provide the basis for extraction of principles from these systems. This approach is also seen more briefly in the earlier judgment of Judge Ammoun in *North Sea Continental Shelf*,[117] and in Judge Weeramantry's Separate Opinion in *Greenland and Jan Mayen.*[118]

In *North Sea Continental Shelf*, Judge Ammoun based support for a principle of equity in African customary traditions on academic works on those traditions.[119] In *Greenland and Jan Mayen*, Weeramantry considered equity as a

[114] *Gabčíkovo-Nagymaros Project* (n 7) 107 (Separate Opinion of Judge Weeramantry).
[115] ibid 107, fn 68.
[116] ibid 107.
[117] *North Sea Continental Shelf* (n 7).
[118] *Greenland and Jan Mayen* (n 7).
[119] *North Sea Continental Shelf* (n 7) 141 (Separate Opinion of Judge Ammoun).

General Principle, discussed in chapter 4. He then discussed equity more generally, focusing on the 'justice and fairness that underlies the meaning of equity'.[120] In doing so, he expanded on Judge Ammoun's list of traditional customs, citing 'modern researches in African, Pacific and Amerindian customary law',[121] as well as Australian Aboriginal customary law.[122] In the context of notions of fairness and fair conduct in relation to management of resources, Weeramantry wrote:

> The first illustration of such a broader perspective comes from traditional legal systems such as the African, the Pacific, and the Amerindian, which contained a deeply ingrained respect for the earth, the atmosphere, the lakes and the seas, which the evolving law of the sea can consider with profit. Among Pacific societies, for example, land had metaphysical connotations which prevented it from being seen as a saleable commodity like items of merchandise. Respect for these elemental constituents of the inheritance of succeeding generations dictated rules and attitudes based upon a concept of an equitable sharing which was both horizontal in regard to the present generation and vertical for the benefit of generations yet to come.[123]

Weeramantry drew on academic texts on chthonic societies, as well as on the Australian High Court's decision in *Mabo (No 2)*,[124] as support for these chthonic practices.[125] In his Dissenting Opinion in the *Legality of the Threat or Use of Nuclear Weapons* three years later, Judge Weeramantry once again used reports on chthonic practices as evidence for those practices at international law,[126] although not in the context of a General Principle of law.[127]

B. Religious Legal Systems

i. Intersections between Religious Legal Systems and International Law

Unlike the chthonic legal systems, modern religious legal systems more readily regulate the same conduct as other secular domestic systems. There are Islamic, Talmudic and Hindu laws covering both civil and criminal law issues.[128] Further, the religious legal systems also intersect with issues of human rights and

[120] *Greenland and Jan Mayen* (n 7) 275 (Separate Opinion of Judge Weermantry).
[121] ibid 277.
[122] ibid 276.
[123] ibid 277.
[124] *Mabo v Queensland (No 2)* (1992) 175 CLR 1.
[125] *Greenland and Jan Mayen* (n 7) 276 (Separate Opinion of Judge Weermantry).
[126] *Legality of the Threat or Use of Nuclear Weapons (United Nations)* (Advisory Opinion) [1996] ICJ Rep 226, 480 (Dissenting Opinion of Judge Weeramantry) (*Legality of the Threat or Use of Nuclear Weapons*).
[127] This case is discussed further in section I.B.iii.
[128] See, eg, VP Nanda, 'Marriage and Divorce in India: Conflicting Laws' (1960) 55 *Northwestern University Law Review* 624; BC Wolf, 'Resolving the Conflict between Jewish and Secular Estate Law' (2009) 37 *Hofstra Law Review* 1171.

gender,[129] as well as international issues such as the laws of war and peace.[130] The subject matter of General Principles that could be drawn from these systems is exactly the same as the General Principles that could be drawn from secular domestic legal systems. The personal laws of religious systems, however, have been criticised as incompatible with notions of equality, particularly the rights of women and girls.[131]

ii. Law and Morality

Given that the religious legal systems previously discussed are fundamentally based on texts that dictate morality, does this mean that any general principle based on these systems will be linked to morality – General Principle resting on natural law?

a. Talmudic

A distinction should be made between morality and rituals. In the Talmudic legal system, there is a clear distinction between the civil part of Jewish law – the *halakhah* – and the ritual portion.[132] Within the study of *halakhah*, there also exists the study of Jewish law from a more secular perspective, the *Mishpat Ivri*.[133] It is recognised, however, that within this study, there will always be links back to the ritual aspect of Talmudic law.[134] Jurisprudence has nevertheless been developed fitting Talmudic law into Western conceptions of positivism and natural law.[135] Debate exists among jurists as to these conceptions, and there are competing views within these discussions based on orthodox, conservative and reform perspectives.[136] Accordingly, it is possible to construct the Talmudic system from either a positivist or natural law standpoint, and principles drawn from this system, although ultimately given validity by the *Torah*, will not necessarily be explicitly linked to morality.

[129] VP Nanda, 'Hinduism and Human Rights' in VP Nanda and SP Sinha (eds), 'Hindu Law and Legal Theory' (New York University Press, 1996) 237; Weeramantry, *Islamic Jurisprudence* (n 68) 113–28; YS Kaplan, 'A Father's Consent to the Marriage of his Minor Daughter: Feminism and Multiculturalism in Jewish Law' (2009) 18 *Southern Californian Review of Law and Social Justice* 393.

[130] Singh, *India and International Law* (n 90) 3–4.

[131] CA MacKinnon, 'Sex Equality under the Constitution of India: Problems, Prospects and 'Personal Laws' (2006) 4(2) *International Journal of Constitutional Law* 181, 191–92. Though note that others such as Dianne Otto argue such marginalisation is not limited to cultural relativists: Otto, 'Rethinking the "Universality" of Human Rights Law' (n 14) 14.

[132] Elon, 'The Legal System of Jewish Law' (n 54) 240.

[133] Shilo, 'The Contrast between Mishpat Ivri and Halakhah' (n 69) 93–94.

[134] ibid 92.

[135] AJ Yuter, 'Legal Positivism and Contemporary Halakhic Discourse' in M P Golding (ed), *Jewish Law and Legal Theory* (Dartmouth Publishing Co, 1994) 55; JD Bleich, 'Judaism and Natural Law' in MP Golding (ed), *Jewish Law and Legal Theory* (Dartmouth Publishing Co, 1994) 85; M Silberg, 'Law and Morals in Jewish Jurisprudence' (1961) 75 *Harvard Law Review* 306.

[136] Yuter, 'Legal Positivism' (n 135) 60–61.

b. Hindu

Any distinction between law, religion and morality is less clear-cut in Hindu law: 'in Hinduism, law, religion and all other topics dealt with … are inextricably intertwined'.[137] As with chthonic systems, attempts to force a Western-style separation of law and morals onto Hindu law forces concepts into 'categorizations that are foreign to the Hindu way of thinking'.[138] This very quality of Hindu law was criticised by the Privy Council during the British colonisation of India: 'All these old text books and commentaries are apt to mingle religious and moral considerations, not being positive laws …'[139] The Privy Council thus found the fundamentals of the Hindu legal system incompatible with Western notions of positivist law – any principles drawn from the Hindu legal system will be intrinsically linked to these 'moral and religious considerations'.

c. Islam

The *Shari'ah* is a comprehensive guide to Islamic life: 'it covers *all* areas of life and not simply those which are of interest to state and society'.[140] Some aspects of *Shari'ah* law have been codified, most notably in the Ottoman Empire with the writing of the *Majullah*.[141] This was 'the earliest and most politically authoritative example of an official promulgation of large parts of the *Shari'ah* by the authority of a modern state, thereby transforming *Shari'ah* into positive law in the modern sense of the term'.[142] The provisions of the *Majullah* have been subsequently applied in other civil codes of modern Islamic countries.[143] For those codes, it is possible to extract principles that are given validity from the code itself, purely positivist in nature. As will be seen, however, many judges look back to the original religious texts when considering Islamic law in the international context. When this occurs, the original statements as to the indivisibility of morals and law in *Shari'ah* law will still apply.

For all three systems, however, even if the domestic rule or principle maintains its link to morality, it does not follow that a General Principle will, as the question will be the rule of recognition on the *international* stage. If that is a comparative methodology requiring horizontal generality then the validity of the General Principle is drawn from this requisite generality across legal systems, rather than the underlying rule of recognition within each legal system.

[137] Rocher, 'Hindu Conceptions of Law' (n 46) 1286.
[138] ibid.
[139] *Rao Balwant Singh v Rani Kishori* [1898] UKPC 1, 6.
[140] Zweigert and Kötz, *An Introduction to Comparative Law* (n 17) 304.
[141] AA An-Na'im, 'Globalization and Jurisprudence: An Islamic Law Perspective' (2005) 54 *Emory Law Journal* 25, 46.
[142] ibid.
[143] ibid 47.

iii. Where Should General Principles be Drawn From?

As with chthonic law, the law of the religious systems does not necessarily sit within the traditional nation state boundaries. While certain countries have incorporated parts of religious legal systems in their domestic laws – for example Talmudic law in Israel,[144] and family and inheritance principles from Islamic law in Arabic countries,[145] as well as codification of certain laws, as discussed – their overall legal systems are often hybrids, fused with the laws imposed by colonial powers.[146] Further, religious laws apply to all peoples of that religion, regardless of national boundaries.[147] Any recognition of religious law that only looks to 'religious law or custom officially recognised by sovereign states … would be seriously misleading'.[148]

In incorporating the religious legal systems into any study of general principles, it is thus necessary to look beyond domestic laws, and often to the religious texts themselves. This approach is seen in some of the cases where the ICJ has had recourse to these laws. The earliest, and perhaps best known, of these is the Separate Opinion of Judge Ammoun in *North Sea Continental Shelf*. Ammoun referenced Islamic law, Hindu law and other laws, in support of a General Principle of equity, and this case has been covered in chapter 4 of this work, as well in section II.A on chthonic law in this chapter. In support of the Islamic principles, Judge Ammoun directly referenced verses of the *Koran*, as well as commentaries on the *Koran*: 'the principle of equity manifests itself … in Muslim law … by the Koran and the teaching of the four great jurisconsults of Islam condensed in the Shar'ia'.[149] In contrast, in support of recognition of the principle of equity in Hindu law, Ammoun cited a secondary source, a comparative law work.[150]

Judge Weeramantry revisited this discussion in his Separate Opinion in *Greenland and Jan Mayen*. As discussed in section II.A, Weeramantry expanded the idea of equity to general concepts of justice and fairness, and in particular fair management of resources. Judge Weeramantry referred to principles from Islamic law, with direct reference to verses from the *Koran*,[151] and from Hindu law, with direct reference to the *Bhagavad Gita*, part of the *Smriti*.[152] Weeramantry also referred to Jewish law, but relied on secondary sources rather than the primary religious texts and commentaries.[153]

[144] See generally Elon, 'The Legal System of Jewish Law' (n 54).
[145] Zweigert and Kötz, *An Introduction to Comparative Law* (n 17) 65.
[146] ibid 65.
[147] ibid 313.
[148] Twining, *General Jurisprudence* (n 1) 362.
[149] *North Sea Continental Shelf* (n 7) 140 (Separate Opinion of Judge Ammoun).
[150] ibid.
[151] *Greenland and Jan Mayen* (n 7) fn2 (Separate Opinion of Judge Weeramantry).
[152] ibid fn 3.
[153] ibid fn 2 (Separate Opinion of Judge Weeramantry).

Judge Weeramantry also referenced Hindu, Talmudic and Islamic law in his Dissenting Opinion in the *Legality of the Threat or Use of Nuclear Weapons*. Unlike the *North Sea Continental Shelf* and *Greenland and Jan Mayen* cases, the discussion in this case was not surrounding a General Principle of law. Rather Weeramantry was providing background context for the humanitarian laws of war. Weeramantry made direct reference to the *Torah*,[154] to parts of the *Smriti*[155] and to passages of the *Koran*.[156]

The teachings of Muhammad (part of the *Sunna*) were referred to by Judge Tarazi in his Dissenting Opinion in *United States Diplomatic and Consular Staff in Tehran*.[157] This case is unusual, in that the judgment of the Court also referred (fleetingly) to Islamic law in its judgment:

> [T[he principle of the inviolability of the persons of diplomatic agents and the premises of diplomatic missions is one of the very foundations of this long-established regime [of diplomatic protection], to the evolution of which the traditions of Islam made a substantial contribution.[158]

The judgment of the Court did not expand on these traditions, or give evidence for them. Judge Tarazi revisited the statement in his Opinion, stating:

> I was pleased to note that the Judgment took particular account of the traditions of Islam, which contributed along with others to the elaboration of the rules of contemporary public international law on diplomatic and consular inviolability and immunity.
>
> … Professor Ahmed Rechid of the Istanbul law faculty gave the following account of the inviolability of the envoy in Muslim law:
>
> > 'In Arabia, the person of the ambassador had always been regarded as sacred. Muhammad consecrated this inviolability. Never were ambassadors to Muhammad or to his successors molested. One day, the envoy of a foreign nation, at an audience granted to him by the Prophet, was so bold as to use insulting language. Muhammad said to him: "If you were not an envoy I would have you put to death." The author of the "Siyer" which relates this incident draws from it the conclusion that there is an obligation to respect the person of ambassadors.'
>
> … In a work entitled International Law, published by the Institute of State and Law of the Academy of Sciences of the USSR, the following is to be read on the conduct in the Middle Ages of the Arabs, the bearers of the Islamic faith:
>
> > 'The Arab States, which played an important part in international relations in the Middle Ages (from the 7th century) had well-developed conceptions regarding the Law of Nations, closely linked with religious precepts. The Arabs recognised

[154] *Legality of the Threat or Use of Nuclear Weapons* (n 126) 479 (Dissenting Opinion of Judge Weeramantry).

[155] ibid 480.

[156] ibid 481.

[157] *United States Diplomatic and Consular Staff in Tehran (United States of America v Iran)* (Merits) (n 6).

[158] ibid 40.

the inviolability of Ambassadors and the need for the fulfillment of treaty obligations. They resorted to arbitration to settle international disputes and considered the observance of definite rules of law necessary in time of war ("the blood of women, children and old men shall not besmirch your victory")'.[159]

Tarazi thus relies on direct examples from the religious documents as well as reports of the law and practice of Islamic groups. This approach is also seen in the decision of the Permanent Court of Arbitration (PCA) in *Eritrea v Yemen*.[160] In that case the PCA cited with approval the writing of Majid Khadduri, a leading Iraqi jurist, who stated that 'the fundamental moralistic general principles of the *Quran* and the *Sunna* may validly be invoked for the consolidation and support of positive international law rules in their progressive development'.[161]

In other cases, judges have referred only to secondary sources – academic writings on the religious systems – as evidence for the principles or propositions drawn from the religious systems. Thus in the *Aegean Sea Continental Shelf Case*,[162] Tarazi considered the basis for the inclusion of Article 2(1) in the Vienna Convention on the Law of Treaties: 'This provision was no novelty. Islamic law had already provided that "in conventions, one must consider the intention of the parties and not the literal meaning of the words and phrases employed".'[163] Judge Tarazi based this principle on an early twentieth-century compilation of Turkish law, compiled by the then Second Secretary of the British Embassy at Constantinople.[164] Similarly, when Judge Weeramantry made reference to Islamic law in his Dissenting Opinion in the *Arbitral Award of 31 July 1989*,[165] he based the evidence for the principle in question (nullity of an act performed without requisite authority) on an academic article on Islamic law.[166] In his Separate Opinion two years later in *Application of the Convention on the Prevention and the Punishment of the Crime of Genocide*,[167] Weeramantry made a brief mention of the possibility of the principle of interim protection's being a General Principle of law, basing this on 'Anglo-American, Roman, Soviet and Hindu law' cited in an academic text on the subject.[168] In an example of close relations in the court, Judge El-Kosheri cited Weeramantry, writing extra-curially for support of his inclusion of Islamic law principles in his Dissenting

[159] ibid 59 (Dissenting Opinion of Judge Tarazi).

[160] *Eritrea v Yemen* (Phase Two: Maritime Delimitation) (1999) 119 ILR 417.

[161] ibid para 94; M Khadduri, 'International Law, Islamic' in R Bernhad (ed), *Encyclopeadia of Public International Law* (North-Holland, 1981) 229.

[162] *Aegean Sea Continental Shelf Case (Greece v Turkey)* (Jurisdiction) [1978] ICJ Rep 3.

[163] ibid 57 (Separate Opinion of Judge Tarazi).

[164] ibid; G Young, *Corps de droit Ottoman* (Clarendon Press, 1906).

[165] *Arbitral Award of 31 July 1989 (Guinea-Bissau v Senegal)* (Merits) [1991] ICJ Rep 53.

[166] ibid 109 (Dissenting Opinion of Judge Weeramantry).

[167] *Application of the Convention on the Prevention and the Punishment of the Crime of Genocide (Bosnia and Herzegovina v Serbia and Montenegro)* (Preliminary Objections) [1996] ICJ Rep 325.

[168] ibid 378 (Separate Opinion of Judge Weeramantry); JB Elkind, *Interim Protection: A Functional Approach* (Brill Nijhoff, 1981).

Opinion in the *Aerial Incident at Lockerbie*.[169] In that case, El-Kosheri derived support for a 'fundamental legal principle' of '*nemo debet esse judex in propria sua causa*' (the rule against bias) from 'the legal traditions of the major systems, particularly Islamic law'.[170] Judge Al-Khasawneh looked to Islamic law as part of a General Principle in *Aerial Incident of 10 August 1999*.[171]

iv. Conceptions of International Law

Writings on Hindu and Talmudic law tend to focus on the internal systems they regulate, and do not extend those principles to public international law as a whole. Jurists writing from a Talmudic perspective have certainly had an impact on the development of international law,[172] but this does not extend to a comprehensive Talmudic vision of international law separate from our modern understanding of international law. Islamic law, however, does have a unique conception of international law. Weeramantry, writing extra-curially, criticises Western jurisprudence for failing to recognise the Islamic system of international law:

> Islamic international law constitutes a vital part of Islamic legal heritage. This is a discipline which was well developed in Islam, contrary to views which generations of prejudiced writing have instilled in the non-Islamic mind, and requires close attention in any study emphasising the international importance of Islamic law.[173]

The Islamic perspective on international law is of a monist system, with international conduct regulated by the same sources that regulate *Shari'ah* law, most notably the *Koran* and the *Sunna*.[174] Thus the sources of Article 38 are irrelevant to Islamic international law – the only sources are those contained in the sources of *Shari'ah* law, which may or may not coincide with those detailed in Article 38. Weeramantry argues that Islamic international law can have a place within modern (Western) international law through the operation of Article 38(1)(c):

> This brief survey [of Islamic international law] will be seen in a practical context when we note that Article 38(1)(b) [*sic*] of the Statute of the International Court of

[169] *Questions of Interpretation and Application of 1971 Montreal Convention Arising From Aerial Incident at Lockerbie* (Provisional Measures) [1992] ICJ Rep 3 (*Aerial Incident at Lockerbie*); Judge Weeramantry was on the bench for the case, but did not mention the principle in his own Dissenting Opinion.

[170] ibid 112 (Dissenting Opinion of Judge El-Kosheri); see ch 5.

[171] *Aerial Incident of 10 August 1999 (Pakistan v India)* (Jurisdiction) [2000] ICJ Rep 12, 57 (Dissenting Opinion of Judge Al-Khasawneh).

[172] For example, the work of H Lauterpacht has been said to encompass the 'elements of a secular Jewish vision' of international law: P Lahav, 'The Jewish Perspective in International Law' (1993) 87 *Proceedings of the Annual Meeting (American Society of International Law)* 331, 333; see also M Koskenniemi, 'Lauterpacht: The Victorian Tradition in International Law' (1997) 8 *European Journal of International Law* 215, 228–30.

[173] Weeramnatry, *Islamic Jurisprudence* (n 68) 128.

[174] ibid 131.

> Justice, requires the International Court of Justice to apply the 'general principles of law recognized by civilized nations'. Having regard to the large number of Islamic nations not members of the United Nations, the international law of Islam is a body of knowledge which the world court cannot afford to ignore.[175]

C. Asian Legal Systems

Accepting the diversity of Asian legal systems, and the dissent between publicists as to whether an overall classification of 'Asian legal systems' is necessary or valid, a comment can still be made for those systems that do have concepts of, or analogous to, *li* and *fa* (or a limited, formalised legal system supplanted by unwritten traditions and customs). In drawing principles from these systems, we should not be limited by the formal structures but also look to custom. In some Asian legal systems such custom is a binding source of law while remaining unwritten, while in others it must be codified through legislation to be binding.[176] An inclusive and global view of General Principles would draw from both scenarios: the unwritten as well as the formalised. Judge Weeramantry did this in his Separate Opinion in *Gabčikovo-Nagymaros Project* when he referred to 'Chinese and Japanese culture' rather than to formal laws.[177]

III. THE COMPARATIVIST'S WARNING

This chapter proceeds on the basis that a comparative methodology is appropriate for finding General Principles (in light of the analysis in the preceding chapters in this book): it takes exception with the *scope* and *selection* of the legal systems for such study. However, it must be noted that there are pitfalls lurking in the use of comparativism without care.[178] Two of these concerns, and how they relate to this chapter, are briefly sketched out below.

A. 'Thin' Law and Legal Cultures

An issue with the comparative approach to General Principles is the need to 'understand the domestic legal principle in any particular system'.[179] Comparativist scholars argue for the need to take into account legal *culture* as

[175] ibid 150.

[176] Black and Bell, *Law and Legal Institutions of Asia* (n 72) 10.

[177] *Gabčíkovo-Nagymaros Project* (n 7) 107 (Separate Opinion of Judge Weeramantry).

[178] See in particular Jain, 'Comparative International Law at the ICTY' (n 21) 486, 490–95. Jain's arguments on transposability are discussed in ch 7.

[179] N Jain, 'Judicial Lawmaking and General Principles of Law in International Criminal Law' (2016) 57 *Harvard International Law Journal* 111, 137.

well as the law itself.[180] While this is true for all legal systems, it is no less the case for the legal systems discussed in this chapter. However, this term itself has met with resistance:

> The term 'legal culture', in its contemporary form, comes to use most frequently from a confused and suspect anthropological tradition. That tradition, in elevating the holistic concept of 'culture' and 'cultures', has been interested in grasping the 'essence' or character of a particular people's (or group's or class's) way of life, seeing these as constituting a systematic totality. The danger of this usage lies in the inherent tendency towards illegitimately monistic, essentialist and functional treatment of the lives, traditions and social mores of people.[181]

One response to both concerns is offered by the use of non-written laws in ascertaining General Principles, as advocated in this chapter. In doing so, it avoids the trap of treating 'customs, traditions and indigenous practices as outside the legitimate concern of legal science, not part of *the* legal system'.[182]

B. Legal Systems as Representatives of Legal Families

One of the vexed problems with categorising legal systems into families is when those families are then used as the basis for a sampling method. In the case of General Principles, this means picking a system from each family and considering their law to find requisite horizontal generality. Sampling across legal families may, as Jain argues, avoid concerns of cherry-picking and 'convenience sampling',[183] but it also places much reliance on the accuracy and suitability of the family classification, which cannot always be found.[184] What then to do if, as some argue, 'carrying out a comprehensive survey of legal systems of the world on a particular issue is beyond the capacity of international courts and tribunals'?[185] A suggested answer is two-fold: first, as explored in section IV, technological advances means that such comprehensive surveys are not (always) as out of reach as once thought. This is particularly true in the case of *written* law: it does not hold so true in the case of *unwritten* laws. Second, if such surveys may be outside the reach of courts, perhaps they are not outside the reach of the litigants. Both Judge Weeramantry and the ICTY have relied upon comparative research presented by parties to the dispute.[186] This has the benefit of avoiding

[180] ibid 138.
[181] Tay and Tan, 'Legal Pluralism in East-Asia' (n 80) 395.
[182] ibid 391.
[183] ibid 490–91.
[184] ibid 492.
[185] J Ellis, 'General Principles and Comparative Law' (2011) 22(4) *European Journal of International Law* 949, 956–57.
[186] However, it must be acknowledged there are also examples of courts choosing *not* to take this opportunity. See, eg, MO Hudson, 'The Fourth Year of the Permanent Court of International Justice' (1926) 20(1) *American Journal of International Law* 1, 6; *EC Measures Concerning Meat*

the inevitable selection bias that occurs when relying on judges' own knowledge and experience.[187]

IV. GLOBAL GENERAL PRINCIPLES IN THE INFORMATION AGE

Requiring a global approach, General Principles must be understood in the context of advancements in access to information and searchability of data. When the PCIJ Statute was being drafted, concepts such as computers, searchable documents and indeed the Internet would have been unimaginable. To undertake a comparative study of even a small number of legal systems would have entailed significant knowledge, skills and resources. Barriers of physical access and language, and simply the sheer amount of time needed to read through legislation, constitutions and case law for the relevant principle, would have been staggering. Little wonder, then, that the earliest cases confined their comparative studies to a small number of countries, and usually those with which the judge was most familiar. A survey of 10 or 20 states would have been practically impossible.

These barriers were not, of course, limited to the PCIJ. They continued to be present for most of the twentieth century. In 1957, Rudolph Schlesinger proposed a 10-year project to determine the substance of many General Principles.[188] This project was supported by the Cornell Law School, and ultimately produced one book, published in 1968,[189] but never resulted in a broad survey as Schlesinger first proposed.[190] Schlesinger warned that the project would be of 'challenging difficulty, to put it mildly',[191] and it foreshadowed a methodology of 'bringing to Cornell University outstanding legal scholars representing the major legal systems of the world'.[192] Originally scholars from eight (predominantly Western) countries[193] were represented, as well as one 'expert on Communist legal systems'.[194] The project involved face-to-face meetings, was 'expensive' and 'time consuming',[195] and was limited in its scope by its methodological

and Meat Products (Hormones), Appellate Body Report (adopted 13 February 1998) WT/DS26/AB/R, WT/DS48/AB/R, AB-1997-4, para 153; H Thirlway, 'The Law and Procedure of the International Court of Justice 1960–1989' (1989) 60(1) *British Yearbook of International Law* 1, 120.

[187] Jain, 'Comparative International Law at the ICTY' (n 21) 490. See further discussion in ch 7.

[188] RB Schlesinger, 'Research on the General Principles of Law Recognized by Civilized Nations' (1957) 51 *American Journal of International Law* 734.

[189] RB Schlesinger, PG Bonassies and Cornell Law School, *Formation of Contracts; A Study of the Common Core of Legal Systems, Conducted under the Auspices of the General Principles of Law project of the Cornell Law School* (Stevens and Sons, 1968).

[190] VD Degan, *Sources of International Law* (Martinus Nijhoff, 1997) 102.

[191] RB Schlesinger, 'Research on the General Principles of Law Recognized by Civilized Nations' (1957) 51 *Australian Journal of International Law* 734, 751.

[192] ibid.

[193] Australia, Egypt, France, Germany, India, Italy, Switzerland and the United States of America.

[194] DW Curtiss, 'Cornell Law School from 1954 to 1963' (1970-1971) 56 *Cornell Law Review* 375, 401.

[195] BF Willcox, 'Rudolph B Schlesinger: World Lawyer' (1974-1975) 60(6) *Cornell Law Review* 919, 923.

constraints: although involved with the initial project, the Egyptian expert was appointed to government office, and withdrew from the project, meaning no analyses of Egyptian or Islamic law was undertaken.[196] Similarly, Spanish and Portuguese systems were omitted after the 'withdrawal for medical and family reasons' of another scholar.[197] The final project surveyed 10 legal systems, and was Western-focused.[198] It seemed to be too much work to be repeated:

> Nine men needed ten years to cover ten systems, on a subject narrowly limited to the mechanics of offer and acceptance … Much time, effort and money will thus be needed to complete this kind of contribution to the bulk of the general principles of law recognized by civilized nations. Assuming that the requisite army of researchers will devote themselves to such efforts … will the funds be available to move such an army about the world for conferences?[199]

Several assumptions arise from this project that are clearly rooted in the technological context of the time – the primacy of face-to-face meetings and the need to collaborate primarily through physical conferences are dated concepts to the Zoom generation (even more so since the shift online during the COVID-19 pandemic). Further, the willingness to rest a study on the experience and knowledge of experts also reflects the difficulty of accessing, researching and understanding national laws of a different country. This same attitude is also prevalent in the suggestions from scholars that the national experience of the bench of the ICJ would be sufficient to determine whether a General Principle existed.

The increasing digitisation of data and global instantaneous access to such data via the Internet, however, have revolutionised legal research. As early as 1986, Robert Berring was exploring the ramifications of searchable full-text legal databases.[200] These databases (the early versions of Lexis and Westlaw)[201] made two critical changes to how previous law had been collected and reported in hard-copy form.

First, they acted to 'eliminate the intervention of *any* editorial judgment … Editors and antiquated subject structures no longer burden the research process.'[202] Because of this, 'every case is equally available to every researcher, limited only by the researcher's training and ingenuity'.[203] Second, full-text database search capability allows searches that would simply have been impossible in hard copy – finding every case within a corpus of cases to use any given unique

[196] ibid.
[197] ibid.
[198] 'American, Australian-Canadian-New Zealand, Communist Legal Systems, English, French, German-Swiss-Austrian, Indian, Italian, Polish and South African': ibid 923.
[199] ibid 925.
[200] R Berring, 'Full-Text Databases and Legal Research: Backing into the Future' (1986) 1(1) *High Technology Law Journal* 27.
[201] ibid 38.
[202] ibid 41.
[203] ibid 42.

term or phrase.[204] Of course, technological development did not stop at full-text searchable databases. By 2000, well into the advent of the Internet, Berring argued that not only did technology make the legal research *look* different,[205] it changed how lawyers and in particular law students *conceived of* the law.[206] Legal researchers no longer had to rely on secondary sources to group, categorise and explain primary sources[207] but had direct access to free, easily accessible primary material.[208]

All of these innovations have direct implications for both the research into and the development of international law.[209] In 1995, the American Society of International Law (ASIL) held a panel discussion on international law resources and information technology.[210] John Gamble suggested:

> The new information age has the potential of redefining the sources of international law in the same way that convention overtook custom as the principal source of international law about 1918. The way in which the sources will be identified and understood will change so radically that it may be impossible to distinguish one from another.[211]

Despite this suggestion of redefining the sources of international law, only custom and treaty were discussed by the panel. In the context of evidence of state practice, Gamble suggested that 'the full text of legislative debates will be available over the internet. It will be possible to complete an exhaustive search of the national legislation of most states in a matter of minutes to assess the congruence between these and international law.'[212] But why limit such information to examples of state practice? The ability to search the national legislation of many nations with relative ease has significant ramifications for ascertaining General Principles. A further question, though, is whether the ability identified by Gamble actually exists? The problem with citing past articles on this area is that with such rapidly changing technology, there is accelerated dating of arguments, examples and data. The cyber landscape such as it was in 1995, or even 2005, is very different from its what it is in 2020 (and indeed, the cyberscape discussed here may seem a hopeless relic of the past before long). Gamble's 1995 prediction of the full text of legislative debates of most nations being available is not a

[204] ibid.

[205] R Berring, 'Legal Research and the World of Thinkable Thoughts' (2000) 2(2) *Journal of Appellate Practice and Process* 305, 305.

[206] ibid 311.

[207] I Gallacher, 'Forty-Two: The Hitchhiker's Guide to Teaching Legal Research to the Google Generation' (2006) 39(1) *Akron Law Review* 151, 161–62.

[208] AM Podbury, 'The Shifting Sands of Legal Research: Power to the People' (2000) 31(4) *Texas Tech Law Review* 1167, 1174.

[209] M Rumsey, 'Gauging the Impact of Online Legal Information on International Law: Two Tests' (2008) 35 *Syracuse Journal of International Law & Commerce* 201, 211.

[210] P Zarins et al, 'Broadening Access to International Law Resources through New Technology' (1995) 89 *American Society of International Law Proceedings* 1.

[211] ibid 2.

[212] ibid.

current reality; however, there have been significant inroads into making something similar a fact. Examples include the free database of English translated constitutions maintained by the International Constitutional Law Project,[213] as well as subscription services available through Hein Online[214] and Oxford University Press.[215] WorldlII is an independent site that provides a searchable database of the laws of over 100 countries,[216] and a catalogue that searches documents from all countries. There are many more databases freely accessible online, often grouped by subject matter – such as anti-corruption law,[217] organised crime and terrorism,[218] labour law,[219] food, agriculture and energy resources law,[220] intellectual property law,[221] the law of the sea,[222] and space law.[223] This access to information not only concerns current laws, but stretches to access to the history and development of laws. The Avalon Project, maintained by Yale University,[224] provides searchable full-text access to documents dating back to the 'ancient' era (the earliest document available is a Roman statement on agrarian law, dating from 111 BC).[225]

The transformation of access to information has also impacted on international materials:

> UN documents – such as Security Council resolutions – which were previously available only to those with access to major libraries in London, Paris or New York, and even then only with great difficulty, are now available to every person in the world with internet access.[226]

[213] 'Countries' (International Constitutional Law Project) available at www.servat.unibe.ch/icl/index.html.

[214] *World Constitutions Illustrated* (HeinOnline) available at https://home.heinonline.org/content/world-constitutions-illustrated-contemporary-historical-documents-and-resources/.

[215] *Oxford Constitutions of the World* (Oxford University Press, 2020) available at www.global.oup.com/academic/product/oxford-constitutions-of-the-world-9780199799848?cc=au&lang=en.

[216] WorldLII, 'Worldlii Databases' available at www.worldlii.org/databases.html.

[217] 'Country Reports on Implementation of the OECD Anti-Bribery Convention' (Organisation for Economic Co-operation and Development, 2020) available at www.oecd.org/document/24/0,3746,en_2649_37447_1933144_1_1_1_37447,00.html.

[218] See, eg, 'SHERLOC: Sharing Electronic Resources and Laws on Crime' (United Nations Office on Drug and Crime) available at www.sherloc.unodc.org/cld/v3/sherloc/.

[219] 'NATLEX' (International Labor Organization, 2020) available at www.ilo.org/dyn/natlex/natlex_browse.home.

[220] 'FAOLEX' (Food and Agriculture Organization of the United Nations, 2020) available at www.faolex.fao.org/.

[221] 'WIPO Lex' (World Intellectual Property Organization) available at www.wipo.int/wipolex/en/.

[222] 'Maritime Space: Maritime Zones and Maritime Delimitation' (United Nations) available at www.un.org/Depts/los/LEGISLATIONANDTREATIES/index.htm.

[223] 'National Space Law: Index by State' (United Nations Office of Outer Space Affairs, 2020) available at www.unoosa.org/oosa/en/ourwork/spacelaw/nationalspacelaw/index.html.

[224] 'Avalon Project – Documents in Law, History and Diplomacy' (Yale Law School: Lillian Goldman Law Library, 2008) available at http://avalon.law.yale.edu/default.asp.

[225] 'The Avalon Project: Agrarian Law, 111 BC' (Yale Law School: Lillian Goldman Law Library, 2008) available at http://avalon.law.yale.edu/default.asp.

[226] P Sands, 'Turtles and Torturers: The Transformation of International Law' (2001) 33 *International Law and Politics* 527, 539.

The point of all this is to illustrate that although Gamble's prediction has not eventuated, the ways of finding a General Principle, now, in the early twenty-first century, are completely different from the resources available to those scholars in the early, mid- and even most of the late twentieth century. This has two significant implications for General Principles. First, it dramatically increases the scope of legal systems from which such laws are drawn. No longer are we content to rest 'mainly on a (superficial) comparison between French, British and possibly German or Italian law only'.[227] Rather, increasingly globalised information mirrors recognition of an increasingly globalised world. Not only are non-Western laws online, but often they are available in free translations. Legal journals also provide increased access to diverse legal traditions – due both to the establishment of many non-Western legal journals in the late twentieth and early twenty-first century[228] and the more general increased access to a large variety of journals through online subscription services.[229]

Second, it increases the ability of specific *rules* to be found commonly across many legal systems. The existence of specific databases grouped by subject matter makes such a task relatively easy. This is particularly evident where new domestic legislation is enacted in many countries in similar or identical format, at the encouragement of a UN agency, an NGO or a corporate body. In these cases, the body will often keep a (freely available) record of such laws, and their status, allowing easy comparison and research. This approach can be seen in the area of laws based on the Council of Europe's Convention on Cybercrime.[230] In other areas, bodies may not be actively advocating for legislative change but monitor domestic legislation and publish results online. As such, the task of identifying a plethora of national laws on a given subject is easier now than it has ever been.

It is this context – the need for truly global General Principles and the modern reality of accessibility of information – that the model for General Principles is constructed in chapter 9.

[227] J Verhoeven, 'Article 21 of the Rome Statute and the Ambiguities of Applicable Law' (2002) 32 *Netherlands Yearbook of International Law* 3, 10.

[228] See, eg, the *African Journal of Legal Studies* (established 2004); *African Human Rights Law Journal* (established 2001); *Asian Journal of Comparative Law* (established 2006); *Asia-Pacific Journal on Human Rights and the Law* (established 2000); *Chinese Journal of International Law* (established 2002); *Chinese Law and Religion Monitor* (established 2004); *Indian Journal of Law and Technology* (established 2005); *Journal of East Asia and International Law* (established 2008); *Journal of South Pacific Law* (established 1997); *UCLA Journal of Islamic and Near Eastern Law* (established 2002).

[229] eg HeinOnline; LexisNexis; Westlaw.

[230] Convention on Cybercrime (opened for signature 23 November 2001, entered into force 1 July 2004) ETS No 185.

9

A Model of General Principles

It is to 'the general principles of law recognised by civilized nations' and to 'the teachings of the most highly qualified publicists of the various nations', in so far as they formulate and develop these principles, that we must turn increasingly for the building and evolution of the new branches of international law, such as international administrative law, international criminal law, or international contract law. Except for the very isolated 'codification' of new principles of international law in international conventions such as the Genocide Convention, practice and precedent will gradually build these systems by drawing, to a much greater extent than before, on the 'general principles'.

Wolfgang Friedmann[1]

WHILE FRIEDMANN'S OPTIMISM regarding General Principles in 1964 may have been misplaced, the derision with which other scholars have historically treated General Principles has no basis. This tide is starting to turn. There is rich history and jurisprudence on General Principles. The concept of source itself – a third source of international law, separate from treaty and custom – has been in existence since the late nineteenth century, and came to the Permanent Court of International Justice (PCIJ) having been included in the most important international Conventions and Draft Conventions up to that date. While the jurisprudence is limited mostly to Separate and Dissenting Opinions in the PCIJ and the International Court of Justice (ICJ), the International Criminal Court (ICC) and the International Criminal Tribunal for the Former Yugoslavia (ICTY) have relied on the source.[2]

Unfortunately, there is also much misclassification of instances where courts have turned to General Principles.[3] This is often due to confusion over the terms 'principles of international law' or similar; but also due to the different formulations of General Principle-like sources in specialised or regional courts and tribunals.[4]

It is vital that a model of General Principles is proposed: one that is both based on historical development and contextualised within theoretical

[1] W Friedmann, *The Changing Structure of International Law* (Stevens & Sons, 1964) 188–89.
[2] Although note the formulation in the ICC is different from the Art 38(1)(c) wording: see ch 6.
[3] Most notably in use of judgments of the PCIJ by scholars: see ch 3.
[4] See ch 6.

discussion of the source. A theme of duality is present throughout this book – the push and pull between positivism and natural law; between the national and the international; between the judge as law-maker and the judge as a law-finder. Duality is present in this chapter as well: first, in the illegitimate, the conception of General Principles that cannot stand; and, second, in the legitimate – a model that proposes a common baseline understanding with nuanced expressions of the tetrahedral framework through the rule/principle distinction.

I. A TALE OF TWO SOURCES: ILLEGITIMATE DUALITY

It is evident, on consideration of the historical development of Article 38(1)(c), its use by courts and tribunals, and the various analysis of it by scholars, that there are two very different types of international norms that are referred to under the auspices of General Principles. The first are variations of a comparative-based General Principle, requiring horizontal generality (of one sort or another) and recognition (of one sort or another) by sub-international legal systems (whether nation-states or otherwise). These norms are found with an objective rule of recognition (of some sort), and if judicial discretion is authorised, it is narrow. These norms are explored in section II.

The second type are norms that are not linked to generality, are not linked to recognition by nations (except in the most tenuous way) and which authorise broad judicial discretion. It is only the first category that are legitimate expressions of General Principles in the sense of Article 38(1)(c). The second, although undoubtedly *used* by courts and tribunals cannot and should not be taken as expressions of General Principles in the Article 38(1)(c) sense. In making this argument, I take a different view from James Crawford, who writes in *Brownlie's Principles of Public International Law*:

> The rubric 'general principles of international law' may alternately refer to rules of customary international law, to general principles of law as in Article 38(1)(c), or to certain logical propositions underlying judicial reasoning on the basis of existing international law. This shows that a rigid categorization of sources is inappropriate.[5]

Although Crawford rightfully separates out the type of norm I am talking about here – the 'judicial reasoning on the basis of existing international law' – from Article 38(1)(c) General Principles, as seen in this book, many others do not.[6] As such, it is not that a rigid categorisation of sources is inappropriate, but that the need for precision of terminology is paramount.[7] As set out in the next section, General Principles as logical deductions cannot be General Principles in the sense of Article 38(1)(c).

[5] J Crawford, *Brownlie's Principles of Public International Law* (Oxford University Press, 2019) 34.
[6] See discussion in ch 7.
[7] The same goes for the conflation of customary international law and General Principles: without due care, references to 'general principles of international law' that are truly references

A. General Principles as Logical Deductions

These are not, harking back to the 1875 Arbitral Procedure Regulations, independent deductions taking into account laws recognised by states.[8] Rather, these are those independent deductions from existing international law – and often the internal legal structure itself.[9] These deductions exist – and are used by judges – this much is certain. But in doing so these judges are *not* employing Article 38(1)(c) as it should be properly understood. Such a conception of General Principles is unsustainable for three fundamental reasons. First, it authorises broad and unfettered judicial discretion, in complete opposition to the historical development of the source from 1875 to its introduction into the PCIJ Statute.[10] Second, it negates the requirement of 'recognised', relying on deduction and inference rather than any recognition. Third, it removes the concept of 'nation' from the source altogether – except as insofar as the nation contributed to the original legal structure from which deductions or inferences are being drawn.

It would be far better if those employed in such deductions labelled them what they were: judicial law making – often necessary, but not linked to any of the formal sources in Article 38(1)(a), (b) or (c).[11] Indeed, many judges do not link such practices to Article 38(1)(c) at all.[12]

II. GENERAL PRINCIPLES AND LEGITIMATE DUALITY

Within a correct use of General Principles duality still exists, set out here along the principle/rule distinction. A common thread in the development and use of Article 38(1)(c) is that little heed was paid by the drafters of the provision, the PCIJ or the ICJ to the distinction between principles and rules. The terms have been used interchangeably throughout for more than 100 years in regard to General Principles. Why, then, return to the distinction for the final model? Simply, it is useful for describing the inherent duality of General Principles under this model. The model I propose here has a baseline with features shared by both types. It then has nuanced manifestations of the four aspects of the tetrahedral framework within its dual expressions.

to custom are taken as references to Art 38(1)(c) by commentators, leading to an over-inflation of perceived use of the source by the PCIJ and ICJ.

[8] L Goldschmidt, 'International Arbitral Procedure' (1874) 6 *Revue de droit international et de Législation Compareé* 421, tr in JB Scott (ed), *Resolutions of the Institute of International Law Dealing with the Law of Nations* (Oxford University Press, 1916) 212; see ch 2.

[9] See discussion in ch 7.

[10] See ch 2.

[11] As framed by Cassesse in A Cassese, *International Law*, 2nd edn (Oxford University Press, 2004) 192.

[12] See, eg, *SS 'Lotus' (France v Turkey)* [1927] PCIJ Series A No 10, 16, 35 (Dissenting Opinion of Judge Loder); *Factory at Chorzów (Claim for Indemnity) (Germany v Poland)* (Jurisdiction) [1927] PCIJ Series A No 9, 21.

A. The Baseline Model

Returning to the tetrahedral framework, the *function* of General Principles is to create binding norms of international law, usually in a gap-filling function but not limited to this.

The source has an objective rule of recognition employing a comparative *methodology*.[13] It authorises only limited judicial discretion,[14] mostly in the exercise of judicial function and going to the appropriateness of the General Principle. It requires horizontal generality, and recognises such generality exists *because* of the normative desirableness of the rule/principle.[15] Tunkin suggested General Principles could never exist because of the fundamental differences between Soviet and non-Soviet legal systems.[16] Rather, General Principles exist *in spite* of the cultural and legal differences between legal systems: due to their inherent value. This model does not, however, have normative desirableness as a constitutive feature of its rule of recognition. In this way the *jurisprudential legitimacy* of the source is mostly positivist, but recognises elements of content driven reason for satisfaction of the rule of recognition.

Horizontal generality, satisfying the comparative methodology, is found in national legal systems.[17] I argue that it should also include non-state legal systems such as Chthonic and Religious Legal Systems.[18] The question of generality drawing from international systems is more vexed: the most consistent use of international materials is as a measure of appropriateness, the 'evidential' process,[19] or used to *augment* General Principles drawn from the domestic system. The *type* of General Principle is not limited to principles or rules (although the distinction is used below), nor to procedural norms only.[20]

[13] In line with the overwhelming majority of practice by the PCIJ and the ICJ: see chs 3–5.

[14] In line with the historical development of the source: see ch 2.

[15] See, eg, *Fisheries Case (United Kingdom v Norway)* [1951] ICJ Rep 116, 147–48 (Individual Opinion of Judge Alvarez); *Interhandel (Switzerland v United States of America)* (Preliminary Objections) [1959] ICJ Rep 6, 116–17 (Dissenting Opinion of Judge Lauterpacht); *Right of Passage over Indian Territory (Portugal v India)* (Merits) [1960] ICJ Rep 6, 136 (Separate Opinion of Judge Koo); *South-West Africa (Ethiopia v South Africa; Liberia v South Africa)* (Preliminary Objections) [1962] ICJ Rep 319, 577–78 (Dissenting Opinion of Judge Van Wyk); *North Sea Continental Shelf (Federal Republic of Germany v Denmark; Federal Republic of Germany v the Netherlands)* [1969] ICJ Rep 3, 135 (Separate Opinion of Judge Ammoun); *Sovereignty over Pulau Ligitan and Pulau Sipidan (Indonesia v Malaysia)* [2002] ICJ Rep 625, 705–06 (Dissenting Opinion of Judge ad hoc Franck).

[16] G Tunkin, 'Coexistence and International Law' (1958) 95 *Recuil des Cours* 5, 26.

[17] In line with the overwhelming majority of practice by the PCIJ and the ICJ: see chs 3–5, and the options considered by the Advisory Committee of Jurists: see ch 2.

[18] See ch 8 for further discussion.

[19] M Akehurst, 'Equity and General Principles of Law' (1976) 25 *International and Comparative Law Quarterly* 801, 818.

[20] As clearly indicated in the use of the source by international courts and tribunals: see chs 4–6 in particular.

B. General Principles as Principles

This variation on the baseline models are those General Principles that are true 'principles' as distinct from rules: abstract and possessing both horizontal and vertical generality. These are principles such as sustainability, as discussed by Judge Weeramantry in *Gabčikovo-Nagymaros*.[21] They develop slowly over long periods of time, and can be considered fundamental or underlying, although not immutable,[22] eternal or unchanging.[23] Their value lies in their flexibility of application to modern situations, and continued application can develop international law in new areas. These principles 'correspond to the Rawlsian concept of the overlapping consensus and should be compatible with many different schemes of life in different countries'.[24]

They are found using a comparative methodology, and look to national laws and judicial practice, and can also be found in non-traditional legal systems, such as chthonic systems or 'living law'.[25] As they reflect long-standing beliefs, customs and laws, the relationship between the normative desirability of the norm and its horizontal generality is clear. Criticism of this type of General Principles is that, without careful justification of application of the principle at each new development in law, they can lead to unfettered judicial discretion and law making, contrary to the authorisation of the source. Accordingly, care must be taken when utilising these types of General Principles to justify their existence based on true comparative methodology, encompassing many legal systems from all major types of legal systems.

C. General Principles as Rules

The second variation on the baseline models are those General Principles that possess horizontal generality but not necessarily vertical generality, or high levels of abstraction (though some degree of abstraction may be required to gain the requisite horizontal generality). Their relevance lies in being drawn directly from specific responses to new global issues and problems, rather than applying long-existing abstract principles to new areas. They are also found using the comparative methodology, looking to national laws and in particular national legislation that is enacted to address new challenges to societies. They can be formed relatively quickly, if there is a global response in domestic legislation to a certain issue.

[21] *Gabčikovo-Nagymaros Project (Hungary v Slovakia)* [1997] ICJ Rep 7, 98–108 (Separate Opinion of Judge Weeramantry).

[22] Akehurst, 'Equity and General Principles of Law' (n 18) 815.

[23] M Bogdan, 'General Principles of Law and the Problem of Lacunae in the Law of Nations' (1977) 46(1) *Nordisk Tidsskrift for International Ret* 37, 44.

[24] S Kadelbach and T Kleinlein, 'International Law – a Constitution for Mankind? An attempt at Re-appraisal with an Analysis' (2007) 50 *German Yearbook of International Law* 303, 342.

[25] *Gabčíkovo-Nagymaros Project (Hungary v Slovakia)* (Merits) [1997] ICJ Rep 7, 109–10 (Separate Opinion of Judge Weeramantry).

The link between normative desirability of content and horizontal generality still stands: even in cases of rapid legislative response to global issues, the commonality of the legislation that must exist to support the finding of a General Principle also suggests there is some underlying 'truth' to the formation of that legislation. This type of General Principle is responsive to social change and global movements, but this is its strength, and is entirely consistent with past development of international law. As the global community progresses and develops, social standards will change and municipal legislation will change to reflect those standards.

'Truth' in this sense is not absolute but is grounded in context. Where a principle or rule contains enough of this quality that it is shared amongst many legal systems from the different legal families, it will be a General Principle in that time. Where social understanding changes so that the rule or principle no longer contains that quality of 'truth' or 'rightness', this will be reflected in the domestic laws of nations, and ultimately the General Principle will also change, or cease to exist. They are thus 'capable of undergoing a process of orderly change, as the municipal laws on which they are based are amended.'[26]

Suggested examples of this second type of General Principle include a minimum age of criminal responsibility,[27] the rule against non-retroactivity in criminal matters,[28] the legal rights of minorities,[29] and generally legal regulation of 'new objective situations which had not previously fallen within the framework of international law', arising because of development of 'international relations, and in particular the development of technology'.[30] The use of such specific General Principles may seem to fly in the face of Lord McNair's caution,[31] and indeed the early expressions of the source prior to the PCIJ.[32] However, the expansion of international law to reach into new areas of regulation means that many matters for domestic regulations are now suitable for international regulation without overmuch abstraction or translation.

III. THE FUTURE OF GENERAL PRINCIPLES

While custom regulates state-to-state conduct (the traditional domain of international law), it often struggles to meet the challenges issued by new areas of

[26] Akehurst, 'Equity and General Principles of Law' (n 18) 815.

[27] D Cipriania, *Children's Rights and the Minimum Age of Criminal Responsibility* (Routledge, 2009).

[28] KS Gallant, *The Principle of Legality in International and Comparative Criminal Law* (Cambridge University Press, 2009) 298.

[29] VD Degan, *Sources of International Law* (Martinus Nijhoff, 1997) 106–107, referring to Budislav Vukas, *Etniĉke manjine i madjunarodni odnosi* (1978), 126–128.

[30] Degan (n 28) 106.

[31] *International Status of South West Africa* (Advisory Opinion) [1950] ICJ Rep 128, 148 (Separate Opinion of Judge McNair).

[32] Goldschmidt (n 8), 212.

international law. These areas are transnational, but do not always involve state-to-state interaction. Yet they still require international regulation. Attempts to retrofit custom to suit ends in a 'self-contained exercise in rhetoric',[33] a twisting conception of state practice and *opinion juris* to meet the 'difficult cases'.[34]

General Principles instead can be used to address such issues. To assess this future, we must first return to the past. Much of Elihu Root's opposition to the inclusion of Baron Descamp's formulation of clauses 3 and 4 into the Statute of the PCIJ (remembering clause 3 as 'the rules of international law as recognized by the legal conscience of civilised nations') has its roots in the unsuccessful earlier attempt to establish the Prize Court, as well as the reluctance of the US Congress to ratify agreements requiring mandatory arbitration.[35] Accordingly, Root argued that 'the beginning must be modest … before conferring broad powers on the Court, it must be permitted to justify the confidence in it which would warrant such an extension'.[36] The state of international law, over 100 years later, is markedly different. While the United States currently does not accept the compulsory jurisdiction of the ICJ, 74 other states do so.[37] Additionally, many bilateral and multilateral treaties contain compulsory dispute resolution mechanisms referring disputes to the ICJ.

I am not arguing for an *extension* of General Principles but merely full utilisation of them as a source of law. In the face of the confidence expressed in the ICJ and in its Statute, such full utilisation is surely justified. Added to this, the growing scope of international law, access to information and globalisation of international law have a momentous impact on General Principles. These factors mean that General Principles are easier to find, quicker to find, and can be found with a higher degree of confidence that they are truly general (that is, they are not simply European norms, or Western norms). This is the case both for rules found in rapidly expanding areas of new law, and for traditional principles.

For emerging or rapidly changing contexts that require transnational regulation, domestic legislatures become the first responders to the new or altered problem. Before a treaty can be negotiated, and certainly before any custom can form, domestic parliaments enact legislation to address the problem within their states. Because the problem is transnational, domestic responses are often homogenised, either through inter-governmental cooperation or by the actions of a non-governmental organisation actively seeking to promulgate harmonised domestic legislation in states.

[33] B Simma and P Alston, 'The Sources of Human Rights Law: Custom, Jus Cogens and General Principles' (1988–1989) 12 *Australian Yearbook of International Law* 82, 89.

[34] ibid.

[35] CR Rossi, *Equity and International Law: A Legal Realist Approach to Decision Making* (Martinus Nijhoff Publishers, 1993) 101; see ch 2.

[36] Permanent Court of International Justice: Advisory Committee of Jurists, *Procès-verbaux of the Proceedings of the Committee* (1920) 309.

[37] See www.icj-cij.org/en/declarations.

While General Principles are of tremendous potential value for *new* problems in international law, they may also be of help in new ways of looking at old problems. Just as Judge Weeramantry was able to draw upon indigenous practices of sustainable development to support a General Principle, there is potential for analysis of other facets of chthonic or indigenous legal systems that may relate to other norms of international law. This will become particularly powerful if there is a generality between chthonic practices and modern legislative responses to the same problems.[38]

General Principles have always been a valid source of international law. While the role of Article 38(1)(c) has been downplayed by some commentators, it is nevertheless true that the source has not been used to its full potential. Such usage was unlikely while doctrinal debate and the jurisprudence itself remained unclear, and at times divided, over the exact nature of the source. Recognising the duality inherent in General Principles allows much of the tension surrounding this source to be eased. This book aims to provide a clearer account of General Principles that is firmly contextualised in their past, present and future.

[38] See, eg, I Saunders, 'International Disaster Relief and Article 38(1)(c) of the Statute of the International Court of Justice: The Forgotten Source of International Law' in DD Caron, MJ Kelly and A Telesetsky (eds), *The International Law of Disaster Relief* (Cambridge University Press, 2014) 29.

Index

www.ingramcontent.com/pod-product-compliance
Lightning Source LLC
Chambersburg PA
CBHW071301180926
51613CB00001B/98